Jekyll and Hyde Dramatized

JEKYLL AND HYDE DRAMATIZED

The 1887 Richard Mansfield Script and the Evolution of the Story on Stage

Edited by Martin A. Danahay
and Alex Chisholm

McFarland & Company, Inc., Publishers
Jefferson, North Carolina, and London

To our long-suffering wives,
Deborah and Jayne

LIBRARY OF CONGRESS CATALOGUING-IN-PUBLICATION DATA

Jekyll and Hyde dramatized : the 1887 Richard Mansfield script
and the evolution of the story on stage / edited by
Martin A. Danahay and Alex Chisholm.
p.   cm.
Includes bibliographical references and index.

ISBN 0-7864-1870-2 (illustrated case binding : 50# alkaline paper)

1. Sullivan, T. R. (Thomas Russell), 1849–1916. Dr. Jekyll and Mr. Hyde.
2. Stevenson, Robert Louis, 1850–1894. Strange case of Dr. Jekyll and Mr. Hyde.
3. Stevenson, Robert Louis, 1850–1894 — Stage history — English-speaking countries.
4. Stevenson, Robert Louis, 1850–1894 — Adaptations — History and criticism.
5. Theater — English-speaking countries — History — 19th century.
6. Mansfield, Richard, 1857–1907 — Literary art.   7. Jack, the Ripper.
I. Danahay, Martin A.   II. Chisholm, Alexander, 1959–
III. Sullivan, T. R. (Thomas Russell), 1849–1916. Dr. Jekyll and Mr. Hyde.
PS2963.D7J45   2005   792.9'5 — dc22   2004014628

British Library cataloguing data are available

©2005 Martin A. Danahay and Alex Chisholm. All rights reserved

*No part of this book may be reproduced or transmitted in any form
or by any means, electronic or mechanical, including photocopying
or recording, or by any information storage and retrieval system,
without permission in writing from the publisher.*

On the cover: Richard Mansfield as Dr. Jekyll and as Mr. Hyde:
a double-exposure photograph by Van der Weyde (*courtesy Library of Congress*)

Manufactured in the United States of America

*McFarland & Company, Inc., Publishers
Box 611, Jefferson, North Carolina 28640
www.mcfarlandpub.com*

Contents

Acknowledgments vi
Chronology vii
Preface 1

Part I: The Characters 5
1 — Richard Mansfield 7
2 — Thomas Russell Sullivan 21
3 — Robert Louis Stevenson 23

Part II: The Scene 27
4 — The American Stage and Popular Entertainment 29
5 — The Jack the Ripper Case 36

**Part III: Richard Mansfield's *Dr. Jekyll and Mr. Hyde*:
The Collated Script** 41

Appendix A: Extracts from Early Mansfield Biographies 81
Appendix B: Press Interviews with Richard Mansfield 100
Appendix C: Reviews of Mansfield's Dr. Jekyll and Mr. Hyde 108
Appendix D: Daniel E. Bandmann's Dr. Jekyll and Mr. Hyde 133
Appendix E: Jack the Ripper 167
Appendix F: H.B. Irving's Dr. Jekyll and Mr. Hyde 191
Select Bibliography 227
Index 229

Acknowledgments

Particular thanks must go to Nick Connell, whose newspaper research has added much to this volume, and Stewart P. Evans, an ever-present source of advice and support. We also gratefully acknowledge the assistance of Professors Sir Christopher Frayling and L. Perry Curtis Jr., Paul Begg, Jeffrey Bloomfield, Paul Daniel, Christopher-Michael DiGrazia, Christopher T. George, Melvin Harris, David O'Flaherty, Adrian Phypers, and Tom Wescott. This edition is also indebted to the pioneering work of C. Alex Pinkston on Mansfield's original production of *Dr. Jekyll and Mr. Hyde,* and to the invaluable assistance of Mr. Stephen B. Hauge, author of the Zane Publishing CD-ROM edition of *The Strange Case of Dr. Jekyll and Mr. Hyde.*

Chronology

1887

9 May	Richard Mansfield first presented T. R. Sullivan's adaptation of *Dr Jekyll and Mr Hyde* at the Boston Museum.
14 May	Mansfield's *Dr Jekyll and Mr Hyde* withdrawn for revision.
12 September	Mansfield's revised *Dr Jekyll and Mr Hyde* first presented at the Madison Square Theatre, New York. R. L. Stevenson's wife, Fanny, attended the performance.

1888

17 February	Lloyd's Weekly Newspaper announced that Mansfield was to present *Dr Jekyll and Mr Hyde* at the Lyceum Theatre, London, during September, October, and November.
12 March	Daniel E. Bandmann's *Dr Jekyll & Mr Hyde* first performed at Niblo's Garden, New York.
11 July	Mansfield and company embarked for England on *The City of Rome* steamer at New York.
19 July	*The City of Rome* steamer docked at Liverpool.
26 July	Scheduled premiere of Howard Poole's representation of *Dr Jekyll & Mr Hyde* at Croydon's Theatre Royal cancelled as a result of legal action for breach of copyright brought by Stevenson's publishers, Longmans, Green & Co.
3 August	Case of Longmans v. Bandmann heard before Mr Justice Stirling of the Chancery Division, in which Bandmann undertook, through his counsel, not to infringe the copyright of the plaintiffs.
4 August	Mansfield opened at London's Lyceum Theatre with T. R. Sullivan's adaptation of *Dr Jekyll and Mr Hyde*.

6 August	Daniel Bandmann opened at London's Opera Comique Theatre with his version of *Dr Jekyll and Mr Hyde*.
7 August	The body of Martha Tabram discovered with 39 stab wounds on a stairway in George Yard Buildings, Whitechapel.
8 August	Bandmann's *Dr Jekyll and Mr Hyde* withdrawn.
9 August	As a result of the Opera Comique performance of *Dr Jekyll and Mr Hyde*, the case of Longmans v. Bandmann was resumed before Mr Justice Stirling in the Chancery Division. At this hearing the defence counsel gave a firm undertaking that Bandmann's play would not be performed again in the U. K. until otherwise ordered by the Court.
31 August	Mutilated remains of Mary Nichols discovered in Buck's Row, Whitechapel.
2 September	Inquest into the death of Mary Nichols opened.
3 September	Second sitting of Nichols' Inquest.—George Grossmith's humorous musical farce *Hide and Seekyll (The Real Case of)* introduced by Lionel Brough to follow *The Paper Chase* at the Royalty Theatre, London.*
8 September	Mutilated remains of Annie Chapman discovered in the back yard of 29 Hanbury Street, Spitalfields.
10 September	Inquest into the death of the Annie Chapman opened.
12 September	Second day's sitting of Chapman's Inquest.
13 September	Third day's sitting of Chapman's Inquest. Evidence given by Divisional police surgeon, George Bangster Phillips, introduces the possibility that the murderer may have possessed a degree of medical expertise.
15 September	An attack of rheumatism resulted in the cancellation of Mansfield's afternoon and evening performances of *Dr Jekyll and Mr Hyde*.—Lionel Brough closed *The Paper Chase* and *Hide and Seekyll* at The Royalty Theatre, before embarking on a provincial tour.
17 September	Third day's sitting of Nichol's Inquest.—Richard Davey's one-act comedy, *Lesbia* introduced to precede *Dr Jekyll and Mr Hyde* at the Lyceum.
18 September	Reviews of *Lesbia*, accompanied by further reviews of *Dr Jekyll and Mr Hyde* appear in Press.
19 September	Fourth day's sitting of Chapman Inquest.— Possibly prompted by the Daily Telegraph's previous day's review, the last 12 performances of Mansfield's *Dr Jekyll and Mr Hyde* advertised, with the final Lyceum performance scheduled for 29 September.
20 September	Mansfield and company give a matinee performance of *Dr Jekyll and Mr Hyde* at London's Crystal Palace Theatre.
23 September	Final sitting of Nichols' Inquest.
26 September	Final sitting of Chapman's Inquest. In his summing-up Coroner Wynne

---

*George Grossmith's one-act parody "*Strange Case of Hyde and Seekyl; or, Through Draughts*" was originally written for presentation by J. L. Toole at his theatre in May 1886. An attack of gout, however, compelled Toole to postpone the London premiere of the new play indefinitely. (*The Era* 22 May & 19 June 1886) It seems to have been this play, slightly amended to take account of Mansfield's and Bandmann's performances, which Brough presented at the Royalty Theatre on 3 September 1888. Pierce (171 n.40) claims that a "musical farce," supposedly based on Stevenson's work, entitled "The Phantom" opened at The Royalty Theatre, London, on 3 September 1888, but there is no evidence that this play was ever performed. No play of this name was presented in any major theatre in London at the time, and it was Grossmith's "*Hide and Seekyll*," not "The Phantom," which was introduced to The Royalty Theatre on 3 September 1888.

	Baxter introduced what became known as the "Burke and Hare" theory, in which it was claimed that the murders and mutilation may have been undertaken to supply body parts to an American doctor.
29 September	Scheduled final performance of Mansfield's *Dr Jekyll and Mr Hyde* given at the Lyceum.
30 September	Elizabeth Stride murdered in Berner Street, St. George's-in-the-East. Catherine Eddowes murdered and mutilated in Mitre Square, Aldgate.
1 October	Inquest into the death of Elizabeth Stride opened.—Mansfield introduces *A Parisian Romance* as the main feature, preceded by *Lesbia* at the Lyceum. This bill was to continue until Tuesday 9 October, with additional performances on Thursday 11, and a matinee performance on Saturday 13 October.—Various newspapers publish details of a postcard and letter, delivered to the Central News Agency purporting to be from the Whitechapel murderer, signed "Jack the Ripper."
2 October	Second day's sitting of the Stride Inquest.
3 October	Third day's sitting of Stride Inquest.—Reviews of *A Parisian Romance* appeared in the daily press. Some of these, most notably the Daily Telegraph, were scathing.
4 October	Inquest into the death of Catharine Eddowes opened.—Press advertisements announce that, due to "continued and great demand," Mansfield's *Dr Jekyll and Mr Hyde* would again be performed at the Lyceum on 10, 12 and 13 October.
5 October	Fourth day of Stride Inquest.—Letter to the City of London Police suggests Mansfield as a likely Whitechapel murder.
9 October	A letter from Mansfield, announcing a benefit performance in aid of night refuges for the poor, appears in the Pall Mall Gazette. The benefit performance of "a comedy" is scheduled for Friday 19 October.—In a letter detailed in various newspapers the Bishop of Bedford urges the establishment of a home where poor women of the East-end could work, offers his services for this purpose, and requests funding.—Henry Irving's Lyceum manager, Bram Stoker, writes to Mansfield advising against introducing a new play as a Benefit.
10 October	Mansfield's *Dr Jekyll and Mr Hyde*, preceded by *Lesbia*, reintroduced to the Lyceum.
11 October	Final day of Eddowes Inquest.—*A Parisian Romance*, preceded by *Lesbia*, performed at the Lyceum.
12 October	The Daily Telegraph commends Mansfield's decision to abandon the "creepy drama" in the coming week.—*Dr Jekyll and Mr Hyde*, preceded by *Lesbia*, performed at Lyceum.
13 October	Mansfield's last Lyceum performance of *A Parisian Romance* was given as a matinee. *Dr Jekyll and Mr Hyde*, preceded by *Lesbia*, performed in the evening.
15 October	*Dr Jekyll and Mr Hyde*, preceded by *Lesbia*, again becomes the regular bill at the Lyceum.
19 October	After a lull of several days in Whitechapel murder news, all major dailies carry reports of a mysterious letter and parcel containing half a human kidney, delivered to George Lusk, chairman of the White-

	chapel Vigilance Committee.—Mansfield introduces his *Prince Karl*, preceded by *Always Intended* to the Lyceum as a Benefit performance in aid of the Bishop of Bedford's fund.
20 October	Final performance of Mansfield's *Dr Jekyll and Mr Hyde*, now preceded by *Always Intended*, presented at the Lyceum.
22 October	*Prince Karl*, preceded by *Always Intended*, becomes the regular bill until Mansfield's Lyceum season closes on Saturday 1 December.
23 October	Final sitting of the Stride Inquest.
8 November	Commissioner of the Metropolitan Police, Sir Charles Warren tendered his resignation as a result of a dispute with the Home Secretary, Henry Matthews, over the responsibilities and authority of their respective offices.
9 November	The butchered remains of Mary Jane Kelly discovered in her room, No. 13 Miller's Court, Dorset Street, Spitalfields.—The Lord Mayor's Show.
12 November	Inquest into the death of Mary Kelly opened and completed.
30 November	Before Mr Justice Stirling in the Chancery Division, counsel for Daniel Bandmann continued the undertaking formerly given not to perform his version of *Dr Jekyll and Mr Hyde* in London or the United Kingdom pending further orders of the Court.
1 December	Mansfield's Lyceum season closes.
3–8 December	Mansfield and company present *Prince Karl* and *Dr Jekyll and Mr Hyde* at the Alexandra Theatre, Liverpool.
10 December	Mansfield presents a matinee performance of *Prince Karl*, followed by an evening performance of *Dr Jekyll and Mr Hyde* at the Grand Theatre, Derby, in aid of his old school's subscription for a new racquet court.
22 December	Mansfield opens at the Globe Theatre, London, with *Prince Karl*, preceded by *Editha's Burglar*, in company with Lionel Brough and Weedon Grossmith.

1889

1 June	Mansfield closes with *Richard III* at the Globe Theatre, London, and returns to America towards the end of the month. He would never act in England again.

1907

21 March	Mansfield's final performance of *Dr Jekyll and Mr Hyde* took place at The New Amsterdam Theatre, New York.
23 March	Mansfield gave his final stage performance in any role, as the Baron Chevrial in *A Parisian Romance* at The New Amsterdam Theatre, New York.
30 August	At 6:40 A.M. Richard Mansfield died in his "Seven Acres" home, New London, Connecticut.

Preface

This edition has its origins in correspondence between Martin Danahay and Alex Chisholm comparing the Smithsonian "prompt book" version of the Mansfield play with the script held in the British Library. Martin Danahay published extracts from the Smithsonian script in his edition of Robert Louis Stevenson's *The Strange Case of Dr. Jekyll and Mr. Hyde* (Broadview Press, 1999). While researching Jack the Ripper, Alex Chisholm located the Lyceum script in the Lord Chamberlain's collection and noted significant differences between that script and the published extracts from the Smithsonian version. From this correspondence emerged a decision to publish a complete and authoritative collated script of Mansfield's *Jekyll and Hyde*, and to explain the historical and cultural context that lead to Mansfield being named as a suspect in the "Jack the Ripper" case when he performed the play on the London stage in the autumn of 1888.

The main text of this edition is therefore comprised of an introduction to the American theater scene and the Jack the Ripper scare, and the collated script of Richard Mansfield's *Jekyll and Hyde*, which has never before been published in its entirety. The introduction begins with Mansfield's biography, focusing on his rise to fame as a star of the American stage. Mansfield's collaborator on the project, Thomas Russell Sullivan, is also profiled, although there is less information available about Sullivan than there is about Mansfield, whose life was chronicled extensively. Finally, a biography of Robert Louis Stevenson gives a brief account of the major events in the author's life, especially in connection with the writing and publication of *The Strange Case of Dr. Jekyll and Mr. Hyde*.

The introduction then gives an account of the historical and cultural context of Mansfield's career, describing the development of American theater in the nineteenth century. Mansfield's performance is compared to other types of popular entertainment, such as quick change artistry, and his style of acting described within the changing conventions of American stage performance in this century. The Mansfield version of *Jekyll and Hyde* uses many of the conventions of melodrama, which was the dominant genre in Victorian theater throughout Mansfield's life. Mansfield is also examined as a transitional figure in the development of a more naturalistic style of acting that emphasized emotion over eloquence and declamation.

Finally, the events of the Jack the Ripper scare and Mansfield's performance are placed in the context of the mounting hysteria in London in the fall of 1888 that was caused by the brutal murders in Whitechapel. Mansfield's performance became an example cited in a general discussion of the role of the theater, through its depictions of murder and other forms of violence, in the Ripper case. Mansfield's power to incite fear in his audience was seen as another example of the pernicious influence of popular entertainment. Mansfield's performance is placed within a general anxiety caused by the proliferation of advertisements for melodramas that contained murder and violence as plot elements. This Victorian debate parallels present-day anxieties about the violence in Hollywood movies and the effect on the general population.

The collated script presents, for the first time, Richard Mansfield's Lyceum version of *Dr. Jekyll and Mr. Hyde* in comparison to his original Boston version and a later American Play Company copy of the play. In addition, by means of extensive footnoting in which significant differences between these versions are highlighted, the collated script section allows the development of Mansfield's performance to be traced through time. The script therefore presents a complete picture of the genesis and development of the Mansfield version of *Dr. Jekyll and Mr. Hyde*.

In Appendix A extracts from the two principal biographies of Richard Mansfield, by Paul Wilstach and William Winter, are reproduced, along with relevant extracts from the journal of Thomas Russell Sullivan. These present first-hand accounts of those who knew well, or were closely involved in Mansfield's production of, *Dr. Jekyll and Mr. Hyde*. In Appendix B, newspaper interviews with the actor himself allow some insight into the public character of Richard Mansfield.

Contemporary newspaper coverage is also presented in Appendix C, where reviews of Mansfield's original Boston performance, his revised New York presentation, and his London season are reproduced. Once again, this allows the development of the play to be traced, this time through the eyes of commentators and critics, while at the same time allowing the differing reactions to the play in these cities to be gauged.

Appendix D offers a brief sketch of the almost Machiavellian machinations that characterized the rivalry between Richard Mansfield and Daniel Bandmann in 1888. It was the publicity surrounding this rivalry that kept *Dr. Jekyll and Mr. Hyde* at the forefront of the news in the weeks leading up to the Whitechapel murders of 1888. In addition to subsequent derisory reviews, Appendix D reproduces the full script of Bandmann's play, ensuring that both dramatic versions of *Dr. Jekyll and Mr. Hyde* presented in London in 1888 are reproduced in this book.

Appendix E places the 1888 London performances of *Dr. Jekyll and Mr. Hyde* in a broader cultural context by reproducing a selection of newspaper reports relating to the Whitechapel murders. It is among such reports that the first signs of the conflation of Jekyll and Hyde and Jack the Ripper can be found. The names of Mr. Hyde and Jack the Ripper very quickly became associated in newspaper coverage of the Whitechapel murders.

J. W. Comyns Carr's adaptation, which Henry Brodribb Irving used when he returned *Dr. Jekyll and Mr. Hyde* to the London stage in 1910, is reproduced in full in Appendix F. Once again, extensive footnoting highlights differences between this script and a partial version held by New

York Public Library, helping confirm that the attribution of the New York Public Library script to R. Mansfield and T. R. Sullivan is, in all probability, erroneous. While this script is assigned to Mansfield, it is in fact a later and much different version of the play.

This book therefore gives a complete picture of the historical and cultural context of the Richard Mansfield version of *Dr. Jekyll and Mr. Hyde*, especially his now infamous performances in the autumn of 1888 that led to him being denounced as a suspect in the Ripper murders. It also allows for a thorough comparison of all the known extant versions of the Mansfield script, as well as with the competing, and much inferior, Bandmann version of *Jekyll and Hyde*. Finally, it helps resolve the confusion over the relationship of the Mansfield version of *Dr. Jekyll and Mr. Hyde* to the 1910 script held by the New York Public Library. While the New York script is interesting in its own right, it is in fact yet another adaptation of the Stevenson novella.

All of the scripts are testament to the enduring power of Stevenson's original vision. The Mansfield version of *Dr. Jekyll and Mr. Hyde* was especially successful in translating the horror of the Stevenson story into dramatic form, and became a model for subsequent film interpretations of the story. Unfortunately, Richard Mansfield died before film became widely popular, so we have no recordings of his performance. This book hopes to reconstruct the power and influence of Mansfield's version of *Dr. Jekyll and Mr. Hyde*, using surviving scripts, contemporary accounts, and photographs of Mansfield, the actor most closely associated with the story during his career.

Part I

The Characters

1

Richard Mansfield

Mansfield's Last Performance

When Richard Mansfield made his last appearance on the stage at the New Amsterdam Theater in New York on March 23, 1907, he had achieved at least some of the fame as an actor that he had sought all his life. Throughout his career Mansfield measured himself against famous actors of his era, such as Edwin Booth and Henry Irving. Mansfield viewed Irving in particular with great envy. When Mansfield took the stage that night, he was an established and authoritative presence in the New York dramatic scene, even if he had not achieved the level of recognition in London that he would have liked. He also had a repertoire of established plays with which his name was connected that he regularly took on tour throughout the United States.

Mansfield's best-known roles were in *A Parisian Romance* and *Dr. Jekyll and Mr. Hyde*. In these plays Mansfield portrayed somewhat disreputable characters, as his biographer William Winter noted:

> It happened that his ultimate choice of principal parts to be represented — a choice, indicative, perhaps, of an inherent temperamental acerbity — fell often upon characters which are, in general, repellent [55].

Winter's ambivalence about Mansfield is obvious here. Winter is not enthusiastic about Mansfield's choice of roles, and he sees his choices as connected to his character. As Winter suggests, these characters were in some ways unsavory or repellent in conventional terms. Winter's judgment in this matter would be authoritative for Mansfield and his contemporaries because he was a well-known and influential drama critic, and the second volume of his biography of Mansfield is comprised of reprints of his reviews of past performances.

For Winter, it was a mark against Mansfield that he played these roles. Winter worked within an aesthetic that equated the true and the beautiful, so that an "ugly" character, whether physically or morally repellent, could never rise to the same level as a beautiful or moral character. Winter ascribed Mansfield's comparative lack of success *vis à vis* such established figures as Irving to his penchant for playing such characters.

Any deficiencies in Mansfield's career,

however, should more accurately be ascribed to his own character. Even a friend and supporter like Winter was ambivalent about Mansfield, and Winter apologized for not being completely enthusiastic in his description of his dead friend. Winter's words reflect the difficulty of remaining Mansfield's friend:

> He was a man of unquiet, undisciplined, impulsive, imperious mind, intent on personal aggrandizement, the acquisition of wealth and fame, and he was so impatient of delay in the fulfillment of his purposes that he scarcely ever allowed a moment of peace either to himself or any person near him [15].

Winter himself had a brief estrangement from Mansfield, but was able to maintain a friendship despite his irascible friend's outbursts.

One of Mansfield's most unpleasant habits was to blame reversals of fortune not on his own deficiencies, but on an amorphous conspiracy to thwart him. This was especially evident in the aftermath of his financially disastrous production of *Jekyll and Hyde* and other plays in London in the fall of 1888. Mansfield blamed his financial losses on Henry Irving, who had helped arrange and finance Mansfield's productions. Winter insisted that Mansfield's suspicions were completely unfounded, and tried to dissuade his friend from repeating his accusations against Irving in public. Nonetheless, Mansfield maintained, often loudly and publicly, that his difficulties in London were due to Irving.

Mansfield never achieved the status of recognized Shakespearean actor, an accolade that he craved. Mansfield's fame rested on his performances in plays that he regarded as light, frothy fare, such as *Beaucaire* and *Old Heidelberg*. While he did stage and play in such Shakespearean dramas as *Henry V*, his longest running and most lucrative engagements were in modern dramas and romantic comedies. Mansfield particularly wished to be recognized as a serious actor in England, and often complained about the difficulty that American actors experienced in trying to extend their fame across the Atlantic. He became the most famous actor of his generation in the U.S., but did not become a transatlantic star.

Early Years

Richard Mansfield was born on May 24, 1854, in Germany. His father, Maurice Mansfield, was English, and his mother, Erminia Rudersdorff, was born in Russia, but spent most of her early life in Ireland and Germany. Mansfield's father is a somewhat shadowy figure who is described by one biographer as "a wine merchant" and a terrible musician (Wilstach, 1) and by another as "a critic of the arts and expert violin player" (Winter, 33). Whatever the father's occupation and musical talents, he had the status of a gentleman and seems to have been able to lead a Bohemian existence without the need to worry too much about working. He died in 1859 when Mansfield was a young child. Wilstach says that Maurice Mansfield died in 1861 "when Richard was only four years old," but this date would make him seven, not four (Wilstach, 13). Winter seems the more accurate biographer, placing Maurice Mansfield's death in 1859, when Richard was four.

Whatever the actual date of his father's death, Richard Mansfield's mother was the most influential figure in his life, and would have been so even if his father had not died when he was so young. His mother came from a musical family. Her own father was a talented violin player who conducted orchestras in Russia, Ireland and Germany, and moved in the circles of high society. As a young girl Erminia spent much of her time in the home of the Duchess Sophia of Baden in Germany as a young protégée. Mansfield's mother passed on to her son both her musical talents and her appreciation for the life that comes with wealth and high social status. In his early years, it was difficult for Mansfield to live up to both his mother's expectations and the aristocratic tastes he inherited from her.

Mansfield's mother had a very successful career in Germany as a singer of opera and musicals, with engagements also taking her to England. It was because of her fame as a singer that Mansfield eventually came to live in America. His mother was asked, on very generous terms, to perform in Boston for the World's Peace Jubilee in 1872. Her performances during the Jubilee were a critical and popular success, and she decided on the basis of this success that Boston would become her permanent home. She bought an apartment in Boston and a country home near Fitchburg, Massachusetts.

Before he was brought to Boston, Richard Mansfield's education had been divided between Germany and England. He was taught by tutors when he lived in Jena, Germany, and then went to boarding school in England. He attended a private school called the Derby School, outside Derby in northern England. It is here that Mansfield had his first acting experience, appearing in a school play, and he returned to the school later in life to appear in a benefit performance.

When Mansfield came to Boston to join his mother, she had wanted him to return to the Derby School for one more year, then to attend Oxford University. Mansfield, however, had had enough of school.

At first he entertained the idea of joining the Indian Civil Service, and living what he imagined would be a life of travel and adventure. With the move to America, however, he abandoned that idea, and instead went to work for Eben D. Jordan, the owner of a department store on Boylston Street in Boston. Jordan became a lifelong friend and patron of Mansfield's acting career, and when Mansfield needed financial help, Jordan was the person he relied on for assistance.

Because Mansfield could speak German and French with some fluency, he was given the job of translating the company's foreign correspondence. He also tried his hand at writing advertisements for the store.

He remained in this position for about two years, but by the time he quit he had decided upon a career quite different from either the Indian Civil Service or business.

Mansfield decided next that he wanted to be an artist. He had appeared in an amateur drama in 1876, but his mother frowned on acting considering it mere entertainment, not a serious artistic pursuit.

His mother was, however, willing to support him in his ambition to be a serious painter, and she agreed to provide him with an allowance so that he could move to London. Accordingly, in 1877, he left Boston and sailed for England. He had moved out of his mother's house when he started working for Jordan, and now he put the Atlantic Ocean between himself and his mother.

His relationship with his mother was always stormy. She taught him to play music and to sing, but she was by many accounts an imperious woman who was used to having her own way. Given Mansfield's own stubbornness, and a fiery temper that could match his mother's, there was inevitably conflict between them. He had also learned from his mother to appreciate the finer things in life, especially fine dining, and almost immediately on leaving his mother's house the young Mansfield was living beyond his means. For example, any money he earned in Boston, from tutoring young ladies in French and German was almost instantly spent.

Mansfield set up his own studio in London and started trying to earn his living through painting. However, he was tempted by the idea of starring on stage, and after a brief appearance one night in a music hall, he engaged to perform in musical comedies at German Reed's "Gallery of Illustration." On the night of his debut he fainted on stage from fright and was immediately fired by the manager. A week of practice and an investment in a new wardrobe were wasted by this overwhelming attack of stage fright. It was not an auspicious start to his professional acting career.

Mansfield was now in dire straits and started performing skits and songs at parties as a way of supporting himself. When his mother learned of his performances from mutual friends she was outraged that her son would demean himself to play for money as a "mere" entertainer, rather than as an actor on stage. She decided to stop his allowance, thus plunging him into a period of poverty and hunger. Mansfield himself said that he would wander the streets of London staring in at the windows of bakers, starving but unable to afford any of the food he saw. As he said, there were times when he "literally dined on sights and smells." It was a desperate time in his life, yet he persisted in his attempts to become an actor.

Mansfield's fortunes finally turned when he auditioned for a part in the D'Oyly Carte comic opera company, which performed the compositions of Gilbert and Sullivan.

Mansfield gained a role in *HMS Pinafore* on the strength of his singing voice and comic abilities. Mansfield was not in the main company that performed at the Savoy theater in London, but rather in the "touring company" that took productions of various Gilbert and Sullivan comic operas on the road to British provincial towns. He had a wealth of stories about the atrocious dressing room conditions that he and the other actors were forced to endure on these tours.

Mansfield was not always the most popular person among his fellow actors because of his love of improvising comic routines. His antics would make life difficult for the rest of the company, either because he strayed from the script, or because the physical comedy he sometimes used would distract the audience from what the other actors were saying. He was never content with a small role, and would try to find ways to make himself more noticeable. While his antics may have pleased his audience, Mansfield upstaged his fellow actors by diverting the audience's attention to himself.

Once, as Mansfield related, he had a small non-speaking role in which he was simply supposed to play a waiter serving wine. However, he pushed the cork down into the bottle so that when he tried to pull it out, he could not do so despite strenuous efforts. He played up the physical comedy of a waiter unable to get the cork out of a bottle. When the cork finally did emerge with an insignificant pop, his efforts brought sustained laughter and applause. Mansfield was dismissed from the company for undermining his fellow actors.

Mansfield performed in the D'Oyly Carte company for a year, but became dissatisfied with the low pay. When he demanded a raise he was summarily dismissed. He was out of work for a while, but just as things were getting desperate an emergency in the company led to his being re-hired to play Sir Joseph Porter in *HMS Pinafore*. Mansfield then went on to play the Major-General in *The Pirates of Penzance*, in which he was a hit.

Despite his success with the company in *The Pirates of Penzance* and *The Sorcerer*, Mansfield was not satisfied with the progress of his career and resigned from the tour to return to London in 1880. He was told by Gilbert shortly afterward that he would never be cast in one of his comic operas again because of his penchant for improvising and departing from the script.

Mansfield did find employment, however, this time in a comic opera by Offenbach called *La Boulangère* (*The Bakeress*). In 1881 and 1882 he went on to play in other light comedies, most of which closed after only a few performances. He stayed in London until the summer of 1882, when he returned to America and took up residence in New York.

The American Scene

Mansfield's mother died on February 22, 1882, and in her will she specified that he was the sole heir to her fortune, but that he was not to inherit until he married. Unfortunately his mother's country home had been destroyed in a fire the year before. Mansfield inherited his mother's money, but many of her prized possessions accumulated during a distinguished singing career had been destroyed.

In September of that year he appeared on the New York stage for the first time in a light comedy role. Mansfield faced stiff competition in New York: Sarah Bernhardt, Ellen Terry and Henry Irving, all actors with international reputations, appeared on stage in the city in 1881 and 1882.

Mansfield later said that he made a mistake in leaving London for New York because the audiences in America were not sophisticated enough to appreciate his acting. He also felt that if he had established himself in London, then come to New York as an established star, like Henry Irving, he would have had an easier time making a name for himself. As it was, he was a young, unknown actor struggling to make himself noticed in the fiercely competitive New York theater scene.

Mansfield's reputation as a player in light operas and comedies preceded him from England. Mansfield, with his usual self-confidence, felt he had the natural ability required for more serious parts in tragedies, but had difficulty persuading theater managers to take a risk with an untried talent.

Consequently, his first New York role was in a light play called *Three Black Cloaks* that opened at the Standard Theater on September 27, 1882. Mansfield was a comic success in this play.

The play itself lasted only four weeks, and the cast started rehearsing another play to replace the failed endeavor. This new play was a dramatization of Washington Irving's telling of the legend of Rip Van Winkle. In an early prefiguring of his role in *Jekyll and Hyde*, Mansfield persuaded the management to let him play the roles of both an old father, Nick Vedder, and his young son, Jan Vedder. He thus played a dual role, but instead of playing a double he played one young and one old version of the same person. This was a tour de force of acting on his part, but also showed his interest in the transformation of the actor into completely different people in the same play.

While Mansfield achieved some success in the play, it did not attract large crowds. The management chose as their next vehicle the new Gilbert and Sullivan comic opera *Iolanthe, or The Peer and the Peri*.

Mansfield was sent to Philadelphia to join a touring group from the D'Oyly Carte company's production of the new piece. He was cast to play the role of the Lord Chancellor, but on the opening night of the play he was struck by acute indigestion and could not go on. It seemed a replay of his stage fright at his first-ever public performance in London. He never did act the role in Philadelphia, but when he had recovered he joined another company performing in Baltimore.

First Fame

In Baltimore, Mansfield aggravated an old ankle injury while playing the Lord Chancellor, and he returned to New York to recuperate and look for another role. He found one in a new play translated from a French hit called *A Parisian Romance*. Initially Mansfield was hired to play a relatively minor character, but he was given the break of his career when the actor playing the male lead, the role of Baron Chevrial, decided that he wasn't right for the part. Mansfield became closely identified with this role in his career. He first performed as Baron Chevrial on January 11, 1883, in New York. He later went with the company to Boston, and appeared on stage as a professional actor for the first time in his home town in April of that year.

The Baron is a dissolute and salacious man at the end of his life who expresses his cynical views on life and love and makes a fool of himself over a much younger woman. Mansfield made the role of a potentially repulsive character fascinating by his sympathetic portrayal of the final moments in the life of a lecherous old drunkard. The play ends with the Baron falling dead, a glass of champagne raised in his hand as a symbol of his commitment to drinking and debauchery. In conventional Victorian terms Mansfield played an immoral and depraved character, but he managed to make him fascinating and also understandable. This was in many ways preparation for his role as Dr. Jekyll.

Mansfield would not appear for his curtain calls after performing the Baron until he had removed his makeup and wig. This was to underscore the way in which he had used his body and face to transform himself into a wizened and dying old man. As he would later in *Jekyll and Hyde*, Mansfield wished to emphasize his ability to use his body and face to transform himself into a completely different person. He could have stayed in character and come out in his wig and makeup, but he wanted his audience to understand the range of expression available to a versatile actor such as himself.

Mansfield was what would now be called a method actor, in that he tried to become the character he was portraying. He would spend a few hours before each performance getting into character, and would not step out of a role until the performance was over. Mansfield's own ability to transform himself is undoubtedly what led him to appreciate the power of Stevenson's story as soon as he read it, and made him an ideal candidate to play the dual role of Dr. Jekyll/Mr. Hyde.

Mansfield spent the summer of 1883 on holiday in London. He returned to New York in the fall to rejoin the Union Square Theater Company, with which he had played the role of the Baron to such effect. Mansfield provoked a good deal of adverse commentary by arriving from England with a business manager, a man named Philip Beck, who he had met in London. He had successful performances on tour with the new company, and began to receive offers from other theaters for roles in forthcoming plays.

Mansfield then announced that he had purchased the rights to *A Parisian Romance* and was going to star in a tour of the play with a cast he had chosen. This was a bold move by an actor who had only one starring role to his name and very little capital to back up his plans. Mansfield performed the play in New York, Montreal and then Albany for Christmas. From that point on his tour was in jeopardy because audiences were small and the money collected was not enough to cover expenses. The tour collapsed in Cincinnati, and Mansfield returned to New York bankrupted by the experience.

Mansfield went back to playing with other peoples' companies, joining the Madison Square Theater for a long run of performances. For the next few years he performed in a series of forgettable plays in both New York and London, not achieving the breakthrough he hoped for; in the words of Wilstach, Mansfield was "born to star," and he was never content to languish in obscurity. These were by all accounts difficult years for him. As a result, he moved between several different companies and seemed always dissatisfied with his position.

A break finally came when in the winter of 1886; he was offered a large salary to play Ko-Ko in a floundering production of a new hit, Gilbert and Sullivan's *The Mikado*. Mansfield, who had experience playing in Gilbert and Sullivan comic operas while in England, was a hit, which helped rescue the production. While in Boston he was approached by the playwright Clavering Gunter, who had written a play about a German prince who acts as a guide for a group of Americans in Europe and falls in love with one of the women. Mansfield, with his knowledge of German high society and his singing ability, saw this as a good vehicle for his talents and decided to produce the play himself.

The play was called *Prince Karl*, and Mansfield was a hit playing the character of the Prince. The play opened in Boston on April 4, 1886, and then moved to New York in May. There was a brief *Prince Karl* craze in New York, with young women wearing Prince Karl rings and photos of Mansfield as the Prince selling at a brisk pace. Mansfield had his next hit after his brief fame as the Baron two years earlier.

Mansfield hired his own company to perform *Prince Karl* in New York, and it was thanks to his casting calls that he met the woman he was later to marry. Beatrice Cameron was an aspiring young actress who had performed several small roles in New York plays. Mansfield hired her for his company and took her with him on his company's tour from the winter of 1886 to the spring of 1887.

Adapting Jekyll and Hyde

It was at this point in his career that Mansfield read Stevenson's *The Strange Case of Dr. Jekyll and Mr. Hyde*. Mansfield was immediately drawn to the dramatic possibilities of the transformation from Jekyll into Hyde. He wrote to Stevenson and asked for permission to adapt the story for the stage, and secured permission for the American and British rights to the play. Mansfield agreed to pay royalties to Stevenson in exchange for these rights.

Mansfield collaborated in the adaptation with Thomas Russell Sullivan, a Boston friend who was early in a career as a novelist and playwright. While Sullivan was dubious that the work could be made into an effective drama, he agreed to help write the dialogue for Mansfield. It was written rapidly and rehearsed in only two weeks before opening at the Boston Museum on May 9, 1887. Mansfield knew it was a race against time to stage the play before others could adapt the Stevenson story, which was a bestseller, and he wanted to do it as soon as possible.

Given the lack of copyright laws in the U.S., anybody could print copies of works published in England without paying royalties, and could also freely adapt such works. Mansfield was aware that managers of other theater groups in the U.S. would recognize the commercial potential of the play and come out with their own adaptations of the story, which was indeed what happened.

His awareness of the competition was what drove him to adapt and perform the story in such haste.

Mansfield was in many ways the most qualified actor to play the dual role of Jekyll and Hyde, given his own interest in what the story refers to as "downgoing men"; that is, men who are about to lose their social status through some scandal or weakness on their part. He had already shown his interest in disreputable or morally questionable characters. Mansfield also appreciated the dramatic possibilities of one actor playing completely contrasting roles and had already shown his ability to carry out such a tour de force. However, in *Jekyll and Hyde* he pushed himself even harder by deciding to have the transformation take place on stage in front of his audience.

By all accounts he was extremely nervous about his ability to pull off this feat of onstage dramatic transformation. Wilstach quotes Mansfield's words about his first performance in the role, in Boston on May 9, 1887:

> That night in the third act where as Hyde I grasped the potion, swallowed it, writhed in the awful agony of transformation and rose pale and erect, the visualized embodiment of Jekyll—

Richard Mansfield. From a portrait by S. L. Stein.

> an ague of apprehension seized me and I suffered a lifetime in the silence in which the curtain fell. In another instant I realized that silence was the tribute of the awe and terror inspired by the reality of the scene, for through the canvas screen came a muffled roar which was the sweetest sound I ever heard in my life, and I breathed again [Wilstach, 145].

Mansfield accomplished his transformation through the use of special makeup and lights, and contorting his body. Dr. Jekyll would be shown by means of conventional lighting from above, but when Mansfield became Hyde another set of lights would illuminate his face from below. The combination of special makeup and the way in which Mansfield contorted both his face and body made it appear that he had been transformed into a new being.

After trying out the play and the role in Boston, Mansfield performed as Jekyll and Hyde for the first time in New York on

September 12, 1887, at the Madison Square Theater. The play was both a critical and commercial success. It was not surprising that the play was a commercial success, because Mansfield understood both how to scare his audience and how to use what was, for that time, state-of-the art special effects. As Wilstach says, Mansfield used all the tricks at his disposal to create suspense and horror for the audience:

> One of Mansfield's purely theatric devices for horror was to convey the suggestion that Hyde was coming. This was effected with an empty stage, a gray, green-shot loom, and oppressive silence. The curiosity was fascinating and whetted every nerve. At such a stage as this (the audience having seen Hyde before) the anticipation and the prolonged anticipation, the searching of the black corners for the demon all begot an hypnotic effect on the hushed, breathless spectators that held them in the fetters of an invincible interest. Then with a wolfish howl, a panther's leap, and the leer of a fiend Hyde was miraculously in view. It was at such a time as that that strong men shuddered and women fainted and were carried out of the theater [Wilstach 146].

In this age before horror movies, Mansfield's performance was the most horrifying entertainment available. There was a great deal of speculation as to how he achieved his transformation, and he countered the speculation by maintaining that he used no trickery, only his own voice and face. According to Wilstach, people left a Mansfield performance too frightened to enter their houses alone. Mansfield understood how to use the resources of the stage to strike terror into his audience, and how to manipulate suspense to heighten the impact of his on-stage performance. Women really were carried fainting out of the theater during Mansfield's performances as Mr. Hyde, because Mr. Hyde, as Mansfield portrayed him, was a figure who threatened women rather than men.

Encouraged by his collaboration with Sullivan, Mansfield tried his hand at writing a comedy for his theater troupe. This was performed under the title *Monsieur*, and the lead role of Monsieur de Jadot, a French gentleman who falls in love with a young New York woman, was played by Mansfield himself.

While the play was a modest success, it was nowhere near as popular as *Prince Karl*. Mansfield blamed its lack of success on the inability of American theater patrons to pronounce the French title, and their reluctance to say the play's name; he felt that had he given it the title "The Frenchman" it would have been much more successful.

Mansfield took his company and his now established repertoire of plays on tour for the remainder of 1887. He returned to New York for the summer season of 1888, and found himself challenged for the role of Dr. Jekyll by the German-American actor Daniel Bandmann, who was performing in another version of the play.

Henry Irving, who had established himself as an international star in England and the U.S., was in New York for the 1887-1888 theater season. Irving saw Mansfield's performance and invited him to bring his plays to his Lyceum Theater in London, and arranged for the opening play in September 1888 to be *Jekyll and Hyde*. Mansfield's plans had to be changed abruptly when he learned that Bandmann had booked his own performance of *Jekyll and Hyde* at the Opera Comique, beginning on August 6. Mansfield immediately set about calling his cast back from their summer vacations early, and gathering them in New York and setting sail for

England in early July. The opening date of his own performance of *Jekyll and Hyde* was secretly moved up to August 4, in order to preempt Bandmann by two days.

In contrast to his earlier stays in London, Mansfield was now wealthy enough to stay in style at a London hotel and expect to be noticed as a visiting American actor. However, London was not New York, and the reaction to his arrival was not as enthusiastic as he might have wished; while he was recognized as a name on the New York stage, his fame did not reach as far as England.

On Saturday, August 4, 1888, Mansfield acted the roles of Jekyll and Hyde at the Lyceum Theater. The play did not enjoy as much success as in the U.S., receiving mixed critical reviews and attracted a low number of customers. Not only were the customers less enthusiastic than in New York, London was also an extremely expensive city in which to perform, and Mansfield was losing money on his production. In order to try to boost box office receipts, he tried staging some of his stock pieces, among them *A Parisian Romance*, which opened on October 1, followed by *Prince Karl*.

The London Stage

Mansfield had much more success with *Prince Karl* and once again found fame by playing the lead romantic role in light comedies. This was not what he had in mind for his London season, and even with the added receipts he was still losing money. Despite his precarious situation, he was determined to make a name for himself as a serious actor.

Mansfield's next idea was to stage a production of Shakespeare's *Richard III* in the Globe Theater. Through this he wished to establish himself as a serious tragic actor, rather than just a player of light comedies and romances. He leased the Globe and began with some of his reliable productions, such as *Prince Karl*. He was planning to open *Richard III* in January, but was suddenly afflicted with respiratory problems and was ordered by his doctor to take a break from acting. He arranged for his company to continue without him while he recuperated, and he spent the time studying for his role in Shakespeare's play, trying to understand his character's psychology.

Mansfield opened *Richard III* on March 16, 1889, at the Globe. This was not a traditional production of the play, but a rearranged and reinterpreted version, staged according to Mansfield's own theories about the character of King Richard. He rearranged the sequence of scenes in *Richard III* and even introduced parts of speeches from *Henry VI* as part of a prologue. Mansfield essentially disregarded all conventional interpretations of the play and as Wilstach puts it, "wiped out three centuries of tradition" with his version (182).

This was Mansfield's attempt to establish himself as a serious tragic actor, equal to the task of tackling the greatest of Shakespearean roles in the capital of English drama. It's a daunting task for any actor to tackle a Shakespearean role, but Mansfield went even further by creating his own version of the play in which to star.

Mansfield brought to the staging of the play the same sensibility that allowed him to exploit the possibilities for horror and suspense in *Jekyll and Hyde*. In this case, however, he used pomp and pageantry to create his effects. The play was designed to be visually appealing, as well as being reworked according to Mansfield's sense of the drama. It ran until June 1, 1889, when his lease of the Globe ran out.

Unfortunately the play was not a financial success, and Mansfield lost more money thanks to his experiment in Shakespearean drama. He left England with a debt of more than $100,000.

Debt, Hard Work and Marriage

Mansfield hoped that his production of *Richard III*, having played in London, would help establish him as a serious tragic actor in the U.S., and enable him to stop performing in romantic comedies like *Prince Karl* and *Monsieur*. He opened *Richard III* at the Globe Theater in Boston on October 21, 1889, and planned to spend a year touring with only this one play. However, he failed to attract enough of an audience in Philadelphia, Baltimore and Washington, D.C., to make the tour profitable. The performances in New York were just as poorly attended, and on January 18, 1890, he closed the production down.

Mansfield had to reevaluate his plans and realized that he still had to perform in popular plays if he wanted to survive financially. He revived his productions of *Jekyll and Hyde* and *Prince Karl*, and started rehearsing a thriller that had been a hit in London and that he hoped would also be popular in New York. This was a melodrama called *Master and Man*, in which Mansfield played a villain called Humpy Logan. It, too, was a financial failure.

Mansfield opened the 1889-1890 theatrical season with a work by a relatively unknown Norwegian writer named Henrik Ibsen; the play was *The Doll House*. Ibsen was poised on the verge of popularity in the United States, and with the production of his play, Mansfield finally had a financial success. Mansfield also created a play as vehicle to play the part of Beau Brummel, the famous eighteenth-century English dandy. Mansfield wrote the play with a coauthor, as he had when writing his adaptation of the roles of Jekyll and Hyde. The resulting play, *Beau Brummel* was essentially a vehicle for Mansfield's talents, and had a very weak plot. It was, like *Prince Karl*, a romantic comedy that relied on the charm of the principal actor— Mansfield.

Beau Brummel was a success, but Mansfield's financial woes continued, and he was forced in the fall of 1890 to sell paintings and furniture to help pay off some of his debts.

He found it impossible to economize, however, and bought even more paintings and furniture. Mansfield's life seemed to be imitating art; Beau Brummel was similarly unable to control his spending, and ended his life deeply in debt, an outcast from the court.

This was to be Mansfield's problem for the next several years. While he made money on *Beau Brummel*, he promptly lost it on his production of *Don Juan*. Wilstach says that it was simply impossible for Mansfield to be economical (220), and that he spent money lavishly on himself and his productions.

He decided that a play based on the downfall of the Roman Emperor Nero, written by Sullivan, would be a hit, and mounted a very expensive production that again lost money.

At this point, Mansfield was in danger of being typecast as a player of villainous characters such as Mr. Hyde, Richard III and Nero. He also felt he was being victimized by the press in reviews of his productions, and found himself in an increasingly antagonistic relationship with drama critics. This, of course, made enemies of many reviewers and guaranteed that he would continue to get bad reviews. He was regarded as a good person to interview because he spoke his mind and had decided opinions on many matters; these qualities also alienated the people who had the misfortune to be criticized by him in print.

Mansfield enjoyed better luck in his personal life, marrying Beatrice Cameron on September 15, 1892. His personal fortunes began to turn as well when, in the winter of 1892-1893, a southern manager offered him a guarantee of $48,000 for 48 appearances in the south. This was, at the time, the largest guarantee ever made to an actor. The tour was a success, and Mansfield finally found himself with a national reputation. As a result of his increasing personal fortune, in 1894 he was able to buy a house in New York, and a yacht so that he could indulge his passion for sailing.

Also in 1894, Mansfield read the manuscript of a play by George Bernard Shaw called *Arms and the Man*. Shaw's play was potentially controversial, but Mansfield recognized it as having commercial potential and decided to produce it, opening the play in New York on September 17, 1894. The play was a great critical success but, as with so many of Mansfield's experiments, initially it lost money and its first run had to be cancelled after three weeks.

When Shaw later wrote a play based on the life of Napoleon called *A Man of Destiny*, he claimed that he had based his character on Mansfield himself (Wilstach, 264). Mansfield's imperious character and his autocratic managing style apparently made him a natural for the role of Napoleon. Mansfield professed himself a monarchist, and enjoyed having his own company so that he could control all aspects of a play's production. He maintained his connection with Shaw for the rest of his acting career, and played the leading role in *The Devil's Disciple* on October 1, 1897.

In 1895 Mansfield suffered a nearly fatal attack of typhoid fever. He had by then assumed the lease of what was once Harrigan's Theater, which he renamed The Garrick and redecorated in sumptuous fashion. Since he was sick and could not perform, Mansfield arranged for a series of plays to be presented, which he organized and advertised as "Richard Mansfield presents." This was an innovation that was later widely adopted in New York theater.

When he had recovered from his illness Mansfield played yet another tortured character, Raskolnikov from Dostoyevski's *Crime and Punishment*. The adaptation of the story in which he performed was called *The Story of Rodion, the Student*. As the title indicates, Raskolnikov's name was changed to Rodion. Mansfield by all accounts was compelling in his enactment of the murder that is the climax of the fourth scene. Critics felt that this was the most compelling performance that he had ever given.

Financial and Dramatic Success

Mansfield had his greatest commercial success with his version of *Cyrano de Bergerac*. The play was a huge hit in Paris, and when Mansfield read the script he concluded that it would also play well in the U.S. He also decided that he was perfectly suited to the lead role of Cyrano. He took a huge gamble on the play, mortgaging his house and everything he owned to finance the production.

A *Cyrano de Bergerac* craze hit the U.S. in 1898, and several English versions were printed, selling out as demand for the story escalated. There were spinoff products of Cyrano figures and recipes based on the almond cream tarts featured in the play.

Such hype before the opening of a play in the U.S was unprecedented (although it is now familiar in the marketing of new movies) and there was pent-up demand for the performance before Mansfield even took the stage. However, there were several rival productions, including one that opened on the same night as Mansfield's, October 3, 1898.

So large were the crowds on the opening night of the performance that scalpers were able to charge well above the face value of tickets. The first night saw numerous curtain calls for Mansfield, and the play was a critical and popular success. The season in New York and the subsequent tour were the most lucrative and successful of his career, and marked the apotheosis of Mansfield's reputation as an actor.

His tours were compared to those of royalty, and were undertaken on a special train that carried him and his company across the country.

In 1900 Mansfield again tackled Shakespeare, mounting a production of *Henry V*. As usual, he did things on a grand scale, with a huge cast and elaborate sets in a four-hour extravaganza. Mansfield was by now an established name in theater, and despite the daunting length of the play it was sold out for its eight-week run in New York.

Mansfield's final new role was in an adaptation of a story called *Monsieur Beaucaire*, in which he played the title role. This was another light comedy and a role very similar to that of *Prince Karl*, and played upon the U.S. interest in European class distinctions. It was a light role in contrast to the tragic roles for which Mansfield wanted to be recognized.

Later in his life Mansfield did achieve some of the recognition he craved as a Shakespearean actor when, in 1904, he played Shylock in *The Merchant of Venice* and *Richard III*. Given his status as a star, he could now stage lavish Shakespearean productions and still show a profit. However, during a performance of *Richard III* he complained of tiredness and was unable to continue. This was the first sign of his failing health.

Final Days

Mansfield was ill throughout the summer of 1905 and had surgery shortly before the opening of the fall theater season. He had hoped to recover quickly from surgery and resume his usual demanding schedule.

The opening of his season was delayed due to his illness, but he eventually started performing, despite warnings from doctors that he was endangering his health. Their advice was for him to retire from the physically demanding work of acting. Mansfield announced that he would retire from acting in 1910, but in the meantime, he intended to continue.

In 1906 Mansfield began playing the role of Peer Gynt in the Ibsen play, but said ominously that "I dig a spadeful of earth for my grave every time I play the part" (Wilstach, 467). He was aware that his health was deteriorating, but he continued to appear on stage every night. His words about digging his own grave were prophetic—he made his last appearance on the stage on March 23, 1907, playing the role in which he had his first success, that of Baron Chevrial.

The next day Mansfield came down with a fever and stomach cramps and was diagnosed with "nervous exhaustion." He was advised to stop working and rest immediately, so the company was broken up and he left with his family to spend the summer recuperating in England. However, his health did not improve and Mansfield grew restless to return to New York, using the chill of the English summer as an excuse to leave.

He returned to his house in Connecticut; unable to walk by this time, he had to be moved around by wheelchair. Mansfield died peacefully in his sleep at his Connecticut home on August 30, 1907. In an obituary the *New York Times* hailed him as "the greatest actor of his hour, and the greatest of all times."

It may be something of an exaggeration to call him the greatest actor of all times, but there was no doubt that he was the most commanding actor in America at the time of his death, especially on the New York stage. While Mansfield did not achieve the reputation he desired in England, by 1907 he was the preeminent male actor in America and at the pinnacle of his profession.

2
Thomas Russell Sullivan

Thomas Russell Sullivan (1849–1916) was born in Boston on November 21, 1849. His father was the Reverend Thomas Russell, a Unitarian minister, and his mother was Charlotte Caldwell. He was educated in the Boston area and found work in the city after his education. He lived in Europe from 1870 to 1873, but returned to Boston and worked as a clerk and cashier for Lee, Higginson & Co., a firm of brokers, until 1888.

In 1888 Sullivan left his job as a clerk to devote himself full-time to writing. Up until this point he had written only after working hours. He aspired to be a novelist and dramatist. Like Richard Mansfield he moved in Boston literary circles, and it was through this connection that he and Mansfield met. Selections from his journals were published in 1917 as *Passages from the Journal of Thomas Russell Sullivan*. Unfortunately these journals only cover the period from 1891 to 1903, so they do not include the composition and staging of the version of *Jekyll and Hyde* that he and Mansfield created. However, Sullivan was moved by the death of Robert Louis Stevenson in 1894 to write in his *Journals* an account of his visit to Saranac Lake, New York, to read the script of his version of *Jekyll and Hyde* to the author. This reminiscence is reproduced in Appendix A.

The journal also records Sullivan's gradual estrangement from Richard Mansfield. After their initial collaboration on *Jekyll and Hyde*, Sullivan wrote a script for a play called *Nero* in which Mansfield was to play the Roman Emperor. Sullivan gives a vivid account of a clash between Mansfield and one of his principle actors during rehearsals of *Nero*. The actor did not take kindly to words of criticism from Mansfield, and the two started an argument which escalated to the point that the other actor was fired. The argument lasted a couple of days and was covered in the local newspapers. Mansfield's high-handed actions showed that he richly deserved the ironic title "His Royal," which Sullivan used to describe him.

Nero was not a great success in New York, and Sullivan felt that Mansfield did not perform the play frequently enough or give it enough publicity. Whatever the case, the play disappeared from Mansfield's repertoire altogether, and its demise signaled the end of the collaboration between the two men.

Nero was not Sullivan's only foray into theater; he wrote two original plays for the

Boston stage, *Hearts Are Trumps* and *Midsummer Madness*. He was only moderately successful as a novelist, and as his experience with *Nero* shows, he had no success as a dramatist after the popular *Jekyll and Hyde*. His novels include *Roses of Shadow* (1885), *Tom Sylvester* (1893), *Ars et Vita* (1898), *The Courage of Conviction* (1902), and *The Hand of Petrarch* (1913). He was esteemed chiefly as a short story writer and had some success with his *Day and Night Stories* (1890, 1893), a two-volume series of short fiction. Sullivan's name now comes up most often in association with *Jekyll and Hyde*, and in lists of Gothic stories and their authors, because many of his short stories contain supernatural elements. His novels have been largely forgotten.

Thomas Sullivan died in Boston on June 28, 1916; he had no children.

3

Robert Louis Stevenson

Robert Lewis (later changed to "Louis") Balfour Stevenson was born in Edinburgh on November 13, 1850. Stevenson, according to most accounts, preferred the French spelling of "Louis," although he retained the English pronunciation. His father, Thomas Stevenson, belonged to a family of engineers that had built most of the deep-sea lighthouses around the rocky coast of Scotland. His mother, Margaret Isabella Balfour, came from a family of lawyers and church ministers. In 1857 the family moved to 17 Heriot Row, in the New Town section of Edinburgh. New Town dated from the late eighteenth century and had wide streets and elegant houses. The Old Town, by contrast, was crowded and contained the city's poverty-stricken slums. In the nineteenth century, Edinburgh, like London, was divided into two distinct areas, close to each other physically but worlds apart in terms of quality of life.

Stevenson's mother, Margaret Isabella Balfour, seems to have suffered from many bouts of ill health from 1850 to 1862, during Stevenson's formative years, and much of his education was left to the family nurse, Alison Cunningham, who Stevenson called "Cummy." Stevenson later called Cummy "my second mother, my first wife." Cummy was very religious and expounded an extreme Calvinist doctrine to the young Stevenson. She also told him many stories of body snatchers, demons, devils and ghosts, which he could draw upon later in stories such as "Thrawn Janet" and "The Body Snatchers." As a child Stevenson was sickly and was often bedridden, and he also suffered from intense nightmares. He imitated Cummy by being a very devout child.

At the age of seventeen, in November 1867, he enrolled at Edinburgh University to study engineering, with the aim of following the family tradition of designing lighthouses. However, he abandoned his engineering studies, making a compromise with his father — he would study law rather than becoming a writer, which was his real desire. His father did not regard writing as a serious enough profession for his son. Stevenson's choice of law, rather than engineering, and then his abandonment of law in favor of becoming a writer, caused contention between father and son. A further breach was opened between them when, in 1873, Thomas Stevenson discovered that his son had joined a socialist club at the university and considered himself an agnostic.

Stevenson was called to the Scottish bar in 1875, but he did not practice. By then he knew that his one desire was to be a professional writer. As a student Stevenson had a reputation for frequenting the areas of the Old Town associated with drinking and vice, as he describes in his poem "Brasheana." He also had the reputation of being a Bohemain in his dress and manner. The term "Bohemian" was used in the nineteenth century to describe anybody who aspired to lead a free, vagabond or in some way unconventional life that set him or her apart from mainstream society. During the university's summer vacations, Stevenson went to France to be in the company of other young artists, both writers and painters. His first published work was an essay on travel called "Roads," and his first books were works of travel writing describing his experiences in France.

In Grez, France, in July of 1876, Stevenson met Fanny Osbourne and her two children. He was twenty-five, and she was thirty-six. Osbourne was estranged from her husband in the United States and was studying art. A romance followed, with Stevenson spending more and more time in Fanny Osbourne's company when she moved to Paris and when she later accompanied him to London. In the summer of 1878 Fanny Osbourne left for the United States, after her husband threatened to cut off her financial support if she did not return. She resumed living with him in San Francisco, while Stevenson lived in London and became more and more despondent. In July 1879 Fanny Osbourne's husband left her, and she sent an urgent telegram to Stevenson informing him of the situation. As a result he expedited plans to visit the United States and bought a cheap steamship ticket to New York. From New York he rode the railroad west to San Francisco, writing of his experiences in the books later published as *The Amateur Emigrant* and *Across the Plains*.

Fanny Osbourne finalized the divorce from her husband in December of 1879 and married Stevenson the following May. During this time Stevenson had very little money and was under a great strain. He experienced several serious illnesses, including the beginning of tuberculosis-like symptoms that would afflict him for the rest of his life. For their honeymoon the couple squatted in a deserted miner's shack in the Silverado Hills. Stevenson chronicled their existence there in *The Silverado Squatters*.

Fanny and Robert Louis Stevenson returned to Scotland together, able to travel first class this time because Stevenson's father had promised him an income of 250 pounds a year. Thanks partly to Fanny's intervention, Stevenson was reconciled with his father. After staying in Davos in Switzerland, where Stevenson could receive treatment for his diseased lungs, they moved to different locations in southern France, finally settling in Hyeres, where Stevenson spent what he said were the happiest days of his life. Persuaded that Hyeres was unhealthy, the Stevensons moved to the Auvergne region for the summer and settled in Royat, which had hot springs and mineral waters. They later returned to Hyeres. They left Hyeres in June of 1884 when an epidemic of cholera was reported in the region, and reunited with Stevenson's parents in England.

The Stevensons then moved to Bournemouth, mainly because Lloyd, Fanny's son, was in school in the area. Bournemouth was a relatively new seaside resort that advertised itself as a healthy place to live because of its mild climate and surrounding pine forests. Initially the Stevensons rented a house in the Bransome Park area called Bonallie Tower. In February 1885 Stevenson's father provided the money to buy and furnish a house in the genteel Westbourne area of Bournemouth. It was in this house that Stevenson wrote *The*

Strange Case of Dr. Jekyll and Mr. Hyde. Stevenson named the house "Skerryvore," after one of the Scottish lighthouses built by his family, and had a model of the original lighthouse built by the entrance to the house. Stevenson lived in Bournemouth for three years. While at Skerryvore Stevenson had frequent visits from Henry James, who had a sister living in Bournemouth, and had his portrait painted by James McNeill Whistler.

Stevenson's father died in May of 1886, and his son as a result inherited a sizeable amount of money and the ability to travel wherever he wanted. The Stevensons left Skerryvore for America on August 21, 1887. He received a warm welcome in New York, thanks to his fame due to the success of *Dr. Jekyll and Mr. Hyde.* Stevenson learned that a stage version of the story was to open in Manhattan the week after their arrival. Stevenson did not see the play, although Fanny and her mother attended a performance. The Stevensons went from New York to Saranac Lake in the Adirondack mountains. Saranac Lake was the site of a sanatorium for consumptive patients and the Stevensons rented a trapper's cottage there. There he wrote *The Master of Ballantrae.*

It was while they were living at Saranac Lake that Sullivan came to visit Stevenson, and read to him the script of *Jekyll and Hyde.* This reading was to establish copyright for the play and obtain Stevenson's approval of the script. According to Sullivan, Stevenson liked what he had done with the original story in adapting it for the stage. Much of Sullivan's visit was taken up with discussions of Stevenson's favorite authors and influences on his fiction.

The Stevensons again abruptly decamped when in May Fanny sent an excited telegram to her husband, saying that she had found the yacht *Casco* for hire. Stevenson immediately told her to arrange for the rental, because he planned to write a series of letters from the Pacific, for which he had been offered a $10,000 commission. When the ship reached Polynesia in July 1888, Stevenson was struck by the beauty of the islands. He decided not to return to America or England, but to spend his time cruising around the Pacific islands. As a writer he needed to find an island with a fast mailship service so that he could keep in contact with his publishers. Stevenson settled on Samoa in 1890, and he lived there for the rest of his short life. He lived on an estate called Vailima that included waterfalls, precipices, ravines and tableland. He died at age 44 on Monday, December 3, 1894, and was buried on the summit of Mount Vaea on Samoa.

Part II

The Scene

4

The American Stage and Popular Entertainment

Richard Mansfield and the American Stage

Richard Mansfield's theatrical career coincided with a profound change in the economic and organizational structure of American theater. The changes took place at several levels, from the management of actors to the booking of plays in theaters. Mansfield embodied elements of both the old way of running theaters and the new, and was thus a key transitional figure in the development of American theater. In his acting, his management of his career, and his choice of plays he bridged the transition from the traditional preindustrial forms of organization, to the commodification of "mass culture" in the twentieth century.

The basic unit of American theater until the 1870s was the stock company. This company would be based in one city and would have an established repertoire of plays and performers. Certain actors would achieve fame in their immediate area and theater patrons would expect to appreciate their favorite actor or actress in a variety of roles. Established, serious theater would concentrate heavily on Shakespearean classics and would perform each for a limited amount of time in a season. While a few actors would become nationally known, most were known only in their local area.

This changed dramatically in the 1870s, marking a crucial turning point in the history of American theater. In a very short space of time the old stock companies were replaced by a new kind of unit, the combination company. Combination companies did not stay in one place, and traveled around the country. They were built around one star, who would assemble a cast of lesser actors and actresses and take them on tours from city to city. These companies concentrated more on popular hits than on Shakespearean classics, and adopted the "long run," which meant that a "successful" play would be performed for an extended engagement to take advantage of its popularity.

As John Frick says, "by the end of the 19th century American theatre had become yet another American industry ... manufacturer of a product prepared and packaged for nationwide distribution" (198). Mansfield adapted to some of these changes with enthusiasm and resisted others. Mansfield took readily to the new combination companies; as his biography shows, extremely early in his career he tried to form his own touring company. Running his own combination company was part of his strategy for achieving "star" status.

Mansfield's biography is peppered with tales of train travel; early stories of his career describe him desperately trying to raise the money required to move his new company from city to city. At times he had to borrow money on the strength of his luggage to pay the train fare to the next city. Anecdotes tell of Mansfield arriving late for engagements, for example one in Texas, and demonstrate his dependence on the rail system. It allowed him to move not only his actors but entire stage sets around, but if the train was delayed, the whole play was delayed because the sets had to be assembled before they could perform. Once Mansfield was established as a star he had his own train and personal carriage, putting him in the company of royalty and robber barons. True to his patrician tastes, he traveled in style in his own carriage and had excellent meals prepared for him. Mansfield's career would not have been possible without the rail system, which helped bring about the combination company and facilitated Mansfield's role in its development.

A change that Mansfield vigorously but unsuccessfully opposed was made in the way in which plays were booked. Initially there was the "theatrical circuit" system. A theatrical circuit was a group of theaters that banded together to coordinate bookings, and a traveling company could arrange its own itinerary by arranging dates with one or more theatrical circuits. These circuits could be a series of nearby cities, or venues on a railway line. Gradually the circuits became centralized, and more and more power became concentrated in the hands of a few theatrical entrepreneurs.

This centralization led, by 1896, to the creation of the Theatrical Syndicate. It was the most monopolistic organization of theaters in the history of American theater, and had a virtual stranglehold on bookings. The Syndicate organized the largest theatrical circuits in the country under the direct control of the country's most prestigious theaters. This power allowed the Syndicate to start dictating terms to other theaters and performers. Independent-minded managers and actors like Richard Mansfield fought the Syndicate and carried out extensive publicity campaigns decrying its effect on American theater, but to no avail.

Mansfield was particularly vehement in his opposition to the Syndicate because he himself tried to maintain two roles that were increasingly divergent: producer and theater manager. He moved back and forth between producing his plays in other peoples' theaters to being the manager and producer, for instance at the Garrick. He was responsible for changing Harrigan's Theater, which had been closely identified with its manager, into the Garrick. With the growth and increased specialization in American theater this combination became increasingly anachronistic, and Mansfield was fighting a steady current of change in trying to remain both the star of his own shows and a theater manager.

While Mansfield may have complained about the Syndicate, he did benefit from the increased integration of American theaters because they facilitated his ascent to star status. He was also helped by the well-developed New York theater scene. Thanks to its elaborate transportation infrastructure and large population, New York supported a thriving and well-established dramatic community that was unrivalled in the country. Mansfield, once he had made a name for himself in New York, could count on the prestige of its theater scene to gain him fame in other cities. While Mansfield aspired to a reputation to equal that of Henry Irving in London, he was by the end of his life the leading man on the New York stage, which guaranteed his status nationwide. While he did not achieve the fame he desired in London, he did achieve it in New York.

New York's theaters were centrally located and very early in the century became a recognizable hub for drama. While its center shifted as the century went on, there was an established theater district throughout Mansfield's career. Theaters often contained a restaurant, and what we would now term "cross marketing" could be carried out. Thus during the first successful run of *Prince Karl*, Mansfield capitalized on his status as a romantic lead by having spoons bearing the words "compliments of Prince Karl" given out to female patrons when they ordered ice cream.

Mansfield also showed himself willing to use a new kind of professional in the theater world, a manager, to coordinate his publicity and engagements. It was a mark of Mansfield's ambition that he chose to do this after his very first successful production, and so early in his career as to provoke some negative commentary in the New York press about an upstart actor presuming to act like an established star. It was a sign both of Mansfield's confidence and his awareness of the growing star system created by the industrialization of the United States. Thanks to increased communication and the expansion of a national system of news due to the telegraph, an actor's reputation could be established on a nationwide basis. Mansfield clearly tried to do this too early in his career, but it showed his awareness of the possibilities of publicity which could turn a New York actor into a nationwide star.

Mansfield from the start was aware of the importance of the media to his career, but his temperament meant that he was often at loggerheads with newspapers. He took criticisms of his performances quite personally, and was quick to defend himself against perceived attacks in print. Mansfield had a touch of paranoia, and often felt that there was a conspiracy to hold back his career. He obviously stood to benefit from having a manager who could handle the media for him. This is the role that Paul Wilstach, one of his biographers, performed during the latter stage of Mansfield's career.

Mansfield and Popular Entertainment

While Mansfield aspired to be a serious tragic actor and to be noted for his portrayal of Shakespearean characters, he also benefited from American tastes for melodrama, the Gothic and light comedies. The dominant dramatic form in the United States throughout the nineteenth century was melodrama. Melodrama emerged as a dramatic form in France, during the Revolution, and was seen as popular and democratic entertainment for the people. Melodrama simplified social issues into good versus bad, and often portrayed evil landlords and other people in positions of power. The form was so diverse that it has to be subclassified into types such as "domestic melodramas" and "melodramas of spectacle." The emphasis in melodrama was on overwrought emotions and actions, and it could be played as either tragedy or comedy.

While Mansfield's plays were not outright melodramas, they were acted within a context in which melodrama was the dominant form. The final scene in *Jekyll and Hyde*, when Dr. Jekyll sees Agnes for the last time, could be a scene from a melodrama. The scene contains overwrought emotions, an individual brought to the edge of despair by a sequence of events, and the conflict between easily recognizable "good" and "evil" characters. In Stevenson's story good and evil are actually contained in one person, but the basic structure of the play is melodramatic since it pits a good but troubled character against an obviously evil force in Mr. Hyde. There is no question that Mr. Hyde is evil and, thanks to Sullivan's adaptation of the Stevenson plot, Dr. Jekyll comes across as a good man at heart.

Melodrama seems artificial and contrived to us now, but this is simply because dramatic norms have changed. Melodrama is in many ways alive and well and appearing on the cinema screen. Films have melodramatic elements in them, and audiences are willing to suspend their disbelief and believe all sorts of bizarre and improbable plot twists when they occur in movies. By the same process nineteenth-century audiences suspended disbelief and enjoyed the plot twists and spectacles of melodrama. Because American theater was above all a popular theater, plays that succeeded in the United States all tended to have melodramatic elements, romance and a moral ending that upheld good against evil.

As the century progressed melodrama also adopted more and more of what we would call special effects. Shipwrecks with real water, horses and a real horse race on stage, a steam engine, and giant battles involving casts of hundreds became selling points for melodramas. Mansfield incorporated some aspects of these special effects in his Shakespearean productions, emphasizing for instance the use of a huge cast to reenact battle scenes. His most notable use of special effects was, however, his transformation from Dr. Jekyll into Mr. Hyde, on stage in front of his audience's very eyes.

Mansfield's sudden transformation from Jekyll into Hyde took him into the realm of performance known as quick-change artistry. Quick-change artists included practitioners of "chapeaugraphy," who could change their appearances through distortions of their faces under different hats, and "shadowgraphy," in which performers used the shadows of their hands to create different shapes. Mansfield did a quick change on stage before his audiences thanks to his own chameleon-like control over his appearance (frequently commented on by friends and critics) and new technical innovations in lighting brought about first by gaslight and then the light bulb. Thanks to improvements in stage lighting technicians could now switch immediately between banks of lights, and Mansfield used two different sets of lights, one for Dr. Jekyll and the other for Mr. Hyde.

Mansfield himself would never have thought of his performance as quick-change artistry. He viewed himself as a serious actor, while quick change artists were performers at carnivals or on streets. However, his performance can be seen in a continuum that includes this kind of street theater, as well as contortionists, magicians and escape artists. Mansfield's control over his face and body was an integral part of his performance, and he depended for his success as much on his physical ability as did these other performers. Mansfield would see himself as an artist and these others as mere performers, but take away the context of established theater and Mansfield was relying on his ability to shock and surprise his audience as much as any street performer. The gasps that accompanied his transformation on the stage of the theater were the same as those sought by any quick-change performer.

The status of his performances was an issue that bothered Mansfield all his life. While he craved the social status of a serious tragic actor who had succeeded on the

London stage like Henry Irving, he was known more for acting in comedies and popular dramas. As a young man he had been forced to perform for money at friends' houses, and it was this kind of low status performance for money that led to the rupture with his mother. Erminia Rudersdorff, thanks to her social connections and the social status of performing classical and operatic pieces, was of a distinctly higher social class than was implied by her son's having to stage small soirees for money. Her outrage at the loss of social status suffered by her son, no matter how desperate his plight, led to her severance of his allowance.

While in his mother's eyes her son had become a mere performer, Mansfield was never in doubt of his own social status. He was known as a gourmet who kept an elegantly furnished home even when he was faced with financial difficulties. Mansfield, raised by a mother who moved in high social circles, had high social aspirations himself. His ambition to be an acknowledged Shakespearean actor was part of his social ambition, reflecting his desire for an aristocratic lifestyle and the status of a star.

Mansfield's difficulties in establishing his status were mirrored in his production of *Jekyll and Mr. Hyde*. While the play was popular and a financial success, a critic and biographer like Winter nonetheless bemoaned Mansfield's choice of characters. Dr. Jekyll seemed to Winter not a tragic character but a repellent one, and despite the apparent moral of the tale, he saw the story as sordid. It was not, in Winter's eyes, high tragedy, but rather a more debased, popular form of entertainment.

The Strange Case of Dr. Jekyll and Mr. Hyde would comfortably be classified now as a horror story; in the nineteenth-century it would have been labeled a Gothic tale. The Gothic in its nineteenth-century form was primarily found in novels and concerned young heroines threatened by dark, possibly supernatural dangers. As the century progressed the genre came to include ghost stories, vampire stories and adventure stories with a fantastic element to them. The original Gothic novels were designed to create a dark, foreboding atmosphere and to evoke emotions of awe and terror in their readers. The action often took place in old buildings or the ruins of medieval (or Gothic in the architectural sense of the term) buildings. Like the term "horror," the term "Gothic" is amorphous, and elements of the Gothic can be found in narratives that do not fit entirely within the classic definition of the genre.

While *The Strange Case of Dr. Jekyll and Mr. Hyde* does not have Gothic buildings or endangered heroines as part of the narrative, it is clearly intended to strike terror into the heart of the reader. The evil double, or doppelganger, element was a classic Gothic device, as was demonic possession and shape changing. These are all found in Stevenson's narrative. Mansfield played up, quite literally, the fear factor in the narrative when he used music and lighting to create suspense before the appearance of Mr. Hyde, and horror at the transformation. The play thus draws on the same emotions of terror and suspense elicited by Gothic fiction.

The Gothic is a precursor to contemporary genre fiction. While Stevenson was using Gothic conventions for innovative ends, it shows how close his own tale of terror was to "shilling shockers" and other mass forms of publishing. Just as with melodrama, the literary Gothic was a popular form that emphasized action and exaggerated emotion over character development. The Gothic can now be found in a residual form in science fiction, horror and detective genres; Stevenson's tale combines elements of horror and the detective genre, drawing upon emotions of both suspense and revulsion. Mansfield's production was more unambiguously located in the horror genre. The appeal of Mansfield's play was entirely in its horror and the awe inspired by his daring quick-change artistry. As newspapers at the time noted, grown men shuddered and women fainted when he carried out his transformation on stage.

Mansfield's Acting

David Holcomb Burr carried out an extensive study of Mansfield's acting based on contemporary reviews and Mansfield's own lecture on the subject, delivered at the University of Chicago in 1898. Burr focused on certain areas of Mansfield's technique, including:

Bodily control — Thanks to his control over his muscles Mansfield could make himself look shrunken and old, as he did when playing Ivan the Terrible, for example. Mansfield was normally large and imposing, so the contrast for audiences was remarkable. He used this ability, of course, to great effect in *Jekyll and Hyde*.

Facial Expression — He had an extremely mobile and expressive face, and could change rapidly from one emotion to another. Again, he used this ability in *Jekyll and Hyde* to switch rapidly from the serene expression of Dr. Jekyll to the terrible leer of Mr. Hyde.

Vocal Expression — Trained as a singer, Mansfield had great control of his voice, and could project it to the back row of the largest of theaters. Indeed, early in his career he would occasionally entertain particularly dedicated audiences by singing as a bonus.

Character — He was by nature a commanding figure, with a strong personality obvious in his bearing. This force of character was amplified on stage. Critics and audiences would refer to his "magnetism" to characterize the power he projected on stage. Mansfield emphasized "force of will" in his own comments on acting, showing his awareness of his use of his own powerful presence in creating a character.

By today's standards, Mansfield's acting would seem exaggerated and overly formal. A more conversational style has come to characterize acting, especially in film, in which the proximity of the camera makes projecting the voice unnecessary. By the standards of his day Mansfield declaimed far less than the "classical" actors who preceded him, such as Booth. These actors would emphasize clear elocution and projection of their voices in even the most heated moments. Mansfield put far more emphasis on the expression of emotion and was accused of being indistinct when he became impassioned.

Mansfield was thus a transitional figure between the more modern and conversational form of acting and the older, declamatory style. This style was declining when he started his career, but because of his voice training and temperament his style resembled the older form. His range of facial expressions and attention to emotion, however, also made his delivery similar to the newer style of acting.

Mansfield was criticized by some critics for being overly stiff and for having a stock set of motions that he used across different characters. What critics saw as his lack of spontaneity was probably the residual presence in Mansfield's acting of the classical approach. Given Mansfield's interest in acquiring status as a serious, tragic actor, his delivery would reflect his desire for a commanding stage presence, rather than a more colloquial and apparently spontaneous form of acting. Critics referred to his acting style as "old" and being "stiff and heavy" (Burr, 88).

Critics were contradictory, however. Those that favored the old, classical style of declamation found Mansfield's delivery too staccato and at times indistinct. Other critics found his way of speaking "artificial" and "dry." The best summary of these conflicting attitudes is found in a quotation from the *New York Times* that Burr reproduces:

> Mansfield's voice is deep, rich and of good compare. He used it well last night, but as a mere elocutionist he is rarely perfect according to the old standards. The thought, the emotion concern him more than the word. In his bursts of fury he sometimes forgets the metre. Your true tragedian never did. He was first of all an interpreter of poets. Actors like Mansfield are first of all impersonators of character as they comprehend it.

Unfortunately for Mansfield he did not, in the critic's eyes, have the delivery of a tragedian. He did, however, show signs of the new kind of acting, what would now be called method acting, in which immersing oneself in the character is more important than eloquent delivery. Mansfield was notorious for remaining in character throughout a performance, and he did not like to have the illusion that he actually was Dr. Jekyll disturbed.

The critic shows some suspicion of this form of acting as impersonation, which makes it sound more like a piece of clever street theater, like a player impersonating a famous figure, than a piece of classical acting. The prejudice against "mere" impersonation showed the hierarchy of values still entrenched among critics even when they could appreciate how different Mansfield's aims and intentions were from the previous model of elocutionary delivery. While the critic at the *New York Times* recognized that Mansfield was trying to achieve an effect that was different from the older form of acting, he could not grant it the same status as the delivery of a true tragedian.

The change in acting methods was part of a cultural shift in American popular entertainment. Whereas earlier in the century the emphasis had been upon language and the delivery of lines, particularly lines delivered as a form of poetry, Mansfield's "impersonation" relied heavily on the visual. Mansfield would physically become his character, and change his body, costume and features to mimic the character he was playing. The words themselves became less important than the emotion conveyed in the performance and the illusion of a transformation of character. Indeed, the lines in Mansfield's *Jekyll and Hyde* are often less than memorable, and rely upon the skill of the actor combined with his command of special effects to give the words their impact.

Richard Mansfield was undoubtedly an accomplished actor and could impersonate a murderer like Mr. Hyde to great effect. Unfortunately, his talents landed him on the suspect list in one of the most notorious series of murders in history. Mansfield found himself playing a fictional murderer on stage when Jack the Ripper was stalking the streets of Whitechapel in East London.

5

The Jack the Ripper Case

Jack the Ripper's Victims

On the same day that unfavorable reviews of Daniel Bandmann's "Dr. Jekyll and Mr. Hyde" appeared in the London press, the *Star* reported "A Whitechapel Horror." This was the murder of thirty-nine-year-old Martha Tabram in George Yard Buildings, Whitechapel. The victim had been stabbed 39 times during a frenzied attack in the early hours of Tuesday, August 7, 1888, but her death attracted little press attention at the time. By the beginning of September, however, this crime had been linked to an earlier assault on Emma Elizabeth Smith and the subsequent murder of Mary Ann Nichols, and the press began to report an apparently related series of Whitechapel murders, which were soon attributed to Jack the Ripper.

Emma Elizabeth Smith, a forty-five-year-old widow, was robbed, raped, and violated with a blunt instrument by a gang of youths in Osborn Street, Whitechapel, during the early hours of Tuesday, April 3, 1888. She was taken to the London Hospital, where she died of peritonitis the next day. The body of forty-three-year-old Mary Nichols was discovered around 3:40 on the morning of Friday, August 31, in Buck's Row, Whitechapel. Her throat had been cut "from ear to ear" and her abdomen ripped open. In the ten weeks that followed, four more East End prostitutes shared a similar fate.

Around 5:45 on the morning of Saturday, September 8, the mutilated body of forty-seven-year-old Annie Chapman was discovered in the backyard of 29 Hanbury Street, Spitalfields. Chapman's throat had been ferociously severed, her abdomen cut open and its contents drawn out and placed on the ground above her right shoulder, while her womb had been removed and taken away by the killer. The nature of these mutilations led to the conclusion that the murderer may have possessed some medical expertise. Together with the missing organ, this gave rise to what became known as the Burke and Hare theory when Coroner Wynne Baxter, in summing up his inquest into Chapman's death, introduced the possibility that the murder may have been committed by someone looking to obtain particular body parts.

At 1:00 in the morning on Sunday, September 30, the body of forty-five-year-old Elizabeth Stride was found in Dutfield's Yard, Berner Street, St. George's-in-the-East. Although Stride's throat had been cut, her body was not otherwise mutilated. This gave rise to the belief that the murderer must have been disturbed before he could complete his work. This view seemed to be reinforced when, only forty-five minutes after the discovery of Stride's body, the severely mutilated corpse of forty-six-year-old Catharine Eddowes was discovered in Mitre Square, Aldgate, within the square mile that constituted the old City of London. Finally, a little after 10:45 on the morning of November 9, the butchered remains of twenty-five-year-old Mary Jane Kelly were discovered in room No. 13, Miller's Court, Dorset Street, Spitalfields. Despite the occasional subsequent scare, it is generally accepted that the death of Mary Kelly brought to an end the killing spree of Jack the Ripper.

Particularly between September 8 and mid–November, the murders were the subject of sensational press reporting. Successive inquests, protracted through lengthy adjournments, helped sustain interest by effectively serializing the developing story of the Whitechapel murders. A letter and postcard, purportedly written by the murderer, were published after the "double event" of September 30, and provided the soon to be eponymous villain with a sensational sobriquet. In between inquest sessions and sensation seeking, however, the official police policy of withholding as much information as possible from journalists often left newspapers with little but rumor and speculation to report. In such circumstances column inches were filled by the often wild theorizing of correspondents, together with Whitechapel-related criticism of government personnel and policy, police administration and methods, and the iniquities of prevailing social conditions, as some newspapers sought to promote their preferred political ideals in the run-up to the first London County Council election.

At the outset it was thought that one of the gangs known to terrorize East End prostitutes could be responsible for the Whitechapel murders. Following Nichols' murder, however, a belief that the murders were the work of a solitary maniac came to be favored. Slaughterers, sailors, policemen, and journalists were all suggested, among others, as possible perpetrators. But it was the medical evidence given at Chapman's inquest that helped foster one of the most enduring popular images of the Whitechapel murderer — Dr. Jack. The notion of the murderer being a deranged doctor, evading detection behind a respectable facade, may also owe more than a little to *Jekyll and Hyde*. After all, given the publicity surrounding Mansfield's Lyceum performance, *Jekyll and Hyde* offered a readily available analogy as the press searched for meaning in the mysterious Whitechapel murders of Jack the Ripper.

Mansfield and Jack the Ripper

We will never know who "Jack the Ripper" really was, although the mystery of his identity continues to inspire innumerable books, television specials and even feature films. We do know, however, that, thanks to Richard Mansfield's compelling portrayal of Dr. Jekyll's transformation into Mr. Hyde, the actor was denounced as a suspect in the Ripper murders. Furthermore, the closing of Mansfield's production was blamed by at least one newspaper on the impact of the Ripper murders, though it seems clear that the impetus that persuaded Mansfield to close *Jekyll and Hyde* and revive *Prince Karl* was financial rather than due to any second thoughts about performing during the Ripper scare.

The letter denouncing Mansfield as the Ripper, which is full of excruciating spelling errors and a hysterical use of capitalization, claims that "*I do not think there is A man Living* So well able to disgise Himself in A moment as he does in front of the Public," which Mansfield would have taken as a supreme compliment. The anonymous and semiliterate writer of this letter was not the only person unnerved by Mansfield's uncanny ability to transform himself on stage. Mansfield managed to claim victims beyond the theater doors. On Saturday, September 29, 1888, the *St. Stephen's Review* reported:

> Between the Whitechapel murders and the weird performance of *Dr. Jekyll and Mr. Hyde*, the mental condition of people with highly-strung nerves is becoming very serious. I was attracted by a crowd in the Strand the other night, and on investigating the matter, found that they surrounded a well-dressed young man who had bolted out of a 'bus while it was going at a rapid rate, and then fallen down in a fit. It appeared he had been to see Mr. Mansfield as Dr. Jekyll, and on getting into the 'bus found himself beside a most repulsive-looking man, whom he immediately concluded must either be the Doctor himself or the Whitechapel murderer. In a fit of fearful nervousness, he jumped from his seat, and came to grief as mentioned.

The hysteria in London over Jack the Ripper was created as much by the media coverage of the events as it was by the murders themselves. While the victims were primarily working-class women who worked as prostitutes, the fear of the anonymous murderer seems to have permeated every level of Victorian society, including "well-dressed young men." Why this young man should have felt so threatened that he leapt out of the bus is unclear. Jack the Ripper never showed a liking for male victims, let alone well-dressed young male victims, and Richard Mansfield was never reported as directly causing the death of any audience member. Nonetheless, the saturation coverage of the murders was enough to make even those sections of Victorian society not directly threatened feel insecure. Mansfield's portrayal of Mr. Hyde quickly and indelibly became confused with the figure of "saucy Jack."

In this new mass media environment, the distinctions between representations of murder on the stage and real violence in London were being eroded. The depiction of murder by actors and the reports of murders in the newspapers intermingled in the circulation of descriptions and images by the press and became confused with one another. This is indexed by how rapidly *Jekyll and Hyde* became a heuristic in journalistic coverage to explain the Ripper himself. For example, the *Pall Mall Gazette* of September 8, 1888, referred to Jack the Ripper as "Mr. Hyde at large in Whitechapel." Even more revealing was the *Philadelphia Inquirer* claim on October 10, 1888, that "the police have started the theory that the Whitechapel murders are the result of a case in real life of "Dr. Jekyll and Mr. Hyde"; the plot of the fiction thus becomes not just another murder story, but a template for the actual murders themselves. In a similar vein a letter printed in the London *Times* on September 22, 1888, suggested that the crimes were caused by the serialized accounts of crimes carried in newspapers, such as *Dick Turpin, the Prince of Highwaymen*. Fiction, the argument ran, causes crime.

The Ripper case caused debate on the connection between media images of violence and violence on the streets; *Punch* cartoons like "Horrible London" and its accompanying poem blamed the rash of murders in the East End directly on plays such as *Jekyll and Hyde* that were advertised by posters throughout the city. Just as there are debates over the connection between violence in the media and violent behavior today, so too in the Victorian period there was a heated debate over the connection between fictional representations of murder and their relationship to the Jack the Ripper case. Even such apparently innocuous fictions as *Dick Turpin*, were blamed for Jack the Ripper's actions.

Richard Mansfield, with his compelling impersonation of a murderer on stage, became a target of suspicion and criticism because of this confusion between real murders in Whitechapel and fictional images of murder. Now whenever lists of possible suspects in the Jack the Ripper case are compiled, Mansfield's name is always included. This is hardly the legacy he had in mind, but thanks to an unlucky piece of timing, this is one of the ways in which he is remembered. Mansfield's name is now indelibly linked to Dr. Jekyll, Mr. Hyde and Jack the Ripper.

Part III

Richard Mansfield's
Dr. Jekyll and Mr. Hyde:
The Collated Script

The Composition of the Script

Richard Mansfield's Lyceum version of *Dr. Jekyll and Mr. Hyde* forms the basis of the following collated script. The Lyceum script was granted Performance Licence No. 196 on July 27, 1888, by the Lord Chamberlain's Office, and is the only known dated script. The script is now held in the British Library's Lord Chamberlain Plays Collection, ref: Add. 53409B. Throughout the collated script the Lyceum version is referred to by the abbreviation LY, while annotations highlight differences between the Lyceum script and two other versions of Mansfield's *Jekyll and Hyde*.

The first of these, held by the Smithsonian Institute, was identified in an article by C. Alex Pinkston, Jr., as a prompt-book for Mansfield's *Jekyll and Hyde*.[1] This prompt-book, essentially a typed script with additional handwritten stage and lighting direction, is undated. However, the absence of a third scene in Act II confirms it to be from Mansfield's original Boston presentation given in May of 1887.[2] As a result, for the purposes of the collated script, this version is referred to by the abbreviation BSN.

The final component of the collated script is an American Play Company copy, held by New York Public Library Research Department, Theatre Collection, ref: RM 4894. Also undated, indications of missing words and phrases within the American Play Company publication suggest this was copied from a script with some indecipherable text. The inclusion of a third scene in Act II, however, confirms that this copy was taken from Mansfield's revised version of Jekyll and Hyde. In annotations to the collated script the American Play Company version is referred to by the abbreviation APC.

For the purposes of this collated script obvious typing and spelling errors in the original sources have been corrected. And, while footnotes highlight more significant differences between the various original scripts, minor variations have been overlooked.

---

1. C. Alex Pinkston, Jr., "The Stage Premiere of *Dr. Jekyll and Mr. Hyde*" *Nineteenth Century Theatre Research* 14:1/2 (1986) pp. 21–44.
2. Act II Scene 3 was the main addition in the revision of the play undertaken between the premier in Boston, May 9, 1887, and the opening in New York, September 12, 1887.

Front and back cover of Lyceum Programme from Mansfield's London performance

ROYAL Lyceum Theatre.

Sole Lessee ... ... Mr. HENRY IRVING.

AT A QUARTER-PAST EIGHT O'CLOCK.

Mr. **RICHARD MANSFIELD**

IN

DR. JEKYLL

AND

MR. HYDE.

The Etchings and Engravings in Act I. supplied by Messrs.
DOWDESWELL & DOWDESWELLS, *Fine Art Publishers,*
160, *New Bond Street.*

DOORS OPEN AT 7.45. PERFORMANCE COMMENCES AT 8.15.
CARRIAGES AT 10.45.

Opera Glasses can be had on Hire from the Cloak-room Attendants, One Shilling each, in all Parts of the House.

The BILL of THE PLAY is in every part of the House SUPPLIED WITHOUT CHARGE.

NO FEES OF ANY KIND.

Stalls, 10s. 6d.; Dress Circle, 6s. 6d.; Upper Circle, 4s.; Amphitheatre, 2s. 6d.; Pit, 2s.; Gallery, 1s.; Private Boxes, £3 2s. to £4 4s.

Box Office open 10 till 5, under the direction of **Mr. JOSEPH HURST**, of whom Seats can be booked Four Weeks in advance, also by Letter.

W. S. JOHNSON—' Nassau Steam Press," 60, St. Martin's Lane, Charing Cross, W.C.

EVERY EVENING,
At a Quarter-past Eight o'Clock,

Mr. RICHARD MANSFIELD

IN

DR. JEKYLL

AND

MR. HYDE

(SOLE AUTHORIZED VERSION),

Dramatized for Mr. MANSFIELD by Mr. T. RUSSELL SULLIVAN.
By kind permission of Mr. ROBERT LOUIS STEVENSON.

Dr. Jekyll }	Mr. RICHARD MANSFIELD.
Mr. Hyde }	
Dr. Lanyon	Mr. HARKINS.
Gabriel Utterson	Mr. SULLIVAN.
General Sir Danvers Carew	Mr. HOLLAND.
Poole	Mr. BURROWS.
Inspector Newcomen ...	Mr. CROMPTON.
Jarvis	Mr. VIVIAN.
Mrs. Lanyon	Mrs. HARKINS.
Rebecca Moor	Miss SHERIDAN.
AND	
Agnes Carew	Miss BEATRICE CAMERON.

Synopsis of Scenery.

ACT I.
SLAVE AND MASTER.
Morning Room in the House of Sir Danvers Carew.

ACT II.
HIDE AND SEEK.
Scene 1.—Hyde's Lodgings in Soho.
Scene 2.—The Old Door by the Court.
Scene 3.—Hall at Dr. Jekyll's.
(*In this Act the Tableau Curtain will be lowered between each Scene.*)

ACT III.
TWO AND THE SAME.
Dr. Lanyon's House in Cavendish Square.

ACT IV.
THE LAST NIGHT.
Dr. Jekyll's Cabinet.

During the Evening the Orchestra will perform the following selection, under the Direction of W. H. Eayres:—

1.—Overture	...	"Der Freyschutz"	*Weber.*
2.— { (a) Duo (No. 4)	...	"Petite Suite"	*Bizet.*
{ (b)	...	"Graceful Dance"	*Sullivan.*
3.—Entr'actes— { (No. 1) in G major	} "Rosamunde"		*Schubert.*
{ (No. 2) in B flat			
4.— { (a) Prelude	"Le dernier Sommeil de la Vierge"	...	*Massenet.*
{ (b) Intermezzo	...	"Loin du Bal"	*Gillet.*

Mr. E. D. PRICE, Manager for Mr. MANSFIELD.
Stage Manager, Mr. FREDERICK PERCY MARSH.

Pages 2 and 3 from inside of Lyceum Programme from Mansfield's London performance.

Richard Mansfield as Dr. Jekyll and Mr. Hyde; double-exposure publicity photograph by Van der Weyde (courtesy of the Library of Congress).

Dr. Jekyll and Mr. Hyde

Play in four acts.
Dramatized for
Richard Mansfield.
*From the romance
of
Robert Louis Stevenson
by
T. R. Sullivan*

CHARACTERS

General Sir Danvers Carew
Dr. Lanyon
Gabriel Utterson
Poole
Inspector Newcome[3]
Jarvis
Dr. Jekyll
Mr. Hyde
Agnes Carew
Mrs Lanyon
Rebecca Moor

ACT I . . . . *Slave and Master.* Morning room in the house of Sir Danvers Carew

ACT II . . . . *Hide and Seek* … Scene i Hyde's Lodgings in Soho
Scene ii A Street in London
Scene iii Hall at Dr. Jekyll's[4]

ACT III . . . . *Two and the same* … Dr. Lanyon's house in Cavendish Square

ACT IV . . . . *The last night* … Dr. Jekyll's Cabinet.

---

3. "*Newcomen*" is the name used here, and throughout in APC and BSN.
4. Act II Scene III does not appear in BSN.

ACT I[5]
Slave and Master

SCENE — Tea-room[6] in the house of Sir Danvers Carew. Handsome interior in 3–4 — at back C. a large French window. Beyond this the trees of a London Square[7] Sunset lights changing to twilight then night with rising moon.

(At rise of curtain Sir Danvers Carew discovered at L. of table near window playing chess with Utterson R. of table. Mrs. Lanyon seated L. of table L.C. Agnes at the open window C. Tea set on table L.[8] H. Music[9])

SIR DANVERS. Don't worry Agnes. It distracts me. (*To Utterson*) Check.

AGNES. (*Sadly*) No Papa.

SIR DANVERS. And shut that window, there's a good child. It grows chilly after sunset.

AGNES. (*Closing window*) Yes, papa.

(She is down behind tea table L.)

MRS. LANYON. (*To Agnes*) Chilly? In August?

AGNES.[10] After India, he means.

MRS. LANYON.[11] There is no heat like the heat of London bricks. I ought to know, my dear: I have passed so many wretched Augusts here in town. Dr. Lanyon will not leave his patients, and his poor wife is of secondary importance. You see what comes of marrying into medicine.

AGNES. (*Seated R. of table*) My dear Aunt, I — (*Looking at window anxiously*) I can't understand why Harry did not dine here as he promised.

MRS. LANYON. My dear, your father is right. To worry is absurd.

AGNES. Yes, but —

MRS. LANYON. As if you were not engaged to the dearest and best man in London. Think of his handsome property, my dear. Dr. Jekyll is very busy. One of his horrid patients has detained him.

AGNES. But he has looked so pale of late — he is overworking, and —

MRS. LANYON. (*Pouring out tea*) Nonsense. The exercise will do him good.[12] Overwork never killed any body but a fool. Look at my husband Everybody calls Doctor Lanyon the picture of health. Yet he works like a slave.

UTTERSON. (*To Sir Danvers*) Check.

SIR DANVERS. Of course. (*Impatiently*) Everybody will keep chattering.

MRS. LANYON. (*To Sir Danvers*) Why, Danvers, how can you say so. Nobody has breathed a syllable (*Sir Danvers growls — aside to Agnes*[13]) He has lost his game.[14]

AGNES. We will speak lower, papa dear, (*To Mrs. Lanyon.*) Aunt, I am sure that Harry has something on his mind.

MRS. LANYON. (*Passing tea cup*)[15] Take some tea.

---

5. Handwritten lighting notes "*At rise house — foots and borders up full fire log lighted L. 2 E. bunch R. 2 E. Calciums — box on drop (Yellow) R. 3 E. Lens L. 3 E. to work on door Lens R.2 E. red (inc fire place)*" are indicated here in BSN.
6. Scene setting begins with "*Morning room*" in APC and BSN.
7. Further scene setting "*Up stage L. of window a chess table. Against wall 3rd entrance, writing desk with writing materials, also a decanter and glasses. Against wall R. front a piano L. of C. table with tea-service, etc. Entrance R 2nd Entrance through window.*" included here in APC and BSN.
8. Stage direction "*Tea set on table L.*" not included in APC.
9. Stage direction "*H. Music*" appears only in LY.
10. Handwritten stage direction "*(coming down L. sits R of table)*" included here in BSN.
11. Stage direction "*L. of table L.*" included here in BSN.
12. "*The exercise will do him good.*" typed but deleted in BSN.
13. "*to Agnes*" typed but deleted in BSN.
14. "*He has lost his game*" contained within previous direction brackets in APC and BSN.
15. Stage direction "*(Passing tea cup)*" not included in BSN.

The Collated Script

dear, and quiet your nerves. And when Dr. Jekyll comes, don't scold him. Keep your criticism until after marriage — you will need them. Don't say I'm malicious. I simply forecast the future with the best of motives. For in spite of his ample fortune, Dr. Jekyll's ideas are quite too far advanced and for such a very young man too, the cleverest and by many years the youngest of them all[16] — my husband[17] says—

(Sir Danvers upsets the chess board, which falls with a crash)

Bless me, what's the matter?

SIR DANVERS. *(Rising to pick up the men, and growling)* All Utterson's fault.

UTTERSON. *(Rising and laughing)* Oh, completely.[18]

MRS. LANYON. *(Rising up C. R. of Utterson)* Why, Danvers, that very thing happened the night before last.

UTTERSON.[19] Just as I — as Sir Danvers was winning.

(Mrs. Lanyon down to Agnes R. whispers to her.)[20]

SIR DANVERS. *(Arranging chess men)* We can never get them back. No matter. Call it a draw. *(Sits again)*

UTTERSON. *(R. of table)* Good. How else could I get over an old Indian campaigner like you? *(Sits again)*

SIR DANVERS. *(Sitting)* You see, Utterson, my next move was this—with the rook.

UTTERSON. And mine was to lose the bishop — or, perhaps, the knight — so.

MRS. LANYON. *(To Agnes)* Mr. Utterson is so clever. Your father really needs a lawyer to manage him.

(Lanyon appears in garden R. C.)[21]

SIR DANVERS. *(To Utterson)* There's Lanyon. We'll leave it to him.

(Enter Lanyon through window)[22]

LANYON.[23] Ah, here you all are. I cut across the square.[24] Jekyll asks me to say that he'll come directly. A patient detained him.

(Agnes crosses to table L.)

MRS. LANYON. *(To Agnes)* There — you see.

LANYON. *(C.)* A splendid dislocation — really fine. I wanted it myself.

AGNES.[25] Ah, you were with him then, uncle.

LANYON. Yes, one of our little discussions. *(Declining tea which Agnes offers)* No, thanks.

SIR DANVERS. No, no, a cigar and a problem.

(Lanyon and other gentlemen go to sideboard up L. for cigars.)

(Enter Jarvis R.)

AGNES. You may take away the tea, Jarvis. *(Going up C.)*

JARVIS. Yes, Miss. *(Handing card)* A card for you, miss. The young person is waiting in the drawing room.

AGNES. Very well, I will see her.

(Jarvis clears the table and exits with tray R. Mrs. Lanyon comes down.)

AGNES. The teacher from the parish school. *(To Door R.)* Will you come, Aunt?[26]

MRS. LANYON. *(Coming down L. C.)* *(Looking at the men absently)* Yes dear. Those men are

---

16. "and for such a very young man too, the cleverest and by many years the youngest of them all" not included in APC.
17. "thinks and" included here in APC and BSN.
18. Another Handwritten "*Completely*" appears here in BSN.
19. Stage direction "*(Down a little L. C.)*" typed but deleted here in BSN.
20. This stage direction is replaced by "*(Mrs Lanyon whispers to Agnes R.)*" in APC, and "*(Mrs. Lanyon, ~~down behind table~~ whispers to Agnes.)*" in BSN.
21. Further stage direction "*(Agnes xs to R.)*" included here in BSN.
22. This direction is replaced by "*(All rise. Lanyon shakes hands with Danvers and Utterson. Then comes down to C. to Agnes who has crossed to greet him.)*" in BSN.
23. Stage direction "*(Entering through window)*" included here in APC.
24. "square" replaced by "park" in APC and BSN.
25. Stage direction "*(xing to Lanyon with tea.)*" included here in BSN.
26. Stage direction "*(Exit)*" included here in APC and BSN.

smoking again. What comfort they get out of it. I'm half inclined to try it myself—but it disagrees with one so.

AGNES. (*At door*) Aunt!

MRS. LANYON. Yes, dear. I'm coming.

(*Exeunt R. Agnes and Mrs. Lanyon—the others come down*)

LANYON. (*Down R. C. sitting*) I have been telling Jekyll a strange story.

SIR DANVERS. (*Down and sitting*) Story? Let us have it. Sit down.

LANYON. Enfield's adventure. You know Enfield?

UTTERSON. (*Seated L.*) Oh, yes. Kinsman of mine.

SIR DANVERS. Jolly man about town, isn't he?

LANYON. Well, hardly jolly. Infernally odd I call him. Fond of pushing his way down by-streets at dead of night after adventure, and by George he got one.

SIR DANVERS and UTTERSON. Well?

LANYON. Well, it was this way. He was coming home from some place at the end of the world about three in the morning, with nothing to be seen but lamps. Everybody asleep—street after street lighted like a procession and empty as a church. All at once he saw two figures one a little man, shuffling along at a good walk and the other a girl—a mere child, running down a cross street. Naturally enough at the corner the two ran into one another—(*Striking hands together*) Like that. And then came the horror of the thing. For the man went on like some damned Juggernaut trampled on the child's body, left her screaming. Nothing when you tell it, he said—but hellish to see!

SIR DANVERS. Horrible! What did Enfield do?

LANYON. He ran after my gentleman. Collared him and brought him back, perfectly calm and offering no resistance. A crowd had collected and the women were wild as Harpies. The man stood in the middle with a kind of black, sneering coolness, frightened, but carrying it off like Satan. He called it an accident. "I'll pay for it," he said. "Name your figure."[27]

UTTERSON. (*Rising crossing C.*)[28] And they let him go?

LANYON. Not till they had made him sweat for it. He took them to a back court by the river, somewhere near the old water gate, there he stopped at a certain door.

UTTERSON. Like a cellar door, low and shabby?

LANYON. Yes, with a gable over the street. So Enfield said. What of that?

UTTERSON. I remember the place that is all. Go on.

SIR DANVERS. Yes, yes. Go on.

LANYON. Well, he opened the door with a key, went in and came back with a cheque for a hundred pounds,—not his own mind you. The cheque of a well known man, whose name Enfield would not tell me.

SIR DANVERS. (*Rising,*[29] *down a little R.*) I see, a forgery.

LANYON. (*Rising,*[30] *down C.*) Not a bit of it. The cheque was genuine.

SIR DANVERS. Come, that's strange.

LANYON. Yes: and how did he come by it? For the fellow was curiously repulsive: so ugly that everyone who saw him turned sick and white at the first look as if an icy finger were tracing out his spine.

UTTERSON. (*Rising—down and C.*) The cheque was genuine, you say. You do not know who drew it?

LANYON. No, Enfield would not give the smallest hint. But he was a person of note, the very pink of the proprieties.

SIR DANVERS. And the name of the man who walked over the child, did he tell you that?

LANYON. Oh, yes. His name was Hyde.[31]

---

27. Handwritten lighting direction "*Change calciums to red*" indicated here in BSN.
28. This direction does not appear in APC.
29. Stage direction "*and placing chair at piano and coming*" included here in APC and BSN.
30. Stage direction "*places chair at chess table, comes*" included here in BSN.
31. At this point "*Sir Danvers*" saying "*Hyde.*" included in BSN.

The Collated Script 51

UTTERSON. (*Starting*) Hyde!

LANYON. (*Looking sharply at Utterson*) Yes, Hyde.

UTTERSON. (*Carelessly*) Um. What sort of a person was he? Did you say?

LANYON. Not easy to describe according to Enfield. "There is something wrong with him," said he. "Something detestable, as if he ought to be deformed and yet he wasn't — all together extraordinary and —"

UTTERSON. Young man?

LANYON. Young — yes — as we men go.

UTTERSON. You are sure he used a key?

LANYON. Enfield said so.

UTTERSON. And you told Jekyll this?

LANYON. Of course. As I tell it to you. Hang it man, I'm not in the witness box. What's the matter with you?

UTTERSON. Nothing, you suggested a problem that I was trying to work out. Your story quite upsets me. (*Up L.*)

SIR DANVERS. And it has given me a cold shiver. B-r-r-. Let us go up to the drawing room. (*Up R.*)

LANYON. (*Crosses to door R., laughing*) Ha, ha! It's not my story, it's Enfield's you know. I thought you would like it. (*Aside*) Utterson knows more of this, I'll swear.

(*Exit Lanyon R. as Sir Danvers waits for Utterson to follow*) (*Utterson detains Sir Danvers*)

UTTERSON. (*Bringing him to C.*) One moment, please, may I write a line?

SIR DANVERS. (*Crosses*) Oh, of course. (*Pointing to desk up stage L.*)[32] There you are. (*Crosses and opens portfolio on desk*) Shall you be long?

UTTERSON. (*L. C.*) Oh no. Just a line.

SIR DANVERS. (*At sideboard*) Here's not a bad glass of cognac.

UTTERSON. (*At desk L.*) Thanks, yes.

SIR DANVERS. (*Crosses to C.*) The whole compound, as we used to say in India is yours. (*Going at door R., stops*) All except that game of chess, that was a draw. (*Exit*)

UTTERSON. (*Crosses in front of table L.*[33] *to C.*) A cellar door, low and shabby, under a gable on the street, near the old water gate too. Surely, surely it was the unused door to Jekyll's laboratory,[34] the old dissecting room of which Hyde had the key. What is the meaning of this strange intimacy. Why is the will that I hold for Henry Jekyll made in favour of his friend and benefactor, Edward Hyde? A man, whom even I, his old acquaintance do not know by sight. Friend and benefactor? Why Hyde must be the fiend himself. There can be no doubt whose cheque he paid, Poor Harry Jekyll, my mind misgives me, he is in deep water now. What if this Hyde were to suspect the existence of the will and grow impatient to inherit? It turns me cold to think of this creature stealing like a thief to the boy's very bedside, it must not be. I'll caution him, and put my shoulder to the wheel. If Harry will only let me. (*Back to desk L.*) I'll write a line at once to make an appointment with him. (*Sits at desk*)

(*Enter Jekyll through the garden.*)

JEKYLL. (*Stopping at window, which Lanyon has left open*) (*Aside*)[35] It must not be. I can never marry her, with this hideous secret, this new danger threatening me at every step. My duty is clear. I must see her no more.

UTTERSON. (*Rising L. and turning towards Jekyll*)[36] Jekyll.

JEKYLL. (*Starting*) Ah. Oh, Utterson — is that you? I —

UTTERSON. (*L. C.*) What is it? You're not ill?

JEKYLL. (*Down C.*) Ill! Oh no: you startled me, that's all. I was never better, never in my life.

---

32. This stage direction appears only in LY.
33. "Crosses in front of table L." replaced by "Alone" in APC and BSN.
34. Stage direction "(*sits R. of table L.*)" included here in BSN.
35. Stage direction "(*which Lanyon has left open*) (*Aside*)" appears only in LY.
36. "*and turning towards Jekyll*" does not appear in APC.

UTTERSON. Um. Well I'm glad to hear it. You come most opportunely. I was writing you a letter. There's no need of it now. (*Goes to Jekyll*[37] *and tears up letter*) If you'll give me a moment. (*Back to R. C.*)

JEKYLL. Business, eh? Well?

UTTERSON. Sit down.

(*Jekyll R. Utterson C.*)

It's about that will of yours.

(*Jekyll looks about anxiously*)

Oh, we're quite alone.[38] Jekyll, I don't like it.

JEKYLL. (*With false gaiety*) My poor Utterson, you are unfortunate in your client. I never knew a man so distressed as you were by my will, except perhaps that hide-bound[39] pedant, Lanyon at my scientific heresies. No man ever disappointed me as Lanyon has.

UTTERSON. (*Sits*) You know I refused to draw up the will, I never approved of it.

JEKYLL. Yes, yes, I know. You have told me so.

UTTERSON. Well, I tell you so again. To one clause in it, I object particularly.

JEKYLL. To what clause?

UTTERSON. You make a large bequest to your "friend and benefactor Edward Hyde" (*Jekyll nods*) So far so good. But you add that in case of your disappearance or unexplained absence for a period exceeding three calendar months the said Hyde shall inherit with out further delay, without further question.

JEKYLL. Yes.

UTTERSON. As your old friend and legal adviser I protest against that provision. It is dangerous— unheard of. Monstrously unjust.

JEKYLL. Unjust?

UTTERSON. To Miss Carew, your future wife— yes. (*A Pause*)

JEKYLL. (*Sighing*) Well, have you done?

UTTERSON. No, I have not done. To-day, I have learnt something of this man, Hyde.

JEKYLL. (*Rising— to C. R.*) I do not care to listen longer. We must agree to drop this matter.

UTTERSON. (*Rising to C. L.*) What I heard was abominable.

JEKYLL. (*C.*) It can make no change. You do not understand my position. (*After pause, more calmly*) I am painfully situated, Utterson: the case is a very strange one, very strange. Talking will not mend it. (*Goes up C.*)

UTTERSON. (*Following him and putting hand on his shoulder*) Harry, you know me thoroughly. I am to be trusted. I will get you out of this. Make a clean breast of it in confidence. I beg of you.

JEKYLL. (*Putting L. hand on Utterson's R. shoulder*) My dear fellow this is downright good of you. I would trust you before any man alive, before myself had I the choice. But it is not what you fancy. The moment I please, I can be rid of Hyde. (*Takes his hand*) There, I give you my hand upon it, and I thank you again and again, but this is a private matter: pray let it sleep. (*Turns up a little C.*)[40]

UTTERSON. (*Crosses R.*) As you please. Are you going up stairs?

JEKYLL. In a moment, yes. One word more. I have really a great interest in poor Hyde …… a very great interest. If I am taken away promise me to bear with him, and to get him his rights. You would, if you knew all.

UTTERSON. (*Gruffly*) I hope I may never see the man. (*Going towards door R.*)[41]

JEKYLL. (*Following him*)[42] It would take a weight off my mind if you would promise.

UTTERSON. (*Same*) You don't want me to like him, do you?

---

37. "*Jekyll*" replaced by "*desk*" in BSN.
38. Stage direction "(*Sits R. of table L.*)" included here in BSN.
39. "*hide-bound*" appears only in LY.
40. This direction does not appear in APC.
41. This direction does not appear in APC.
42. This direction does not appear in APC.

JEKYLL. (*Laying his hand on Utterson's arm*) No, only to do him justice for my sake when I am gone.

UTTERSON. (*After pause, sighing*) Well I promise. (*They shake hands — going aside*) Much good that interview did either of us.

(*Exit R.*)

JEKYLL. (*Alone*) Poor human kind. Bound by laws as rigid as the sheepskin covers of the book that holds them.[43] And I, who have toiled for man am doomed to eternal wretchedness, the possessor of a secret I dare not even whisper. Ah, Heaven help me, Heaven help me![44] (*Falls into chair R. of table L. C. his face in his hands.*)[45]

(*Enter Agnes R.*)[46]

AGNES. (*At door*) Harry!

JEKYLL. (*At table, not hearing her — aside*) In the power of the monster I myself created — in its power What if it[47] should present itself here — before them all. What if —

AGNES. (*Aside*) What does he say? (*Crosses to*[48] *him, aloud.*) Harry!

JEKYLL. Agnes! (*Shrinking from her*) Is that you? (*Rise*)

AGNES. (*Round in front of chair.*) Yes, there is something wrong. I have seen it in your face for days. What is it Harry?[49] You must let me share in this. How else am I to help you?

JEKYLL. (*Turning away his face.*) You cannot help me. There is no help for me on earth.

AGNES. Harry![50]

JEKYLL. We are at the cross roads — we must part before it is too late. (*Crosses to R*) I must go on alone.

AGNES.[51] Part!

JEKYLL. Yes.

AGNES. Are you out of your senses? Do you know me? I have promised to be your wife — I love you. Look! This is I — Agnes Carew. (*Arms round his neck.*)

JEKYLL. (*Breaking from her.*) It is you who do not know me. I am unfit to live upon the same earth as you. (*Crosses to L.*) You do not know me, I tell you.

AGNES. (*Following him*) Are you not Henry Jekyll?

JEKYLL. The philanthropist, the man of science, the distinguished surgeon — before the world — yes. How if it were all a lie? If I were like one possessed of a fiend — wearing at times another shape, vile, monstrous, hideous beyond belief?

AGNES. (*Hiding her face in hands.*) Oh, be silent.

JEKYLL. Yes, a fiend, without a conscience, and without remorse — inventing crimes and longing only to commit them.

AGNES. This is horrible. Who accuses you? You are ill and tired. You are not yourself.

JEKYLL. That is true. I am but half myself — the other half is —

AGNES. Mine. You have no right to accuse it, falsely.

JEKYLL. You will not believe — if I dared to tell you —

AGNES. You shall tell me nothing.

JEKYLL. You are right, it is best to part so.

AGNES. (*Following him*) Part? How little you know me! If you have sins to conquer, I have mine. Who is there without sin in all the world? We are born into it to help one another. And when you need me most, am I to give you up — to leave you?

---

43. "*of the book that holds them*" not included in APC.
44. "*Ah, Heaven help me, Heaven help me!*" not included in APC.
45. This entire direction is replaced by "(*Stands at fire*)" in BSN.
46. This direction does not appear in BSN.
47. Typed dialogue "*my worser half*" deleted and replaced by a Handwritten "*it*" in BSN.
48. Further stage direction "*chair, bending over*" appears here in BSN.
49. Typed stage direction "(*Sinking at his feet*)" deleted here in BSN.
50. Handwritten lighting direction "*Change cals to blue* and *start lowering house foots* and *borders*" indicated here then deleted in BSN.
51. Stage direction "(*Following him*)" included here in APC and BSN.

JEKYLL.[52] You can say these things? You ask me nothing?

AGNES. No, you have won my love, you must accept it.

JEKYLL. But if you knew—[53]

AGNES. (*Drawing nearer, tenderly*) How much I might confess to you. You would not listen.

JEKYLL. Darling, I—No—I cannot[54]—(*Falls in chair L.*)[55]

AGNES.[56] Who ever lived that was not tempted by the fiend. To be tempted is not to yield. We will resist. (*Putting her arm round his neck.*)[57]

[58](*Jekyll embraces her.*)

JEKYLL. You are an angel.

AGNES. (*In his arms*) Harry, do you remember where I met you first?

JEKYLL. In the ward of the hospital, yes.

AGNES. Where you watched by my poor old nurse who was dying. You were there night and day, with all that human skill could do, with more than human patience and devotion. I tried to thank you for your kind looks, your gentle words, I could not speak.

JEKYLL. But your eyes said it all. And then I loved you. It was a strange courtship.

AGNES. That is the man I know. There is no other. Drive away these morbid fancies—for my sake—for my sake.

JEKYLL. (*Kissing her*) For your sake, yes. You shall teach me to control myself. I will take courage.

AGNES. To me you are without fear, without reproach.

JEKYLL. To you at my best, always. (*Embracing her*)[59] See. The stars are coming out. Which among them all is ours. (*Going up to window, arm around her waist*)[60]

AGNES. The brightest. I will show it to you.[61] Come!

(*Exeunt, through window into garden*)

(*Enter Sir Danvers R.*)

Dr. Jekyll and Agnes Carew (*The Illustrated Sporting and Dramatic News*, August 18, 1888).

52. Handwritten "*Jekyll*" replaces typed but deleted "*Agnes*" in BSN.
53. Handwritten lighting direction "*Start lowering house foots and borders and cals*" indicated here in BSN.
54. "*tell her that*" included here in APC and BSN. Followed by an additional handwritten "*never that*" in BSN.
55. Typed direction "(*Up to window falls in chair*)" deleted and replaced by handwritten "(*X's down L. sits R of table.*)" in BSN.
56. Stage direction "(*Following and detaining him.*)" appears here in BSN.
57. This typed direction deleted and replaced by handwritten "*Kneeling R of Jekyll*" in BSN.
58. Handwritten lighting direction "*Change calciums to blue*" indicated here in BSN.
59. This stage direction appears only in LY.
60. This stage direction appears only in LY.
61. "*I will show it to you*" appears only in LY.

SIR DANVERS. Agnes! Jekyll! (*Up at window*)[62] Oh, I see—there they go! Poor dears (*Crossing to L.*) Just as I was at their age. (*Sits L. in arm chair at fire*) It is for this that we come into the world, and when a man gets beyond love it is time for him to be mustered out. Heigho! Here I sit like a one legged fowl upon his perch, waiting for the old butcher, Death to despatch him.

The Good die first
And they, whose hearts are dry as summer dust
Burn to the socket.

I dare swear I shall live to be a hundred. My poor wife! I tried her sometimes with my quick temper but I have never outgrown my love for her, thank God, though she has been gone these twenty years.

(*Re-enter Agnes from window C.*)

AGNES. (*At window*) Papa! Has everybody gone? (*Coming down a little*)[63]

SIR DANVERS. Yes, Agnes. What? And Jekyll too?

AGNES. (*Back to window, looking out*) Yes, he was called away—an important case, he said. There he goes now, through the trees.[64] Look papa. The moon is coming up, it is beautiful.

SIR DANVERS. Yes, darling. Almost like a moonrise in the East.

AGNES. (*Same, closes window*) A falling star! They say, for every star that falls, a mortal dies on earth. (*Down to L. back of arm chair in which Sir Danvers is sitting*) Do you believe that, Papa?

SIR DANVERS. (*Sadly, leaning back in chair.*)[65] Why not? There is no earthly moment without death. it is very near us always. Agnes do you remember Mangalore? (*Takes her hand from behind him and puts her arms round his neck.*)[66]

AGNES. Not clearly. Strange things come back to

A sketch depicting Richard Mansfield as Dr. Jekyll (*The Illustrated Sporting and Dramatic News*, August 18, 1888).

me—trifles that mean nothing: the shore of the river, a red macaw that always swung on the verandah, a tall brown man who carried me sometimes, and—and—

SIR DANVERS. Your mother, Agnes?

AGNES. Yes, dear mamma. How large her eyes were: what slender wrists she had, what tiny little hands. (*Sir Danvers moved*) Oh papa, papa. (*She throws her arms about his neck*)[67]

62. Additional Handwritten dialogue "*What, gone!*" inserted here in BSN.
63. This direction does not appear in APC.
64. Additional handwritten dialogue with "*Sir Danvers*" saying "*Ah, yes, I see*" inserted here in BSN.
65. Stage direction "*leaning back in chair*" appears only in LY.
66. Stage direction "*from behind him and puts her arms round his neck*" appears only in LY.
67. Further handwritten direction "*Kneels, sobbing.*" inserted here in BSN.

SIR DANVERS. Now it is strange that a great blustering trooper like me should have even one tear left in his dry old eyes. There — there — play something, dear.

AGNES. (*Going to piano R.*) What, papa?

SIR DANVERS. The Indian air.

AGNES. Mamma's?

SIR DANVERS. Yes.

(*She plays. At the finish Hyde appears at window Coming R. C.*)[68]

AGNES. (*Turns L., looking at Sir Danvers*) I do believe Papa has dropped asleep. (*She rises up R. sees Hyde, and draws back with a low cry R.*) Ah!

SIR DANVERS. (*Waking, rising L. C.*) How cold it is! Ha! (*Sees Hyde and rising*) What's this. (*Draws back with a shudder*)

AGNES. (*Recoiling to R. with arms extended towards her father*)[69] Papa! papa!

SIR DANVERS.[70] Leave the room, Agnes.[71] (*After pause more gently*) Do as I bid you child.

(*Exit Agnes silently R.*)

And now, Sir, what business brings you to my house?[72]

HYDE. Agnes, why did you send her away? (*Down a little*)

SIR DANVERS. My daughter's name! Why, what's that to you?

HYDE. Your daughter, yes.[73] Call her back. I must speak with her.[74]

SIR DANVERS. (*Furious*)[75] How dare you?

HYDE. (*Fiercely*) Call her back, I say. I saw her face through the window, and I like it.[76]

SIR DANVERS. Scoundrel, leave my house!

HYDE. (*Laughs*) Eh? That's good[77] (*Laughs defiantly*)[78]

SIR DANVERS. Monster! Who and what are you. Go, or —

HYDE. (*To C. laughing*) Go? I. Why, I will make the house mine, the girl mine if I please.

SIR DANVERS. (*Springing at him*) (*L.*) Infernal villain, I'll —

HYDE. (*Throwing him off*)[79] Hands off, or it will be your death, I warn you.

SIR DANVERS. By Heaven! I'll —(*Grapples with him C.*)

HYDE.[80] Eh? Good! One more, one less, what does it matter? There! If you will have it![81]

(*They struggle*)[82]

SIR DANVERS. Help! Help![83]

(*Hyde throttles him*[84]— *Door R. thrown open and Agnes rushes in*)[85]

---

68. Handwritten lighting direction "*Change lens R and L to green*" indicated here in BSN.
69. Stage direction "*with arms extended towards her father*" appears only in LY.
70. Stage direction "(*Pushing her off*)" included here in APC and BSN.
71. Additional dialogue with "Agnes" saying "*Papa, papa.*" included here in BSN.
72. Handwritten lighting direction "*As Hyde enters green cal on in fire place*" indicated here in BSN.
73. "*Your daughter, yes*" not included in APC.
74. "*I must speak with her*" replaced by "*I saw her face through the window and I like it*" in APC.
75. Stage direction "(*Furious*)" replaced by dialogue "*Villain!*" in APC.
76. "*I saw her face through the window, and I like it*" not included here in APC.
77. At this point there appears to have been a hiatus in the original source for APC, with the APC script noting "(*There is a speech missing here, but it is just to end the act*). The APC transcript then ends Act I with the direction "*Hyde jumps on Sir Danvers — strangles him and withdraws through the window as Agnes and the others rush in at the door. CURTAIN*"
78. This stage direction, and all remaining text in Act I does not appear in APC.
79. This stage direction does not appear in BSN.
80. Additional dialogue "*Tired of life*" typed here but deleted in LY and BSN.
81. This entire line of Hyde's dialogue is typed but deleted in BSN.
82. This direction is typed but deleted in BSN.
83. This entire line of Sir Danvers' is typed but deleted in BSN.
84. Additional direction "*Agnes rushes in R and throws herself upon the body.*" typed but deleted in BSN.
85. Stage direction "*Door R thrown open and Agnes rushes in*" replaced by "*Hyde up to window.*" in BSN.

Quick Curtain.[86]

(N. B. If there is a call Agnes bending over her father. Hyde in window up C.)[87]

Right: Mr. Hyde, at the window, terrifies onlookers (*The Illustrated Sporting and Dramatic News,* August 18, 1888).

ACT II
Hide and Seek[88]

SCENE 1 *Mr. Hyde's Chambers in Soho. Doors R. and L. 3rd entrance and L. in flat. In flat R. a large mirror to swing open for door. (Mirror opens out) R. 2nd entrance, fire place with fire burning. L. 2nd entrance a desk. Table with lighted candle L. C. The room is richly furnished but sombre in tone. At rising of curtain, door R.*[89] *stands open showing a landing with plain white-washed wall.*[90] *Lights down.*

(*Enter Hyde door R. He waits upon the threshold, listening.*)

HYDE. Still as death! Not a sound! I thought some one followed me[91] in the street. I saw the shadow. (*Seeing his own shadow on wall of landing*) It was my own. Shut it out! Shut it out! (*Closes door and laughs, crosses to L.*[92] *sees himself in mirror C. and starts*)[93]

86. Additional handwritten direction "*as Hyde leaves Sir Danvers*" inserted here in BSN.
87. Handwritten lighting direction "*Green cal. in fire place off*" inserted here in BSN.
88. Handwritten Lighting direction "*At rise house foots and borders out green foots ½ up. Green calcium through window L. 2 E. on door R.* ~~*green cal. off. Hyde's exit*~~ *Green lense in fire place to work on at cue—"To the ghost of Sir Danvers Carew" Follow Hyde until cue—"Gone gone," then shut off quickly—Green lense L. C. behind flat to work up and off gradually as he exits. Lense = "* indicated here in BSN.
89. "*shut*" included here in APC and BSN.
90. "*stands open showing a landing with plain white-washed wall.*" appears only in LY.
91. Handwritten "*followed me*" replaces typed but deleted "*tracked my footsteps*" in LY.—"*tracked my footsteps*" remains the text in APC and BSN.
92. Stage direction "*(Turning towards door.)*" included here in BSN.
93. "*sees himself in mirror C. and starts*" does not appear in BSN.

[margin note: Talking to himself / reflect]

Who's there? (*Trembles and then laughs, indicating himself*) Why it is this—this that I love. Who would suspect harm of this? That this could kill, and kill and kill, for the sport of killing? Why no one. My own self is my sanctuary. I need not fear. But no more shadows, no more shadows. (*Lights candles on tables L. C.*) Fool! She has forgotten the brandy.[94]

(*Enter Rebecca door L. 3. with decanter and glasses.*)

Oh, you're there, are you? The brandy?

(*Rebecca to L. of table L. C. puts brandy down*)

REBECCA. Here.

HYDE. (*Eyeing her R. of table*) You have something to tell me.

REBECCA. A man has asked for you.

HYDE. (*Starting*) A man, when?

REBECCA. An hour ago.

HYDE. What did he want?

REBECCA. You.

HYDE. What was he like?

REBECCA. A man—like any other. (*One step front of table*)[95]

HYDE. Like me?

REBECCA. No. Thank Heaven!

HYDE. (*Sneering*) Heaven! Choose your words better.

REBECCA. The other place, then.

HYDE. Curse your tongue. Go!

(*Rebecca starts to go*)

Stop.

(*She returns.*)

[margin note: interrogate]

What's their gossip at the street corner?

REBECCA. What should they talk of? The murder.

HYDE. Murder? What murder?

REBECCA. The old man—the rich General.

HYDE. And they say?—

REBECCA. That the murderer is discovered.

HYDE.[96] Discovered? (*Recovering himself*) What's that to me. I do not know him.[97]

REBECCA. Nor I. If I did—

HYDE. Well?

REBECCA. It would be worth money to me.

HYDE. What could you do with money?

REBECCA. Count it and keep it to count again.

HYDE. (*Throwing coins on the floor*) There's money for you. (*Laughing at her as she springs to the coins.*) Hark ye. If I am asked for again say I'm gone.

REBECCA. (*Busy with coins*) Gone?

HYDE. (*Fiercely*) Gone away. Do you hear? (*Rising and threatening*)

REBECCA. (*Retreating*) Ay, I have ears.

HYDE. Use them and spare your tongue. Go.

(*Rebecca up to door L. shakes her fist at him*[98] *and Exits.*)

HYDE. (*Alone at table*) They're after me.[99] I must destroy all clues and be gone. (*Crosses to desk L.*)[100] (*Locks and bolts door R. 3.*)[101] So. (*Stops listening*) Hark! (*Growling at his own fear*) Why do I tremble so? Brandy. (*To table, fills glass and gulps it down*)[102] Sir Danvers Carew is in his grave. No, beyond it. In Heaven or—[103] (*Fills glass again*) To the ghost[104] of Sir Danvers Carew.[105]

---

94. Stage direction "(*Xes to chimney and pulls bell R.*)" included here in APC.
95. This direction does not appear in APC.
96. Stage direction "(*Trembling*)" included here in APC and BSN.
97. Further handwritten "*I don't know him*" included here in BSN.
98. "*shakes her fist at him*" appears only in LY.
99. "*They are after me*" is typed but deleted in BSN.
100. Typed dialogue "*First to lock the door*" deleted here in LY but remains in APC and BSN.
101. Stage direction "(*Locks and bolts door R. 3*)" does not appear in APC.
102. This direction appears only in LY.
103. "*down there*" included here in APC and BSN.
104. Stage direction "(*doors open wide*)" included here in BSN.
105. Handwritten lighting direction "*Lense in fire-place on quickly*" indicated here in BSN.

(Door R. 3 opens wide and shuts again without visible agency Hyde looks about fearfully, then relieved at seeing nothing laughs.) (He turns and starts)[106]

Are you there, are you?[107] This is a merry meeting. Your hand. (*As if shaking it*) A little nearer to the fire. The night air is cold. Your health, sir and a warm grave to you in the morning.

(Door opens and closes. He drinks and puts glass down)

He's gone, gone,[108] — Hark!

(Rebecca and Newcome[109] *heard in discussion outside L.)*

REBECCA. (*Outside L. 3. E.*) He's gone away, I tell you.[110]

(Newcome forces his way in at door. Hyde Exits through glass down R. l.)

NEWCOME. I say I must come in. Aha. Snug quarters—very snug. And the lodger?

REBECCA. (*Who has come quietly to C.*) He's not here.

NEWCOME. And if a friendly gentleman should come to call upon him and couldn't for the life of 'im recollect his name—

REBECCA. (*R.*) I do not know his name.

NEWCOME. Ha, ha![111] That's a good un so it is.

REBECCA. I have many lodgers. I ask no questions and am well paid for it.

NEWCOME. Ah! (*Takes out pocket book*) I am Inspector Newcome, from Scotland Yard.

REBECCA. (*Drawing nearer to him, eagerly*) He is in trouble. What has he done?[112]

NEWCOME. (*Pushing her off*) Gently, now, gently.[113] (*Counting bank notes and watching her joy at sight of them*) Now, these are bank notes— notes— money. Dy'e see?

REBECCA. Yes— yes, I see.

NEWCOME.[114] And they're yours.[115]

REBECCA. Mine — Mine! (*Snatching notes and counting them*) Why, this is £20.[116]

NEWCOME. All yours and as much more — if you will help me to a few words with this gentleman. He's a very popular character, don't you see.

REBECCA. (*Putting up money*) I hate him.

NEWCOME.[117]Come, that's business. Oh, we're getting on.

REBECCA. Hush, hush! speak lower, there are mice in the walls.

NEWCOME.[118] Ay! And out on 'em too! (*Aside*) The old she-devil.

REBECCA. (*Moving to L. of table to R. and beckoning Newcome who follows softly. After looking cautiously about she whispers*) His name is[119] Hyde.[120]

(Newcome up R. of table, writes in his note book.)[121]

NEWCOME. (*Whispers*)[122] Hide![123] And he's here?

---

106. This entire direction replaced by "*Looks about fearfully*" in APC, and "*Hyde turns and starts*" in BSN.
107. Handwritten "*are you?*" replaces typed but deleted "*old boy*" in LY.
108. Handwritten lighting direction "*Lense in fire-place off quickly*" indicated here in BSN.
109. "*Newcome*" is replaced here, and throughout the text, by "*Newcomen*" in APC and BSN.
110. At this point a *handwritten* dialogue insertion with "*Newcomen*" saying "*I tell you, I must come in.*" followed by typed text with "*Hyde*" saying "*Hark*" included in BSN.
111. Handwritten "*Don't know his name. Dear, dear.*" inserted here in BSN.
112. "*What has he done?*" is repeated here in BSN.
113. Additional *handwritten* dialogue "*No love making*" inserted here in BSN.
114. Handwritten stage direction "*(R. C.)*" followed by typed additional dialogue "*Five, ten, fifteen, twenty—* " included here in BSN.
115. Stage direction "*(Gives notes to Rebecca)*" included here in BSN.
116. "*twenty pounds*" repeated here in BSN.
117. Additional dialogue "*Hate him. Dear, dear me.*" included here in BSN.
118. Additional dialogue "*Mice in the walls; dear, dear me.*" included here in BSN.
119. Additional dialogue with "*Newcomen*" saying "*His name is*"—included here in BSN.
120. Stage direction "*(scratching on wall outside)*" included here in BSN.
121. This stage direction appears only in LY.
122. Additional dialogue "*Dear, dear. My*" included here in APC. Typed "*Dear, dear, me.*" is deleted in BSN.
123. Newcome's "*Hide*" arrived here and elsewhere in LY by the typed "*'ide*" being amended with a *handwritten* "*H*".

REBECCA. No. But he will come back. Go to the street door and watch. When the right man comes I will hold the light in his face so. (*Takes up candle and holds it in Newcome's face.*)

NEWCOME. You're an angel[124]— of light.

(*Rebecca laughs and replaces candle*)

A real out and outer, blest if you ain't.

REBECCA. And the money?[125]

NEWCOME. Wages paid weekly — regler, when earned.

REBECCA. Not so loud! Go!

(*She points to door L. towards which Newcome crosses L. she runs after and detains him*)

£20 eh? 20 pounds?

NEWCOME. (*Nodding*) Mum!

(*Rebecca is wildly delighted*)[126]

Easy now, easy![127] No love making.[128] (*Aside*) Lord! Lord she'll hug me next![129]

(*Breaks from her and Exits by door L. 3. E.*)

(*Rebecca crosses behind table to C.*)[130]

REBECCA. (*Alone taking out money*) Five — ten — fifteen —

(*Enter Hyde R. creeping down softly*)

Twenty — twenty pound.

(*Hyde snatches notes. Rebecca recoils in terror*)

HYDE. What did you whisper there?

REBECCA. (*L.*) The money — give me the money.

(*Hyde tears notes into bits and throws them down. Rebecca drops and fumbles for them, wailing. He catches her by the throat*)

HYDE. You sold me, did you?

REBECCA. (*Freeing herself and rising*) No— no!

HYDE. (*Catching her again and shaking her.*) What did you tell him? Answer!

REBECCA. (*Gasping*) Nothing, nothing!

HYDE. (*About to strangle her*) That's a lie! (*Throwing her from him*) Another word and I'll kill you — Now go.

(*Rebecca to door L. H. and Exit sobbing*)

(*Hyde follows her and locks the door — then rushes to desk and throws it open tossing out papers in confusion.*)[131]

HYDE. They're after me.[132] (*Burning papers in the fire*) But I leave no clue, no trace but ashes[133] (*He laughs*)[134] Aha,[135] too late, too late.[136]

(*Knock heard.* HYDE *extinguishes candles opens Mirror and stands laughing and rubbing his hands as knock repeated louder and louder. Hyde vanishes through mirror. Rebecca Enters L. D. holding light above her head, followed by Newcome.*)[137]

---

124. "*a hangel*" is the typed text, with "*a*" overwritten by a *handwritten* "*an*" and "*h*" deleted in LY. The typed text "*a hangel*" remains in APC and BSN.
125. "*the money*" is repeated here in APC and BSN.
126. This direction appears only in LY.
127. "*Dear, dear me*" is included here in APC and BSN.
128. "*Dear, dear me! I'm a married man, wife and children. Dear, dear me.*" included here in APC and BSN.
129. "*(Aside) Lord! Lord she'll hug me next*" appears only in LY.
130. This direction appears only in LY.
131. This direction appears only in LY.
132. "*They're after me*" is replaced by "*I must be gone*" in APC and BSN.
133. Handwritten lighting direction "*As Hyde puts out candle green foots out*" indicated at this point in BSN.
134. Stage direction "*(He laughs)*" is replaced by "*(Footsteps outside)*" in APC and BSN.
135. "*Aha,*" is replaced by "*Hark!*" followed by stage direction "*(Extinguishes candle as he goes through mirror)*" in APC and BSN. Handwritten lighting direction "*Work Lense L.C. up and off gradually*" then indicated at this point in BSN.
136. Stage direction "*(Rebecca and Newcomen enter with lighted candle) CURTAIN*" is included here in APC and BSN. Further *handwritten* direction "*Call Curtain up and down on picture.*" included in BSN. Handwritten lighting direction "*As Rebecca enters green foots up full.*" also indicated here in BSN.
137. This entire direction appears only in LY.

SCENE 2[138]— *A street in London. In flat R. C. a low door with knocker. Light down*

Description of Scene: "Two doors from the corner the line was broken by the entry of a court: and just at that point a certain sinister building thrust forward its gable on the street. It was two stories high, showed no window nothing but a door on the lower story and a blind forehead of discoloured wall on the upper and bore in every feature the marks of prolonged and sordid negligence"

(Quotation from book.)

(*Enter Utterson R. 1. E.*)

UTTERSON. Jekyll still absent, out of town, on an important case, the servants say: and leaving no address: he can know nothing of the murder. It is unaccountable. No matter: he gives me the better chance to investigate his friends. There is the laboratory door, as dark and ugly and mysterious as ever. Night after night I haunt this place, as the story of that human Juggernaut haunts me. I have sworn never to rest until I learn the cause of this strange friendship. I must see Mr. Hyde — meet him face to face — and this is the only way. Hark! (*Looks off L. listening*) There's some one coming — if it were he. Let him be Mr. Hyde, I'll be Mr. Seek. (*He withdraws hastily into the shadow of the buildings R.*)

(*Enter Hyde, hurriedly L. He crosses, taking out a bunch of keys, goes to door R. C. and crouches before it his face turned away from Utterson L.*)

UTTERSON. (*Stepping out and touching him on the shoulder*) Mr. Hyde, I think.

HYDE. (*Shrinking back and hissing, his face turned away.*) What do you want?

UTTERSON. I see you are going in. I am an old friend of Dr. Jekyll. Mr. Utterson of Gaunt Street — you must have heard my name.

HYDE. (*As before, blowing in the key*) You will not find Dr. Jekyll: he is from home. How did you know me?

UTTERSON. On your side will you do me a favour?

HYDE. With pleasure. What shall it be?

UTTERSON. Will you let me see your face?

(*Hyde Hesitates, then faces about and glares at Utterson, who recoils — recovering with an effort.*)

Now I shall know you again. It may be useful.

HYDE. (*Down a little*) Yes, of course. You should have my address.

UTTERSON. (*Aside*) Horrible. He, too, was thinking of the will.

HYDE. That reminds me. You are Jekyll's man of business.

UTTERSON. So far as he consults me, yes.

HYDE. It was you then who drew up his will?

UTTERSON. (*Aside*) Oh, infamy! (*Aloud*) By no means. It was I who declined to draw it up.

HYDE. (*Sneering*) Ha! You don't like me.

UTTERSON. No, why should I?

HYDE. Wait till you know me better. The will is in your keeping.

UTTERSON. Yes.

HYDE. Have a care! Were it to be lost or destroyed.

UTTERSON. You forget yourself — I am not likely to betray my trust.

HYDE. So much the better. And a word in your ear. Jekyll is not long for this world.

UTTERSON. What do you mean?

HYDE. He is far from strong. I am anxious — most anxious. Should he be taken away — suddenly — you will —

UTTERSON. I need no professional advice. At the proper time I shall do my duty.

---

138. Handwritten lighting direction "*At rise house foots* and *borders out, green foots up ½ single green light L. 3 E*" indicated here in BSN.

HYDE. If you are prudent: if not, it will go hard with you.

UTTERSON. Spare me your threats if you please.

HYDE. Not so fast: the wise man thinks twice before making enemies. You left my question unanswered. How did you know me?

UTTERSON. By description.

HYDE. Whose description?

UTTERSON. We have common friends.

HYDE. Common friends! Who are they?

UTTERSON. Why, Jekyll, for instance.

HYDE. He never told you (*Utterson bites his lips*)[139] I did not think you would have lied,[140]

UTTERSON. Come, sir, this is not fitting language.

HYDE. (*Laughing*) Ha! Ha! (*Back at door—Utterson to L.*) You don't like me, eh? No matter: I like you. Call upon me and I'll pay you compliments.

(*Laughs savagely and Exits into house Door in F.*)

UTTERSON. Ugh. He made my flesh creep. What does it mean? Why has he that key. I must know more. (*Up to door*) No window, not a loophole. (*Listens*) But I hear his step—a light shines through the crevice. What is his business there in Jekyll's absence. (*Listens again*) Silent as a coffin. (*Down C*[141].) A devil's mystery this. Oh, Harry Jekyll, if ever I read Satan's signature in a man's face it is there in the face of that new friend of yours!

(*Rebecca Enters, he sees her*)

What do you want? I have nothing for you.[142]

REBECCA. Have you seen him? Which way did he go?

UTTERSON. Seen him, seen whom?

REBECCA. I followed him through the glass[143]—street after street. Turning and twisting—up and down. And now, he is lost—lost. (*Crossing to R.*)

UTTERSON. (*Following her*) What do you mean? Whom did you follow?

REBECCA. (*Starts to go R.*)[144] The murderer.

UTTERSON. (*Catching her by the wrist*) Murderer!

REBECCA. Let me go. He has robbed me—he tore up the notes before my eyes. But I'll find him, as sure as I'm a starving woman. Let me go—let me go. (*Struggling:*)[145]

UTTERSON. There's money for you! (*Rebecca snatches the coins*) What man do you want?[146]

REBECCA. £20 he stole from me—£20.

UTTERSON. Speak, who is it?

REBECCA. I know—I know. He lied, but I heard the officers whispering it. I know—I know. He murdered Sir Danvers Carew.

UTTERSON. Who did this? Where does he live?

REBECCA. At my house—the police are there—the best lodgings in Soho! (*Breaking away*) He has robbed me—robbed me—

UTTERSON. (*Following and detaining her*) Soho! His name—his name

REBECCA. Hyde! (*Utterson staggers back with a loud cry*) Hyde! Hyde! I'll cry it in the streets—I'll write it on the walls. He shall swing for it—I'll find him. Hyde! Murderer and thief—thief—

(*Exit R wailing.*)[147]

UTTERSON. He murdered Sir Danvers Carew! Hyde! Edward Hyde!—he has the key of Jekyll's house—Jekyll's bosom friend—and he is there at this moment. Horrible!

---

139. This direction appears only in LY.
140. "*to me*" is included here in APC. "*to me*" also appears as *handwritten* addition in BSN.
141. Further stage direction "*as Rebecca enters L.*" is included here in APC.
142. "*I have nothing for you*" appears only in LY.
143. "*through the glass*" is typed but deleted in BSN.
144. This direction does not appear in APC.
145. Further stage direction "*(goes to R.)*" is included here in BSN.
146. Stage direction "*(Lets go her hand)*" included here in APC and BSN.
147. Further stage direction "*and shouting*" followed by additional dialogue "*Hyde, Hyde. Murderer, thief, Murderer.*" included here in BSN.

Why do I stand here? I must rouse the servants. He must be taken. (*Rushes to door in flat*) Locked — locked, of course. (*Putting his shoulder against it*) To be here, with only this plank between us. I can not break it down, but he is mine for all that. (*Rapping door violently*) Open, open, I say. (*Rapping again*) Oh, you shall answer, or I will wake the dead. (*As before*) Open! Open!

(*The door opens and Jekyll appears at the lighted entrance*[148]) (*Utterson staggers back amazed*) (*L.*)

UTTERSON. Jekyll![149]

JEKYLL. (*Very calmly*) Utterson! Is that you?[150]

UTTERSON. Jekyll, here — and alone!

JEKYLL. Why not?

UTTERSON. And you do not know — the murder — you have heard nothing?

JEKYLL. Yes, all. Just now, from the servants.

UTTERSON. (*Drawing nearer — in a whisper*) What have you done with Hyde?

JEKYLL. (*Shudders, then recovers himself*) Hush! Come in!

(*Exeunt into house. Utterson first, then followed by Jekyll. The door closes*)

SCENE 3[151] — Hall in Jekyll's house. Brilliant[152] interior in 3. At back C. a large fire place with fire burning R 2 entrance, large door leading to street. Smaller door L. 2nd entrance. Large table R. C. Sofa L. front.[153]

(*Poole Discovered l. C. looking at door L. 2. E.*)[154]

POOLE. The doctor has come back. The news of this murder has been a terrible shock to him — but there is something else, something that is driving him to his grave. He is in the laboratory where he locks himself up for days and days and sees nobody but Mr. Hyde.[155]

(*Knock outside D. R. 2. E. — Poole crosses to door R. and opens it. Enter Lanyon R.*)

LANYON. (*Down R. C.*) Any word of your master, Poole?

POOLE. (*Crosses round behind table and down L.*)[156] Heaven be praised, he's back at last. I heard him just now in the laboratory. He came that way, I think.

LANYON. (*Putting hat and gloves on table R. flat*) Say I must see him — say at once. (*Sits R. of table*)[157]

POOLE. Very good, sir.

(*Exit L.*)

LANYON. (*Alone.*) He knows nothing, who should have been the first to know, and I must break the news. (*Taking out newspaper*) This, of to-night, is strange indeed. That fiend, Hyde, the murderer We might have guessed it. And, as usual, the police have muddled the affair. He is scot free. (*Rising.*)

148. "*at the lighted entrance*" replaced by "*with lighted lamp*" in APC and BSN.
149. Stage direction "CURTAIN" appears at this point, bringing Act II, Scene II to an end, in APC. At this point in BSN *handwritten* lighting direction "*Unmask green lense L. 1 E, throw light on Jekyll but be careful not to have light too strong*" is included, followed by typed "CURTAIN." There then follows *handwritten* but deleted lighting direction "*Lights up sufficiently to see Mr. Mansfield's face*" after which the *handwritten* direction "*Calls in front of curtain Utterson and Rebecca 1st then Dr. Jekyll*" completes Act II Scene II in BSN. In the absence of a third scene, Act II concludes at this point in BSN.
150. This and all subsequent Act II Scene II dialogue and direction appears only in LY.
151. Act II Scene III does not appear in BSN.
152. "*Brilliant*" is replaced by "*Oak*" in APC.
153. "*Sofa L. front*" does not appear in APC.
154. This direction appears only in LY.
155. This entire dialogue appears only in LY.
156. This direction does not appear in APC.
157. This direction does not appear in APC.

(*Enter Jekyll R.*)

JEKYLL. Ah, Lanyon.

LANYON. (*Going to fire.*)[158] I bring news — bad news.

JEKYLL. Yes, I know, I have seen Utterson. (*Offers chair, they sit*)[159] You have taken Agnes to your house.

LANYON. (*Sits R of table.*)[160] Yes, the change will do her good. But she asks constantly for you.

JEKYLL. (*Sits L. of table.*)[161] Poor child — poor child! The murderer has been traced it seems.

LANYON. Yes, to certain lodgings, which were found deserted. (*Handing paper*) Here's the story, never fear, we shall get him.

JEKYLL. Let us hope so. (*Looks at paper.*)

LANYON. The man is mad, of course.

JEKYLL. (*Throwing paper down.*) Strange, very strange. And yet, I doubt—

LANYON. What?

JEKYLL. The underlying madness.

LANYON. What else could it be?

JEKYLL. You know my views, Lanyon — that every man has two natures, a power for good and an evil power. One, pure, noble divine. The other, working in darkness—

LANYON. Your old hobby horse — not unsaddled yet.

JEKYLL. No. Call it what you will. I still believe that by some means, the good and evil in man may be housed in separate identities.

LANYON. In short, that you or I may walk out of that door, not one man, but two distinct creatures, with substance, form, reason, all the rest of it.

JEKYLL. Yes.

LANYON. (*Rising*)[162] Pardon me. Are you serious?

JEKYLL. Never more so. Look at your shadow. It is black and ugly, horrible in its distortion. Knowing only your shadow one could be forgiven for declining to know more of you, Lanyon.

LANYON. (*Laughing*) True, we might dispense with our shadows and be none the worse.

JEKYLL. Think then, how we might dispense with those that lie hidden here. (*Touching his breast*) If our unjust half could hold his course without remorse — if the just could do good free of all disgrace, untrammeled, unhampered.

LANYON. Why this is like the ounce of black powder turning quick silver to gold. Perpetual motion is a fool to it. (*Sits in chair*)[163]

JEKYLL. Steam and electricity were sneered at once. Think how such discovery would benefit the world.

LANYON. Bah! Let discovery go. Perfect that which is discovered, and throw overboard your delusions. They lead nowhere.

JEKYLL. Or to fame and immortality — to cures of which Hippocrates never dreamt.

LANYON. Preposterous. You have no right to dabble in these occult sciences. It is unprofessional.

JEKYLL. Unprofessional. That word kills enterprise. (*Rises to C.*)[164]

LANYON. (*Rises to him — after pause*) We won't quarrel, my dear fellow. Study these things if you will, but don't discuss them with me. I am an old fogy. There, there, say you forgive me.

JEKYLL. (*Taking his hand*) With all my heart. But if the murderer —

LANYON. We'll dissect him together when he's taken. Until then, hang him, say I.

---

158. This direction appears only in LY.
159. Typed dialogue "*Poor Sir Danvers!*" is deleted at this point in LY, but remains in APC.
160. This direction appears only in LY.
161. This direction appears only in LY.
162. This direction appears only in LY.
163. This direction appears only in LY.
164. This direction appears only in LY.

JEKYLL. He will never be taken.

LANYON. (*Taking up paper*) We shall see. We are forgetting Agnes. You will come to her? (*Takes up hat &c.*)

JEKYLL. Yes, I will follow you.

(*Enter Poole L.*)

Ah. Poole!

POOLE. I beg pardon, sir. Are you to dine at home?

JEKYLL. No. I shall dine out.

(*Poole going R. to door which he opens.*)

POOLE. Very good, sir[165]

LANYON. (*Going R.*) Jekyll has gone stark mad. Enterprise! Bosh!

(*Exit angrily R.*)

(*Poole crosses to L. D.*)[166]

JEKYLL. Poole![167]

POOLE. Yes, sir.[168]

JEKYLL. Is Mr. Utterson still there?

POOLE. In the laboratory? Yes, sir.

JEKYLL. Say I am alone.

(*Exit Poole — Jekyll up C. sighing.*)

(*Enter Utterson L.*)

UTTERSON. (*Folding arms and eying Jekyll*) What have you done with Hyde?

JEKYLL. He has entered this house for the last time.

UTTERSON. That is no answer. Have you been mad enough to conceal this fellow.

JEKYLL. I swear to you that I have done with him. He will never be heard of more.

UTTERSON. (*Coldly*) As you please. (*Crosses to R. turns.*) Remember if this comes to a trial your name must appear inevitably.

(*Utterson starts to go*)[169]

JEKYLL. (*C.*) I know, I know. Stay a moment: I want your advice.

UTTERSON. (*R.*) Advice?

JEKYLL. Yes. (*Taking letter from table R. C.*)[170] This letter received from him to-night assures me of his escape. It should perhaps be shown to the police. Will you advise me.

UTTERSON. A letter — from Hyde.

JEKYLL. Yes.

UTTERSON. (*Taking the letter C.*) Let me see it.

(*Jekyll to L. front, Utterson reads letter and starts.*)

UTTERSON. (*Aside*) Great Heaven! A forgery! The hand clumsily disguised but Jekyll's own!

(*Utterson goes up to fire place C. throws letter into it.*)

UTTERSON. That is my advice. (*Aloud*)

JEKYLL. What have you done?

UTTERSON. Saved your neck, it may be. So you forge for a murderer — and such a murderer! God forgive you!

(*Jekyll falls upon sofa L. hiding his face. Utterson going R. meets Agnes who Enters R.*)

UTTERSON. Miss Carew!

AGNES. Harry. Where is he?

UTTERSON. He is there.

(*Agnes crosses to C.*)[171]

UTTERSON. Poor girl! Who shall tell her this!

(*Exit Utterson R.*)

AGNES. (*Throwing her veil on table R. C.*) Harry!

JEKYLL. (*Rising and meeting her*) Agnes? Here?

AGNES. You did not come. I could not wait.

JEKYLL. Agnes — but how sad, how pale!

---

165. Stage direction "(*Jekyll and Poole talk apart L.*)" included here in APC.
166. This direction appears only in LY.
167. This dialogue appears only in LY.
168. This dialogue appears only in LY.
169. This direction appears only in LY.
170. This direction appears only in LY.
171. This stage direction is replaced by "(*Aside*)" in APC.

AGNES. Have they not told you?

JEKYLL. Yes—just now—but it is all strange, unreal. (*Falls back upon L. of sofa agitated*)

AGNES. (*She sits beside him*)[172] Harry, I have come here for your help.[173] They told you did they not that the police are on the track of—of that man—

JEKYLL. Yes, yes. I know.

AGNES. But there is something more. Harry! It was I who saw him.

JEKYLL. (*Shuddering*) Saw him? Saw whom?

AGNES. The man—Hyde.

JEKYLL. You saw him? When?

AGNES. That night. I remember every line of his face. No other ever wore a look so wicked. It haunts me everywhere. I see it in my dreams. Here at your side, I see it even now.

JEKYLL. (*Turning away and trying to escape—aside*) No, no! No!

AGNES. (*Clinging to him*) Harry, I can never rest till he is taken. He must be traced, identified by my description. Come with me to the police. (*Rising*)

JEKYLL. (*Rising—disturbed*) The Police—

AGNES. (*Drawing him to C.*) Yes, come—come.

JEKYLL. Impossible.

AGNES. What do you mean?

JEKYLL. Not now I mean. It is too late—to-morrow.

AGNES. No, at once. (*Jekyll hesitates*) What, you hesitate?

JEKYLL. No, no. Let us go! (*To C.*)

AGNES. Ah! (*To table, takes up veil, then to door R.*) Come!

(*Enter Poole L.*)

POOLE. I beg pardon sir, in the laboratory I found these keys. Surely, sir, they would be Mr. Hyde's.

(*Agnes runs quickly to Jekyll*)[174]

JEKYLL. (*In a hoarse voice*) Give them to me. (*Poole hands keys*)

AGNES. Mr. Hyde! Harry, what is this? You know him?

(*Jekyll tries to speak then nods*)

My father's murderer, your friend?[175] Harry! Harry![176]

(*Falls at Jekyll's feet—as she falls Jekyll over her.*)[177]

[*The following additional Act II Scene III dialogue and direction appears only in APC.*]

JEKYLL. No! No! I spoke the truth—he is gone forever.

AGNES. And you let him go! (*Jekyll approaches her*) Don't touch me! If you really speak the truth, if you are honest and sincere, prove it to me now.

JEKYLL. Prove it? How?

AGNES. A word will do. Promise to have no thought but this. Promise to follow up this man, to hunt him down with all your heart and soul. Find him. Promise that—no swear it!

JEKYLL. Oh, not that—not that—

AGNES. Swear it!

JEKYLL. I cannot.

AGNES. You cannot! Why?

JEKYLL. Because—he is my other self!

(*Agnes with a cry, falls fainting. Jekyll stooping over her in despair*)

CURTAIN.

---

172. This direction appears only in LY.
173. Additional dialogue with "*Jekyll*" saying "*My help!*" is included here in APC.
174. This direction appears only in LY.
175. Additional dialogue "*You have concealed him*" in APC.
176. "*Harry! Harry!*" appears only in LY.
177. This direction appears only in LY, followed by "*CURTAIN*" bringing Act II Scene III to an end in LY.

ACT III[178]
Two and the Same

Consulting room in Dr. Lanyon's house in Cavendish Square, handsomely furnished. In flat R. a low window, backed by view of London Street, to which a small door in flat L. leads. The window curtains are closed,[179] doors 2nd Entrance R. and 1st entrance L.[180] Fire place with fire 2nd entrance L. book-shelves at back C. other shelves containing books, glasses bottles etc. Against wall at 1st and 3rd entrance R. L. C.[181] Library table with lamp, decanter and glasses R. C. sofa, small table against wall 1st Entrance R. clock on mantel-piece L.[182])

(*Enter Lanyon and Poole hurriedly R.*)

LANYON. (*To C.*) Come in—come in. What is this? Your master is away?

POOLE. Yes, sir: and he wrote me word to bring you this parcel—which I've done, sir. (*Hands package wrapped in white[183] cloth*)

LANYON. (*C.—opening package at table L. C.*) A drawer—with powders and a phial, where did you get this?

POOLE. (*R.*) In the doctor's cabinet—all just as I found it, sir. The orders written me was to give it to your own personal self—with this letter (*Hands letter*)

LANYON. I see: it is from Jekyll. He never came to dinner yesterday. You say he is gone—where? (*Pockets letter unopened*)

POOLE. I don't know—but I don't like it, sir. He's mostly away, sir and when at home, he locks himself up in his cabinet alone.

LANYON. With his infernal discoveries, I suppose.

POOLE. I wish I may die if I[184] like it, sir. There's something wrong.

LANYON. Wrong?

POOLE. Mischief's a brewing in our house. I don't know what it is, but I'm afraid, sir—I'm afraid.

NEWCOME. (*Outside, R.*) Quite right, Miss. Quite right.

LANYON. The inspector! There, there, Poole, we'll talk of this another time. I'll call tomorrow upon your master.

POOLE. (*Going R.*) Very good, sir. (*Returning*) But, sir, if he asks you into that cabinet of his, don't you go.[185]

LANYON. Nonsense! You're a fool. Not another word, go home, and go to sleep.

POOLE. Very good, sir. God grant we are as we are—all of us—to-morrow, sir, at this time.

(*Exit Poole R.*)

LANYON. Stupid old fool! Like master, like man. What's all this rubbish? I'll put it out of the way.

(*He wraps up drawer and carries it to table crossing C. as Newcome Enters R, with open note book*)

LANYON. Well, you saw Miss Carew?

NEWCOME. (*Down R. C.*) Quite right, sir. By her account the murderer wasn't one to fall in love with. (*Puts up book*) We shall get 'im.[186]

LANYON. (*C.*) You will print the hand-bills?

---

178. Handwritten lighting direction "*At rise house foots and borders up full fire log lighted L R 3 R E. bunch R. 2 E. Calciums box on drop R. Yellow. Lens C. door L. Dressing case***? R.*" indicated here in BSN.
179. "*closed*" is replaced by "*open*" in APC and BSN.
180. "*and 1st entrance L*" appears only in LY.
181. "*other shelves containing books, glasses bottles etc. Against wall at 1st and 3rd entrance R. L.C.*" appears only in LY.
182. "*to indicate 5 minutes to twelve*" included here in BSN.
183. "*white*" is replaced by "*black*" in BSN.
184. Typed "*wish I may die if I*" deleted and replaced by *handwritten* insertion "*don't know, but I don't*" in BSN.
185. Additional dialogue "*Sir, don't you go!*" included here in APC and BSN.
186. "*We shall get 'im.*" is repeated here in APC and BSN.

NEWCOME. At once. All the world will know my gentleman before the week is out. He 'asn't the ghost of a chance. Good night, sir. (*Going R.*)

LANYON. One moment. (*Crossing to table L. C.*) Here's a bit of a night-cap for you.

NEWCOME. Thank you, sir.[187]

LANYON. (*Fills glasses*) Old port.[188] I give you — the tanning of Hyde! (*Drinks.*)

NEWCOME. The tanning of 'Ide. (*Drinks and smacks his lips*) That's a one'er, so it is![189] (*Up C.*) Oh, Damme, I quite forgot her Ladyship!

LANYON. (*L. C.*) Her ladyship?

NEWCOME. (*L. by door*) The old hag, Hyde's housekeeper. She swears she'll see you and the young lady. I made her wait outside.

LANYON. (*C.*) What does she want?

NEWCOME. (*Slapping pocket*) The needful, she lost the notes I paid her — or says so.

LANYON. Let her come in, she may be useful.

(*Newcome opens door R. H. and calls off*)

NEWCOME. Come in, beauty

(*Enter Rebecca R. she crosses and stands R.*)

NEWCOME. (*Down a little R.*) She ain't much to look at.

(*Lanyon calls "Agnes" R. D. goes to L. and sits L. of desk.*)[190]

NEWCOME. P'raps the young lady would rather not —[191]

(*Enter Agnes R.*)[192]

Oh, I beg pardon, Miss—(*Retires up C.*)

AGNES. I will see her.[193] (*To sofa R. Rebecca down C.*) What is your name?

REBECCA. Rebecca, Miss— Rebecca Moore.

AGNES. You have asked for me?

REBECCA. It's the money, Miss, the money — he tore it up bit by bit — before my eyes.

AGNES. Who did this?

REBECCA. Hyde (*Agnes shivers.*)

NEWCOME. (*Down a little*) She keeps the lodgings, Miss. Hyde's lodgings in Soho.

AGNES. Yes, yes. (*To Rebecca*) And this money —

REBECCA. Twenty pound, Miss, twenty pound. I am a poor woman — my trade is ruined — only twenty pound, and if I find him.

AGNES. Let her have the money, uncle. She may help us.

REBECCA. Yes, that's it — that's it The money![194] (*To table L. C.*)

LANYON. (*Taking notes from pocket book*) There!

REBECCA. (*Clutching money, greedily*) Ah! (*Leaning over table to Lanyon*) Help you, yes.[195] He burned his papers— but I found this bit in the ashes, there's writing on it, d'ye see. (*Shows paper*)

LANYON. Let me have it. (*Takes paper and starts — aside*) Great Heaven! Jekyll's hand! (*Rises —*)

REBECCA. (*To C.*) Bless you, Miss— Bless you for these! (*Kisses notes, Agnes has risen and watches Lanyon closely*)

NEWCOME. (*Down to L. F. to Rebecca.*) There, there, that will do. You've got the money — keep it.[196] Go![197]

REBECCA. Keep it, yes![198] (*Crosses up to C. door*

---

187. This line of dialogue does not appear in APC.
188. "*Old port*" appears only in LY.
189. Additional *handwritten* dialogue "*good night, sir.*" inserted here in BSN.
190. This direction is replaced with "*(Enter Agnes)*" followed by dialogue with "*Lanyon*" calling "*Agnes*" in BSN.
191. Additional *handwritten* dialogue with "*Agnes*" saying "*I will see her*" inserted here in BSN.
192. This direction does not appear at this point in BSN.
193. "*I will see her*" is typed but deleted at this point in BSN.
194. "*The money!*" does not appear in APC.
195. Stage direction "*(To Agnes)*" included here in BSN.
196. Additional *handwritten* dialogue "*That's what they do with money, keep it.*" inserted here in BSN.
197. "*Go!*" is a *handwritten* insertion which appears only in LY.
198. Further dialogue "*I should think so.*" is typed but deleted here in BSN.

laughing) Till doom's day!¹⁹⁹ (*Laughing*) Five, ten! fifteen²⁰⁰ —

(*Exit C. D.*)²⁰¹

NEWCOME. (*To L. C.*) I beg pardon, sir, that bit of paper —

LANYON. (*Controlling himself with an effort*) I will examine it. You shall have it to-morrow.

NEWCOME. Very well, sir. At your orders, sir. You'll find me at Scotland Yard (*Up to door — looking at Agnes*) Poor young lady!²⁰²

(*Exit Newcome door in flat C. and L.*)²⁰³

AGNES. (*To C.*) Uncle. (*He turns to her*)²⁰⁴ that paper —

LANYON. (*R. C.*) It is nothing. Part of a cheque to Hyde's order — The signature burned away — not of the smallest consequence.

AGNES. I must see it.

LANYON. Yes — another time — I —

AGNES. No, I insist —

LANYON. What! For such a trifle!

AGNES. You are wasting time. I know who signed the paper. Give it to me!

(*Lanyon looks at her in surprise then hands the paper reluctantly*)

AGNES. His hand, I thought so.

LANYON. You knew? Was it for this that you broke with Jekyll yesterday.

AGNES. Do not speak his name. I learnt things that I cannot understand — that are hard to believe. (*Sits on sofa R. her face in her hands.*)

LANYON. (*Up to her*) He gave Hyde money, why?

AGNES. I do not know — Oh, Uncle, see him — make him tell you.

LANYON. Yes, to-morrow. I will see him — force him to confess —

AGNES. (*Rising*) Confess? Then you, too, believe —

LANYON. No, I cannot believe, that paper — let me have it.

AGNES. (*About to hand it, looks at him a moment, then refuses*) No!

LANYON. Agnes!

AGNES. You promised this to the police and they shall have it.

LANYON. Child, think what you are doing! If Jekyll should be innocent? Will you bring evidence against him?

AGNES. No. Against my father's murderer. Who else should bring it.

LANYON. (*After pause — sighing*) You are right — it is best.

(*Agnes shudders — Lanyon up C.²⁰⁵ turns back and seeing Mrs. Lanyon from R.*)²⁰⁶

Hush! Your aunt, not a word of this to her! (*Down L. C.*)

(*Enter Mrs. Lanyon R.*)²⁰⁷

MRS. LANYON. (*R.*) Agnes. I have been looking for you everywhere.

AGNES. (*C.*) For me?

MRS. LANYON. To tell you I cannot bear it, I say it is absurd and wicked.

LANYON. (*L.*) Wicked? What is it? Who is wicked?

MRS. LANYON. Why, Agnes. It is all her fault, I am sure, she has quarrelled with Dr. Jekyll — broken the engagement for no reason, at such a time too! I say it is positively sinful! Poor man, I feel for him so!

---

199. "*Till doom's day*" repeated here in APC and BSN.
200. "*(Laughing) Five, ten! fifteen*" appears only in LY.
201. This direction appears only in LY.
202. "*poor young lady*" is repeated here, followed by stage direction "*(as he exits)*" and additional dialogue "*Dear, dear, dear.*" in BSN.
203. This direction appears only in LY.
204. This direction appears only in LY.
205. Additional stage direction "*Mrs. Lanyon coughs outside*" included here in BSN. Further stage direction "*Looks off*" included here in both APC and BSN.
206. "*turns back and seeing Mrs. Lanyon from R*" appears only in LY.
207. Additional *handwritten* stage direction "*Agnes sits on sofa R.C.*" inserted here in BSN.

What good will all his money do him now. (*Sobs.*)

AGNES. I can not help it, Aunt. (*On sofa.*)

MRS. LANYON. She will be the death of us all! (*To Lanyon.*) Why do you stand here and take her part? Do something.

LANYON. There is nothing to be done.

MRS. LANYON. Nothing? She will die an old maid in a black frock, and he calls it nothing. (*Crossing to L.*)

LANYON. She is perfectly right. (*Up L. C.*)

MRS. LANYON. To break her word like a weather cock? Write to him, Agnes, call him back: think of your family—think of your worldly prospects! (*Down L. C.*)

LANYON. (*Down L. of Agnes R. to Mrs. Lanyon.*)[208] She is right, I tell you.

AGNES. I can never see him, never hear of him again.

MRS. LANYON. (*L. front.*) What! You do not love him then? (*Agnes hesitates.*)

LANYON. (*Speaking for Agnes*) No! she does not love him.

MRS. LANYON. That is not true.

AGNES. No, it is not true. I do love him—I cannot help it. (*Crosses to fire, burns cheque*[209]) There!

LANYON. (*To Agnes*) What have you done? (*at table.*)

AGNES. (*Crossing to R. centre.*) I have saved his life, but I must never see him—never! (*Hides her face in Lanyon's arms.*)

LANYON. Go, my child, go. We will talk of this to-morrow.

(*Exit Agnes R.*)

MRS. LANYON. (*To C.*) It is shameful. (*Sits R. C.*)

LANYON. (*Down L. C.*) Let her alone. In these matters it is best not to interfere.

MRS. LANYON. Interfere! I interfere? How dare you say such things?

LANYON. Why, just now—

MRS. LANYON. Just now, I did my duty.

LANYON.[210] (*L. C.*) Granted, but—

MRS. LANYON. (*L. C.*) It is a point of honour, poor Jekyll.[211] I could almost marry him myself to save the family reputation.

LANYON. (*Nettled*) Oh, well, well! As you please! Don't mind me. (*Up and down L.*)

MRS. LANYON. And you uphold her!

LANYON. (*Angrily—L. of table.*) Be calm—be calm.

MRS. LANYON. (*Crosses and down in a passion R.*)[212] Calm! You have no feeling, no sympathy—

LANYON. (*Same*) Don't provoke me!

MRS. LANYON. No sense of propriety!

LANYON. (*Furious, slamming book*[213] *down on table L. C.*) Damn it, Madam!

MRS. LANYON.[214] Brute! (*Runs off R.*)

LANYON. (*To C.*) Propriety! I object to bigamy in the family, and she calls me a brute—and Agnes, too—a man is always in the wrong. What does all this mean? What has Jekyll to do with Hyde? (*Seeing*[215] *the package on table.*) Why did he send me those powders. (*Sits L. of table.*) Ah, his[216] letter. (*Taking letter from pocket, reads.*) "Dear Lanyon, You are one of my oldest friends: and although we may have differed on scientific questions, I remember no break in our affections. There was never a day when I would not have sacrificed my left hand to help you. Lanyon, my life, my honour, my reason

---

208. This direction does not appear in APC.
209. "*burns cheque*" is replaced by "*and destroys paper*" in APC, and "*tearing check and throws in fire*" in BSN.
210. Handwritten lighting direction "*Lower house foots and borders gradually*" indicated here in BSN.
211. Handwritten dialogue "*I feel for him so*" inserted here in BSN.
212. This direction appears only in LY.
213. "*book*" is replaced by "*hand*" in APC and BSN.
214. Stage direction "*Rises, shrieks, goes to door R.*" included here in BSN.
215. "*Seeing*" replaced by "*Placing*" in BSN.
216. "*Ah his*" replaced by "*and this*" in APC and BSN.

> [handwritten: Interjection of Lanyon's thoughts ↓]

are all at your mercy." (*Speaks*) Life! Honour! Reason! what is this? "At midnight, wait alone in your consulting room, and admit with your own hands into the house a man who will present himself in my name, place the drawer which Poole brings you in this man's hands. If you then insist upon an explanation, he will satisfy you that these arrangements are of capital importance. Think of me in a strange place, labouring under a blackness of distress that no fancy can exaggerate: yet if you will punctually serve me, my troubles will roll away like a story that is told. If not, you have seen the last of

Your friend

Henry Jekyll."

(*Rise and up to table C.*)[217] He is mad. No doubt of it, what are these things. (*Looks at powders etc.*) Unmarked, of Jekyll's own manufacture, then, why does he send them here. It is plain that I have to deal with a madman — or, rather with his messenger. I don't half like it, I'll unchain my watch dog. (*To table L. C. takes pistol from drawer and puts it in pocket*)[218] There, now I feel truly hospitable. That clock wants but a moment off twelve — it must be fast. (*Looks at watch*) No — or I am wrong. I'll open the window and take my time from the bell of St George (*To window which he opens, gusts of wind and rain without*) By the Lord Harry! what a night, it rains waterspouts! And not a soul to be seen, ah, yes there goes the bull's-eye of a policeman. My good friend, I may want you yet. *Distant bell strikes*) The hour! ([219]*Listens — closes window — back to C.*) Well, here I am[220] — he can't complain of me — but the other.

(*Knocker raps gently at door in flat, startled, in a low whisper*)

Bless me! There he is already.

(*Goes to table takes up the lamp and moves towards door in flat — the Knock repeated gently,*[221] *as he opens the door a gust of wind blows out the lamp leaving stage lighted by the fire.*[222] *He retreats with a cry of alarm to C. and puts the lamp on the table as Hyde Enters cloaked, from door in flat.*[223])

HYDE. (*Springing after Lanyon R. and catching him by the arm.*) Have you got it?

LANYON. (*Shaking him off with a shudder*) Not so fast, sir — the lamp —

HYDE. No matter.[224] Have you got it?

LANYON. Come, sir. You forget that I do not know you. (*Motions Hyde to chair C. — aside*) His hand was like ice!

HYDE. (*To C.*) I beg your pardon, Dr. Lanyon. You are right. My impatience has shown its heels to my politeness.

LANYON. Be seated, sir.

HYDE. A little nearer your fire, I am wet to the skin. (*Crosses to fire L. and crouches before it.*)

LANYON. Very good, and meantime I — (*As if about to light lamp.*)

HYDE. Do not light it, let it alone.

LANYON. (*Aside down C.*) He is ghastly as the grave. (*Aloud*) Excuse me, I do not know your name.

HYDE. (*Disturbed*) My name!

LANYON. Yes. (*Aside*) Good Heavens! What a suspicion! The distorted face — the evil look — the impression of disgust he makes upon me —

HYDE. I come at the instance of your colleague, Dr. Jekyll —

LANYON. (*Aside, R. of table*) It can be no other!

---

217. This direction does not appear in APC.
218. Additional stage direction "*(Flash of light)*" included here in BSN.
219. Further stage direction "*Flash of lightening. He*" included here in BSN.
220. "*Well, here I am*" does not appear in APC.
221. "*the knock repeated gently*" does not appear in APC.
222. Handwritten lighting direction "*As lamp goes out white foots out — green foots up. Green calcium on in fire place (Lens)*" indicated here in BSN.
223. Further stage direction "*Flash of lightening*" included here in BSN.
224. "*No matter*" replaced by "*Let it alone*" in APC and BSN.

(*Aloud*) Then you are the wretched criminal — the murderer — now hunted for in every corner of the land! You are his friend, Edward Hyde!

HYDE. (*Starting up — advancing to Lanyon*) Silence! Silence or —

LANYON. (*R. C.*) Why how dare you venture back into the very heart of London. I have but to open that door and call in the police.²²⁵ Ah! You would like to kill me, too. But I am armed, you see. (*Shows pistol*)²²⁶ and within an hour I will have you safely lodged in Newgate. (*Up C. — moves.*)

HYDE. (*Following up C.*) Wait — wait — (*Catching him by the sleeve.*)

LANYON. (*Recoiling C.*) Hands off, fellow!

HYDE. (*Getting between him and the door.*) Stay! I say, I am here to save Henry Jekyll, by your friendship for him, I charge you to carry out his orders. For his sake, I beg it of you. I implore you to do his bidding, or his life must answer for it, if you refuse.

LANYON. His life? — Pshaw!

HYDE. Did he not tell you so?

LANYON. (*Recoiling in disgust*)²²⁷ Wretch! He paid you money! What is the bond between you?

HYDE. You shall²²⁸ know all.²²⁹ Do but grant his request — Then deal with me as you please.

LANYON. Speak for him, then, if that is your mission.

HYDE. But first I understood — I understood — a drawer —

LANYON. (*Taking drawer from table R. C.*) Yes, here it is.

(*Holds out drawer, Hyde springs towards it, then stops with distorted face and lays his hand upon his heart.*)

What is the matter, man? Compose yourself.

(*Hyde smiles at him — he recoils again in horror. Hyde snatches the drawer and crosses to L. Tears off the white covering, and dropping upon his knees pulls over the contents with a sob of relief.*)

HYDE. Here — everything — safe! Safe!

LANYON. (*R.*) All exactly as I found it.²³⁰ (HYDE. *looks about nervously*) What more?

HYDE. (*L.*) A graduated glass — If you have one.

LANYON. What? That you may drink and cheat the gallows with your devil's mixture.

HYDE. (*Rising with one of the powders and phial*) Man, Man. Were it only that, why should I trust myself with you? Has the river Thames run dry? I tell you, Jekyll at this moment is in deadly peril. Read his letter. Is there not agony in every word.

LANYON. It is like the cry of a lost soul. He is in your power, now?²³¹

HYDE. He only²³² is to blame, you shall see and know all.²³³ Give me the glass, I cannot answer for delay.

LANYON. (*To R. finds, glass on shelves R. to C. with it.*) Here!

HYDE. (*Snatching glass*) (*He goes to table L. C. measuring out powder and liquor in the glass by the light of the fire. As he measures he crouches over the fire.*)

LANYON. (*Aside, looking at his own hand that* HYDE. *has touched*) There is death in that hand of his. The devil's own could not have a touch more terrible.

---

225. Stage direction "*(Hyde moves at Lanyon)*" included here in BSN.
226. This direction does not appear in BSN.
227. This direction does not appear in APC.
228. Handwritten "*see and know*" inserted here in BSN.
229. Handwritten "*if you must*" inserted here in BSN.
230. Handwritten stage direction "*(Long pause)*" inserted here in BSN.
231. "*now*" replaced by "*how*" in APC and BSN. — May be error in LY.
232. Typed "*only*" deleted and replaced with handwritten "*a skeptic he alone*" in BSN.
233. Handwritten "*all*" replaces typed but deleted "*if you must*" in LY. "*if you must*" remains the text in APC, and is typed, with "*if you*" deleted and replaced by handwritten "*But*" in BSN.

HYDE. (*Back to fire — smiling and looking closely at Lanyon*) And now to settle what remains. Will you be wise? Will you be guided? Will you suffer me to take this glass in my hand and leave your house without further parley?

LANYON. (*Putting hand on pistol*) By the night above us, no!

HYDE. (*L. C.*) Ah! the greed of curiosity has too much command of you.

LANYON. (*R. C.*) Curiosity? What has that to do with it? You ask me calmly to let a malefactor loose upon the world. I refuse. You are my prisoner.[234]

HYDE. (*Crosses to Lanyon — Lanyon recoils to R.*) Foolish words. You rather are in my power now. Again I give you the choice. Think before you answer, for it shall be done as you decide. As you decide,[235] you shall be left as you are now and neither richer nor wiser, unless the sense of service rendered to a man in mortal distress may be counted as a kind of riches of the soul, or, if you so prefer, a new province of knowledge and new avenues to fame and power shall be open to you, here in this room upon the instant: and your sight shall be blasted by a prodigy to stagger the unbelief of Satan.

LANYON. (*Aside*) What does he mean? It seems as though my heart stopped beating. (*Aloud*) You speak enigmas, and I hear them with no impression but that of doubt. You cannot wonder at it. (*Recoils to R.*)

HYDE. (*Following him to C.*)[236] Choose! Sleep in peace: or learn that all your science is a cipher. Learn marvels of which Hippocrates never dreamed!

LANYON. (*Aside in terror.*) Why, those were Jekyll's words! (*Aloud*) I have gone too far to retreat. At last, I own to the greed of curiosity. Go on! I must know the end.

HYDE. Good. Lanyon you remember your vows. What follows is under the seal of your profession, and now, you who have so long been bound by narrow and material views, you who have denied the virtue of a medicine for the soul — Behold! Man of unbelief! Behold!

(*Drinks from the glass which he puts down with a loud cry. He reels, staggers and clutches the table calls out in Jekyll's voice "Lanyon! Lanyon! Then straightens himself and walks erect to C. as Jekyll.*)

LANYON. (*Over come with horror, retreating to extreme R.*) Jekyll!

QUICK CURTAIN.

[*The following handwritten lighting and stage direction appears here in* BSN]

~~White foots up~~ Calcium on ~~R~~ L. I. E. quickly just high enough to see Mr. Mansfield's face, bunch on R I E.

Calls in front of curtain

Dr. Lanyon 1st.

then Mr. Mansfield.

---

234. Handwritten stage direction "(*Starts to C.*)" inserted here in BSN.
235. This "*As you decide*" is a *handwritten* insertion in BSN.
236. This direction does not appear in APC.

ACT IV[237]
The Last Night

Dr. Jekyll's cabinet.[238] *Interior in 3-4 In flat C. a large curtained window backed by wall of court. Double doors with heavy bolts 2nd Entrance R. Mantel piece with clock, fire place &c 2nd entrance L. Glazed presses against wall R. and L. of fireplace. L. C. an office table on which writing materials and several saucers containing chemicals.*[239] *Smaller table with bottles upon it up stage R. of window. Up stage C. a large cheval glass with brackets containing lighted candles. Books Papers &c are scattered about in confusion.*[240] *Late afternoon, changing to twilight and dusk.*

(Jekyll discovered alone at window C. He holds in his hand a glass into which he drops liquor from the phial.)

JEKYLL. *(Putting phial on table at window and holding glass up to the light.)* It will not do. Experiment is useless. Failure, succeeds failure. The salt is not the same. A curse upon the science that can reveal half truths and then betray us. *(Down C.)* Without this tincture I am doomed. I were better in my grave.

(Clock strikes six.)[241]

Six o'clock![242] so late and still Lanyon does not come. It is foolish to wait longer. I know already the answer that he brings. My hope is but the merest thread — and on that depends my life. I am like the condemned wretch who has taken his last look of earth, yet still hopes for reprieve.

(Knock at door R. He trembles and catches at the table.)[243]

JEKYLL. He is there! No, that is not his knock. What then? *(He goes to door,*[244] *the knock is repeated.)* Who's there?

POOLE. *(Outside R.)* Only me, sir. — Poole

JEKYLL. *(Aside)* I cannot see him. He half suspects my secret. *(Aloud)* You have the answer from the chemist?

POOLE. Yes, sir — a written message.

JEKYLL. Very good, pass it to me — Quick. *(Draws paper from aside the door and down C. — reads.)* "Mr. Whitelock regrets that he can only fill Dr. Jekyll's order with a sample like the last one. *(Tears paper to pieces angrily)* Useless! Useless! And Lanyon's word will be the same.[245] Why wait to hear him say it, rather let me die now in my own shape which even as I speak may be taken from me. *(Shuddering)* Ah, anything but that! Let the dead man's face they look at be Henry Jekyll's not the face of Hyde. *(up C.)* I laid the poison ready for the time when it should come. It has come now. *(Shudders.)* That shudder again! Is it the warning, am I too late already?[246] *(Waits a moment as not daring to look into the glass, looks with a cry of joy.)*[247] Ah, thank Heaven! My own self still. *(Supports himself, panting by table R.)* Oh what horrors incredible this glass has seen and known, and yet with what wild joy I first looked here upon the face I hate and loathe, believing my discovery a bless-

---

237. Lighting direction "*At rise house foots and borders up full. White lense R,I,E. Red box on drop R. Red lense on window C. from L, 4, E*" indicated here in BSN.
238. "*Dr. Jekyll's cabinet*" is the only part of this entire scene setting included in BSN.
239. "*and several saucers containing chemicals*" appears only in LY.
240. "*with brackets containing lighted candles. Books Papers andc are scattered about in confusion*" appears only in LY.
241. This direction does not appear in APC.
242. Stage direction "*(Strikes six on steel bar)*" included here in APC.
243. "*and catches at the table*" does not appear in APC.
244. "*He goes to door*" does not appear in BSN.
245. Dialogue "*No remedy! No remedy!*" deleted here in LY.
246. Typed "*am I too late already*" deleted and replaced by handwritten "*Have we changed places already?*" in BSN.
247. This stage direction appears as dialogue in the form of "*What a moment — as not daring to look in the glass, looks. What a day of joy!*" in APC. — perhaps an error in original transcription.

ing to mankind. Alas It was dreadful in its incompleteness! (*Taking up poison*)[248] But stay, what if Lanyon has found the lost ingredient that will give me new power to control and conquer these fiendish transformations I might live, be happy, to marry as I promised. (*Covers his face with his hands.*) Coward, what right have I even to think of her — no right — no right. (*Takes up poison again.*) Now!

(*About to drink, gentle knock at door R. he stops.*) (*Knock is twice repeated, puts down the phial.*)[249]

Lanyon's knock! What! Can Heaven be merciful! (*Goes to door R. and draws back the bolts.*[250] *Enter Lanyon*)

LANYON. (*At door.*) Harry!

JEKYLL. Come in.

(*Lanyon to C. bolting door and looking eagerly at Lanyon's face*)

You have not brought it. (*To R. C.*) (*Lanyon shakes his head.*) I saw it in your face. Sit down, my poor Lanyon, you are trembling.

LANYON. (*Sitting R. C.*) It is nothing. I have not been myself since — since —

JEKYLL. (*Crosses to C. sitting in arm chair*)[251] Since that night[252] — I understand. You saw the Chemists?

LANYON. Yes, they remembered your first purchase of the salt, but assured me that the old supply was long ago exhausted, that furnished you lately was from a fresh invoice.

JEKYLL. And it is useless like all the others. With Poole's help, I have ransacked every chemist's shop in London. This last interview of yours was my forlorn hope. Did you beg them to search their cellars?

LANYON. More than that. I searched with them. Praying to find some crate that had been overlooked, but in vain.[253]

JEKYLL. All is over then. The first supply was impure, I am persuaded that unknown impurity[254] gave the drug its power, we cannot reproduce it. (*Rising*) I am a dead man Lanyon.

LANYON. (*Crossing to him*)[255] Courage, what you fear may never take place after all.

JEKYLL. Do not believe it. I have trifled too long with my conscience. I have destroyed the balance of my soul The evil power within me has the mastery. It is Hyde now that controls Jekyll — not Jekyll, Hyde.

LANYON. What do you mean?[256]

JEKYLL. (*Sits in arm chair C. Lanyon sits on front of table by R. of Jekyll*) Let me tell you.[257] Three days ago I dropped asleep in this chair where I am sitting. How long I slept I do not know, but waking my eyes fell upon my hand as it lay there — not this that I now hold up before you — but a distorted hand of a dusky pallor — I turned, and saw in the glass not my face — but his — the monster's — Hyde's.[258]

LANYON. You were transformed without the drug then?

JEKYLL. Yes, as often of late. I have slowly lost the hold upon my original, my better self. To restore it then was the work of a moment. I had only to mix the draught and drink it but for that I used the last of the old powders: without them I am help-

---

248. This direction appears only in LY.
249. This direction appears only in LY.
250. Stage direction "*and draws back the bolts*" omitted and replaced with dialogue "*Come in, come in.*" in APC and BSN.
251. This direction does not appear in APC.
252. "Since that night" is typed but deleted in BSN.
253. "*but in vain*" is a *handwritten* addition in BSN and does not appear in APC.
254. "*unknown impurity*" is omitted and replaced by a single typed line, indicating indecipherable text in APC.
255. This direction does not appear in APC.
256. Typed stage direction "(*Clings on table*)" followed by handwritten "(*Bus, Jekyll fainting*)" appears here in BSN.
257. "*Let me tell you.*" typed but deleted in BSN.
258. "*there*" included here in APC and BSN. Further *handwritten* "*there*" followed by typed direction "(*Business*)" included in BSN.

less[259] — once transformed again only death can save me.

(*He rises, Lanyon sits in chair R. of table. Jekyll crosses to Lan.*)[260]

LANYON. My poor Harry.

JEKYLL. To prolong my own agony I have destroyed your peace of mind Forgive me Lanyon.[261] The nightmare which has haunted you will soon be over — soon I shall trouble you no more.

LANYON.[262] You must seek a place of safety. Here, new dangers threaten you.

JEKYLL. What new danger can I fear?

LANYON. Utterson has found a clue.

JEKYLL. The forged letter — I had forgotten that.

LANYON. He believes you to be Hyde's accomplice. At any moment the police may search the house. You must leave it at once and go with me.

JEKYLL. To whom do you say this — to Dr. Jekyll or to Mr. Hyde?

LANYON. Harry, I entreat you — (*Step forward.*)

JEKYLL. To force you to compound felony and make that monster your companion? Why? To what end? He is proscribed and branded. He would not be safe one hour. No, leave him[263] to himself. The police for Hyde have no terrors, he will escape them in his own time, in his own way.

LANYON. But here you cannot escape from yourself. There is danger for you even in the sight of these surroundings.

JEKYLL. (*To C.*) That is true, there is not an instant to be lost.[264] Lanyon I have one last request to make to you.[265] If you were ever my friend you will hear and grant it.

LANYON. Speak, what must I do?

JEKYLL. It concerns one whose name I hardly dare to breathe — Oh, you have guessed it.

LANYON. Agnes!

JEKYLL. Do not fear. While I live, I would not have her know my story, I dare not speak with her, I might betray myself. It is not that, but yet I must see her, Lanyon — once, only once, while I am still myself.

LANYON. But how?

JEKYLL. I have found the way. From that window, I could see her face. The court is narrow — we are high above it. Bring her there upon some pretence, no matter what, she will never see me, will never know. But I may look at her for one moment. — one moment before —[266]

LANYON. I understand, and I will do it, but on one condition. Give me your promise first?

JEKYLL. What promise?

LANYON. That until this change you fear has come you will make no attempt upon your life.

JEKYLL. I promise. (*Gives his hand.*) There's my hand upon it. Once more, I promise.

LANYON. (*Holding his hand — other hand on shoulder*)[267] Meantime have faith, do not give way, do not despair.

JEKYLL. Farewell, old friend, whatever happens, pity me and forgive me if you can.

LANYON. Whatever happens, my place is here with you.

JEKYLL. (*Crossing and unbolting door R.*) Yes. First bring her there: and come to me afterwards alone. I will watch for your signal.

---

259. "*without them I am helpless*" does not appear in BSN.
260. This direction does not appear in APC.
261. Handwritten stage direction "*rises X to table*" inserted here in BSN.
262. At this point additional dialogue "*No, no. It can't be. This awful presence is gone; it will not return again. The end has come. Have you not suffered already as no man ever did.*" is included in APC and BSN.
263. The following dialogue "*himself. The police for Hyde have no terrors, he will*" is not typed but indicated as a handwritten insertion at this point in BSN. The full handwritten insertion reads: "*to himself. The police for Hyde have no terrors, he will know how*" in BSN.
264. Stage direction "*(Bus. with poison)*" included here in BSN.
265. "*to make to you*" does not appear in BSN.
266. "*at her for one moment — one moment before —*" typed but deleted and replace with handwritten "*upon her once; only once — before —*" in BSN.
267. "*other hand on shoulder*" does not appear in APC.

The Collated Script

LANYON. (*Crosses to door.*) Courage! Courage!

(*Exit R.*)[268]

JEKYLL. (*Bolting doors behind him*) And so farewell, for we shall never meet again — I know it. I am left to face my death alone. Ah, were death all! (*Up R. C.*) It is the other nameless terror that racks me, terror of myself — for we are one. (*Shivers and supports himself by chair up stage R.*) Again that shudder of the grave![269] Have we changed places already.[270] (*Looks in glass*) No, not yet —[271] (*Sits in chair R. and burst into tears*) Poor fool! To waste time like a woman in tears (*To table L. C. sits and takes paper from drawer*)[272] This my full confession. (*Looking over it*) I have not spared myself. (*Writing*) For Gabriel Utterson Let him deal with it as he pleases. And here my will revoking the other which he holds. (*Laughing bitterly*) He will like this better — it cancels the bequest to HYDE — what could Hyde do with money. Poor Hunted wretch, the wealth of London would not save him now. (*Writing*) This too for Utterson. (*Rises, shivering*)[273] It has come,[274] the devil's hand is at my throat. No, it is past. (*To C.*) Agnes — where is Agnes, he promised that I should see her. (*Up to window, which he opens.*) She must come quickly or I shall be gone. Night is closing in! The stars are coming out. How often together Agnes and I have wondered at them! And now, for me, no dawn, no twilight — only the outer blackness of the grave. Will they never come? Footsteps! (*Looks out and draws back hastily*) An inspector of police Well and why not? Dr. Jekyll surely may take a breath of air unchallenged. I am like a child and start at nothing. He is gone again. No sound but[275] the roar of London. Hark! I heard voices. Lanyon has kept his promise. She is there.[276] They pass. She knows nothing. I will not have it so. I must speak[277] if only one word. Agnes! Agnes! look it is I Henry Jekyll! (*Down a little*) She has seen me, she will come! Thank Heaven! (*Falls into chair R. C.*) She will come![278] I shall hear her voice! Shall see her once — only once, before! — (*He has slowly turned into Hyde and now sees himself in the glass and rises with a shriek.*) Ah!

(*Murmur of voices swelling louder until all on stage. Hyde crouches C. trembling. Loud knocking at doors R.*)

UTTERSON. (*Outside R.*) Jekyll! — Jekyll!!

HYDE. (*Aside in terror*) Utterson — the Police —

(*Knocks repeated.*)

UTTERSON. (*Same*) Jekyll! I demand to see you. If not of your consent then by brute force.

HYDE. (*On floor C.*) Utterson — for God's sake have mercy.

UTTERSON. (*Same*) That's not his voice — down with the doors.

(*Heavy blows on door R.*)

HYDE. (*Aside*) The poison — here — (*Up to table R. takes up phial doors R. are broken down and Utterson Enters R. followed by Poole, Lanyon and Agnes*)

(*Hyde down C. drinks and throws away phial*)[279]

UTTERSON. (*Crosses to front of table — all the others in doorway*) Murderer! what have you done with Jekyll?[280]

---

268. Handwritten lighting direction "*Lower house foots and borders change cals. to blue*" indicated here in BSN.
269. "*Is it over?*" included here in APC. The same dialogue is typed but deleted in LY and BSN. This dialogue is replaced with *handwritten* stage direction "*(bus)*" in BSN.
270. "*Is this the hand of Hyde?*" typed but deleted in LY.
271. Further "*not yet*" included here in APC and BSN.
272. This direction does not appear in APC.
273. "*shivering*" replaced by "*shuddering*" followed by *handwritten* lighting direction "*Green foots on*" in BSN.
274. Typed "*It has come*" deleted in BSN.
275. Typed "*No sound, but*" deleted and replaced by *handwritten* "*All is still, only*" in BSN.
276. Further *handwritten* "*She is there*" inserted here in BSN.
277. Typed "*with her*" included here in APC and BSN.
278. "*She will come*" and subsequent dialogue "*I shall see her face — I shall hear her voice*" appear as *handwritten* insertions in BSN.
279. Further stage direction "*coughs and falls C*" appears here in BSN.
280. This direction and dialogue does not appear in APC.

HYDE. Gone, gone!²⁸¹

*(Hyde dies. Lanyon advances. Poole crosses to back of table.²⁸² Newcome near door. agnes running in to Lanyon.)*²⁸³

AGNES. Who is there?²⁸⁴

*(Lanyon tries to prevent Agnes seeing Hyde.)*²⁸⁵

POOLE. It is my master!²⁸⁶

CURTAIN.²⁸⁷

Mansfield as Hyde. *The Theatre*, September 1888

---

281. Stage direction "*(Laughs and falls in C. dead)*" included here in APC.
282. This direction does not appear in APC.
283. "*Newcome near door. Agnes running in to Lanyon*" appears only in LY.
284. "*Who is there?*" replaced by "*Harry! Where is he? (Enters) What is there?*" in BSN and APC. This is immediately followed by "*CURTAIN*" in BSN. The APC version continues with stage direction "*(Utterson entering and xes to front of table. All others in doorway)*" followed by additional dialogue by "UTTERSON" saying "*Murderer, what have you done with Jekyll?*" This is followed by dialogue from Hyde "*Gone! Gone!*" and the closing stage direction "*(Dies) (Lanyon advances — Poole xes to back table) CURTAIN*"
285. This direction appears only in LY.
286. This dialogue appears only in APC.
287. Handwritten direction "*Lights up quickly as soon as curtain falls. Calls in front of curtain — Mr. Mansfield only*" included here in BSN.

Sketch of Mansfield's Lyceum performance of *Dr. Jekyll and Mr. Hyde* (*Penny Illustrated Newspaper*)

Appendix A:
Extracts from Early Mansfield Biographies

The first biography of Mansfield to be published following the actor's death was *Richard Mansfield, the Man and the Actor* by Paul Wilstach, in 1908. In the latter years of Mansfield's career, Wilstach was his business representative and theatrical press agent.

WILSTACH, CHAPTER 12 (1887–1888)
Pages 143–148

Mansfield was eminently catholic in his reading, his devotion to the classic and standard authors in no way precluding an interest in the latest novel. He dearly loved a mystery tale, if of the sea so much the better. Among the books he picked up the previous spring was Robert Louis Stevenson's new story, "Dr. Jekyll and Mr. Hyde," and it held him captive to the very end.

He foresaw an extraordinary triumph if his powers could visualise to an audience, as his imagination presented to him, the contrast between Dr. Jekyll and Mr. Hyde, the weird transformations of the man into the fiend and back again, and the gradual absorption of the good man by the evil man as expressed in the increasing difficulty of controlling the reversion from Hyde to Jekyll. He foresaw not only his opportunity to project a powerful performance on the stage, but the ethical effect of the noble moral which underlies this fable of the struggle between good and evil in man and the inevitable control of the good by the evil if experimented with instead of being firmly curbed in the beginning.

When he laid the book down it was to write to the author for the privilege of making a dramatisation. Stevenson concurred heartily, and the English and American rights to any play from this source were soon contracted.

Mansfield was playing in Boston at the time, and he urged his friend, Thomas Russell Sullivan, to make the play. Sullivan doubted the possibilities of a drama in the little story which offered all the difficulty of duality in the hero and no hint of the conventionally prescribed love interest and lighter relief. Mansfield at once exposed a scenario which his imagination had already conjured up, repeated a few of the Hyde passages with ghastly gutturals and in demonic posture that frightened his friend out of several nights' sleep, and urged him to read the book again, with the gentle warning, "If you don't dramatise it, some one else will." Sullivan accepted the commission and delivered the play during the winter.

It departed from the book only in the elaboration of merely suggested detail, and in developing a love story between Dr. Jekyll and a beautiful young creature, Agnes Carew, the daughter of Sir Danvers Carew, who is murdered by Hyde. In essence it reflected faithfully the duality of the character, the transitions, and the tragic moral of the final submersion of Jekyll in Hyde.

It was rehearsed barely two weeks while he played "A Parisian Romance," but he brought to the first rehearsal, as he did always when preparing a production before or after, a perfectly composed characterisation. His rehearsals were largely to set up the environment of the completed central figure. "Dr. Jekyll and Mr. Hyde" was first acted on any stage at the Boston Museum, May 9, 1887.

With this cast:

Sir Danvers Carew	Mr. Boyd Putnam.
Dr. Lanyon	Mr. Alfred Hudson.
Gabriel Utterson	Mr. Frazer Coulter.
Poole	Mr. James Burrows.
Inspector Newcomer	Mr. Arthur Falkland.
Jarvis	Mr. J. K. Applebee, Jr.
Dr. Jekyll & Mr. Hyde	Mr. Richard Mansfield.
Mrs. Lanyon	Miss Kate Ryan.
Agnes Carew	Miss Isabelle Evesson.
Rebecca Moore	Miss Emma Sheridan.

Mansfield approached the experiment with grave forebodings. Could he in the presence of a vast audience effect the transformation from Hyde to Jekyll in such a manner as to strike absolute conviction? He afterward confessed: "That night in the third act where as Hyde I grasped the potion, swallowed it, writhed in the awful agony of transformation and rose pale and erect, the visualised embodiment of Jekyll — an ague of apprehension seized me and I suffered a lifetime in the silence in which the curtain fell. In another instant I realised that silence was the tribute of the awe and terror inspired by the reality of the scene, for through the canvas screen came a muffled roar which was the sweetest sound I ever heard in my life, and I breathed again."

At this time he played "Dr. Jekyll and Mr. Hyde" only one week. It was far too emotional, tragic, and absorbing either for himself or for his audiences during the summer. He kept it in the background from May 14 to September 12, that same year, 1887, when he acted it in New York City, first at the Madison Square Theatre. The praise his performance received from the press was in most quarters unreserved, and his audiences did him the compliment to pack the theatre and proclaim the unforgettable effect of his acting.

He was sometimes criticised for not making Jekyll more normal, affable, companionable. But this would not have been in harmony with his conception. He believed in simplicity and directness. His aim was to mark the contrast between the two entities, but without losing sight of the salient, dominant point of each character. He conceived and exhibited Jekyll as a man haunted by the most terrible loathsome fiend that the mind could conceive in human form. He had to indicate yet restrain the cracking secret of his soul, the ceaseless terror of the uncontrollable change which might come at any moment — in the street, in the house of his friends, in his sweetheart's presence. Jekyll was a haunted man. A man set apart. Only an unimaginative actor would have played him for ease, indifference, geniality.

One of Mansfield's purely theatric devices for horror was to convey the suggestion that Hyde was coming. This was effected with an empty stage, a gray, green-shot gloom, and oppressive silence. The curiosity was fascinating and whetted every nerve. At such a stage as this (the audience having seen Hyde before) the anticipation and the prolonged anticipation, the searching of the black corners for the first evidence of the demon all begot an hypnotic effect on the hushed, breathless spectators that held them in the fetters of invincible interest. Then with a wolfish howl, a panther's leap, and the leer of a fiend Hyde was miraculously in view. It was at such a time as that that strong men shuddered and women fainted and were carried out of the theatre.

People went away from "Dr. Jekyll and Mr. Hyde" afraid to enter their houses alone. They feared to sleep in darkened rooms. They were awakened by nightmare. Yet it had the fascination of crime and mystery, and they came again and again.

Such an effect as that described, while a testimony of his stage management, he deprecated as no gauge of his quality as actor. It was to the last act that he pointed with all the pride which he took in this performance. During twenty minutes he held the stage alone with only one interruption. The scene represented Dr. Jekyll's cabinet in broad daylight, and disclosed the harassed man overwhelmed with the knowledge that the drugs with which he had controlled the changes were accidental in composition and not to be duplicated. The transitions to Hyde were increasingly recurrent, in fact Hyde controlled Jekyll and Jekyll no longer controlled Hyde. His soul-sadness, his tender despair, his haunted anticipation of the reversion to bestial Hyde as the convulsions seized him, his pitiful, agonised attitude as he stood before the mirror dreading to remove his hands for fear of the demon's face they would reveal, his cry of joy as he discovered that the change had not yet come and he was still Henry Jekyll — these were all accomplished by Mansfield with simple, lofty, and invincible art, and produced effects on the spectator more profound and quite as thrilling as the theatric scenes preceding.

Every one speculated on the secret of the transformation which they saw yet could not believe. He was accused of using acids, phosphorus, and all manner of chemicals. The mystery spread to London, where some one declared it was "all perfectly simple. He uses a rubber suit which he inflates and exhausts at pleasure!" Mansfield told the simple facts and caused them to be repeatedly published, that his only change was in the muscles of his face, the tones of his yielding voice, and the posture of his body, which as Hyde he poised in a crouching position on his toes, swaying and bounding with an agility which gave a weird, spectral quality in the half lights of the night. Believe him? Of course not. Such candour was too transparently suspicious and only further stimulated the amateur theorist.

Pages 154–156

It has been said that Mansfield repudiated any artificial means in effecting his marvellous transformation from Dr. Jekyll to Mr. Hyde. His friend, De Wolf Hopper — for whose comic skill on the stage and irresistible personal good-fellowship off the stage, Mansfield always entertained sincere admiration — attests the facts in this anecdote:

I was supping with Mansfield one night in his rooms at the Continental Hotel, Philadelphia, after our respective performances, while his Jekyll and Hyde was in the first bloom of its terror-spreading triumph. There was a single heavily hooded green lamp over the table at an angle which lighted our faces and threw the rest of the spacious chambers into cavernous shadows. I remember there was even a bell in a neighbouring tower which broke into the subsequent recital with weird opportuneness. Mansfield seldom talked shop and never off the stage exploited his professional achievements. He sang, played, narrated with a witchery of expression and improvised scenes with alluring fecundity. But the sock and buskin was far away in his dressing-room. This night, however, he yielded to my plea and told me of his sensations when he appeared first as Dr. Jekyll and Mr. Hyde in Boston; of that critical make-or-ruin first change from Jekyll to Hyde; of the ghastly silence of the audience for seconds that seemed minutes and shrieked failure in his heart; and then the whirlwind of applause; the exhilarating, overwhelming sense of success. I was spellbound by his graphic eloquence. The shadows tightened all about us, and I saw nothing but his luminous countenance. In a burst of sympathetic enthusiasm I asked what he did and how he did it. And then and there, only four feet away, under the green light, as that booming clock struck the hour — he did it — changed to Hyde before my very eyes — and I remember that I, startled to pieces, jumped up and cried that I'd ring the bell if he didn't stop!...

The great popularity he established for "Dr. Jekyll and Mr. Hyde" disclosed the fact early in the season that the book was insufficiently protected under the copyright law. Other versions of every type, from indifferent to unmentionable, sprung up like mushrooms all over the country. One manager, touring in the remote sections of New England, advertised that his Mr. Hyde was the most terrible of all and had to be kept chained in a box car en route and in the theatre. He had the town hall crowded every night. The only one, of all those at this time playing "Dr. Jekyll and Mr. Hyde," who at all threatened Mansfield's interests was a German-American actor named Daniel Bandmann. Of the two performances, the Lounger in the New York *Dispatch*, of July 18, 1888, says: "Bandmann, whose prominence in this matter is next to that of Mansfield, could not stand the test of comparison with the young actor. New York saw both of them essay the rôle, and while it shivered at Mansfield, it only smiled at Bandmann. The former was weird, the latter grotesque."

Henry Irving was again in America for the season of 1887-1888. On every hand he heard of the young genius whose rise was meteoric. Firmly entrenched in his own position at the head of the London stage, by a diplomacy which drew every one to him and held them in bonds of sweet fealty, Irving's wisdom foresaw a rival artist, if in any one in America, in Mansfield, whose published programme included Nero, Shylock, Richard III, and Cagliostro.

He saw the younger actor and invited him to come to London and appear in his own Lyceum Theatre. Flattered beyond measure, Mansfield paused to consider no expediency, deferred readily to Irving's terms, and agreed to begin his season in London on the third of September next following. "Dr. Jekyll and Mr. Hyde" was announced for the opening bill....

Page 157

But he was to leave earlier than he anticipated. His rest was cut short, his work trebled, and his sweetest hopes threatened with dire disaster by the announcement that Bandmann had engaged the Opera Comique in London, and would act "Dr. Jekyll and Mr. Hyde" there, on August 6 — one month before Mansfield!

Mansfield had faith in himself, but he believed that "faith without works is dead." He girded for the fight! Hundreds of dollars were spent in spirited cables, the date of his opening was advanced to August 4 (two days before Bandmann), though the fact was not announced. His company was scattered to the mountains and seashore for their vacations, but he hurriedly gathered them together, and they quietly slipped away for England, on the steamer City of Rome, early in July!

Chapter 13 (1888–1889)
Pages 158–159

On his arrival in London, Mansfield established himself at Long's Hotel in Bond Street, and visiting royalty rarely surrounded themselves with more luxury. America had recognised him first, and, coming to England as an American, he assumed the obligation of sustaining American dignity.

The difference between the two countries in extending welcomes was brought home to him with unforgettable directness. There was a total absence of the exuberant journalistic hysteria which in those years seized a visiting actor at American quarantine and trumpeted him into a success of curiosity days before his début. Mansfield found London perfectly calm. His old friends called and there were renewals of former friendships, cementing of new ones, many merry parties and quiet pilgrimages to spots hallowed by youthful memories. The truth is, however, that his prevailing sentiment was one of anxiety not alone about the impression he hoped to make, but lest Bandmann succeed in getting his "Dr. Jekyll and Mr. Hyde" before the public first and remove the cream of novelty from his presentation. He harassed himself, too, with an alleged belief that Bandmann might walk off with the honours in spite of the fact that New York had repudiated the imitator and laughed with derision when it should have been hushed with awe. It was ever his disposition to magnify obstacles, however inconsequential, and fancy them where they did not exist at all.

The first Jekyll–Hyde in the field appeared, however, from a completely unexpected quarter. On Thursday, July 26, an actor-manager of several minor theatres and of some provincial repute, named Howard Poole, produced a dramatic version of the Stevenson story at the Theatre Royal, Croydon, about ten miles out of London. He attracted no attention and made no impression. He was immediately enjoined, and Stevenson and his publishers, the Messrs. Longmans, repudiated all versions of "Dr. Jekyll and Mr. Hyde" other than Mansfield's, as unauthorised.

Appendix A: Extracts from Early Mansfield Biographies

Henry Irving concluded his performances at the Lyceum Theatre on July 7. Sarah Bernhardt followed him at once on July 9 in Sardou's newly produced "La Tosca" and others of her great rôles. She held the stage until Mansfield assumed his tenancy of the theatre with the initial performance of "Dr. Jekyll and Mr. Hyde," on Saturday evening, August 4.

The cast of the play on this occasion was:

Dr. Jekyll & Mr. Hyde	Mr. Richard Mansfield.
Dr. Lanyon	Mr. D. H. Harkins.
Gabriel Utterson	Mr. John T. Sullivan.
Genl. Sir Danvers Carew	Mr. Holland.
Poole	Mr. J. C. Burrows.
Inspector Newcomer	Mr. W. H. Compton.
Jarvis	Mr. F. Vivian.
Mrs. Lanyon	Mrs. D. H. Harkins. (Helen Glidden)
Rebecca Moore	Miss Emma Sheridan.
Agnes Carew	Miss Beatrice Cameron.

Page 160

The London critics at once confessed that on the plane of what is weird, sombre, saturnine, and mystical there had been nothing in the experience of living theatre-goers comparable to Mansfield's performance, excepting Henry Irving's Mathias in "The Bells." Mansfield's triumph was complete after Bandmann's effort the following Monday, August 6, of which Clement Scott wrote in *The Theatre*:

> This version is bad.... Only in the first and last acts is there any dramatic interest.... The adapter has made Dr. Jekyll in love with Sybil Howell the daughter of a clergyman who is murdered by Hyde in presence of the audience. The principal incidents of the story are closely followed, but in doing so there are introduced comic scenes, such as are witnessed only at pantomime time.... Mr. Bandmann's Dr. Jekyll is a canting, sanctimonious humbug of Pecksniffian appearance; his Mr. Hyde a malevolent dwarf-like creature with large teeth, that was ridiculous from its monkey-like tricks which only prolonged laughter and derision where they should have inspired terror.

The piece was withdrawn by Bandmann after the second performance!

The most distinguished people in London acknowledged the spell of Mansfield's performance, and among them came United States Minister Phelps, who wrote him: "I am proud of you, of the American company and of the perfect taste of the whole production. It was an eminent success." The public, however, remained away with heart-breaking persistency. Vogue, based even on the highest, soundest, and most vigorous achievements, is not attained in a night in London. The English are slow to yield either their interest or their affections; but once they bestow either, they are constant as the stars.

Page 161

There appeared to be a turn in the tide later and he wrote to his friend, E. A. Dithmar.

> I suppose you think I am unkind, unmindful, and ungrateful not to have written to you once I have been over here — or perhaps you will understand how hard worked I have been and how tired when I reached home and was unable to sit still and write to my friends. It has been a hard fight, with much against us, but I think we have conquered. At all events, "Dr. Jekyll and Mr. Hyde" is in for a long run and will not be taken off during my tenancy of the Lyceum Theatre. The audiences are very enthusiastic, much more so than in America, and it does seem as if the profession here had a desire to acclaim me. Terris has been twice and wrote me a note saying: "I thank you for the most artistic treat since Irving's 'Louis XI.'" Everybody writes and speaks in the same vein. Frith, the painter, who is an old man and has seen everybody, told me (I hope he meant it) I reminded him much of Macready and that my voice was finer.... I have just received a card from the Hon. Louis Wingfield notifying me that at a special meeting of the Garrick Club I was elected an honorary member. Toole, Beerbohm Tree, and Wingfield were my sponsors.... I need hardly tell you that the expenses here are enormous, and I would warn any American actor to think twice before he tackles the British lion — every hair of his tail costs gold, and we are safely through it, thank God! I have ventured, perhaps, where angels would have feared to tread, and succeeded; but had I known exactly — well, I might have been frightened away....

Pages 162–163

In spite of his optimistic letter to Dithmar, "Dr. Jekyll and Mr. Hyde" limped no further along than the end of September, and "A Parisian Romance" received its first London presentation at any hands on October 1.

...Peering out nightly at the empty benches, Mansfield saw a crisis approaching. Unwilling at any time to expose in the English capital so vaporous a trifle as "Monsieur"—for he had no vanity about certain of his own accomplishments—he played his last card on Friday evening, October 10. The run of "A Parisian Romance" was interrupted for one night, and "Prince Karl" received its first London performance, preceded by Horace Wigan's one-act comedy, "Always Intended."[1]

The occasion was made the benefit for a Whitechapel charity, and his patrons included: the Princess Christian of Schleswig-Holstein, the Duchess of Teck (Princess Mary), the Duke and Duchess of Westminster, the United States Minister, and Mrs. Phelps, Sir Richard Taylor, Sir Philip Cunliffe Owen, Sir Morell Mackenzie, Henry Labouchere, M.P., Joseph Hatton, Edmund Yates, and a score of other prominent persons.

Pages 165–167

"Prince Karl" became the evening bill on the Monday evening following, in spite of the somewhat severe blow to his pride that his former more serious efforts as an artist should be less popularly received than a light comedy which he held far below the standard of his ambition.

The attendance was now larger, but not yet profitable. The performances were still given at a loss. This, added to the huge indebtedness which had piled up during the preceding twelve weeks, presented an obligation and an outlook to distress the stoutest heart. It was really all along a struggle from hand to mouth. Every shilling went to his company, and a weekly promissory note for $3,000, bearing interest, was handed Mr. Irving for the rental of the Lyceum. One week, Mansfield's manager, Mr. E. D. Price, came to him with the news of a crowning catastrophe. Two hundred pounds, their share of the week's receipts, had been stolen from the safe in the office of the theatre. Too late he realised what he overlooked in his spontaneous eagerness to do great things when Irving offered him time at the Lyceum — that he had allowed himself to be booked in London at the wrong time of the year; that financial success there is a growth and not a shower; and, finally, that, on the same boards with the most popular actor England had doted on for generations, and a man in the full flower of his important achievements, and, preceded by the greatest living actress at the zenith of her power and fame, he had challenged criticism with three mediocre, unpretentious plays, displaying two characters essentially repugnant to the sympathies, and a third which defined only the superficial elegancies of his art.

Impoverished and exhausted, his material depleted, and nothing ahead, apparently, but to close his season and, as he had prophesied, "swim home," his mettle was challenged. He was ever a man for an emergency, never more undaunted than in seeming defeat. He now manifested his courageous spirit and his indomitable pluck. He would not leave London defeated. The hoped for success of Chevrial, Karl, and Hyde, even at the best, could not have been comparable to the triumph he now determined to wring from the intolerable situation. It is not drawing the long bow to say that London was profoundly astonished the morning it read Richard Mansfield's announcement that he had leased the Globe Theatre and would, before he left the British capital, act the Duke of Gloster in Shakespeare's tragedy of "King Richard III." He would measure himself at the shoulder of the greatest English actors....

He was not able to secure the Globe immediately on the termination of his lease of the Lyceum, December 1. One week he devoted to seven appearances at the Alexandra Theatre, Liverpool, and on his way back to London indulged himself in an enterprise which had been near to his heart ever since he arrived in England. One of the first to rush to greet him on his arrival was his dear old master, the Rev. Walter Clark, from whom he learned that the Derby boys were struggling with a subscription

---

1. The introductory benefit performance of *Prince Karl* took place at the Lyceum on October 19, and interrupted for one night *Dr. Jekyll and Mr. Hyde*, not a *A Parisian Romance*.

for a new racquet court. Mansfield at once promised to come and play in Derby and devote the entire receipts to the boys' subscription. This he accomplished, on his way back from Liverpool to London, Monday, December 10, 1888, at the Grand Theatre, where he gave not only one performance, but two!—"Prince Karl" in the afternoon and "Dr. Jekyll and Mr. Hyde" in the evening. He afterwards spoke of this as one of the proudest occasions of his life.

A Derby paper of the next day said: "At the close of the evening performance Mr. Mansfield had quite an ovation, being again and again recalled, and, a speech being insisted on, he in a few well-chosen words expressed the pleasure he felt in being in Derby once more, and the pride he had always felt and should continue to feel in his old school. He felt especial gratification at the enthusiastic reception he had received at their hands. The audience included, of course, scores of Derby-School boys, and some of them found a vent for their enthusiasm by taking the horses from Mr. Mansfield's carriage and dragging him in triumph up to the school." Once there he did not fail to look up the platform of his boyish histrionic experiments.

Returning to London he opened his tenancy of the Globe Theatre, "entirely refurnished during a possession extending over thirty-six hours," Saturday evening, December 22.

Chapter 20 (1894–1895)
Pages 265-266

There were, indeed, constant inquiries why he did not return to act in London, but Mansfield replied that he had not been successful there. A truer indication of the London sentiment is conveyed in this passage from a letter from Norman Forbes, written to him at this time:

> I have just received your long and interesting letter that you have so poor an opinion of the way London treated you when you produced, so beautifully, "King Richard III" at the Globe Theatre. I must, however, differ from you somewhat on this point. It is impossible for any man who has achieved the success you have in your art to do so without making enemies. Believe me, you are as much admired in England as in America. I don't mean, of course, that you have so large a following, but the best people in London, those whose opinions carry weight and influence, and are therefore worth listening to, have over and over again proclaimed your great ability. I was dining with Alfred Gilbert, R.A., the other day. His praise of you could not have been more enthusiastic. Surely his opinion bears out what I say, coming as it does from one of England's greatest living sculptors.

This was true, and when Mansfield died, the British press acknowledged the "loss to the whole English-speaking stage" in the same terms as the American press.

Perhaps a truer indication of Mansfield's sentiment about remaining away from London is found among his papers in his own endorsement on a letter from Sir Francis Knollys, Secretary to the Prince of Wales, at whose suggestion the manuscript of "Beau Brummell" was submitted to the English Examiner of Plays when Mansfield thought of returning to London to act.

Mansfield's endorsement reads: "H. R. H. finally decided that he would prefer that I did not present 'Beau Brummell' in England and I returned to America—especially that during my absence Henry Irving had secured all acting rights to 'Dr. Jekyll and Mr. Hyde' with which I might have hoped for renewed success. R. M."

Chapter 30 (1904–1905)
Pages 425–427

His performance of a rôle—even of those which he retained in his repertoire from his early successes—whether in comedy or tragedy, was to him a sacred work, almost sacramental. He was first in the theatre, never less than two and sometimes three hours before his first entrance. This time he spent in the seclusion of his dressing-room.

But the preparation did not begin there. In the afternoon he took a long walk. When he returned he would see no visitors, none of his household, and his servants attended him in silence. He ate a light repast at five o'clock with a book for company at table. Then he retired to his own apartment for a short nap and a bath, and rode away in his unbroken silence to the theatre. At this hour he wore an old great-coat with cape, a slouch hat well down over his eyes, and a muffler over the lower half of his face. He made it imperative that the carriage be draughtless.

And so into the dressing-room. When the call came for his entrance and he emerged from his room a metamorphosis had taken place. It was not the actor who went upon the scene, it was the character. By some process, and it has been called self-hypnotism, he became the person he was playing.

He carried the manner to and from and into his dressing-room. He acted the rôle all the evening on and off the scene, and it fell away from him only as he put aside the trappings and emerged from the dressing-room his own self bound for home. He preferred not to see any one during a performance. The nights he played certain characters it was inviting trouble to attempt to bring him out of the character with disassociated topics, however important in themselves.

...There was always a cloud over the stage on Richard, Ivan, and Hyde nights. Undistracted, all went well, but disorder, inattention, wrong lights were met in the spirit of the imperious characters who had possession of him.

No critics knew half so well as he how much the effects produced in the early acts of "Dr. Jekyll and Mr. Hyde" depended on the lights. He never went on the stage for the transformations that he was not in an agony of apprehension lest the effect be spoiled. This apprehension stimulated his imagination and he grew to suspecting always that the lights were wrong, so that "Dr. Jekyll and Mr. Hyde" nights became the same terror to him and all about him on the stage, though for a different reason, that they were to audiences. He often said that on these nights he suffered actual martyrdom. The part was not long. Yet such was his distress that repeatedly he declared that he could not live through Hyde another night. In these last years he acted it only when the other pieces of the repertoire were overplayed. This performance had a remarkable hold on the public, and it held the record for attendance and receipts in nearly every theatre in which it was acted. It drew to the Walnut Street Theatre, Philadelphia, the oldest theatre in America, the record audience since it was opened in 1806.

After a night of Jekyll and Hyde he usually saw no one and supped alone. His friend, "Jack" Lincoln, had this in mind on the last night of Mansfield's Chicago run this winter of 1904-1905, when he was invited to come to have a farewell supper, and pleaded an indisposition, adding that he was coming to see him play, however. Mansfield gave finality to the invitation with this note: "Caro mio Jacko: I think if you are well enough to see Jekyll and Hyde you are well enough to see me — and if I can endure playing Jekyll and Hyde I can stand seeing you."

The second biography to appear was *Life and Art of Richard Mansfield* by William Winter, in 1910. Winter, a respected dramatic critic and author, was Mansfield's close friend and advisor throughout most of the actor's career. He began his biography in 1905 in fulfilment of a promise made to Mansfield to produce a comprehensive record of the actor's life and art. (Although not included here, Winter ends his biography by forcefully commenting on the plagiarism of his earlier writings found in Paul Wilstach's work.)

WINTER VOL. 1, CHAPTER III
(1883–1888)

Pages 56–58

Thoughtful examination of Mansfield's professional career at once impels inquiry as to the place in dramatic art that should be allotted to things that are gruesome or terrible, and opens the old, perplexing controversy as to artistic use of ugliness and beauty. In the vast, incomprehensible scheme of creation evil appears to be as necessary as good is. If there were not the one there could not be the other. Life is a struggle between good and evil, and it is through the victory of good over evil that everything great and glorious is produced. In what proportion those antagonistic elements ought to be mingled and contrasted, in a work of art, dramatic or otherwise, judgement often finds it difficult to determine. There are, however, cases in which instant decision becomes readily possible. Monstrous and hideous things exist, that ought never to be included or considered in a play for public presentation. When *Cornwall* plucks out the eyes of *Glo'ster* and casts them on the ground, exclaiming "Out, vile jelly!" the reader of "King Lear" is repelled with a sickening consciousness of disgusting atrocity: the spectator of such a proceeding, seeming to be literal, would be convulsed, not with terror but with loathing. There must be a limit somewhere. Unmitigated horror or monstrosity is absolutely barren of valuable result. One of the best examples of the wrong use of evil, in a play, is "Titus Andronicus,"—that sickening rag of pollution attributed to Shakespeare. One of the best examples of the right use of evil in a play is the melodrama of "The Lyons Mail." Mansfield presented controversial examples, in *Jekyll* and *Hyde*, in *Ivan*, in *Rodion*, and in *Nero*; but it was not to be reasonably expected that those presentments, however finely displayed, would enlist the affection of mankind.

The interval between Mansfield's striking achievement as *Chevrial* and his more determinate success as *Dr. Jekyll* and *Mr. Hyde*,—a period of upwards of four years, extending from January, 1883, to the autumn of 1887,—was one of incessant effort and continuous activity, but it was entirely formative. His fortunes fluctuated, being sometimes propitious and sometimes adverse. The part of *Prince Karl*, which he acted for the first time on April 5, 1886, at the Boston Museum, although he did not highly value it, either then or later, helped to advance him in public favor. From May 3 to August 14, 1886, he acted at the Madison Square Theatre, New York, giving 117 successive performances of that part. It was not, however, until he had made a decisive hit with the drama of "Dr. Jekyll and Mr. Hyde" that he gained an authoritative position in the broad field of theatrical enterprise, and at last was able to assert himself in active competition with the potential leaders of the stage. That play was first presented on May 9, 1887, at the Boston Museum, and in the following autumn, after it had undergone severe revision, it was brought out, September 12, at the Madison Square Theatre, New York.

Pages 61–62

During the period that intervened between the production of "Monsieur," July 11, and the production of "Dr. Jekyll and Mr. Hyde," the work of revising the latter play and preparing it for presentment largely occupied his attention. The first draft of "Dr. Jekyll and Mr. Hyde" had been made for him, more or less under his immediate advisement, by Thomas Russell Sullivan. The play had not entirely pleased his audience in Boston, yet he had faith in it and was resolute to push it to a further trial. He earnestly wished and requested that I should advise him as to the revision of it, prior to its presentment in New York, and various letters on that subject passed between us, and occasionally we met and conferred about it.... As the time drew near for the fresh venture with *Jekyll* and *Hyde* his anxiety steadily increased: success in that dual personation meant everything to him, for, already, he was meditating an English expedition as well as the American tour.

Pages 64–65

It was at all times difficult to make Mansfield understand that other persons often were heavily burdened with exacting tasks and compelled to be quite as busy as himself. At the first opportunity, however, I called on him, discussed with him every detail of the play of "Dr. Jekyll and Mr. Hyde," and suggested such changes as seemed desirable. Later I attended a rehearsal of it and wrote to him additional words of counsel and cheer, to which he replied:

The Westmoreland, New York,
September 2, 1887.
My Dear Winter:
Thank you for your kind letter, and thank you again for coming over here to listen to a

dreary rehearsal. Your opinion has encouraged me immensely and I have not felt downhearted since. I have made the changes and adopted the suggestions you make in your letter. Even I have cast Miss Kate Rogers for the old hag *Rebecca Moore*. Emma Sheridan is still too weak to work....

It is quite impossible for me to play Dr. J. & Mr. H. next Saturday, simply because the scenic artists, although employing extra hands, can barely be ready by Monday.

The Dress Rehearsal will be on Saturday Evening, and if you care to come and accept a bed and all else here, you know how truly welcome you will be!

God bless you, and believe me
Sincerely and always gratefully yours,
RICHARD MANSFIELD.

Pages 66–69

One incident of a humorous character chanced, at this time, to intervene, slightly diversifying the monotonous complexion of care and strife. Robert Louis Stevenson was in New York in the summer of 1887, and I learned from Mansfield that each of them made several ineffectual attempts to see the other. "It happened that he was not at home when I called on him," said Mansfield, "and it happened that I was not at home when he called on me. At last, one day, I was fortunate, as I thought. I sent in my name, and a person whom I understood to be Mr. Stevenson's adopted son presently appeared, and, after the customary exchange of civilities, said that Mr. Stevenson wished to know whether I had a cold, because, if I had, he could not venture to see me. I told him to tell Mr. Stevenson, with my kindest regards, that I had an exceedingly bad cold, which I should be most happy to communicate to him, and so took my leave. We did not meet. Later I heard that Mr. Stevenson had promptly left town — probably to escape infection, — and me!"

That incident is characteristic of Mansfield's eccentricity, but no words can express the humor with which he related it. The following letter, after mention of friendly counsel as to the production of "Dr. Jekyll and Mr. Hyde," then imminent, refers to that occurrence:

My Dear Winter:

How am I to thank you for your kindness to me?! I will do my best to follow your advice, the wisdom of which I thoroughly appreciate. You are the only man I can turn to for such help. It is impossible to do quite what you say, for I can only depend upon *myself* for stage-management.

I have *not* seen Mr. Stevenson and I do not *know* him. An acquaintance of his called at the theatre and asked for seats for his (Stevenson's) wife and sister, for the first night of Dr. J. & Mr. H., and said that Stevenson had instantly left town. It seems, however, that he is a great friend of Mr. Henley's — a man I do *not* think I should care for. When are you coming over? Sunday?
Yours always,
RICHARD MANSFIELD.

The production of "Dr. Jekyll and Mr. Hyde" was accomplished on September 12, with gratifying success. Public applause was abundant, and, in general, the press was favorable, in some cases even to the extent of enthusiasm. The fulfilment of my professional duty on the occasion, although a serious task, was an agreeable one, because it is always pleasant to see merit rewarded with recognition, to give praise where praise is due, and to contribute, though ever so little, to the encouragement of worthy endeavor and high ambition. The feelings of the actor, were, naturally, animated, and he was quick to express them.

The Westmoreland, Tuesday.
Mr Dear Winter:

How am I to thank you and what can I say?!!! How *splendidly* you have proved your kindness and your friendship!

Such a criticism — such a magnificent review of my effort to please you above all others, is ample payment for all the work of latter years — it wipes out all disappointments and bitterness and above all it ENCOURAGES — it fortifies me — it makes me feel that with more hard work in the right direction (and I do not think you will permit me to go off on the wrong track) — I may ultimately succeed. I need hardly tell you what *you* know and what *you* meant! that you have to-day done more for me than any other man alive could do. You have my heartfelt gratitude and my absolute devotion. I must see you and speak with you; when and where shall it be?

Yours affectionately and gratefully,
RICHARD MANSFIELD.

I understood that you could not come last night and yet I waited until three o'clock! Name *some* night this week and come to supper — it is the best meal, after all! The work is done and we draw nearer together.

The first run of "Dr. Jekyll and Mr. Hyde" in New York lasted only from September 12 to October 1, when his season ended. The weather was exceedingly hot, and Mansfield suffered much from the heat and from the severe strain imposed on his nervous system by acting the dual part. His impersonation of *Hyde*, upon which, at that time, he customarily expended a disproportionate volume of physical exertion, greatly exhausted him.

Pages 70–71

The Westmoreland,
New York, September 22, '87.

My Dear Winter:

The Doctor warns me that I am threatened with a nervous disease, likely to endanger my life! I cannot say that I care much — and in fact I have always shown such remarkable ability to recover from any drain upon my system, after a few weeks of rest, that I have no doubt I shall give the Doctor the lie. However, this "Dr. Jekyll and Mr. Hyde" is a disagreeable nightmare to me just now, and when evening comes I assure you I am anything but happy. There can be no doubt that just at present I am in a very nervous condition. We must be able to change the bill often — but with dignity and credit to ourselves — and I feel that "Monsieur," although well enough at the time, is not the thing. I must see you and consult with you over many matters. You know I have absolutely no one — no one but *you*— I am forced to appeal to you in all matters of importance.... In the meanwhile what can I play that will rest me and yet be good? Something bright, light, airy, exquisite — not necessarily modern? Let me know when to expect you.

Your sincere and grateful friend,
RICHARD MANSFIELD.

CHAPTER IV (1888–1890)

Page 83

Mansfield, at this time, had reached a most important stage of his professional career. His immediate attention was fixed upon the enlargement of his means of appeal, — it being his conviction that the public is ever craving something new, and that no actor can long prosper who does not gratify that solicitude, — but his "darker purpose" was to seek renown beyond the ocean, to act in London, and to return home a conqueror. With that intent he determined not only to acquire new parts, especially *Nero,* — upon which he had long brooded, and which, though never popular, became one of his most characteristic embodiments, — but to form a strong company and challenge all competitors.

Page 85

N. Y.
April 23, 1888.

My Dear Winter:

...I am getting together a strong company, I think a very strong one, but it is the Devil's own work and fearful are the terms they all ask, being stars themselves, to support such a poor thing as myself. However, as it is a question of winning the battle, I am to lead veterans into the field and shall not trust to raw recruits — so you may look out for an array of talent.

RICHARD MANSFIELD.

Pages 87–93

It was characteristic of Henry Irving that he felt a lively interest in every phase of human activity and, particularly, that he was sympathetic with every courageous and novel adventure undertaken in his profession. No man could be more fervently desirous than Irving was that other actors, supposing them to be meritorious, should meet with the recognition and practical reward that merit deserves. He had known and had befriended Mansfield when that much younger actor was struggling through an arduous novitiate in London, and he failed not to observe, with sympathy and satisfaction, his intrepid and striking enterprise, as shown in the choice and practical utilization of "Dr. Jekyll and Mr. Hyde." Mansfield, in meditating a professional visit to London, with his new plays, believed that if he could successfully appear in that capital, preferably at the Lyceum, his success abroad would much accelerate his advancement at home. That belief he made known to me, and it was subsequent to my mention of the subject to Irving that a correspondence ensued between the two men, resulting in an arrangement for Mansfield's appearance at Irving's theatre, in the course of the season of 1888-'89. It had already been arranged that Irving, on his return from America, would make his re-entrance at the London Lyceum on April 14, and a contract had been made with the eminent French actress Sarah Bernhardt, providing for her advent at that house in the following July. The opening for Mansfield, who, on February 14, 1888, had leased the Lyceum for a period of several weeks, was assigned for September 4. The prospect seemed entirely auspicious, and both Irving and Mansfield viewed their plan with pleasurable expectation of a happy result. The way, however, was not to be smooth. Mansfield's prosperity with "Dr. Jekyll and Mr. Hyde" had fired emulation, and as Stevenson's story of "The Strange Case" was not, in America, protected by copyright, several plays on the basis of it were speedily manufactured, in imitation of Mansfield's drama, — which, as already mentioned, was to a large extent his own work. One of those plays was produced in New York, on March 12, 1888, at Niblo's Garden, by Mr. Daniel E. Bandmann (1840–1905), an actor of considerable ability and long experience, and that performer afterward announced that he would proceed with it to London, intending to present it there, in advance of Mansfield's arrival. Opportunity in London, however, is not readily found. The only theatre that Mr. Bandmann seemed likely to have any chance of securing for his purpose was one called the Opera Comique. The situation, of course, soon became known to Irving, and necessary steps were immediately taken to command it. A cable message was sent to Mansfield, advising his presence in London in season for the making of all needful preparations to appear at the Lyceum early in August instead of early in September, as first proposed, and the Opera Comique was leased by Irving, for a considerable time. I remember the amused and amusing voice and manner of Irving, when, on one of Sarah Bernhardt's "Tosca" nights, he came into the Lyceum box where I was sitting, and, showing me a slip of paper, remarked: "I have protected our friend. I have hired the Opera Comique, for some extra rehearsals. This is my receipt. If Mansfield comes over at once, we shall have no trouble." Mansfield did come over at once. From June 4 to June 30 he was acting in New York, at the Madison Square Theatre, but, after the close of that engagement, and on receipt of Irving's message, he sailed for England.

It happened that Irving was, at this time, rambling in Cumberland, with friends, — among them the writer of this memoir, — and Mansfield presently joined the party, at the cosey old hotel at Patterdale, on the shore of Ullswater; and I remember we sat up all night, discussing his budget of American news and his plans and prospects for a London season. The meeting was a delightful one. The relations between Mansfield and Irving were then friendly. They did not always remain so. They fluctuated, considerably; and although, at the last, the two men remained on ostensibly amicable terms of social intercourse, the feeling existent between them was that of disapprobation on the part of Irving and antipathy on the part of Mansfield. It is necessary to allude to this subject, because those actors, eventually, became professionally opposed, and because circumstances in the stage career of Mansfield would otherwise remain unexplained. The subject, furthermore, is an essential part of theatrical history, — a record which should tell the truth, and not be encumbered with sentimental eulogium and obscuration of facts. Mansfield had no reason to blame any one but himself for the loss of Henry Irving's active friendship. It was an infirmity of his mind that he ascribed every mishap, every untoward circumstance, every reverse of fortune, to some external, malign influence, — never to any accident, or any error of his judgement, or any ill-considered act or word, or any fault of his own. Accordingly, when the total result of his London ventures had proved disastrous to him, as by and by it did, he accounted for it by adopting the fantastic, ridiculous notion that Irving, out of jealousy, had, from the first, intended to ruin him, and by great social influence and control of the press had accomplished that purpose. There has been a liberal superfluity of that kind of reproach against Henry Irving, in association with the names of several distinguished actors who have appeared in London and, according to some of their admirers, have been dissatisfied with the measure of commendation there accorded to them;—for example, Edwin Booth, Lawrence Barrett, Mary Anderson, Helena Modjeska, Ada Rehan, and Charles Coghlan. The disseminators of that frivolous gossip, meanwhile, have never explained how Irving found time to attend to his own complex and exacting business, while attending so industriously to the destruction of professional rivals, or how it ever happened that, possessing such imperial control over the society and the press of London, he could not avoid occasional disastrous failures and, at times, a newspaper defamation of his own acting quite worthy of the pens of Kenrick and Pasquin. The fact is that Irving earnestly desired that Mansfield should meet with great success in London, believed that he would meet with it, and did all in his power to promote that result.

Two letters that Mansfield wrote to me, one shortly before and one immediately after the arrangement had been made for his appearance at the London Lyceum Theatre, display in a clear light the respect and affection with which he then regarded Irving.

The Croisic, New York,
January 9, 1888.

My Dear Winter:

...You will be startled, I know, when I tell you what my project is, and you will, probably, tell me that I am a fool—and, frankly, I believe I am.

It is *good* of you to give yourself this trouble for me! Yes, *Henry Irving is a great, good man, and I am entirely devoted to him*. He was charming to me. I received a little book from him, the other day, which I value highly....

RICHARD MANSFIELD.

The Croisic, New York,
February 17, 1888.

My Dear Winter:

...*This is a great thing Irving has done for me—pray God he sees the good work he intends for me accomplished!* But I am a bad actor, and I feel it more and more every day....

If you see Irving, tell him how I feel about this—it is the greatest good thing a great man ever did for a youngster.

Always yours,
RICHARD MANSFIELD.

Pages 94–103

After our festal night at Patterdale Mansfield immediately proceeded to London, to begin rehearsals of "Dr. Jekyll and Mr. Hyde." At first he lodged at 118 Jermyn Street, "over a hen-shop," as by an early post he facetiously informed me: later he moved to 183 Piccadilly. "I think we are in a good way," he wrote, "to crush the tragedian Bandmann. At all events I have the sole rights to the play,—from the publishers, Longmans, Green & Company, to whom Stevenson sold his rights. They protect me and I indemnify them. The same lawyers who succeeded in the 'Little Lord Fauntleroy' case are engaged and very busy. Bandmann is to be met, and served with papers, upon his arrival."

Long afterward Mansfield described to me the call on those publishers that he made, in company with Irving, to adjust the copyright business. Irving, who sometimes spoke indistinctly, mentioned his name to an elderly clerk who was in attendance and who neither understood nor recognized him, so that he was obliged to repeat the name several times. When that dense person had left the room, to announce the visitors, Irving walked to and fro, for a few moments, musing; then, turning to his companion, he said, reflectively: "Mansfield, I believe there are some persons who are ignorant of the history of their own times." Irving, it should be noted, was a figure so universally known in London that, as a rule, when he happened to call a cab and wished to go to his residence, all he said, or needed to say, was "Home."

Mansfield's production of "Dr. Jekyll and Mr. Hyde" was effected at the Lyceum Theatre on August 4, 1888. On the morning of that day he addressed to me the following letter, which indicates the vexations to which he had been exposed and the obstacles that he supposed to exist. His notion that rapid changes of scenery could not be made at the Lyceum Theatre, and were not customarily made there, was incorrect. It is possible, however, that the mechanics, scene-shifters, etc., did not care to make them for *him*. Ungenial "Sons of Martha" do sometimes behave in a peculiar manner when working for strangers, or for persons whom they do not like.

>   183 Piccadilly, London,
>   August 4, 1888.

My Dear Willie:

Just a line before undergoing execution! I am sorry to say I am hoarse, very hoarse; how could I be otherwise, with what I have undergone and the weather we have had?

It would have been quite enough work for any one man to parry the attacks of Herr Bandmann. He has kept my hands completely full for the last week. *Last night* he announced a full dress rehearsal at the Olympic, and issued over 1,500 invitations, — all without the consent of the management! Of course they stopped it, and he then had the audacity to send to me for permission to give it at the Opera Comique! Of course we were compelled to decline! All the same, he issued slips of paper to the crowd which had assembled before the Olympic, inviting them to the Opera Comique, and he would have *forced his way in, had I not placed commissionaires and police around the building.* Lively, is it not?

I am sorry to say, like all great things and most great men, the Lyceum is not faultless. I have had, and am having, a hard time. They are, of course, accustomed to slow work — to taking months to prepare a play. They do not understand my rapid methods and swift action. There is no discipline, and crowds of loafers about the stage, who trip over one another and do nothing. The men are slow to obey and argumentative, and full of importance and the conviction that they know it all, or, at least, much better than we do. The company complain of the darkness of the dressing-rooms and inadequate conveniences, compared with our American theatres. Scenery which has arrived in St. Louis or Grand Rapids at four in the afternoon, and been used, without a hitch, at eight in the evening, and without a dress rehearsal, required all Thursday night, all day Friday, and a scenic rehearsal which lasted from eight yesterday evening until two this morning! and was the most imperfect, at that, it has been my bad fortune to attend.

I am much distressed, very weary, very hoarse, and very anxious, and I have had too much work and too little play for a small boy.

God bless you — I shall see you to-night. Pray God, all may yet go well!

>   Ever yours,
>   RICHARD MANSFIELD.

The legal measures that were taken to protect Mansfield's rights to the use of "Dr. Jekyll and Mr. Hyde" proved decisively successful, and Mr. Bandmann's attempt to forestall him was foiled, — much to the satisfaction of all fair-minded persons. Mr. Bandmann had falsely proclaimed himself, in America, the original representative of *Dr. Jekyll* and *Mr. Hyde*, — the fact being that Mansfield had acted the dual part ten months before it was assumed by any other person. It should also be observed that the plan, — likewise stolen from him, — of weaving a love-story into the analysis of *Jekyll's* complex nature, as set forth by Stevenson, was original with Mansfield, and that it was he who led the way, and showed other actors how the abstruse theme could be made practically dramatic. Four days before Mansfield appeared, Irving, who was leaving home, for a tour in Switzerland, and who had seen a rehearsal of the play, signified his auspicious view of our friend's advent at the Lyceum by this message to me: "Mansfield will be splendid." That augury was fulfilled. I remember the occasion as one of exceptional interest. The audience was numerous and of a brilliantly intellectual character. Upon his first entrance Mansfield was welcomed with two distinct, hearty rounds of applause, and he was recalled to the stage five times in the course of the representation. His voice was a little hoarse and once or twice his movement was slow and artificial, because of extreme nervous excitement, but he acted with intrepid spirit and, generally, with amazing vigor. The crowning artistic charm of his impersonation was its preservation of unity. The two sides of the one nature were clearly shown, — the concrete result being one man, not two. The element of terror was made duly prominent, but the element of pathos was made to exceed that of terror. *Jekyll* was invested with poetic sentiment: *Hyde* was embodied as loathsome and venomous, but very awful. *Hyde's* perception of the invisible ghost of his murdered victim was made to provide a moment of truly infernal exultation, and it gave the assemblage a thrill of horror. In the scene of the transformation of *Hyde* to *Jekyll* Mansfield's splendid outburst of passion, combined with his startling demeanor and ever-increasing volume of vocal power, caused a prodigious effect. Often as he afterward played that exacting dual part, I do not think he ever played it in a more inspired mood than he did on that critical and important night. He did not win the public heart: hearts are not won by horrors: but he made it clear that he was a unique actor and one entirely worthy of high intellectual consideration.

On the next morning I sent to him this message, — interesting, perhaps, as conveying first impressions of a memorable occasion.

Hammersmith,
August 5, 1888.

Dear Dick:

I am off for Scotland. I expect to be absent for about ten days. I congratulate you on your success. The piece was thought dreary and tiresome, but *you* were greatly admired, and I think the public will grow to be very fond of you. Don't feel hurt at the criticisms, if any of them are sharp. The Second Act should be carried more rapidly. Miss Sheridan should be told to let herself out a bit. The hag needs more effect. There is a little too much of *Jekyll's* misery—and misery never was popular, on the stage,—or off! I wish you would get a new wig. Fox could make a much better one than that you now wear. And you ought to make *Jekyll* a more picturesque fellow,— more "taking,"— even at a sacrifice of strict correctness. He is heavy now, at least he was, last night, in act second. Your first entrance should be made striking, and there the *appearance* becomes of vital importance. I was delighted with your first act and with the scene of the change. Your Speech was in excellent taste. Miss Cameron played better than ever before, because so moderate and symmetrical. But tell her to be distinct and vigorous. She needs great care of her health, — exercise and good sleep, so that she may not be weak and seem fragile. I was surprised by the good judgement and the grace of her acting. Sullivan also was tasteful and judicious.

Ever yours,
W. W.

After one of those *Jekyll* and *Hyde* nights he wrote to me:

…Frith, the painter, who remembered my having been to him once, for his opinion upon some sketches of mine, came to see me last night—came to my dressing-room, after the play, — deeply moved and impressed, and said I reminded him of Macready! And he thought my voice was finer. He's a bluff old fellow, and I think he meant it. I am foolish enough to be quite happy over it!

Always, dear friend, yours,
RICHARD MANSFIELD.

On his return from Switzerland Irving attended a performance of "Dr. Jekyll and Mr. Hyde," and after it had ended he and Mansfield met, for supper, at the Garrick Club, where one of those trivial incidents occurred which sometimes are more conducive than acts of positive hostility could be, to the disturbance of friendly relations between individuals. Attendance at the Lyceum, large at first, had begun to dwindle, and Mansfield, dissatisfied and somewhat depressed in mind, and no doubt weakened by the prodigious exertions that he had been making, spoke much of his discontent and of the tremendous strain imposed upon him by the acting of such painfully difficult parts and of the warnings given to him by physicians. Irving, at most times prone to more or less playful satire, listened observantly, and then, in his bland, piquant way, replied: "Ah—yes—interesting—very: but, Mansfield, my boy, if—*if it isn't wholesome, I wouldn't do it.*" No unkindness could have been intended, but a sensitive man, especially one in whose temperament there is much of the woman, will sometimes remember with resentment the satirical pleasantry of a friend, long after he has forgotten a substantial kindness. It was about this time that I received from Irving (Monday, August 27, 1888), a letter in which he said:

Poor Mansfield! He's a little hipped just now, and thinks the world's against him. But I did my best to "shake him up" and to show that he's everything to be grateful for. He's made a thorough success with the public—not every man's good fortune. I'm very fond of him and hope his boat may ever sail as freely as it does now.

The boat, however, was not sailing as freely as it might have done and as the actor's friends assuredly wished that it might do. The trend of his fortunes and the direction of his thoughts, at this time, are well evinced in the following letter, received in Paris:

August 30, 1888.
My Dear Winter:

I have your good kind letter: you are, thank God! always the same. Some of my idols here, however, have fallen. It resolves itself into a hard struggle,—and a struggle it shall be. I have youth and strength on my side. Our friends are rather inclined to advise me to finish up quickly and go home. I shall *not* finish up quickly, and I shall *not* go home—just yet—altho' I know that very powerful forces will be, probably, arrayed against me. Business is slightly improving and will doubtless grow better as we reach the middle of September and October.

I want some charming first piece, and I am looking for it; nothing in which to appear myself, but for five or six ladies and one or two men; it is difficult to find. I should then begin, as the nights grow longer, at 7:30, and with Dr. J. & H. at 8:30. I think the play will draw a good business, in spite of all. I shall have the "Parisian Romance" knocked into shape and do it (I think at the Globe), and follow it with "Nero" and "Richard III." Voila!

Please say not a word to any one: what I say to you I say to myself. Would you could be with me and by my side always! I shall get all the money I can, and make myself as strong as possible in that particular. I have seen Irving but that one day, and heard nothing of him since.

I hope Daly is doing finely in Paris. Will you remember me most kindly to Miss Rehan? When do you return?

Always, dear Winter,
RICHARD.

Mansfield's season at the Lyceum extended from August 4 to December 1, and, financially, it was a failure. On October 1 he presented "A Parisian Romance," and gave his fine performance of *Baron Chevrial.* October 10 he made the mistake of presenting "Prince Karl" for a Benefit (for the poor of the East End), so that when it was brought forward, on October 13, as his regular attraction, it lacked the gloss of novelty and did not attract much notice.[2] He had been wisely advised relative to the Benefit expedient, but the good counsel,—contained in the following letter,—of one of the most experienced and judicious of London managers had been disregarded:

Theatre Royal, Manchester,
October 9, 1888.
My Dear Mr. Mansfield:

Mr. Irving asks me to say for him that he would be delighted to aid in any way he can. He thinks, however, that to make him a *patron* of a performance in the *Lyceum* would do harm instead of good, as it would look like a "put up" thing. He quite thinks, as I thought myself, that you would do very much better *not* to have a benefit for a charity on your first night, as such is so often done in London that it has come to be taken by the critics and the public as a bid for favor. You make your play more important by giving it on its merits, and *friends*, in London, in such matters, do not count for a row of pins. Very much better have the good results of a fortnight yourself, and, as the Yellow Fever benefit seems to be off, from your having another subject, you need not have a Charity Benefit at all. We all certainly think that you would do better *not* to have a benefit.

Yours very truly,
BRAM STOKER.

Pages 104–105

After his season at the Lyceum had ended Mansfield acted for one week in Liverpool, by way of reinforcing his purse, and before returning to London he visited Derby and gave two performances there, for the benefit of the school which he had attended when he was a

---

2. The introductory benefit performance of *Prince Karl* took place at the Lyceum on October 19, and interrupted for one night *Dr. Jekyll and Mr. Hyde*, not a *A Parisian Romance*.

boy, and which he always remembered with affectionate interest. "I had one bright day in Derby,"—so he wrote to me,—"where, at the old school, I met with a welcome worthy of a King—a packed house and endless cheers and calls. After the play the boys took the horses out of the carriage and dragged me,—they yelling like Comanches,—to the school. I played twice, and netted a handsome sum, for a new racquet court and a new chapel." To that visit his thoughts often reverted, and more than once he told me it was the one unalloyed happiness of the year he then passed in England. The Lyceum season, while it had increased his prestige as an actor, had left him in debt, to Irving, for rent of the theatre and other expenses, £2675. With that situation he had now to contend. He did not lose heart, however, but determined on another and still more onerous venture,—the resumption of the plan he had formed before leaving New York, of acting in London in one of the great plays of Shakespeare. With this purpose he hired the Globe Theatre and began preparations for a magnificent production of "Richard III."

Chapter VII, (1893)
Page 193

Mansfield had been driven into a sort of frenzy, by failures, disappointments, care, and incipient sickness. The following is a mild specimen of his epistolary productions at that time, addressed to me:

> ...Damn your criticisms! *No* man can keep me back for long! You can injure my pocket, and you certainly have — on occasions! I had a deuce of a time getting our only patrons, the Jews, to come and see "The Merchant," because *you* made me out a fiend and a vulture. $8,000 more of my hard-earned dollars gone; and you impractical Devil—what do I—am I—can I, live on? Air? Do you think I am eternally to sweat and labor for no earthly return?...
> I have been harassed and worried and hounded, beyond all endurance. It seems I must even suffer in silence! It seems that I must never look forward to anything but a life of work!...
> Irving has been fêting the critics here (in Chicago) and I have again found the trail of the serpent and its slime! I have even an accurate and verbatim report of his conversation with them, — one of his not least amazing declarations being that he is to present "Dr. Jekyll and Mr. Hyde," in London. That being the play in which I should make my re-entrée there, his Snake-ship will, snake-like, forestall me!...

Pages 195–196

In giving his first performance of "Dr. Jekyll and Mr. Hyde," for example, — when that play was produced in Boston (1887), — at the moment in the first act, when *Hyde* leaps upon *Sir Danvers Carew*, hurls him to the floor, and strangles him, Mansfield lost control of himself and so maltreated the representative of *Sir Danvers*, the late Mr. Boyd Putnam (1865–1908), that the injured victim of realism fainted, repeatedly, and was with difficulty recovered. At another point in the same play, when *Hyde* interrogates the hag, *Rebecca Moore*, as to the personal appearance of a man who has called to see him, Mansfield suddenly turned up toward her a distorted, hideous, diabolical countenance, and, growling forth the inquiry, "Like *me*?", druled at the mouth. Such "real" expedients are not only unnecessary but unartistic.

Pages 199–201

When he left England, in 1889, he was in debt to Irving, and it seems to have been his conviction that his lack of sufficient public patronage had been caused by the insidious hostility of that actor. The notion was as deplorable as it was fallacious, and, eventually, it caused much unhappiness. Mansfield was impulsive, and, when excited, prone to reckless speech. There is no reason to doubt that he believed what he said, at the time he said it, when he attributed his ill-fortune to enmity on the part of Irving; but he had no reason to believe it, his talk was wild, and more than once, after his arrival home, in 1889, I besought him to restrain his words, to discard his delusion, and to make all possible haste in the settlement of the Lyceum business. That counsel he then received in kindness: "I will, and have borne in mind all you say about Irving" (so he wrote, October

25, 1889); "I will have none but the kindest feelings: the business part of it shall be attended to at once." His sensible resolution did not prevail over his fretful ill-humor. He continued to inveigh against the phantom foe of his angry fancy. His censorious words drifted to Irving's knowledge,—calumny, as usual, being carried by "the birds of the air,"—and that actor (a loyal friend and a "good hater"), bitterly resentful of injustice, retaliated by taking legal steps for the recovery of the money that Mansfield owed to him, and also by purchase, from the London publishers, of the rights to use the story of "Dr. Jekyll and Mr. Hyde" on the English stage. The debt was paid. Mansfield, much as he sometimes grumbled and vapored, never intended to wrong Irving, or to wrong anybody else. The following entry, copied from the Ledger of the London Lyceum Theatre, appears in the copious, minute, interesting "Life of Henry Irving," by Austin Brereton:

£1675 left owing by Mr. Mansfield for rent. Also £1000 Loan.

£2675.

1894 Recv'd loan and interest £1180 16 8
1896 Recv'd rent and interest,
      Less law fees £1476 14 10

£2675 11 6

The good news of the adjustment of this affair, by the removal of an irksome cause of mutual discontent was communicated to me by Mansfield, and was recognized with these words:

I received your letter, this day, about your relations with Mr. Irving. I am very glad to hear that the money is paid and the business part of it settled. Perhaps you and he will, one day, understand each other. I hope so. I never heard *him* say an ill word of *you*. I wish that the papers had not represented you as saying hard words of him. It is a great pity that two men, whom God has blessed with such genius, and such power for the good of the stage and society, should not agree, and get on in kindness. But, in Heaven's name, never open your lips about him again, for any paper to hear!

W. W.

The final extract in this Appendix is taken from "*Pages from the Journal of Thomas Russell Sullivan 1891–1903*," published by Houghton Mifflin Company in 1917.

T.R. SULLIVAN (1895)
Pages 119–122

January 1. The news of Stevenson's death is unhappily confirmed, and I am moved to record here some remembrances of my association with him. When, in 1886, I undertook to make a drama out of "Dr. Jekyll and Mr. Hyde" for Mr. Mansfield, who saw the theatrical effect of such a dual rôle, I wrote to Stevenson, asking his consent to the scheme. He replied at once, granting permission, and wishing me success in what he felt to be a difficult undertaking. The play first saw the light, in Boston, on the 9th of May, 1887. It was an undoubted hit, and I wrote again to the author of the story, giving him a full account of the first performance. In the summer of 1887 he left "Skerryvore," his Bournemouth home, forever, and came to the United States, bringing with him his wife, mother, and stepson, Lloyd Osbourne. We met first at Newport, where he was visiting the Fairchilds. Upon calling, I was taken to his chamber, where he lay in bed, reading and smoking cigarettes. It seemed to me that I had never seen so strange a figure. He was not only very thin and very pale, but had an uncanny look in his bead-like eyes; and his long, brown hair hung around his face like strings. He received me most courteously, sat up in bed, and wrapping himself in a red silk blanket, began to talk. Our interview lasted, perhaps, a quarter of an hour, and I went away strongly impressed by his friendliness, his unaffected modesty, his wit, and his very marked individuality. But the lean, blanketed figure haunted me, and I felt as if he must be on the brink of the grave. This was in August, I think, and in the following month the play was produced for the first time in New York. Stevenson, though in the city, was too ill to go to the theatre, but the box I sent him was occupied by his family, who gave me hearty congratulations. The play proved to be a financial triumph, making an enormous success in all the cities. Later in the year came other Richmonds into the field with new versions of the story. And an old stager, Daniel Bandmann, early in 1888, brought out his own pretentiously absurd one, which ended with an apotheosis of the repentant Dr. I saw, *incognito*, the first performance of this at Niblo's. The play had no merit whatever, and was coldly received by a very thin house. But certain papers, the next morning, were sufficiently friendly to cause Mansfield uneasiness, and it was known that Bandmann had corresponded with Stevenson, who was passing the winter in the Adirondacks. I reminded Mansfield, as I had often done before, of a promise made me by him, to the effect that in case of a great success he would pay Stevenson royalties. "Now is your time to give him an earnest of your good faith," I said, and Mansfield, accordingly, made him a remittance on account. Then, still uneasy, he suggested that I should visit Stevenson, read him my play, and obtain his signature to a formal announcement of it as "the authorized version." To this plan I assented very willingly, and started without delay for Saranac, where I arrived early one gray March morning. I put up at the hotel, and then went directly to the Stevenson cottage, which was very near. Mrs. Stevenson welcomed me warmly, "But I hope you haven't a cold," she said. "No," I answered. "Good!" she continued; "then you may go in. Louis never sees any one who has a cold. His mother has been three days in quarantine." Upon my reassurance, I was shown to Stevenson's chamber. He was sitting up in bed, smoking cigarettes as usual, and at work on a page of manuscript. He explained that this was a portion of a story (it proved, afterwards, to be "The Wrong Box") which he was then writing with Lloyd Osbourne. "I never write long at a time," he added; "and when I stop work, I amuse myself with this," — pointing to a flageolet which lay on the bed beside him. I told him why I came. "Yes," he said, "I have heard from Bandmann, but have not answered his last letter. What is his play like?" I described it in detail, and he laughed heartily. "Mrs. Stevenson liked yours, you know." "Well, then," I said, "perhaps you would be willing to hear it. Here is the manuscript in my hand." "Of course I would like to hear it, and the sooner, the better." I then sat down at the bedside, and read the play from beginning to end at a single sitting which lasted nearly two hours. He listened most attentively, so far as I can recollect, interrupting me but once, at the end of the third act, which closes with the transformation scene in Lanyon's office — much the strongest thing in the whole play.

The scene is described in the story, and my work upon it had consisted in extending the very brief dialogue, and in turning narrative into action. "Good!" said Stevenson. "You have done precisely what that scene needed for stage effect. It is very strong." I went on with the fourth and last act, at the end telling him frankly that I had never in my life found anything more trying than this little reading. "Yes," he said, laughing. "I saw you were very nervous, and I should have been so, too, in such circumstances. I might not have liked it, you know. But I do like it, all through. Now, let us go to luncheon."

Appendix B:
Press Interviews with Richard Mansfield

New York Sun, January 1, 1888

MANSFIELD VS. STEVENSON
New and Interesting Conceptions of Dr. Jekyll and Mr. Hyde.

When his remarkable book was first produced in New York as a drama, Robert Louis Stevenson was in the city. His delicate health, since so much improved that he has now become a robust mountaineer up at Saranac, prevented his going to see "Dr. Jekyll and Mr. Hyde," great as was his desire to see Mr. Richard Mansfield create the parts. The difference between the conceptions the writer of the book and the actor of the play seemed to have of the dual character was striking enough to be generally commented on by many people, who confessed themselves fascinated by each of those conceptions. Mr. Stevenson was appealed to for his ideas of the virtuous monster of his dream, and gave them in writing.

The book, he said, is ugly, it is true, but just enough to the modesty of facts. Hyde in the book is younger than Jekyll. Not good looking, and so not a mere voluptuary, but the embodiment of cruelty and malice and selfishness and cowardice, "which are the diabolic in man."

The hypocrite in Jekyll let out the beast Hyde. The evil of Hyde's being is inconsistent with the idea of a mere voluptuary; "there is no harm in a voluptuary; Hyde is no more sexual than another; bad and good, even to human eyes, has no more connection with what is called dissipation than it has with flying kites."

Mr. Mansfield has heretofore declined to give his reasons for forming the conception he enacts of Hyde and Jekyll. On learning Mr. Stevenson's views, Mr. Mansfield said he did not wish to put himself *en evidence* against the author of the marvellous book. Mr. T. Russell Sullivan dramatized for him. At length he has reluctantly consented to write the following:

"Mr. Stevenson's ideas have afforded the basis for ideas of my own. A man may dream a dream, and, telling it, another may be so powerfully impressed that he may also dream a dream of his own, founded, however, upon the dream which has been related to him. Thus far I am indebted to Mr. Stevenson for his dream.

My dream is thus: A very young physician, possessed of great wealth, and following his profession, consequently, from pure love for it, has by dint of unremitting study, by an unlimited burning of the midnight oil, and to some degree also by the power of his great wealth and his philanthropy, which without this wealth he could not possibly exercise, risen to the very foremost rank of his profession. He is in love with science; that branch of it, especially, is fascinating to him which has any tendency toward the occult. *Jekyll* is a dreamer and a visionary. While his every inclination is toward the good, while he himself is inclined toward all that is honorable, pure, and noble, he still recognizes in himself the germs of sin and evil, the desire to satisfy, to let loose a passion, no matter what it may be, and that it is only the restricting force of good, the power of the discriminating conscience, which deters him from indulgence. Analyzing this he simply finds the good eternally hampered by the bad, and he sets himself to discover, to create a distinct separation of the two. He succeeds, and concocts a draught which absolutely expels all that is good in him and leaves only the purely bad — the quintessence of badness. The form shrinks to fit the spirit, which remains, and the form and features accommodate themselves to the likeness of the being within. The creature thus created is the embodiment of evil, and, being possessed of no restraining force whatever, is irresponsible. A child in its way is trampled upon, the pure and holy love he entertains as *Jekyll* for *Agnes* becomes in *Hyde* a simple lustful desire; an old man (the father of the girl) standing between him and the object of his passion is instantly murdered. Drink now possesses its charm for him, for it heightens and enhances the enjoyment of his unrestricted passions. Unable, by reason of his hideous shape, to indulge the dreams of his disordered imagination, he surrounds himself with such pictures of vice as may best add continual fuel to the flames of his desires. There is no crime that he is not ready to commit, and cowardice alone is capable of binding and deterring him, and cowardice alone and the instinct of self-preservation which exists in the lowest form of brute causes him to return to the shape of *Jekyll*.

"The bad in *Jekyll*, having had unlimited indulgence, is exhausted for the time, and leaves the good in him almost as pure as the bad was in *Hyde*. *Jekyll* is now an unhappy and a most wretched man; the very fact of his goodness makes the knowledge of his badness the more overwhelming. The terrific strain upon a once powerful system begins to tell, and he finds himself generally less and less able to withstand, both physically and mentally, the encroachment of evil. He is bowed down with remorse at the thought of the monster he has conjured up betwixt himself and the beautiful woman to whom he is engaged; he cannot but feel himself responsible for the crimes which he has committed in his other self; he finds too late that the good in him must now suffer for the indulgence of evil in him. Worse is added to worse. *Jekyll* becomes the victim of *Hyde*; vice gradually gains the mastery, and, to pile Ossa on Pelion, the drug gives out, and cannot be reproduced.

"To me the last act is immensely touching. *Jekyll*, aroused to the full horror of his situation; *Jekyll*, the loved, the admired, the wealthy; *Jekyll*, who had the world at his feet and all the pleasures and all the happiness the world could afford, if he chose, in his grasp; *Jekyll*, in his youth, in his strength, with the knowledge that he is closeted with death, and such a death! It seems to me that if there ever was a moral powerfully taught it is here. I wish I could act it as well as I feel it.

"The gentlemen who say in the journals that there is no necessity to make the play so strong, that there is no use in displaying so horrible a character upon the stage or of lingering over the agony of *Jekyll*, seem to forget that as long as the actor acts he will consider the highest form of his art the display of the most powerful passions of men, and that he will strive at all times to choose such subjects as will best afford him opportunity to sway and impress his audience. It is our aim and our end in view. I do not delight to hear that just so many women have fainted of an evening in the theatre, but I, my art, and my nature, receive a fresh stimulus and inspiration from the breathless silence and the rapt attention of my auditors. As long as the dramatic art flourishes, despite all men may say or write from private motives of their own, the world will go to see that which stirs and moves it; and it will ever support the actor who puts his whole heart and soul, all his enthusiasm, his energy, his earnestness, his sincerity into his work. In reply to the criticism that the moral contained in the story of *Jekyll and Hyde* could be taught equally persuasively by gentler and prettier means, I have only to point to the great masters, and ask why Shakespeare piled horror upon horror in 'Richard III' and 'Macbeth,' why *Othello* smothers the beautiful *Desdemona*, and then cuts his throat or stabs himself, why everybody is killed in 'Hamlet,' and why even 'Romeo and Juliet' carries us to the tomb? You may say, 'the thoughts and the language of Shakespeare,' and I stop you. Find me a Shakespeare to-day and I will certainly engage him. In the meanwhile I am satisfied, for want of better, with the thoughts of Stevenson and the dramatization of a young American scholar, Sullivan. It is the best I can find, and the best I can give you. For myself, I give all I have. In time, if God spares me, I hope it will be better. I shall try."

Pall Mall Gazette, London, July 24, 1888

"THE REAL DR. JEKYLL AND MR. HYDE."
AN INTERVIEW WITH MR. RICHARD MANSFIELD.

THE interest and curiosity with which Mr. Richard Mansfield's promised production of "Dr. Jekyll and Mr. Hyde" is looked forward to, are not the result of Mr. Robert Louis Stevenson's weird fancy alone. They depend on several circumstances, chief among which are the extraordinary popularity achieved by Mr. Mansfield in the part during twelve months' representation in America; to the reports of the handsome fortune already realized through it by the lucky actor; to the improvement and strength—(rare occurrence!)—added by the adaptor to the written story, which, after all, was more or less of a sketch; and, in no small degree, too, to the report that Mr. Bandmann had been poaching on his preserves and had announced his (Mr. Bandmann's) intention of producing a second edition of the book a month before Mr. Mansfield's advertised date of opening. But, as will be seen by what follows, Mr. Mansfield is not a man to be beaten; he is about to open at the Lyceum Theatre two days before his rival. Our representative, who had an interview yesterday with Mr. Mansfield, sends us the following report of the conversation: -

As I entered the managerial room I found Dr. Jekyll and Mr. Hyde settling his arrangements with his *chef-d'orchestre*. "Whatever music I have," he was saying, "must be fine; it must be fit for the concert-room, and to the taste of the *dilettante*." The programme, and the number of performers—twenty-eight, I think—decided upon, Mr. Mansfield put himself on his guard for a journalistic chat. He was now wholly Dr. Jekyll.

"How did you come to put this 'Strange Case' upon the boards, Mr. Mansfield?"

"I had read the book, like every one else, and laid it on one side, and not till a long time afterwards did it occur to me that it might be transformed into a piece with all the dramatic interest necessary to a stage-play, but uncalled for in a book. So, without re-reading the story, I took the idea to a very delightful and powerful writer (at least, so I think him), Mr. T. Russell Sullivan—a great favourite in the States. According to my plan he dramatized it."

"In what way have you cut it into acts?"

"Like this. The first act represents the house of Sir Danvers Carew; the second act contains three scenes of which the first is Hyde's secret lodgings in Soho; the second, the street scene, showing the back entrance; and the third, the hall in Dr. Jekyll's house. The third act shows Dr. Lanyon's office, where Hyde, you remember, comes in quest of the potion to transform himself back into Jekyll; and the fourth act represents Jekyll's laboratory, where the final catastrophe takes place."

"And what is Mr. Stevenson's attitude towards his child, which you've adopted?"

"Benignant. Although, according to American law, I need not recognize his rights in any way, I have, since the first production of the piece, paid him £20 a month, besides certain other heavy charges to which I have been liable, and that money he has accepted, not as 'royalty' exactly — as he had no hand in the dramatization — but as 'honorarium.' And that sum, I have no doubt, will be largely increased during the coming run of the piece."

"But you must surely have had to introduce some other characters in addition to those mentioned in the piece?"

"Yes; we've introduced the love interest in the first place, and a very strong interest I think it will be found. We throw in Agnes Carew, daughter of Sir Danvers, and Mrs. Dr. Lanyon. Then Mr. Stevenson's sketch of the housekeeper has been filled out, and Poole, the man-servant, has been assigned a more important share in the action."

"And how does the love come in?"

"You see, Dr. Jekyll is in love with Agnes Carew, and what makes the story the more tragic is that when he is himself he, a good man then, feels what a base scoundrel and inhuman villain he is while he's Hyde, and his grief becomes accentuated, for he is for ever thinking 'I'm not worthy of her — I'm not worthy of my darling.' That is where I believe I've improved on Mr. Stevenson's conception. All he wanted to do, as Balzac, Daudet, and Théophile Gautier have done before, was to give one man's soul two bodies — only Stevenson developed the idea so far as to so divide the soul as to put the better and worse halves in different (and typical) bodies. But where, I think, he made a mistake was in making Dr. Jekyll a jovial, happy, amiable, dinner party giving, jolly-good-fellow. Now, on Stevenson's assumption that Hyde was the impersonation of all that was *bad* in his character, how could Dr. Jekyll (who was the *good*) be otherwise than shocked at the enormities he committed when his other self? How could he be otherwise than remorseful and moody, in spite of all his goodness and loving-kindness? Could such a man, who knew well he had committed murders and outrages in the morning, be the smiling, benignant host in the evening? Of course not. Now, rightly or wrongly, I have a theory that all that is good in a man's character — his affection for others, his love of truth and mercy, his self-sacrifice, patience, and other virtues — all come to him from his mother; and so I make Jekyll somewhat effeminate, that is to say, gentle in his manner and passionate and self-sacrificing in his love."

"What do you consider the strongest situation in the piece?" — "I think there are two — the one in which, as Hyde, I spring upon the woman. That is the point where, more than once, nervous women, and men too, have fainted with emotion."

"Your 'fainting lady' that has been so industriously paragraphed, Mr. Mansfield?"

"Well, the origin of that 'base invention of the enemy.' And the other is the whole of the last act, which is practically a monologue for me."

This scene Mr. Mansfield then described for me, half acting it as he sat in his chair; but I refrain from disclosing the exact nature of this extraordinarily powerful and sorrowful scene, lest I spoil the pleasure, by anticipation, of those who will go to judge for themselves. But as he finished I found myself clutching at the table edge, and, raising my gaze to the actor's face, I saw his eyes filled with tears.

"It is a terribly tiring part for me," continued Mr. Mansfield; "for all the time the nerves are trembling and in a state of great tension; and the case is a harder one as Mr. Bandmann, who started a version of his own about ten months after I had been running mine, tried to cut the ground from under my feet by opening before me. But as it is," he went on with a smile, "I open on the 4th of next month."

"Now, Mr. Mansfield, will you say how you effect the transformation?"

"Absolutely without adventitious aid — which is mere clowning, certainly not artistic in its method. As it will be given 'in another place,' you will see that the impersonator will be furnished with another wig and a set of teeth by a man stationed underneath the table. That is all very well in its way, but I think I can show you as complete a transformation as is necessary and permissible to the case by acting pure and simple; by change of features, disarrangement of the hair, and collapse of the figure — all in sight of the audience."

"And your company and scenery?"

"The company will be the same as I have had with me all along, and the scenery identical in design and arrangement as has served me hitherto."

The Star, London, July 27, 1888

A CHAT WITH RICHARD MANSFIELD.
How "Dr. Jekyll and Mr. Hyde" Grew from a Novel to a Play — The Cause of its Extraordinary Success — A Word on English Audiences — The Cost of "Macbeth."

There is very little of the theatrical about Mr. Irving's business office at the back of the Lyceum. Were it not for a sheaf of "property" swords in one corner and an ex-Academy portrait of the lessee himself in another, you would imagine this soberly furnished, Turkey-carpeted apartment to be the sanctum of some bank-manager or smug solicitor. Nor is there ought to dispel this illusion in the dapper, nattily-attired little gentleman who rises to greet a representative of *The Star* and modestly confesses his identity with Mr. Richard Mansfield, of "Dr. Jekyll and Mr. Hyde" fame. Mr. Mansfield's is the latest instance of those sudden flying-trapeze leaps into fortune which only America can show. A year ago he was a comparatively unknown, unfriended young actor lost in the drudgery of provincial tours. Today, thanks to a moment of happy inspiration that prompted him to develop a sketch of Mr. Robert Louis Stevenson's, and still more to the vivid power with which he has brought this expanded sketch to the footlights, the same young actor is swimming in a pactolos of dollars, and furnishing after-dinner gossip for two continents.

"So, Mr. Mansfield, you have stolen a march upon your rival after all, and are coming out at the Lyceum two days before his appearance at the Opera Comique. But is not that a game at which two can play? What is to hinder Mr. Bandmann from advancing the date of his first performance, as you yourself have done?"

Here Mr. Mansfield's eye twinkles merrily. "Well, sir, until my first night at the Lyceum the Opera Comique has been taken — *by me*; and before Mr. Bandmann can enter that house, even for a rehearsal, he will have to ask my leave."

"Which of course he will get?"

Again a merry twinkle.

"It has been said over here, Mr. Mansfield, that you are an Englishman and served your apprenticeship in the rank and file of Mr. Irving's company."

"No, sir, though I was born in an English possession — Heligoland — I am not an Englishman. I did come over here some years ago as an artist — or, perhaps we had better say (another twinkle), as a painter. I drifted on to the comic-opera stage, under Mr. H. B. Farnie and others. But it was in the States I got my first real start on the boards, and I owe it to Mr. W. S. Gilbert."

"And when was it you burst upon the world with 'Dr. Jekyll and Mr. Hyde'?"

"In the spring of last year, at Boston. In the fall we took it to New York, and our first night at the Madison-square Theatre was the biggest ever known at that house. In three weeks we had netted 16,000 dols."

"Who is responsible for the play?"

"The plan — the *scenario* — is my own. The details have been filled in by a popular American dramatist, Mr. Russell Sullivan."

"And Mr. Stevenson?"

"Has had no hand in it. We submitted the rough draft to him, and here you have a letter from him saying, 'I may be able to lick up the piece a little.' But here is another, later on, highly approving the play, and deciding that it would be a mistake to add anything. I must tell you, however, that Mr. Stevenson has from the first had a hand in the proceeds. Here you see his endorsement to a number of 100 dollar cheques, one of which is sent to him every month."

"To what do you ascribe the success of your play?"

"Well, in the first place, it creates a profound moral impression. It brings out, as no other play I have ever seen brings out, the awful contrast between the good and evil natures which co-exist in every man. From this, the ethical, point of view it has been made the theme for sermons in every pulpit in New York. Then I find my treatment of Dr. Jekyll — which is something different from Mr. Stevenson's treatment, as you will see next week—undoubtedly effective. It is there, I think, that the scores of other actors who have tried the part in America have all come to grief. There are Jekylls and Hydes in every dime museum in the States—all starving. Mr. Bandmann travelled from New York to San Francisco, 3,000 miles, to produce his version. He opened on Monday—and closed on Wednesday. The fact is, they can all find Hyde in Mr. Stevenson's book, but my Jekyll they cannot find, for he is not there."

Is the play all Jekyll and Hyde?"

"Nearly. We give the doctor a sweetheart, so introducing a love interest, and there is a little, a very little, comic relief. But the play, as a play, is really a series of episodes. That, from the nature of the subject, was inevitable."

"A chaplet of pearls—black pearls, say—strung upon a rather weak thread?"

"Precisely."

"And is there any truth, Mr. Mansfield, in the current gossip about the mechanical devices by which you accomplish the transformation from Jekyll to Hyde; the shrinking elastic garment, and so forth?"

"None whatever. Come into my dressing-room next week, and you shall see for yourself that my change is simply a change of style, a change of posture and facial expression."

"What other novelties have you in store during your four months' tenure of the Lyceum?"

"We intend to follow with our adaptation of a play of Octave Feuillet's, already very successful in the States, "A Parisian Romance." Later on I shall produce an entirely new classical drama, in the mounting of which I hope to get the aid of Mr. Alma Tadema—a version of the Italian play of "Nero."

"Now, Mr. Mansfield, you have made experiment of both English and American audiences. What, if any, is the difference between them? Madame Bernhardt told *The Star* the other day she found the London public as sympathetic as any in the world."

"Well, I think American audiences are more difficult to please—or, at least, more slow to express their pleasure. I have played in Boston to a house that has been silent through a whole evening, and have found that everyone was really delighted. On the other hand, American audiences never hiss. If they do not like a play they simply walk out."

"But if satisfaction with a good actor may fairly be expressed aloud—and I have never heard an actor grumble at that—why not dissatisfaction with a bad actor?"

"Because your bad actor, however bad, is doing his best. If you must hiss, go round to the office and hiss the manager, who is to blame for supplying a bad article—or, better still, let the critics, whose business it is, do the hissing in print next morning."

"The critics! But successful actors give us to understand that they never read criticisms. To name no others, M. Coquelin and Madame Bernhardt have both told me so."

"Depend upon it, even they read them on the sly. As for myself, a *critique* of my friend William Winter's was, in this very "Jekyll and Hyde," of the greatest service to me. Henry Irving, I know, carefully reads all criticisms."

Parler d'un ange, &c.! At this moment enter Mr. Irving himself, full of friendly interest and cheery encouragement for his young tenant. "By the way, Mr. Irving," says the *Star* man as he takes his leave, "M. Damala has told me that you say you expect to spend £12,000 over 'Macbeth' next December. Is not that rather steep?"

"M. Damala must have got confused with our English currency," is the smiling answer. "The real figure will probably not amount to a third of that sum."

Sunday Times, London, August 26, 1888

CHATS WITH CELEBRITIES.
MR. RICHARD MANSFIELD.
WITH "JEKYLL AND HYDE" AFLOAT.
"A Wet Sheet and a Flowing Sail."

A spick and span new boat beating up the reaches of the river between Richmond and Putney Bridge. No cockle-shell, but a small Thames yacht with centre-board and a white sail with a reef in it, for the wind is strong and gusty. In the bows a smart waterside boy in jersey and scarlet cap. At the helm, a tight, well-built young fellow in flannels, and in full charge of the dancing yacht.

Lying prone in the stern at the yachtsman's feet smoking a cigar and enjoying the fun, the present writer, a representative of the SUNDAY TIMES.

The skipper at the helm is Richard Mansfield, the Jekyll and Hyde of the Lyceum Theatre.

I wanted to have a chat with him. I found that he leaves London every morning for an out-of-the-way retreat of the most unostentatious kind, and that in the intervals of study and reading he spends his time sailing his little yacht hither and thither, most pleased with the exercise when the wind is dead across the river and he has to tack about with the added danger of being run down by a steam-barge, or capsized by a more than ordinary gust of wind. I found him at this occupation. He invited me on board, and we had a very pleasant time.

How to Take Care of Yourself.

"And this is how you keep yourself in form?" I asked.

"When I came to London," he said, "I took a chill, had a sore throat, had to consult Sir Morell Mackenzie. He advised my taking great care of myself. One day I struck a little tavern away down the river, and I found there pleasant and private quarters, I came upon this boat, it was for sale, I like boating, I bought it, and I bought my juvenile skipper with it."

"Bought him!" I said.

"Did I say bought—I mean hired—and I said to myself if I retire every day for a certain number of hours to this retreat and live in the open air as much as possible I shall take care of myself, get rid of my sore throat, and keep equal to my nightly work. And all that has come to pass. I sail about, breathe pure air, drink soda and milk, eat the plainest of food, and to-day I am as strong as a lion."

And he looked it.

"You like the river?"

"Like it! I love it," he said, "and I love it all the more that it has cured me, and made me 'fit,' as you say."

"And what about Jekyll and Hyde?"

"Jekyll and Hyde are both very well, thank you. Jekyll and Hyde have not had a bed of roses; the criticism has been a trifle hot here and there, but the controversy is doing good, our business is growing, and to be able to say that in August is a big thing they tell me; theatrical people who know. I think everybody has been very kind; the critics who don't like the play are good enough to say they like me, and to recognise the fact that to act Jekyll and Hyde is no child's play; what some of them do not recognise are the technical difficulties of the two parts, for example, I am obliged to treat Jekyll somewhat mildly in order to get the contrast with Hyde; I am obliged—"

Here the sail gives a tremendous tug, and a Thames steamer comes swishing past, enforcing the skipper's attention to the navigation of the boat, and compelling the guest to change his position in order to trim the vessel, whose nose is right up in the wind, and whose sail is wet with flying spray.

Critics and Criticism.

"Where was I?" Oh, I know—I am obliged even to dress Jekyll as I do because I have certain arrangements to make touching the dress of Hyde; I dare not put vigour and 'go' into the character of Jekyll, because then I should be intrenching upon the character of Hyde."

"Some of the critics seem to think you should prepare the audience for the appearance of Hyde."

"I don't think so; the element of surprise

would then be knocked out of the first act, and the later acts would also be injured."

"You don't think the play is perfect?"

"By no means."

"You don't think it is a good play?"

"I think it is a good representation of a very strange story, and a very difficult story to tell; I think it might be improved here and there, and I try to improve it just as I try to improve my dual part. You mentioned, for instance, in the last SUNDAY TIMES, that I now wear a silk hat as Jekyll; it is a small matter, but it shows you that I am not a mule, that I am open to suggestions, and that I am anxious to consider criticism that is instructive, as all criticism should be."

"And you are satisfied with your reception?"

"More than satisfied, I am delighted; that was a close shave; did you see how quickly she came round; my centre board's up or I dare not have run in so close."

"What Next?"

We had run as it were right ashore, to turn as sharp round as if wind and waves were entirely at our control. Yes, there were waves. A steam barge with other cumbersome craft had just swung by us, threatening, it almost seemed at first, to occupy every bit of river space; but the skipper cleared the lumbering fleet, and at the point, as it seemed, of running us ashore we slewed round and were beating along our next tack with a ripple of muscle at our bow that was delightful. I lighted a fresh cigar, and if you imagine I care whether these notes are consistently written in the present tense or the past you are mistaken; I do not. I am spinning them out on a typewriter which goes pegging away, and almost with as much noise as the tug that puffed and snorted by the Beatrice yesterday. Didn't I say it was the Beatrice? No; well then it was, and the name is painted in blue and gold at the bow of the tightest little Thames sailing boat afloat.

"Go on talking I say; tell me anything you like; and shout."

"I am shouting," he said, but he was shouting to the occupants of a wherry, the said occupants, a girl and boy, being very much occupied with each other, and letting their wherry drift with the tide, and just right across our tack, and right a-starboard where we did not want them; and what a pretty pair of blue eyes looked up and smiled as we went scudding by!

"Oh, I don't know that I have any more to say," he answered, "except that I have come to London to stay until next year; that I shall run 'Jekyll and Hyde' as long as the public care to come and see it, and I believe they will be more and more interested in it as the pleasant summer weather comes to an end, and we get into autumn and dark nights; and when they are tired I think I shall give them a Parisian romance, 'Prince Carl,' 'Nero,' or other plays new and old, but that is looking too far into the future."

"Meanwhile you are quite content and happy?"

"Quite."

"I am very glad to hear it."

"Stand by, Tommy," says the skipper, and as I turn to see why Tommy is ordered to stand by, the sail drops and we run into a picturesque slip near half a dozen wooden steps, a nimble boatman catches our bow, and "We have arrived" says Mansfield.

I am not at liberty to say where we had arrived; but it was a simple if dainty little luncheon; and the moment I was ready my carriage was announced, and I hope this brief, hurried, "dot-and-go-one" kind of sketch of my interview with our newest celebrity may not be considered quite unworthy of the occasion.

Appendix C: Reviews of Mansfield's *Dr. Jekyll and Mr. Hyde*

Reviews of Mansfield's Original Boston Performance, May 9, 1887

Boston Post, May 10, 1887

"DR. JEKYLL AND MR. HYDE."

An audience that any actor might be proud of assembled at the Museum last evening to witness the first production of "Dr. Jekyll and Mr. Hyde," the play which Mr. T. Russell Sullivan has prepared from Mr. Stevenson's story and in which Mr. Richard Mansfield assumes the strange dual characters for whom it is named. It was an audience whose favorable judgement was well worth securing; and even its evident entire friendliness, both to actor and to author, did not essentially impair the worth of that judgement. Having said so much, the further statement that the applause throughout was long and loud, and that nearly every one remained seated at the end of the performance until Mr. Mansfield had appeared several times to bow his acknowledgements, indicates what measure of success was secured by the new production. The presence of Mr. Sullivan was also emphatically demanded, until Mr. Seymour was forced to appear in his stead, with the assurance that he could not be found. It is certain that such modesty on his part was not demanded by circumstances, since the congratulations which the audience were so willing to bestow were well deserved.

It would be idle to claim on behalf of the play that it has quite the power or the fascination of the story. There is, indeed, in Mr. Stevenson's narrative an inherent lack of dramatic force which it must have cost no little effort to overcome. We do not mean by this to disavow or to underrate the very high degree of moving power which that narrative undoubtedly possesses. But, however melodramatic (using the word in its best sense) it may be in substance, it is obviously quite the reverse in form. Its weird improbability is hardly more marked than the essentially modern and scientific manner in which the psychic problem it formulates is stated. In fact, the very problem itself — at least in this form — belongs distinctly to the century. Alchemic transformations were favorite subjects with our earlier romancers; we meet with the magic potion which can alter the very currents of life even in the primitive fictions of every race. But in such cases the great and mystic truth is clumsily stated; it is the duality of mankind rather than the duality of man that is perceived. In Mr. Stevenson's story it is this "thorough and primitive duality of man" that is the basis of interest. *Henry Jekyll's* efforts are all directed toward the separation of the two contending elements. "If each, as I told myself, could but be housed in separate identities," he is made to say, "life would be relieved of all that is unbearable; the unjust might go his way, delivered from the aspiration and remorse of his more upright twin; and the just could walk steadfastly and securely on his upward path, doing the good things in which he found his pleasure, and no longer exposed to disgrace and penitence by the hands of this extraneous evil." It is to an elaboration of the theory thus propounded that the story is mainly directed; and its incidents, therefore, partake less of the artistically inevitable than of the psychologically indispensable. In other words, it is, as the title page suggests, not so much a story as a "strange case." The peculiar glamour which surrounds it is due largely to the inherent awfulness of a dual existence like *Jekyll's*; the individual incidents, clever in their weird conception as they are, are of subordinate importance, and this is why Mr. Stevenson's narrative may be imperfectly and roughly described as modern and scientific in its real significance.

This lack of ideality — and we must ask the reader to remember the distinction between ideality and imagination and not misunderstand our meaning — gives the dramatist a very serious problem to consider. Mr. Sullivan proves that the problem is not unsolvable, though even his clever pen has failed to resolve it quite into its prime factors. Of the incidents of the story he makes very good use, though he has to transpose them to secure anything like dramatic unity. The murder of *Sir Danvers Carew* is the chief incident of the first act; in the second, *Hyde* is traced to his lodgings in Soho, tracked to *Dr. Jekyll's* laboratory, and then made to resume again the form of *Jekyll* himself, baffling for the moment all inquiry; the third act is devoted to the discovery of the mystery to *Dr. Lanyon* and here the account of that interview, as given in the story, is very cleverly interwoven with other details; in the last act the death in the cabinet takes place. This final scene is by all odds the most impressive in the play. It omits the vivid and picturesque interview between *Utterson* and the old butler, substituting a brief scene with *Dr. Lanyon* and a remorseful monologue on the part of *Jekyll*. Whether this change materially betters the dramatic effect is at least an open question; but as it helps the audience to a better understanding of *Jekyll* himself, it is, perhaps, permissible. This climax is very striking and vivid, and it comes with a sharpness and suddenness that is worth many minutes of mere melodramatic agony.

The wholly extraneous characters and circumstances supplied by Mr. Sullivan show commendable tact and invention. His development of the character of the lodging-house keeper in Soho — though hardly in accordance with the brief hints furnished by Mr. Stevenson — is generally excellent, and the revolting cupidity of the old harpy and her feverish anxiety to wreak injury on *Hyde* are very effectively portrayed. The introduction of *Sir Danvers Carew* and his daughter *Agnes*, on the other hand, has its disadvantages. That *Jekyll* should be in love with the latter does not strike us as quite natural or probable, even though his affection is made to add not a little to the intense human interest of the closing scene. Of course, too, the murder of *Carew* becomes particularly revolting under this condition of affairs, the more so as it seems to some degree incongruous with *Hyde's* conduct elsewhere. The question necessarily arises whether or not *Jekyll* retains control enough over his other self to have led him to avoid the house of his betrothed. Even so late as the night of the interview with *Dr. Lanyon*, when the two are becoming more and more closely interfused, the voice of *Jekyll* now and then seems to speak through *Hyde*. Why, then, at a comparatively early stage of his mental and moral decline, does *Agnes Carew's* lover deliberately seek out and murder her father? The crime as related in the story has quite another bearing upon the case. Mr. Sullivan has a perfect right to discard this, if he must, in the face of dramatic necessity, but he should, at least, select another aspect of the matter equally clear and logical. The question is not one likely to strike an audience, and so far it is, perhaps, comparatively unimportant; but it has, nevertheless, a significance that ought to be considered. Beyond this—and our objection may be hyper-critical—we have small fault to find with the play. It is coherent, compact, intensely and even oppressively exciting; the dialogue is clever, and at times brilliant, and the situations, as we have already indicated, are stirring and impressive. Altogether, Mr. Sullivan is to be warmly congratulated upon his work.

We have left ourselves but little space in which to speak of Mr. Mansfield's impersonation of the difficult dual character of *Dr. Jekyll* and *Mr. Hyde*. The distinction which he makes between the two is in every way admirable. Up to a certain point his task is a comparatively easy one; it is where *Hyde* is actually transformed to *Jekyll* in the very presence of the audience that the chance of failure becomes momentous. As *Dr. Jekyll* we do not think Mr. Mansfield struck precisely the right key; the awful consciousness of his dual personality is too palpably carried about with him. He discards entirely Mr. Stevenson's conception of the man, and never represents him as "quite at ease," as we are told he was on at least one occasion; and the alteration gives Mr. Mansfield's first moments upon the stage a melodramatic insincerity that rather depresses the spectator. Any wide physical difference between *Jekyll* and *Hyde* could obviously only tend to burlesque upon the stage; but at least the mental distinction of some attempt at ease or gayety of manner might be made with very great advantage.

The failure to make such a distinction keeps the impersonation altogether too near a dead level of melancholy. But if Mr. Mansfield is not wholly satisfactory as *Dr Jekyll*, little but praise can be given to his *Mr. Hyde*. His stooping, slouching gait, that suggests deformity without actually being such; his glittering leering eyes, his distorted features, his twisted and gnarled hands that perpetually suggest the strangler; his harsh, cold and malignant voice, –all these details are elaborated with marvellous and realistic precision. When the change from *Hyde* to *Jekyll* comes, in the scene with *Dr. Lanyon*, he throws back his overhanging hair, runs his hands across his face, and immediately the visible evil spirit dies out of his eyes and lips. It is in every way a psychological transformation, which it is worth while to have witnessed, as powerful, as significant, as impressive, as it is free from mere contortion and grimace. Even the awful closing scene does not outdo this in its vividness of conception and strength of execution.

The members of the Museum company gave efficient support in the other roles of the play. Mr. Hudson leading with some of his characteristically best work as *Dr. Lanyon*. Miss Emma Sheridan, who is specially engaged, gave a clever and at times brilliant impersonation of the voracious and terrible old lodging-house keeper. Mr. Coulter was dignified and impressive as *Mr. Utterson*, and Miss Evesson played the part of *Agnes Carew* with gentle grace and sweetness. Mr. Putman was rather extravagant as *Sir Danvers Carew*, and Miss Ryan shared something of the same fault as *Mrs. Lanyon*. The stage settings were, in the main, excellent.

Boston Globe, May 10, 1887

Mansfield's Triumph.

"Dr. Jekyll and Mr. Hyde"
Win Plaudits
Loud, and Long Continued, from a Brilliant Throng.
A Great Piece of Character Acting at the Boston Museum.

Cheered to the echo by one of the most brilliant audiences of the dramatic year, and recalled many times to bow his acknowledgements to enthusiastic plaudits, Richard Mansfield achieved last evening another and most signal triumph in character portrayal.

Who has not read "The Strange Story of Dr. Jekyll and Mr. Hyde"? That this tersely told narrative, however, should be made the subject of a play, hardly entered the mind of a single one among the earlier readers of Stevenson's enthralling romance. Not to mention other obstacles, the difficulties that stood in the way of one who would attempt to set forth on the stage both Jekyll and Hyde — the embodiment of high purpose, the thing of evil — seemed assuredly enough absolutely insurmountable.

The young actor whose Chevrial was recognized as such a marvel of portrayal, and whose skill in his chosen art has found such varied and successful illustration, undertook what most of his associates would unhesitatingly pronounce an impossible task. Dr. Jekyll and Mr. Hyde should, he determined, be added to his repertory — the judgement of the public to decide whether it should there remain, or be classed among the courageous but unsuccessful dramatic essays of the time.

The Work of Preparing a Play from Stevenson's story was entrusted to Mr. T. Russell Sullivan, whose aptness as a translator of dramas had been pleasantly shown on the stage where Mr. Mansfield purposed to make his first bow in his new and dual character.

Inevitably, in play as in story, interest centres in the Jekyll-Hyde character study. The dramatist has changed, in a good many details, the development of events. He has introduced a young girl, daughter of the General Carew who is struck down by Hyde; and this maiden, betrothed to Jekyll, finally breaks her engagement in grief and despair, and comes in at the close of the play to find, not the old lover whom she expects to see, but the dying murderer of her father.

The character of Hyde's housekeeper — drawn by Stevenson in a few, a very few lines — is in the play much elaborated. Rebecca Moor has intense hatred for her master, but her great passion is the love of money. She is a miser of misers; and when Hyde tears from her hands the notes for which she had agreed to deliver the fugitive to the police, that act does more to make her his unrelenting foe even than the terrible crime for which he is sought by justice. On the whole, Mr. Sullivan certainly added a strong, though not altogether an original character to the Jekyll-Hyde play in this Rebecca Moor. Carew's daughter is made a sweet tender-hearted creature, and her presence at least supplies the "love element" which is thought so essential to the success of any stage production.

Dr. Lanyon as the novelist drew him and Dr. Lanyon, as the playwright sets him forth are not altogether one and the same. One of the most remarkable changes made by Mr. Sullivan is that which not only presents the physician as recovering from the shock of the change from Hyde to Jekyll, but later on introduces him into Jekyll's office, knowing his dread secret, and giving him words of hope and cheer. Utterson and Poole remain "undeveloped" — indeed, neither character in the play seems as important as in the story. General Carew is only a sketch, but there is some excellent work in the opening scenes, where his daughter recalls memories of days when her mother was yet alive. Possibly for the purpose of giving a touch of comedy to the drama, Mr. Sullivan offers to attend on Mrs Lanyon, wife of the doctor, who loudly bemoans the obduracy of Agnes in breaking off the engagement with Jekyll, and who is a humorously mercenary sort of person of rather a familiar type.

The Hyde and Jekyll Story Is Told in four acts. The first is almost all the dramatist's own. Jekyll meets his affianced, wanders away with her for a moonlight stroll, and is called away on business of his profession. Then Hyde appears at the window of Carew's house. Seeking for the daughter, he meets the father. There is a brief struggle; Carew is trampled to death by the fiendish visitor, and Agnes returns to the scene just in time to catch a glimpse of the murderer's face before he flees away. The second act opens with a scene in Hyde's lodgings in Soho. Rebecca Moor, his housekeeper, bribed at first to keep the presence of the murderer a secret, is persuaded later on by an inspector's gift and promise to betray her master into the hands of the authorities. But Hyde detects her purpose, snatches from her grasp the money she has been paid, and hurries away. At the door of the Jekyll labratory (as in the story) Hyde is confronted by Utterson. The scene closes with Jekyll's appearance to his astonished friend. The fourth act brings the climax of the play, the midnight visit to Dr. Lanyon's house in Cavendish square, his eager draught of the tincture, and the transformation before the eyes of his friend from Hyde to Jekyll.

It would probably have been impossible for the dramatist to avoid the effect of anticlimax in arranging the closing act of the play. At any rate this is the least interesting in all the drama. The introduction of Dr. Lanyon in these closing scenes certainly weakens the character as Stevenson drew it. Nor does it serve, apparently, any special purpose. Jekyll confesses nothing to him that would convey to one who was unfamiliar with the story any real idea of the purpose and motive that actuated him in his strange course. There is something too much of Jekyll's soliloquies; and even when the moment of danger came, and the eager party break in the door, only to see Hyde dying before their eyes, the effect is less than might be expected. A rearrangement of this closing act, with a better "leading up" to the death of Hyde, would certainly add not a little to the impressiveness of a play that is, on the whole, arranged so skilfully and well. It only remains to note that Mr. Sullivan has followed as far as possible the language of the character of the story, and that his own dialogue is all excellently written.

Mansfield's Wonderful Art has never been more strikingly illustrated than in his dual performance as Hyde and Jekyll. He departs widely from the character of the physician as drawn in the story. In his hands Dr. Jekyll is made a man already suffering from the influence of an evil genius whom he has evoked, and whom, like Frankenstein, he cannot lay. In his sadness and suggestion of weakness there is scarcely a hint of the robust Lanyon whom Stevenson imagined. But none the less is it the embodiment of high thought and purity; so that Mr. Mansfield has preserved perfectly the spirit of the character, while making it possible for him to set forth, also, that "other self" of Jekyll.

And what a marvellous portraiture is that of Hyde. In his Jekyll there is a hint now and then of certain other personations which this artist has given the stage — only a hint however. But Hyde is a creation absolutely new. He seems the very embodiment of evil. As he creeps along the stage one seems to feel that strange sense of repulsion for the uncanny creature whom this actor's skill has so perfectly embodied on the stage. Singularly effective is Hyde's first entrance upon the scene, his cruel, sensual face lit up by the moonlight, as he stealthily advanced towards Agnes Carew, only to be confronted by the angry father, whose life is trampled out a moment later in furious passion.

What a great actor and master of facial expression can do, without recourse to anything like charlatanism, was admirably shown in the scene in Lanyon's house, where, under the spell of a potent drug, Hyde's personality is shaken off and Jekyll once more walks among his fellow men. One moment and the audience sees Hyde, with trembling hands, stooping form and satanic face. A hand is passed over the forehead, and in an instant the figure seems to rise to new height and dignity — the face is changed, one scarcely knows how, and Dr. Jekyll, weak and trembling, but still Jekyll's own, unmistakable self, stands on the stage. Hyde has vanished as utterly as though he had been in very truth spirited away.

Cheer on cheer followed the curtain's fall on the great third act of the play. There had been recalls and most generous recalls, too, after the other acts; but now there was a scene of enthusiasm rarely paralleled within the walls of the Boston Museum. Four and five times was the artist summoned to make his acknowledgements to plaudits that gave abundant assurance that his great endeavor had been gloriously successful in its most exacting scene.

The Consistency and Skill of Mansfield's portrayal, from Jekyll's first appearance until the death of Hyde, should by no means pass unrecognized in reviewing his most remarkable performance. One may wish that exigencies of personality permitted a closer following of the Dr. Jekyll of the story than Mr. Mansfield's setting forth of this part of the role. But it is impossible not to admire the art with which the conception of the character, once studied out is carried through.

"Dr. Jekyll and Mr. Hyde" does not afford great opportunities for any in the cast save Mansfield. It is a one-character play, essentially like "The Bells"; and the success of the drama will be, as it should be, chiefly the success of the leading actor, here and elsewhere.

Emma Sheridan, especially engaged for this production, made a strong impression as the avaricious housekeeper of Hyde, winning deserved applause after the scene where her master robs her and she vows vengeance on the man she hates most of all in the world. Isabel Evesson was pretty and sympathetic as Jekyll's affianced.

The Museum was packed last evening to the doors. Such a reception from such a noteworthy assemblage assures to play and star a week of high success for the first production on any stage of "Dr. Jekyll and Mr. Hyde."

Boston Evening Transcript, May 10, 1887

"Dr. Jekyll and Mr. Hyde."

"Dr. Jekyll and Mr. Hyde," Mr. T. R. Sullivan's four-act dramatization of Mr. Robert Louis Stevenson's romance of the same name, was given for the first time on any stage at the Boston Museum last evening. The cast was as follows:

Dr. Jekyll/Mr. Hyde	Mr. Richard Mansfield
General Sir Danvers Carew	Mr. Boyd Putnam
Dr. Lanyon	Mr. Alfred Hudson
Gabriel Utterson	Mr. Frazer Coulter
Poole	Mr. James Burrows
Inspector Newcomen	Mr. Arthur Falkland
Jarvis	Mr. J. K. Appleby Jr.
Agnes Carew	Miss Isabelle Evesson
Mrs. Lanyon	Miss Kate Ryan
Rebecca Moor	Miss Emma Sheridan

If current report be credible — and in this case it is very credible indeed — it was entirely at the instigation of Mr. Mansfield that Mr. Sullivan applied himself to the task of dramatizing Mr. Stevenson's story. That Mr. Mansfield should have seen in the double personage of Dr. Jekyll and Mr. Hyde material for a telling character-part was natural enough. Natural enough, also, that he should not have cared to look beyond what affected himself personally in the proposed play; for Mr. Mansfield, although an admirable actor, is still a young man, and must have other fish to fry than are implied in the elevation of the stage. If Mr. Sullivan felt any hesitation in undertaking the task offered him, it came probably from a pretty shrewd appreciation of its difficulty; that is, of the difficulty of working up the story into an effective acting play. For, if we mistake not, he is, both by instinct and conviction, an impenitent romanticist, and has no naturalistic sympathies which could breed scruples on the matter of having to do with the purely imaginary. Mr. Stevenson's story is an allegory, as was quite correctly seen by Mr. Payne when he wrote of it in the Quarterly Review, "A noble moral underlies this marvellous tale," for, if the story were not allegorical, it would have no moral nor meaning whatever. The plot hinges on a physical impossibility. This being the case, neither the romancer nor his dramatiser can be held bound to any purely realistic adherence to Nature, but merely to that psychological truth to Nature which must underly all allegories, if they are to have real worth. They are perfectly free to use any means in their power to give point and significance to their allegorical picture. They thus, in one sense, enjoy greater freedom than the naturalistic writer, who has to hold fast not only by the moral but by the physical truth. But this seemingly greater freedom brings with it a condition which in no wise affects the naturalistic writer. With the moral impression his characters make upon his audience he has nothing to do; he draws them as true to life, and invests them with as much vitality, as he can; but whether they excite love or hatred, reverence or contempt in the minds and hearts of his public, lies wholly without his reckoning. The romanticist, on the other hand, especially the writer of an allegory, is in duty bound to consider the physical relations between his characters and his public; he must make his virtuous heroes sympathetic, and his villains hateful, for, if he does not make them so, he misses his mark. This is even more necessary in drama than it is in romance, for in drama the first instinct of the spectator is to individualize the people he sees moving visibly before his eyes on the stage, to take each one of them first in the concrete, and to apprehend their ethical or philosophical significance only afterwards. And here we come to the point which, most of all, makes the story of "Dr. Jekyll and Mr. Hyde" an exceedingly hazardous theme for dramatic treatment. We, the audience, cannot fully sympathize with Jekyll, because we know all the while that, beside being Jekyll, he is also Hyde; for the same reason we are unable perfectly to hate Hyde, because we know that he may turn back into Jekyll again at any moment. Hyde is Jekyll's malady, and our abhorrence of the disease is lessened by our pity for the sufferer, for, in this case, disease and sufferer are one. Then, too, as the disease is essentially shameful, and, to a certain extent, voluntarily incurred, our sympathy with and pity for Jekyll is not quite free from a dash of contempt. We feel toward this double incarnation of the virtues and vices much as we do toward a periodical drunkard. You may tell us that his failing is a disease and convince our understanding that it is so; but in our heart of heart we do not quite respect him, even in his sober days. Perhaps we ought to, but the fact is that we do not. That impenetrable veil of mystery behind which Mr. Stevenson hides the identity of his two heroes in the story and which is drawn aside only at the *dénouement*, might have helped matters here, had it been possible to keep it up. But Mr. Sullivan wisely abandoned all attempts at mystery; wisely, because, on the stage, the thing was plainly impossible. Still, the unfortunate fact remains that we are less interested in the double character of Jekyll and Hyde than in the manner in which Mr. Mansfield acts the two parts. It is, perhaps, a sort of retributive justice that what was written for acting should be looked at from a histrionic point of view. We heard the opinion expressed in the lobby last evening that Mr. Sullivan had weakened the story by introducing the love passages between Jekyll and Agnes Carew. With this opinion we can by no means agree. On the contrary, we think that this hapless love adds an important element of dramatic interest, which the play could ill afford to forego. It was not only a happy inspiration, but is very cleverly introduced and worked out to excellent purpose. The development of the character of Rebecca Moor, the plutomaniac old housekeeper, is also felicitous, and adds, if not variety of mood, at least variety of horror; and, in so dark a story, any variety is welcome. The murder of General Carew by Hyde must, however, be called at thought clumsy; it is all too sudden and unexplained. Hyde is a phantasm, to be sure, but, on the stage, even phantasms must account for themselves. The literary part of Mr. Sullivan's work is excellent, and the play increases in interest as it progresses, the last two acts are fairly thrilling. And yet we could not help thinking more than once of what Wagner wrote of Berlioz's recitatives to Weber's "Freischütz"; "Had M. Berlioz been willing to forget his reverent veneration for Weber, and thrown the reins upon the neck of his fervid imagination, instead of effacing himself in honor of his idol, as he has done, no one can doubt that he would have written recitatives of the most brilliant effectiveness." It seemed to us that Mr. Sullivan had allowed himself to be unnecessarily hampered by a too strict adherence to the original story. Had he written his play as a certain eminent writer is said to "translate" German novels—read the original carefully through, and then never look at it again—we think that it was in him to do better. His scenic instinct is often fine, and could have been trusted to work unshackled. He would have introduced more elements of variety into a play which, as it now stands, is terribly sombre from beginning to end. Still, and, after all, this was perhaps the main point, he has written for Mr. Mansfield a character-part which may be said, in many ways, to seek its superior. Of the way in which Mr. Mansfield acts the part much is to be said in high praise, and one thing in decided criticism. Both in his make-up and in his acting he makes Dr. Jekyll too inveterately gloomy. Kotzebue presented this suffering world with the Stranger, and actors upon actors have delighted in embodying this incubus. But one Stranger is quite enough, let us have no more avatars of this Cimmerian spectre! If Mr. Mansfield's Jekyll would but keep some of his mental misery to himself! This perpetual gloom becomes tiresome, and, at times, borders on the ludicrous. But this is the one flaw; for the rest his Jekyll is marked by depth and sincerity of feeling, and great finish of execution. But his Hyde—ah, there is a triumph! The feline attitude, the cruel, protruding chin, the sharp eyes, the rasping voice, and, above all, the mouth, with its leering bestiality, all contribute to form a picture irresistibly forcible and vital. All the evil passions are here portrayed with the sure hand of a master; it was superb. Miss Evesson acts Agnes Carew with great sweetness, simplicity and dignity. Miss Sheridan, if perhaps a little conventional, gives a very strong and striking impersonation of Rebecca Moor, and the other parts are well taken, Mr. Hudson deserving an especially good word for his Dr. Lanyon. The piece is exceedingly handsomely and artistically staged. The house was packed full by a brilliant audience, and expressions of enthusiasm were both frequent and hearty. Mr. Mansfield was repeatedly called before the curtain, and at the close, the audience clamored loudly for Mr. Sullivan, who, however, as Mr. Seymour, the excellent stage manager, had to announce, was nowhere to be found.

"Dr. Jekyll and Mr. Hyde" will run through this week, when Mr. Mansfield's engagement terminates.

Reviews of Mansfield's First New York Performance, September 12, 1887

New York Herald, September 13, 1887

DR. JEKYLL AND MR. HYDE
Mr. Mansfield in the Dramatization of Mr. Stevenson's Narrative.

MR. MANSFIELD AS "DR. JEKYLL AND MR. HYDE."

Dr. Jekyll	
Mr. Hyde	Mr. Richard Mansfield.
Gabriel Utterson	Mr. John T. Sullivan
Dr. Lanyon	Mr. D. H. Harkins
General Sir Danvers Carew	Mr. E. B. Bradley
Poole	Mr. Harry Gwynette
Inspector Newcomen	Mr. C. E. Eldridge
Jarvis	Mr. Thomas Goodwin
Mrs. Lanyon	Miss Katherine Rogers
Rebecca Moor	Miss Helen Glidden
Agnes Carew	Miss Beatrice Cameron

Dr. Jekyll changed to Mr. Hyde and the latter reverted into the former several times at the Madison Square Theatre last evening, both before and behind the scenes, to the intense interest of a large "first night" audience.

Mr. Richard Mansfield, who first brought out the piece in Boston last spring, was the actor who sustained with brilliant skill and wonderful command of facial and bodily expression what may in literary license, though incorrectly, be called the dual role.

The two changes made in view of the audience were really wonderful, and the whole impersonation was, on the whole, so powerful and consistent that the actor had most numerous and hearty curtain calls, mingled on one occasion by many shouts of "Bravo," both during and at the close of the play.

The author — Mr. R. L. Stevenson — of the original remarkable physiological study in narrative and statement form was not present, but his mother and wife were. Mr. T. R. Sullivan, the dramatist, was on hand, but though called for with considerable persistence, did not respond. He was finally persuaded to go on the boards, but it was too late, for the double stage was working.

The play of "Dr. Jekyll and Mr. Hyde" is a clever and scholarly semi-perverted amplification, theatric in form rather than truly dramatic in substance, of the English author's presentation in realistic mental and bodily yet supernal shape of a spiritual dualism in man. It is interesting, fascinating, and yet at times rather wearisome. The last arises somewhat from a lack at times of sufficient action, and from the facts that the fourth and last act is hardly more than a monologue and that there was a state of expectation of the lightning changes which, while it did not interfere with the intellectual enjoyment of the doings of hideous Mr. Hyde, certainly did with that of much of the other material.

Then, again, as presented last night, Dr.

Jekyll did not thoroughly interest, while Mr. Hyde most emphatically did. The latter had the call every time. There are some remarkably strong scenes in the play, and some fine scene and act climaxes. The introduction of the female element, which the original lacks, is happy for stage purposes, but the almost entire absence of comedy was strongly felt. Then the end of the first act is irrational. Hyde comes like a beast of prey is search of Jekyll's affianced, Agnes Carew. Brought to bay by her father, Mr. Danvers, he murders him. Then, when the girl appears on the scene, he slinks away. She should not come on.

The general impression made by the performance was undoubtedly strong and as undoubtedly weird and peculiar. Mr. Mansfield was so masterly as Hyde that it is a pity he was not more in contented frame of mind at the opening as Jekyll. He was melancholy from the beginning, not the fine, portly doctor of the original story, but a morose, pale, long, black haired youthful misanthrope. His speech, hard, grating, yet powerful as Hyde, was monotonous often as Jekyll, reminding occasionally of Wilson Barrett, and with every now and then suggestions of himself as Prince Karl and Monsieur. As Hyde his makeup was marvellous.

The cast was good all round, though Mr. John T. Sullivan did not make a very strong impression as Utterson. Miss Cameron was a pleasing and effective Agnes Carew, and Miss Katherine Rogers a capital Mrs. Lanyon, while Miss Helen Glidden made a hit as Rebecca Moor.

The stage was thoroughly well set and managed and the excellent scenery is by Messrs. Hawley and Emens.

New York Tribune, September 13, 1887[1]

RICHARD MANSFIELD AS DR. JEKYLL AND MR. HYDE.

It is about two years since Mr. Robert Louis Stevenson's grotesque and grisly story of the "Strange Case of Dr. Jekyll and Mr. Hyde" was published in this country. It soon began to attract attention; it is now in everybody's hands, and everybody may be presumed to know something about it. As a literary composition it is sketchy, fragmentary, almost curtly written, and roughly jointed. No doubt the form intended was the form of the documentary memorandum. There are readers who will think that a conception so fine and so absorbing ought to have been considerably expanded and symmetrically shaped, and that its text — which now reads like a first draft — ought to have been carefully rewritten. Nevertheless it is a work of originality and power, and one for which — as for all works of originality and power, especially in these days of excessive criticism — we ought all to be grateful. That such a story should have suggested a play is not surprising. Yet it is purely narrative in structure, and its dramatic elements, numerous and uncommonly strong, are all — as a chemist would say — in solution. Facts and incidents are merely stated. The culmination of the plot is reached in the middle of the narrative, and is then supplemented with an explanation. Perhaps also, the testimony and the description would have been truer to human nature, and thus more directly in the vein of the dramatists, had the author made a more thoroughly logical analysis of his own conception. Perhaps the *Dr. Jekyll* whom he has described is a sort of man who would be but little likely to take the mystic and transcendental track and turn into *Mr. Hyde*, and perhaps no man, having once travelled that dark road, could afterward exist without giving more numerous and more harrowing denotements of it — even in the brief interval that precedes his ruin and extinction — than are given by the *Dr. Jekyll* of the book. However this may be, the story has been turned into a tragic drama, which is a thoroughly good one — alert with incident, rapid and cumulative with action, various in character, fluent in

---

1. This review was written by William Winter, and forms the basis of Winter's assessment of Mansfield's *Jekyll and Hyde* in Vol. II of his "*Life and Art of Richard Mansfield*," pp. 35–46.

style, and graphic and vitally significant in picture and in meaning. This play was planned and sketched out by Mr. Richard Mansfield and made and written by Mr. Thomas R. Sullivan. It had its first representation on May 9 at the Museum in Boston. Last night it was brought out at the Madison Square Theatre in this city.

The thought upon which Mr. Stevenson built his story, and which likewise is made to sustain the fabric of this play, is stated in the words of the novelist, here extracted from *Dr. Jekyll's* confession:

> I saw that, of the two natures that contended in the filed of my consciousness, even if I could rightly be said to be either, it was only because I was radically both.... I learned to dwell with pleasure, as a beloved day-dream, on the thought of the separation of these elements. If each could be housed in separate identities, life would be relieved of all that was unbearable.... I began to perceive ... the trembling immateriality, the mist-like transcience, of this seemingly so solid body in which we walk attired. Certain agents I found to have the power to shake and to pluck back that fleshy vestment, even as a wind might toss the curtains of a pavilion.... I not only recognized my natural body for the mere aura and effulgence of certain of the powers that made up my spirit, but managed to compound a drug by which these powers should be dethroned from their supremacy, and a second form and countenance substituted, none the less natural to me because they were the expression and bore the stamp of lower elements in my soul.

In the allegorical sense there is a basis of significant truth in that fantastic reasoning. Human nature is composite. Human goodness would sink supine in sloth if there were not evil in the warp of things to compel it to action — evil being the agent in creation which never rests and cannot rest. Many persons no doubt go through life without ever once lapsing into vicious conduct. But most persons who from the summits of middle life look back upon the past are aware that they have sometimes had the consciousness of evil moods and impulses — a tendency in themselves so wrong that had it ripened into wicked acts, instead of ending in the conquest of good over bad, it would have alienated them from their better nature, and thus might almost be said to have changed their identity. When a good man consciously does wrong he has, for the time, ceased to be his actual self. The man who keeps on consciously doing wrong must eventually blunt his moral sense and weaken his power of resistance to evil, till at last he becomes incapable of reverting to his former state of virtue. The old theologians called this catastrophe the ultimate triumph of "original sin." The wiser scientists of today declare it to be the temporary predominance of that remnant of the brute in the human which evolution has not yet entirely eradicated and cast away.

In order to build a play upon this analysis or minute allegory of imagined, emblematic experience, it was necessary, first, to reject the intention to dramatize the book in such a manner as to reproduce it, and, secondly, to devise a scheme of innovation upon the original. There is a narrow order of the critical mind which, in a case of this sort, seems to feel a savage delight at finding discrepancies betwixt the play and the novel upon which the play is founded. Of course there are discrepancies. They exist in every similar case; they are inevitable; and, furthermore, they are essential. Just as a lecturer is not an actor, although each may treat a dramatic theme, so a novel is not a play, although both may relate to the same subject. The novel describes. The play exhibits. The novel is character in picture, clothed with description. The play is character in action, clothed with scenery. Once in a while somebody writes a novel so dramatic that it can, with just a few touches, be turned into a play; but this is rare. More often the novel must be greatly altered before its dramatic aspects can be released. Frequently portions of its material must be rejected to make way for material absolutely new. This was the necessity of the case in dealing with "Dr. Jekyll and Mr. Hyde." The dramatist has taken the essential idea of the book, its ground plan and its dramatic situations and incidents; but he has modified its characters and displayed them under changed conditions, and he has environed "the Strange Case" as well with an atmosphere of domestic life and love as with the otherwise unrelieved and monotonous investiture of weirdness and horror.

The movement begins in the home of *Sir Danvers Carew*, who is present in company with his daughter and their guests. Among the latter are *Mr. Utterson* and *Dr. Lanyon*. The time is evening and the scene is one of domestic comfort and repose. The theme of the play is opened by a talk between *Dr. Lanyon* and *Mr. Utterson*, in which *Hyde* and his savage cruelty are described. *Dr. Jekyll* comes upon this scene — a pale, sad man, forlorn and wistful, over whom it is instantly observed that trouble has cast an indescribable blight. But *Dr. Jekyll* and *Agnes Carew*, the daughter of *Sir Danvers Carew*, are betrothed lovers, and it is intimated that they are soon to wed. The girl cheers her lover, and will not hear his self-reproachful words. Presently the scene is cleared of all but *Sir Danvers Carew* and *Agnes*, who linger awhile, in affectionate talk of the past. Just as they have said "good-night," and are parting, the grisly and sinister figure of *Hyde*, emerging from the moonlight, glides into the room, through a great window at the back of it — a figure like *Jekyll*, yet most unlike him; shrunken, malevolent, repulsive, stealthy, insolent in demeanor, horrible in facial expression, irritating in voice, a loathsome image of depravity and menace. This wretched reptile coarsely commands the father to call back his daughter, and being repelled by the intrepid baronet, suddenly springs upon him and chokes and mauls him to death. The spectacle is very hideous, but happily it is soon over. Mr. Mansfield is an artist, and he does not linger upon any point that once is made.

The second act consists of three scenes. *Hyde* is shown in his secret lodging, where, with blood-curdling glee, he fills a cup of wine and pledges the ghost of *Sir Danvers Carew*. Mr. Mansfield has wisely and widely deviated from the novel by surrounding this miscreant with profuse, disorderly luxury — not that of taste, but that of exuberant sensuality — just as Ben Jonson indicates for *Volpone* and *Sir Epicure Mammon*. This scene shows the police in pursuit of *Hyde*, and ends with his escape through a secret door artfully devised within a mirror. He is next encountered entering the mysterious postern of *Dr. Jekyll's* cabinet, and there he is accosted by *Utterson*. The subsequent scene is within the cabinet, and *Dr. Jekyll* once more becomes the central figure.[2] Act third is occupied with the startling scene in *Dr. Lanyon's* house wherein *Hyde* mixes and swallows his drug and is visibly transformed into *Jekyll*. In act fourth *Dr. Jekyll*, immured in his cabinet, and shuddering on the verge of involuntary transformation into the brute that lurks within him, beseeches *Dr. Lanyon* to bring *Agnes* beneath the window, so that he can look upon her face for the last time. Mr. Mansfield here portrays a dying man. *Jekyll* is now doomed, and his better nature must take leave of all things that are good and lovely in this world. The tragedy and the pathos of it are that the parting is eternal. The girl is brought, but at the moment when he looks upon her the transformation is accomplished, and the imbruted *Hyde* — aware of his danger — swallows a quick poison and sprawls horribly into death.

In any field of art the portraiture of the monstrous is comparatively easy. A good actor can fill the measure of *Caliban* more readily than he can fill the measure of *Lear*. But the portraiture of the monstrous, if comparatively easy, is superlatively fruitless. Doubtless it enables the actor to make a startling display of his skill. The monstrous is almost always powerful. It is the crocodile or the cobra, and it frightens, or sickens, or horrifies. But a spectator derives no lasting benefit from a display of power and skill in this direction. Horror is barren, except of disgust. The late E. L. Davenport, in the full maturity of his extraordinary powers, set out to conquer a national popularity by playing *Sir Giles Overreach*. He played it marvellously well, and his great ability in it was recognized and admired; but, the better his performance was the more it was avoided. The character is a monster, and being merely monstrous it is hateful. Such creations, devoid of a human side — being neither brilliant, fascinating, conscience-stricken and rueful, like *Richard*, nor awful and pathetic, like the fiend-driven *Macbeth* — cannot be redeemed and commended to sympathy by any felicity, however great, of artistic treatment. Henry Irving's great performance of *Dubosc* — who, however, is more a human savage than a monster — derives its greatness partly from the actor's humor, but far more from its association with that superb image of beautiful purity and lofty heroism, the companion character of *Lesurques*, which is concurrently embodied by this same

---

2. After closing in Boston *Jekyll and Hyde* underwent "severe revision." See Appendix 1 (Winter Vol. I p. 58) The addition of this third scene in Act II appears to have been the most notable product of that revision.

man of genius. The two works are taken together, and they are felt and accepted as a wonderful and thrilling example of the variety of attributes which may exist within the scope of one and the same human mind. It is not simply a hideous aspect of reptile vitality that awakens our sympathy and wins our admiration; it is the potency of that manifold, impressive and touching significance which is expressed and conveyed to us in the correlation of beautiful and terrible attributes in one and the same being, and that being a human creature, made of the same materials that compose ourselves.

Mr. Mansfield depicts, with horrible animal vigor and with intense heat and reckless force of infernal malignity, the exultant wickedness of the bestial and frenzied *Hyde*—displaying herein a carnal monster of unqualified evil. It is an assumption remarkable for startling intensity and tremendous power. This actor possesses great volume of voice and great impetuosity of nervous force, and if this effort of his be viewed simply as execution, it furnishes brilliant and conclusive evidence of his exceptional resources and rare proficiency in the dramatic art. But Mr. Mansfield rises to a far nobler height than this—for he is able, in the concurrent and associate impersonation of *Dr. Jekyll*, to interblend the angel with the demon, and thus to command a lasting victory, such as his baleful image of the hellish *Hyde* could never, separately, achieve. This is the basis of his remarkable success. He is distinctly individual in each of the two characters. His dramatic art and his temperamental quality are as cogent in the one as in the other. But by concurrently embodying the two—by at once contrasting his two studies and blending them into one,—he has, substantially, displayed, under dramatic circumstances of unique and unflagging interest, a single image of human nature—the image of a man who is convulsed, lacerated, and ultimately destroyed by a terrific and fatal struggle, upon the theatre of his own soul and body, between those forces of good and evil which are inherent in himself, even as they are in each one of us. Here again the two works are taken together, and so taken they enthrall the imagination and deeply thrill the heart. This presentment is an awful and pathetic picture of a remorseful human soul, whelmed by the sin to which it has yielded, while struggling to avert the terrible consequences of its own self-murder. The actor's work diffuses the unfailing charm of spontaneous dramatic action, and in its magnetic quality, not less than in its strong enforcement of the essential moral truth that the deadliest peril of the immortal spirit lies in successive surrender to conscious iniquity, it is a distinct revelation of genius.

Three points might especially be indicated at which Mr. Mansfield conspicuously manifests imagination, creative dramatic power, and sympathetic emotion. The sardonic malignity of *Hyde*, when he pledges the ghost of *Sir Danvers Carew*, the inspired exultation with which *Hyde*, controlled by *Jekyll*, exhorts *Dr. Lanyon* before drinking the magical mixture, and the lamentable pathos of *Jekyll* when, as he takes his eternal farewell of beauty and goodness and life, he gathers into his hands a few flowers and tenderly gives them a parting caress, are in the most exalted mood and the highest manner of acting. The actor's transitions, also, are wonderfully fine. In act third *Hyde* changes to *Jekyll*. In act fourth *Jekyll* changes to *Hyde*. The transformation is wrought in physical bearing, in stature and demeanor, in facial expression, and above all, in what can only be indicated as the magnetic radiation of an interior spirit. As denotements at once of the man's soul and the artist's faculty this effect is eloquent and impressive in no common degree.

But the essential and abiding superiority of his impersonation is in his fine analysis of the nature of *Dr. Jekyll*, and his splendid adjustment of that nature to its terrible and most miserable conditions. Here were involved the retrospective quality—the quality in acting which discloses a whole life-time in a single glimpse—the sympathy, the redeeming humanity, the poetry, in one word the *justification* of the whole work. *Dr. Jekyll* in the book never inspires sympathy, but he constantly wins it in the play. Mr. Stevenson marks him out as "a large, well-made, smooth-faced man of fifty, with something of a slight cast, perhaps, but every mark of capacity and kindness"; and Mr. Stevenson makes him say; "It was rather the exacting nature of my own aspirations than any particular degradation in my faults that made me what I was and severed in me those provinces of good and ill which divide and compound man's dual nature." This recalls

Brinsley Sheridan's standard of virtue, which he said was so high that he could not possibly live up to it. Mr. Mansfield both rectifies and exalts the ethics of the subject by his finer ideal of *Jekyll*—who, a poetic enthusiast for occult science, has conjured up a spectre that he cannot lay and subjected himself to an impending doom that he cannot, by any self-sacrifice or expiation, avert. There are certain works—and works of merit, too—which stop short at personal display of the actor. They are pyrotechnics, brilliant while burning, but gone for ever as soon as they cease to burn. The supreme merit of this work of Mr. Mansfield's is that it far transcends personal display; that it comes home to every human heart and has a meaning for every human soul; and it at once gives him a place, as a tragic actor, among the men who are radically important to the age in which they live.

There are technical defects which no doubt will disappear. The tones of *Jekyll's* voice should be sweeter and not, as now, too often metallic. The love scenes lack passion. The make-up of *Jekyll's* face in the first scene should be less like the lineaments of a bandit. It was not till the death scene that his face seemed wholly true to his nature. The aspect of *Hyde* was a little defective in being over gruesome, suggesting that of a gnome in a fairy spectacle. It ought to be sinister and deadly—for dramatic purposes—and possessed of the hideous fascination of the adder. The general effect, however, was powerful and thrilling. There were four recalls at the end of act third and six at the end of the play. Miss Beatrice Cameron acted with deep feeling and sometimes with surprising force, to depict the growth of harrowing doubt and distrust in the bosom of a woman who deeply loves. Mr. Harkins played a difficult *Dr. Lanyon*, with studious and exemplary care. Katherine Rogers and Helen Glidden in the introduced characters of *Mrs. Lanyon* and *Rebecca Moor*, did good service to the piece. There are six sets of scenes, all good; and on appropriate air of mystery was artfully diffused over the entire drama.

Reviews of Mansfield's London Performances, 1888

Illustrated Sporting and Dramatic News, London, July 28, 1888

On Saturday week, August 4th, we are to see Mr. Mansfield's famous representation of Hyde and Jekyll at the Lyceum. With regard to the adaptation the *Spirit of the Times* has some remarks which may explain the remarkable success of the work: "One reason why Mansfield's Jekyll and Hyde has succeeded, while all others have failed, is quite apart from the acting of the dual part. Mansfield excels in that, but he displays his genius in the conception of the character. His Jekyll and Hyde is not in Stevenson's book, and therefore his imitators cannot get at it by dramatising the book. As it reads, the story is not dramatic. A proof of this is that nobody except Mansfield thought of dramatising it. If there had been a drama in the book itself, either the author—who is longing to be a playwright—or some other clever person would have dramatised it for Irving. Hyde is in the book, and how grand Irving would have been as that inhuman human monster! But Jekyll was the difficulty. The weak point of Stevenson's work as a story and as a psychological study is Dr. Jekyll. He is represented as a jovial, charitable, dinner-giving, alms-giving personage, except when he transforms himself into Hyde. This is Balzac's idea, and Gautier's and Daudet's, and after reading their tales of the transmigration of souls Stevenson dreamed out his Jekyll and Hyde. But it is the idea of two distinct souls in two distinct bodies, not of one soul divided between two bodies—the good part in one, the bad part in the other. Mansfield took Stevenson's suggestion, derived from the French authors, improved upon it, elaborated and completed it. Consider for a moment what Stevenson's Dr. Jekyll would be upon the stage without the veil of printed words. Here is a man who, as Hyde, murders, robs and ravishes,[1] and then, as Jekyll, becomes jolly, holds out to his friends the hand that has killed their friends, and jauntily gives away the wealth he has stolen. Why, thus represented, Jekyll would be more monstrous than Hyde himself. Mansfield, as we study his performance, evolves a nobler, subtler, and more logical conception. Hyde is all the base, brutal, vile, wicked part of Jekyll — that is, of human nature — eliminated and reincarnated. Consequently Jekyll becomes more and more pure, feminine, angelic as the play proceeds. He could not be jolly — he is crushed by remorse for the crimes he has committed as Hyde; he is in despair at the inexorable fate that binds him to his baser part and renders his resistance to the noxious drug weaker and weaker. Jekyll longs to die, to rid himself of a duality that he loathes, but were he to act as if he enjoyed himself he would appear to be a willing accomplice in Hyde's criminalities. This exquisite philosophical and psychological conception is the keynote of Mansfield's acting, and explains why, in spite of the unpleasant story, all audiences are fascinated by his Jekyll and Hyde. Alone, Hyde would horrify them. A jovial Jekyll in partnership with the hideous Hyde would revolt them. But we all sympathise with poor Jekyll as Mansfield impersonates him; we pity him; we know that he feels the same horror of Hyde that thrills us, and having thus won our hearts with one side of his dual character, Mansfield can make the other as terrible as possible. Ladies may faint when Hyde leaps upon his victim; but they will not leave the theatre while the fate of the gentle Jekyll remains undecided.'

According to the same authority the story goes that Mr. Bandmann decided to play Jekyll and Hyde because he was refused free admittance to Mansfield's performance. The doorkeeper did not know him — though not to know Bandmann argues oneself unknown — and thereupon he vowed revenge. "Ha! If I cannot see Jekyll and Hyde without paying, I will act it myself and make other people pay! Let M-m-mansfield tr-r-remble!" Revenge, like ice-cream, is sweet, but expensive, the narrator of this anecdote observes, and he goes on to suggest that Mr. Bandmann would have found it cheaper to put his pride in his pocket and take out the price of a ticket. Here, too, is another Hyde and Jekyll story: "What Stevenson thinks of the various versions of his book nobody knows. He has seen none of them acted. He receives regular payments from Mansfield; but he declines to call them royalties, as he had nothing to do with the dramatisation. The suggestor and creator of Jekyll and Hyde have never met. An interview was once arranged, at the untimely hour — for an actor — of 9 a.m., and Mansfield kept the appointment. A stepson of Stevenson received him and mysteriously said, 'I beg pardon, but I must really ask you one question before introducing you to Mr. Stevenson — Have you a cold?' 'Yes,' replied Mansfield, rather astonished, 'I have a cold, and it is a very bad cold.' 'Then,' said the stepson, 'I regret to say that it will be impossible for you to see Mr. Stevenson. He is in delicate health, and so sensitive that he takes any disease with which a visitor may be afflicted. You see for yourself, sir, that —' 'But,' interrupted Mansfield, his humour getting the better of his amazement, 'I have been suffering for some time with this cold, and I should like somebody to take it — in a friendly way, of course.' 'It is quite impossible,' said the stepson, unsmiling, 'quite impossible,' and he bowed Mansfield gravely and quietly away."

---

1. Although not explicit in either Stevenson's original or Mansfield's performance, it appears that Mr. Hyde was being thought of as some kind of "sex fiend" even before the confusion with Jack the Ripper.

Sunday Times, London, August 5, 1888

LYCEUM THEATRE.

After much preliminary advertising, in the form of adaptor's quarrels and legal injunctions, the first version of Mr. R. L. Stevenson's weird psychological romance, "The Strange Case of Dr. Jekyll and Mr. Hyde," was presented last night to an English audience; and in a most generous and patient spirit was it received, for the sake of the young English actor, Mr. Richard Mansfield, who, fresh from histrionic triumphs in America, has come to stand the test of English criticism under the generous and friendly auspices of Mr. Irving. It is not necessary to enter into any discussion as to the dramatic merits of "Dr. Jekyll and Mr. Hyde"—at all events, as adapted by Mr. T. Russell Sullivan—for this piece is not a play at all, but a series of episodes designed to give the actor opportunities for depicting the two distinct personalities of the dual man as conceived by Mr. Stevenson. The result, dramatically considered, is dismal and wearisome in the extreme, but as a study in strongly emphasised character-acting it is remarkable. Mr. Mansfield makes Dr. Jekyll a very maudlin and lugubrious young man, and the love interest is consequently incongruous and unsympathetic, for it is difficult to imagine any young lady, other than a sickly sentimentalist, putting up with such a sweetheart, much less adoring him to distraction, as Miss Agnes Carew is supposed to do. But contrast is everything in a case like this, and the complete change to the repulsive demoniacal and Quilp-like Hyde is all the more striking on account of the bland melancholy of the virtuous other self, Dr. Jekyll. Mr. Mansfield's first entrance in the character of Hyde created a profound impression, the hideous yelps and hisses of the loathsome creature, the sudden inhuman leap and murderous attack, and the fiendish gloating over the body of the murdered general, all combined to produce a startled and astonished sensation, mingled with admiration at the surprising cleverness of the actor. The applause was accordingly very genuine. The first scene of the second act was a repellant but remarkably skilful embodiment of Hyde in his own weird lodging, waited upon by a miserly old hag. And here and in the next scene, and again in the third act, the wolfish nature of the horrid creature was depicted with imaginative realism of a very powerful kind. Indeed, Mr. Mansfield won an undoubted triumph in the guise of Hyde, his quick change in the third act being extraordinary; but his acting as the maudlin Jekyll rather added to than diminished the deadly dulness of the play. The last act revealed some powerful touches on the part of the actor, but there was much monotony in it, and the audience seemed rather relieved when the curtain fell. Apart from Mr. Mansfield, the best acting was shown by Mr. Burrows as the old butler, Poole; while Miss Sheridan revealed some rugged force as the weird old hag. Miss Beatrice Cameron was as pleasing as possible in the part of the heroine. Mr. Crompton supplied a clever suggestion of comedy as a detective with a catch phrase; and Messrs. Harkins, Sullivan, and Holland played the other parts. Mr. Mansfield was loudly called, and addressed a few words of thanks to the brilliant audience, which included the Duke and Duchess of Teck, and many literary, dramatic, artistic and social celebrities. Mr. Mansfield achieved a great personal success.

Appendix C: Reviews of Mansfield's Dr. Jekyll and Mr. Hyde

The Daily Telegraph, London, August 6, 1888

LYCEUM THEATRE.

Mr. Richard Mansfield, the young actor of English birth and origin, of whom America is so justly proud, and who started on his career of management on Saturday night, has come to this country to win a success of esteem under conditions the most formidable and arduous that were ever self-imposed by an ambitious artist. Feeling the strength that was in him, conscious of a power yet undeveloped, and a fierce intensity that could not be restrained, his attention was—we think unfortunately—called to the morbid, unhealthy, and wholly undramatic brochure by Mr. Louis Stevenson, entitled "Dr. Jekyll and Mr. Hyde." Literary nightmares of the kind abound in fiction; but they have never in one single instance been found successful on the stage. Yet here was one in form, in design, in outline, in colour, in idea, about as ill-suited for dramatic representation as any story could possibly be. It need not be unsuccessful because it was weird; but the weirdness must be contrasted with the picturesque. "The Bells" has a weird subject; but how romantic and idyllic is the setting of the story! It need not fail because horror is accentuated; but then the horror must be tempered with human interest. How often must it be urged and insisted on that the startling in fiction is not dramatic as regards stage representation! In the stage sense, there is not one page in Mr. Stevenson's story that is dramatic. It is a morbid, unsatisfactory, gruesomely uncanny chapter of useless psychological analyses, unrelieved by one touch of humanity and unenlightened by the bright contrast that the stage properly demands. It is a tale of terror told in the dark, a creepy romance recited with the lights turned down. Such grim speculations as these are to be enjoyed by the dim light of the library lamp; but they are wholly foreign to the purpose of the footlights. We will not go so far as to say that an audience cannot be interested in a good ghost story, or that the pulses cannot be stirred with psychological problems and tales of mere terror, though it is on record that the Frankensteins and Vampires and all their uncanny brood have never been made welcome except in pantomimic form. But in "Dr. Jekyll and Mr. Hyde" we get far away from ordinary ghosts, goblins, sprites, and banshee warnings; we are admitted to the portals of the madhouse, whose shrieks and gibberings ring in our ears, we are led by the confiding dramatist into an "inferno" of unreason; the arch-fiend of this terrible story is no calm and mysterious ghost, no fascinating and impressive spirit, no friend from the other world, but is as he is presented to us—a sickening compound of greedy Ghoul, of hideous Leprechaun, and of dream-haunted Jabberwock. The mere contemplation of such a monster is enough to make any audience shudder and go home terrified in the dark watches of the night. Unfortunately again for Mr. Mansfield, the dramatist who has undertaken to popularise Mr. Stevenson's story on the stage has taken it for granted that everyone present has read the book. This is exactly what no practised dramatist ever does. It is not until we arrive at the middle of the play and listen to a dialogue between Jekyll and Dr. Lanyon that any one present unfamiliar with the story can make head or tail of what has occurred. It is as unsatisfactory as a dream, as disturbing as a nightmare. It is of the first importance that the whole scheme should be suggested in a prologue. The curtain should not have arisen five minutes before everyone's mind was satisfied of the double nature existing in one frame; of the awful wrestling between the good in Jekyll and the fiendish in Hyde; of the power to change shapes conveyed by a potent drug; of the soul-torturing of Jekyll when he finds that the evil instincts raging within him have instituted a morbid craving more potent than those caused by alcohol or lust. It should have been explained beforehand how it comes about that the wretched Jekyll has such lines of agony in his face, and by what extraordinary process all on a sudden a face more awful than any depicted by Gustave Doré appears in the moonlight at a window, and in another second a bat-like brute is springing at an old gentleman's throat, and doing him to death with his claws, amidst mumbled ululations and grim groans that can never have been heard before outside a padded cell in Bedlam. Of course, it was necessary to do something for Louis Stevenson's story, a love episode must be dragged in somehow, and it was useful in a dramatic sense to make Henry Jekyll in love with the daughter of Hyde's victim; but granted that these additions and suggestions help the lame story on to the stage, still the play remains no play at all, but an uninteresting jumble of ill-assorted scenes, a dramatic scheme prolonged by tableaux curtains, a mere vehicle for the display of the remarkable talent of a young actor, who elects to give an entertainment consisting of certain episodes in the life of Dr. Jekyll and Mr. Hyde.

It will be well, then, to dismiss the play from further consideration. It could not have lasted an hour had not the attention of the audience been arrested by the dominant power of the actor, who forced the story by the intensity he displayed in elaborating the revolting Hyde. Mr. Mansfield has, in the course of the piece, three great opportunities. The first is the murder of General Carew, which will be pronounced the most powerful and horrible thing ever seen on the modern stage. Jekyll has gone out with his pale, sorrowful face, and his airs of a melodramatic æsthete; Jekyll, so unlike the Jekyll of the book, has departed with his wavy gestures and transpontine flourishes, beloved no doubt in America. He is not a genial Jekyll, but a man already half consumed with the evil that is preying upon him, a modern Prometheus with the vulture of baseness and depravity gnawing at his liver. This dark-haired man with the ashen countenance has made his farewell to the family circle where he is beloved, the guests are gone, the lights are almost extinguished, and Hyde's victim is left alone in a semi-darkened room. Suddenly a face of terror appears at the window, a face so revolting in its ugliness and hideous depravity that a shudder seems to run round the house. It is not a man, or a beast, or a bird, but a nameless thing. It does not walk; it hops. It is a nightmare vision suggested by the bird of prey and the kangaroo. And yet it must be a beast, for it growls like an angry animal, and it has the suggestion of a man, for it jabbers and mows like a maniac. The thing, whatever it is, thirsts for blood. It shrieks for the love and possession of the old soldier's fair daughter; with impotent rage it hops and flaps about the room like an exaggerated bat; and then, without warning, it leaps from the floor straight at the old man's neck, the claw-fingers meet in his throat, and the ugly mass of fiend and man drop down to the floor with a soft thud. Then comes the horrible part when this demon-haunted man tears and kneads his victim to death, uttering meanwhile the most horrible groans, and muttered roars and dreadful imprecations. On this astounding picture the curtain falls. That such a scene could ever be palatable, that such morbid excess could be conscientiously recommended, that art has any fellowship or common ground with such gratuitous ferocity, we need not insist. It can only be pardoned by the extenuating circumstance of the actor's power — it can only be forgiven in that it foreshadows great gifts in the future which may be of immense assistance to the stage. The actor triumphed, for he held the audience. His nervous electricity caused silence throughout the house — the surest test of power. Badly done, such a scene would have created roars of laughter or have been hooted from the stage. But the curtain fell upon a shock of silence, followed by a roar of sympathetic applause, not for the scene, for it is indefensible, but for the actor, who is unquestionably clever.

The next chance came with the transformation of Hyde into Jekyll on the stage, before every inquisitive eye and apparently without any trick, adventitious aid, or help whatever. Hyde, as the hunted murderer, has fled for refuge to his friend Lanyon, who is in possession of the drug that can alone restore the brute to the man. It is a long, passionate, and perhaps the most interesting scene in the play. The fiend grovels and begs for the priceless drug; the man of the world, somewhat of a sceptic, for a time refuses. At last Lanyon yields, and the deformed, shapeless, withered Hyde sinks in a heap on the floor, feverishly mixing the drug by the light of the winter fire, the red glow falling upon his towsled hair and revolting features. There is a pause but of an instant, when, to the surprise and admiration of everybody, there arises, without screens, or gauzes, or traps, or anything, from the grovelling, ill-dressed jabbery mass on the ground, the well-knit frame, the well-dressed body, and the pale, calm, clear-eyed face of the renewed Jekyll. All this is most admirably done; and, though long ago the story had lost all interest, and its effect had been gravely discounted by that powerful first act, the audience once more broke out into applause, and talent, however unwisely exercised, received its reward. The third opportunity comes in the final act, when Jekyll, almost at death's door with despair, is under such mastery of the evil influence that he takes the last drop of the fatal drug that remains on earth, and for the last time becomes Hyde, who poisons himself before the law can arrest this inhuman monster and murderer. Were Mr. Mansfield as successful or as convincing in the character of Jekyll as he is as Hyde, this should be the most interesting and dramatic moment of the play. The torture of the good man overmastered by the preying and corroding evil; love, honour, respect, love of existence all sacrificed for the mad fascination of transformation; the sight of a strong man weakened and debased by a taste for depravity which has undermined his better nature and made him a drunkard in crime; the awful oncoming of the temptation; the feeling that the brutal Hyde is oozing through the pores and racking the frame of this poor distracted creature; the sudden rush to the looking-glass to see how much was demon and how much was man; all these things were foreshadowed, but not wholly grasped by the actor, who would be a genius indeed if he could be as impressive here as he is alert and pantomimic elsewhere. Here, at least, was a chance for that higher imagination which is the gift of great actors, and this scene, brilliantly played, might have mitigated some of the horrors that had gone before. But in effect this was Mr. Mansfield's weakest scene; it was clever in intention, feeble in execution. Everyone knew what the actor meant, but he had not quite mastered the difficulty of the position. There was naturally a pause of surprised horror when the shrivelled Hyde dropped on the floor, a debased and despised suicide, and the curtain fell; but whatever disappointment might have been caused by the recital of so uncanny and gruesome a tale, every possible encouragement was given to the actor, whose skill and power were clearly shown by the way he surmounted his difficulties. Those present soon recovered from the shock of the play; with an effort they pulled themselves together and generously turned to the actor whose talent is so pronounced. He was called out amidst every sign of appreciation for his cleverness; and, in reply to the inevitable demand for a speech, Mr. Mansfield, in a few earnest and sincere sentences, thanked the audience for its attention and encouragement, and said some graceful things about Mr. Henry Irving, who has taken him by the hand with a loyalty and generosity not usually found in this domain of art.

It will have been guessed that this is a one-part play, designed wholly for the exhibition of Mr. Mansfield's idiosyncrasies. But he was supported with great care and credit by a useful and clever company. Mr. Harkins, an actor of the old school, was of much value as the didactic Dr. Lanyon, and Miss Sheridan gave a very striking sketch of the miserly and revengeful Rebecca Moor, who hates and loathes the monster she is bound to tend. This strange person reminds one of the "dumb cook," Hester Dethridge, in Mr. Wilkie-Collins's romance of "Man and Wife." There is one thing that English actors and actresses might well learn from our American cousins, and that is the art of distinct speaking and clearness of enunciation. Every word spoken on the stage is heard, the sentences are not mumbled, and none of these American artists dream of dropping the voice at the end of the sentence. It is delightful to hear the text that is put down to be spoken not slurred, and if the modern English actor and actress could only occasionally listen to their muffled utterances, they would appreciate the rare merit in expression of Mr. Daly's and Mr. Mansfield's American companies.

Mr. Mansfield has come, he has been seen, and he has conquered as an actor of remarkable power and intelligence. Everything is before him, and we are glad to hear that he has yet to produce Octave Feuillet's "Roman Parisien" (a Parisian Romance) and a new play called "Nero." But let him be warned by experience, and turn his back upon so-called psychological studies that are gloomy, horrible, and without relief of tenderness, on the one hand, or cheerful comedy on the other. The modern stage does not require a dose of hideous stories, nor does it demand the dramatisation of dreams caused by painful indigestion or a course of opiates. These things may be clever, but they are not for the stage. They may interest the few, but they shock and disturb the many. However clever Mr. Mansfield may be in this *tour de force*, it would be unfortunate if his remarkable skill gave a taste for the vampire drama, or a succession of idealised nightmares and morbid horrors suggestive of the churchyard, the madhouse, and the bedside of the inebriate. The stage that welcomes all to its doors rightly eschews the appalling and welcomes all that is wholesome, natural, sympathetic, and merry. Except as a chance for bringing out a clever actor, "Dr. Jekyll and Mr. Hyde" could not possibly amuse, and will very probably shock many who are not particularly sensitive or fastidious.

Pall Mall Gazette, London, August 7, 1888

The Nightmare at the Lyceum.

Nothing more horrible has ever been seen on a stage than the appearance of Mr. Hyde in the moonlight at the drawing-room windows of Sir Danvers Carew. Imagine a crouching imp of stunted stature, misshapen and crook-backed, halting in his gait, a mass of towzled black locks covering his forehead, his eyes glowing like coals, without teeth, and varying his raucous bass tones with hisses and gasps, and you have a feeble idea of the compound of Quilp and Caliban which leaps with an awful cry on the breast of the terrified baronet, bears him to the ground, and chokes the breath out of him. Who can wonder that a murmur of fear and horror runs through the shuddering audience? This scene concludes the first act of the Lyceum version of Mr. Stevenson's psychological study, and is far the most striking of the three chief situations in the play. The second of these is the extraordinary change before the eyes of the audience from Jekyll to Hyde, the third being the highly effective scene in the laboratory in which Jekyll is in momentary expectation of becoming the obscene Hyde, the one occasion when Jekyll rises above the walking gentleman. We believe that Mr. Mansfield claims to have improved the original character of Jekyll by making him grieve for the hideous sins of his evil half, but it is difficult to understand how an actor who is possessed of such abilities as Mr. Mansfield should show us a Jekyll who is a mixture of a smug young shopwalker and an aesthetic curate, who wishes to be well with the ladies. That is Mr. Mansfield's idea of Dr. Jekyll, whom we have hitherto regarded as a clever scientific gentleman with the very devil inside him. In the last episode of a play that is only a series of episodes, Jekyll becomes for once a remarkable man. Imagine him locked up in his laboratory, fitted up, by the way, like the retreat of a mediaeval Faustus, pacing to and fro in mortal agony. The drug, which was once so potent in effecting convenient transformations, cannot be procured in its native purity, and with its purity its potentiality has gone. Hyde has become the master of Jekyll, who is in momentary fear of the terrible transformation, and once Hyde he knows he is a doomed man, for Hyde is wanted for the murder of Carew. So great is Jekyll's agony that he writhes in unutterable torments before he dares to lift his hands from his face to test his features by the mirror. Fine as was this effort, it does not bear repetition, and Mr. Mansfield will be wise if he consults the glass once only. The horrible struggle continues until Jekyll sees through his window the figure of Agnes Carew, the daughter of the baronet whom as Hyde he has murdered, and to whom he was betrothed. A fearful cry of despair is heard, and Jekyll disappears for ever. The malignant Hyde leaps down the stage, swallows the poison which is on the table, and falls in his death throes just as the door is broken in and the detectives enter the room.

It would be impossible to make an effective stage play of Mr. Stevenson's little book. Mr. Sullivan, who is responsible for this version, has assumed that every one is familiar with the grim story, which is surely a great mistake. Until the third act no one, unless he happens to have read the book, could for the life of him appreciate the fiendish pranks of Hyde, or the melancholy rhapsodies of Jekyll. A young lady and a little love were supposed to be necessary, and Sir Jasper Carew is given a daughter, to whom Jekyll is engaged. And thus are the horrors piled up, higher and higher, as

Jekyll becomes through Hyde the murderer of the father of the girl whom he is to marry. One of the best passages in Mr. Stevenson's book is the description of the search for Hyde in Soho. This den, exterior and interior, is the scene of the second act. "Two doors from one corner, the line was broken by the entry of a court; and just at that point a certain sinister block of buildings thrust forward its gable on the street. It was two storeys high; showed no window, nothing but a door on the lower storey and a blind forehead of discoloured wall on the upper; and bore in every feature the marks of prolonged and sordid negligence. The door, which was equipped with neither bell nor knocker, was blistered and distained. Tramps slouched into the recess and struck matches on the panels; children kept shop upon the steps; the schoolboy had tried his knife on the mouldings; and for close on a generation no one had appeared to drive away these random visitors or to repair their ravages." Such is the exterior of Hyde's den in the purlieus of Soho, admirably reproduced on the stage, in which part of the second act takes place, shifting presently to the interior, which presents a striking contrast to its external aspect, with its lofty walls, and an equipment which is apparently luxurious. Hither comes Hyde, pursued by detective and lawyer, and another horror is added in the person of the raving miseress who acts as Hyde's housekeeper. The third act takes place in Lanyon's consulting-room, in which as the neighbouring clock strikes twelve Hyde appears, in compliance with Jekyll's note, to obtain the transforming drug from Lanyon. Here, amid thunder and lightning, Hyde swallows the powder and becomes Jekyll before the audience. The murder of Carew is the most terror-striking of Mr. Mansfield's efforts, because it is so grotesquely horrible, and takes the audience by surprise, but it is over in a few seconds. The scene with Lanyon is prolonged, and calls forth all the actor's powers. The facial change, which is made with extraordinary rapidity, is a remarkable *tour de force,* and is effected without the intervention of the wigmaker. And not less remarkable is the change from the penetrating, raucous tones of Hyde to the musical but sonorous voice of Jekyll. Then comes a brief episode in Jekyll's hall, followed by the final scene in the laboratory, upon which the curtain drops. So ends a most horrible play, which will, we believe, attract all playgoers by the extraordinary impersonation of the abominable and apish Hyde. It makes your flesh creep; the auditorium is in semi-darkness for the greater part of the evening, there is absolutely no relief from the sombre, but we venture to prophesy Hyde will draw crowds in London just as it has done in America. The critic may curse the morbid and the horrible, but the craving for them is deeply rooted. Scratch John Bull and you find the ancient Briton who revels in blood, who loves to dip deep into a murder, and devours the details of a hanging. If you doubt it, ask the clerks at Mr. Smith's bookstalls, ask the men and women and boys who sell newspapers in the street. They will tell you. For the same reasons, then, a great many people will go to see Mr. Mansfield's Hyde. The Lyceum nightmare, by the way, lends itself admirably to burlesque. Hyde's hiss (produced by a respiration through his clenched teeth) may become as familiar as the war-whoop of Buffalo Bill's Indian warrior. We may perhaps express a hope that the 'possum-like leap with which he pounces on his victims, and the claw-like paw with which he strangles them, may not suggest a new method to the garrotter.

The Sunday Times, London, August 19, 1888

THE LYCEUM.

Mr. Mansfield gave his first morning performance yesterday. There was a full house. Many prominent actors and actresses were present. "Jekyll and Hyde" was given, it seemed to us, with more "go" and better effect than heretofore. Mr. Mansfield, as Jekyll, had discarded the Hyde hat and wore the silk *chapeau* of ordinary life.[2] His Jekyll was more vigorous and manful than on the first night, and the working of the entire play has improved. The dual studies were yesterday received with great favour. Mr. Mansfield has now quite recovered from his hoarseness, and the management intimates that the paragraph announcements of "The Parisien Romance" are premature.

Pall Mall Gazette, London, September 1, 1888

THE TRANSFORMATION IN "DR. JEKYLL AND MR. HYDE."
HOW IT IS DONE BY ONE WHO KNOWS.

Now that half stay-at-home London has been thrilled by Mr. Mansfield's tremendous impersonation of Mr. Hyde, everybody is asking how the marvellous transformation from Mr. Hyde to Dr. Jekyll before the very eyes of the audience is accomplished; but no one has yet been forthcoming to explain the mystery. Let me step into the breach — not with the immediate intention of showing "how it's done," but rather with a view to warning the play-going public off the usual track, and telling them how it is *not* done.

It may well be imagined that so startling, and withal so powerful and artistic, a feat could hardly have been performed nightly for twelve months in the United States without the inquiring and ingenious American mind being set vigorously to work to penetrate the secret. Such, indeed, was the case; but so well was that secret kept, that no hint escaped to the outside public, and even the keenness of the ferreting journalist was for once at nought. At Louisville (so runs the record in an American paper) its dramatic critic sat out the play for three consecutive evenings, armed with strong opera-glasses; but to no purpose. At last a reporter of St. Louis burst forth upon a relieved world with what he called "Mr. Mansfield's Exposure," publishing a statement that rapidly went the round of the press.

Here is his story, together with his alleged discovery. Having been refused admittance as a reporter at the rehearsals, he disguised himself as a workman, and obtained a situation as scene-shifter. When in this capacity he kept his eagle eye fixed on the actor during the course of the play, arriving thereby at the following conclusions: "To begin with, the face is made up for Dr. Jekyll. Above the eyes and about them the cavity is coloured a dark red — not the red that is put upon the face for health, or used on the cheeks for the actors, but a dark red used for lining wrinkles." After some more very detailed description of this sort, he went on to explain that a mask of thin rubber fixed on to the wig, and is so made as to remain in position over the face as required. The wig, he said, is a trick wig, with the hanging hair (for Hyde) on a spring piece that allows this fringe to turn over back or down over the forehead. "The spring of the wig that turns down holds the top of the mask in place. The bottom of the mask is attached to two rubbers that are intended to draw it out of sight and into Jekyll's collar. These rubbers are extended, but are kept from acting by being fastened to his collar-but-

---

2. This change of hats clothed Dr. Jekyll in the fashion that was to become the classic image of Jack the Ripper.

ton, which takes the pressure from the mask. As Hyde (in the scene in Dr. Lanyon's office) is taking the medicine, he clutches at his throat, releases this button, and with the next movement, the spring of the hair and the mask flies out of sight. The play of the hands over the face conceals its passage. As for the hands, they are white and simply turn green in the light — a calcium light being thrown through a green gelatine plate.

Now all this sounds very ingenious and plausible, but, in spite of the circumstantial character of this description, *there is absolutely no truth whatever in it*— more's the shame to "journalism."

I can affirm (1) that there is no rubber mask, or mask of any sort, kind, or description; (2) that there are no rubbers or springs; (3) that there is no spring to the wig. There may be a collar-button — there probably is; I won't quarrel about that; but I know that it has absolutely nothing to do with the "change."

The wig is an innocent wig, in which there is no guile. I examined it only yesterday, when it was being re-dressed by Mr. Fox, the maker, and so I know. The only peculiarity I noticed was that it is rather heavily pomaded — that, in fact, the hair which is brushed back from the forehead on either side of the parting was somewhat weighty with grease; the effect being that, whether the matted hairs were brushed back or pulled forward, they kept their place with curious docility. I stuck the wig on my closed hand, and, amused at the experiment, I made my fist a Hyde or a Jekyll one at will.

How then does Mr. Mansfield make so extraordinary a change in his person without mechanical aid? How, from the yellow, shiny-faced, impish, deformed, twisted, shock-headed, hateful, diabolic thing, as he first appears at the window (a mixture, he has been called, of cold shiver, nightmare, and *delirium tremens*, which may well account for the fainting of a lady last Tuesday night), how does he become before our eyes the tall, well-made, eminently respectable and well-cared-for professional man? By means of six things: (1) the change of attitude, (2) of facial expression, (3) of voice, (4) of make-up, (5) of arrangement of his coat, and (6) by the manipulation of the gas. Thus, when he cries "Behold!" and swallows the potion out of the *empty* glass, he straightens himself, allows his poor distorted features to return to the places appointed by nature, opens the coat and turns down its collar, rubs the outside coat of "make-up" off his face (leaving that of Dr. Lanyon underneath visible); and, as he changes from the gurgling and raucous "Ah! ah! ah! ah! ah! ah! ah!" to the plaintive and deeply-musical "Lanyon! Lanyon!" the gradually-rising gaslight is turned on full.

Now, when I had an interview with the actor some weeks ago and asked him what apparatus or other unusual appliance was used, he replied, not without a touch of reproof in his voice, that the change was effected entirely without adventitious aid. The use of masks or other appliance, he declared, would not only be inartistic and illegitimate, but downright farcical; and that he only used such materials as in every actor's make-up box — grease-paint, rouge, lining-pencil, and powder. But on the ground that he objects, for the sake of art, to too intimate a relation between actor and public, considering that the footlights should be between them, and the public not invited into the actor's dressing-room, he declined to explain his little secret. Satisfied that I have solved it by other means, I give my explanation without fear of contradiction, either from the actor himself or from those of the public who have already witnessed, or will go to witness, this remarkable performance.

So far as I am aware, this play is the only one in which an actor tries to double two parts, which in character, appearance, and individuality are at opposite poles. Mr. Irving as Duboscq and Lesurques in "The Lyons Mail," Mr. Righton as the Bishop and the drunken waiter in "Twins," and many other dual characters, from Shakspeare downwards, have oftentimes been done before, and the method of their quick changes explained in print. But "Dr. Jekyll and Mr. Hyde" form a precedent as interesting from the curiosity of the transformation as it is from the psychological study presented by this "strange case."

The Era, London, September 1, 1888

Mr. Richard Mansfield

To the Editor of the Era.

Sir,—It has been reported that Mr. Mansfield, as Dr. Jekyll and Mr. Hyde, employs a trick wig and a rubber mask, or close-fitting skin cover, for his face. Permit me to say that Mr. Mansfield's wig is of the ordinary kind, without springs or other mechanical devices, and that he does not use a rubber mask, a skin cover, or adventitious aid of any kind. The transformation in the third act is accomplished by change of facial expression and of bearing, and with such trifling effects of make-up—including the powder-puff—as are employed by every actor. Mr. Mansfield throws back his hair, brushes the pallor from his face with a swift movement of the hands, stands erect, and Edward Hyde has given place to Dr. Jekyll.

I am, Sir, your obedient servant,

E. D. PRICE.
Lyceum Theatre, Aug. 30th.

The Daily Telegraph, London, September 18, 1888

Lyceum Theatre.

Mr. Richard Mansfield has happily recovered from the sharp attack of rheumatism which kept him a prisoner on Saturday, and compelled him to close the theatre. That grim but fascinating nightmare known as "Dr. Jekyll and Mr. Hyde" is well worth a second visit by all who would attentively study the finished detail and daring realism of the young actor's art. It is well-nigh impossible to take the mysterious dose at one gulp. The imagination is so stirred, the nervous system is so quickened, and anticipation is so alert that it is very difficult to preserve the critical faculty during the hurried scenes of so extraordinary a play. What nervous woman can attend to the dialogue when she knows a pistol is going off on the stage? We can describe the result, but cannot properly analyse the method while we are waiting for Mr. Mansfield's bogey. It is, however, worth studying, and the high praise he has received is well deserved. He has acquired fame at one bound, as Mr. Irving did when he astonished every one with his performance in "The Bells," and now he may safely and conscientiously be advised to bid a kindly adieu to Mr. Louis Stevenson and all his morbid imitators. The beautiful and not the horrible is the highest attainment in art after all. The recent outrages in the East of London, the dread of a sudden presence, the horror of the unexpected, may have given a fillip to the mouthings and jabberings of this loathsome Hyde; but those who admire Mr. Mansfield's observant power and sudden intensity must long to see him well clear of the moral deformities that will be pressed into his artistic service. His next play will be anticipated with interest, for, however much we may deplore the realistic force expended on such monstrosities, and the employment of stage devices for the elaboration of such inhuman distortions, the actor who can conquer us into attention is one of no ordinary capability.

The Era, London, September 22, 1888

"DR. JEKYLL AND MR. HYDE."

The production, on Monday last, of a new "first piece"[3] at the Lyceum Theatre, gave us a second chance of seeing Mr. Richard Mansfield as Dr. Jekyll and Mr. Hyde, in Mr. T. Russell Sullivan's dramatisation of Mr. R. L. Stevenson's novel. Our opinion of the talent displayed by the actor in following the lines he has either laid down for himself or had laid down for him by the adaptor was in no way altered by another hearing. Mr. Mansfield's Hyde is as ghastly a mixture of Quilp, Quasimodo, and the "Man Cat" of the old Victoria Theatre as can be imagined, and his acting on Monday, after his enforced absence, attributed to an acute attack of rheumatism, from both performances on the previous Saturday, was as thrilling as before. Any criticisms we now add to our previous notice apply more to the adaptation than to the histrionic talent of the principal performer; but as Mr. T. Russell Sullivan dramatised the piece "for" Mr. Mansfield, the latter can hardly be excepted entirely from the range of our gentle objections. The vital defect of the authorised dramatisation of the novel is that the grim and deep moral suggestiveness of the book is eliminated. The value of Mr. Stevenson's work was that, without any deliberate or obtruded moral lesson, he preached an awful sermon to all of us. It is distinctly stated that before Jekyll discovered the drug he tampered with vice, and with vice in its more reprehensible forms. His ultimate subjection to and absorption by the Hyde section of his divided personality was the terrible punishment of his first secret sins and subsequent devotion of his occult science to evil purposes. It was for these, and not, as Mr. Sullivan's Jekyll says, "for the benefit of mankind," that Jekyll first used the drug. There is too much of the melancholy and virtuous martyr about the stage Jekyll, and hardly enough of the sombre gloom of the remorseful sinner. Nor, throughout the whole of the play, are Jekyll's character and motives explained or demonstrated, or the depiction of the man carried below the surface. The same characteristically "stagey" defects are necessarily found in the actor's embodiment of the personage. His Jekyll is as much too sentimental as his Hyde is, to our taste, too grotesque. The Hyde of the book is not an ordinary theatrical monster of the *For Ever* sort, but an individual with an extremely repulsive expression and personality. A creature wheezing, jumping, and twinkling his hands and fingers as the stage Hyde does would be followed by crowds through the streets of London. In Mr. Russell's adaptation probability has been sacrificed to startling theatrical effect. Something may have been gained in the way of immediate success by the alteration, but much is lost; for the melodramatic peculiarities of Hyde come at times very near to being comic instead of horrible. Of course, in all stage work it is impossible to omit a certain graphic and necessary exaggeration; but the spirit which humours popular taste in advance may be carried too far, and we cannot help wishing that, in dramatising Mr. Stevenson, Mr. Sullivan and Mr. Mansfield had given us a little more moral and intellectual depth, and rather less striking exaggeration. But, accepting the views taken by the adaptor and actor as wise ones, there can be no two opinions as to the excellence of Mr. Mansfield's impersonation. Particularly fine, indeed, was his facial expression in the last act, in the scene where Jekyll feels the terrible change coming over him against his will. This piece of acting, on a second acquaintance, seemed to us the most emphatic and undeniable, as it was certainly the most legitimate and important, item of Mr. Mansfield's success. By convulsive twitches of the muscles of the face, the features and expression of Hyde could be seen actually invading the mask of Jekyll; then, after a terrible and intense effort, the surface became calm again. Mr. Mansfield's work in this otherwise rather monotonous act reached a high level of histrionic achievement, and showed that he was capable of better things than the clever "quick-change" trickery and apish horrors of previous portions of the play.

---

3. This new "first piece" was Richard Davey's one-act classical comedy, "*Lesbia*," introduced by Mansfield to precede *Jekyll & Hyde* on Monday September 17, 1888.

Mr. Harkins as Dr. Lanyon.— Mr. Harkins's Lanyon, with its bluff matter-of-factness, is an excellent contrast to Mr. Mansfield's sad and sickly Jekyll; and is consequently very valuable to the cast.

Mr. Sullivan as Gabriel Utterson.— Mr. Sullivan has a peculiar accent, or trick of delivery, as though, so to speak, he were trying to swallow a brogue, which, at times, detracts from the finish of his performance; but his friendly lawyer, though not much resembling the Utterson of the book, is a decidedly creditable piece of work.

Mr. Crompton as General Danvers Carew supplies a useful and valuable comedy character to the piece; and Mrs. Sol-Smith as Mrs. Lanyon is mildly amusing.

Mr. Burrows as Poole and Miss Glidden as Rebecca Moor may be bracketed in praise for the agreeable absence of exaggeration, and the quiet carefulness and finish of their respective performances.

Mr. Frankan as Inspector Newcomen devotes much pains to his brief part, and does not over-emphasise a catchword which might easily have been made tiresome.

Miss Beatrice Cameron as Agnes Carew.— Miss Cameron, though seldom before the audience, plays so earnestly and intelligently in the scenes in which she does appear as to leave a very favourable impression, a result all the more creditable considering the poorness of her opportunities.

Appendix D: Daniel E. Bandmann's *Dr. Jekyll and Mr. Hyde*

Richard Mansfield's rivalry with Daniel E. Bandmann, played out in the pages of the London press during the summer of 1888, helped promote Mansfield's production and ensured that *Jekyll and Hyde* remained in the news in the weeks leading up to the Whitechapel murder sensation.

Mansfield's proposed tenancy of the Lyceum was first reported in London in February 1888:

> A New York correspondent telegraphs that Mr. Henry Irving has offered the tenancy of the Lyceum theatre, London, for the months of September, October, and November, to Mr. Richard Mansfield, who will produce *Dr. Jekyll and Mr. Hyde*, with American artists, himself taking the title-roles. Mr. Mansfield is one of the most versatile actors of the day.[1]

Later reports confirmed September 3, 1888, as Mansfield's Lyceum opening. By July 6, however, *The Star* was reporting: "We may possibly have Mr. Bandmann's version of 'Dr. Jekyll and Mr. Hyde' at the Opera Comique in a week or two. Mr. Richard Mansfield will not like this." At this time London's Opera Comique Theatre was occupied by Mrs. Bernard-Beere's presentation of *Masks and Faces*, which was to end on July 21.[2] This theatre would then be vacant until Bandmann assumed his tenancy on August 6. In order to prevent Bandmann advancing his opening night, temporary tenancy of the Opera Comique was secured from July 22 until August 5.[3] Mansfield's scattered company were hurriedly reassembled and embarked from New York aboard the *City of Rome* steamer on July 11, arriving in Liverpool on July 19.[4] The circumstances attending this embarkation were related in *The Star*:

> MANSFIELD JEKYLL, AND BANDMANN HYDE.
>
> There is such a spice of enterprise in the sudden departure of Richard Mansfield and his "Dr. Jekyll and Mr. Hyde" company for England a few days ago, says the New York World, that its recital will prove interesting. The facts of the flight have not been given previously. It was a thing that was done on the spur of the

---

1. *Lloyd's Weekly Newspaper*, February 19, 1888.
2. *Lloyd's Weekly Newspaper*, July 15, 1888.
3. See Appendix A (Winter Vol. 1, p. 90) and Appendix B, p. 104.
4. The ship's departure and arrival dates are taken from the *Daily Telegraph's* Shipping Intelligence, July 12 and 20, 1888, respectively.

moment. There was no long premeditation about it. Mansfield and his manager, Mr. Price, had a conference on Monday last regarding the move made by Daniel Bandmann to get to London in advance and open there one month ahead of Mansfield's date at the Lyceum. A portion of the Mansfield company had already secured passages in the City of Rome, which was to sail on Wednesday. They were going over to spend their vacation in England prior to commencing their fall campaign of acting. They did not dream for a moment that they would be called upon to act until the date originally fixed. Mr. Mansfield and Mr. Price came to the conclusion that something should be done to euchre Bandmann, and that something was to get to London as quickly as possible, and, when there, endeavor to alter the date at the Lyceum, and instead of giving "Dr. Jekyll and Mr. Hyde" to the London public after the Bandmann version had been seen, to let them have it before. The "Dr. Jekyll and Mr. Hyde" company, or the greater portion of them, were scattered all over the country—some at Lake George, another in Maine, and two in the mountains. Then the passenger list of the City of Rome was full. This difficulty was quickly straightened out and by midnight Mansfield and all his people were aboard the steamer.[5]

On July 16, advertisements in the London press announcing Mansfield's Lyceum appearance, at some still indeterminate date, began to appear:

> LYCEUM.—DR. JEKYLL AND MR. HYDE.—In preparation, the drama, in which Mr. RICHARD MANSFIELD will appear, founded, by the author's permission, on Mr. Robert Louis Stevenson's novel.[6]

The following day advertisements announcing Bandmann's intention to open at the Opera Comique on August 6 began running in the press:

> OPERA COMIQUE.—Mr. F. J. Harris, Lessee; Mr. John Lavine Manager.—Every Evening, at 8.15, commencing MONDAY, Aug. 6 (Bank Holiday), MR. DANIEL E. BANDMANN in his successful version of DR. JEKYLL AND MR. HYDE, supported by Miss Louise Beaudet and a London company.[7]

It was only from July 21, however, two days after his arrival in England, that a definite date of August 4 was advertised for Mansfield's Lyceum premiere:

> LYCEUM.—SATURDAY, August 4, at 8.15, appearance of RICHARD MANSFIELD in the dramatisation by Russell Sullivan, by permission of Robert Louis Stevenson, of THE STRANGE CASE OF DR. JEKYLL AND MR. HYDE.—Box-office (Mr. J. Hurst) open Wednesday next, July 25, from ten till five.[8]

With Mansfield's primacy seemingly regained, attention turned to Croydon's Theatre Royal where provincial actor/manager Howard Poole intended to stage his representation of Stevenson's weird tale on Thursday, July 26, 1888.[9] Timely court action on the part of Longmans, Green & Co., however, foiled Poole's aspirations, ensuring his version was never staged, and establishing Mansfield as the sole person authorised to present *Dr. Jekyll and Mr. Hyde* in dramatic form in the United Kingdom. *The Star* reported the details on July 27:

> NO JEKYLL AND HYDE AT CROYDON.
>
> A version of "Dr. Jekyll and Mr. Hyde" was advertised for first performance for yesterday evening at the Croydon Theatre, but owing to the action taken by the solicitors to Messrs. Longmans and Co., who are the owners of the copyright, the performance was withdrawn at the last moment. Mr. Justice Stirling granted special leave to serve notice of motion for injunction on Mr. Bandmann, in conjunction with the performance advertised at the Opera Comique.[10]

The same day the following notice began appearing alongside Mansfield's advertisements:

> DR. JEKYLL AND MR. HYDE.—Messrs. Longmans and Co., as owners of the copyright of "The Strange Case of Dr. Jekyll and Mr. Hyde," beg to state that Mr. RICHARD MANSFIELD, of the LYCEUM THEATRE, London, is the SOLE PERSON AUTHORISED to present it in dramatic form

---

5. *The Star*, August 1, 1888.
6. *Daily Telegraph*, July 16, 1888.
7. *Daily Telegraph*, July 17, 1888.
8. *Daily Telegraph*, July 21, 1888.
9. *Croydon Advertiser*, July 28, 1888.
10. *The Star*, July 27, 1888.

Appendix D: Daniel E. Bandmann's Dr. Jekyll and Mr. Hyde

in Great Britain and Ireland, and that, under the recent decision in the High Court of Justice, any other person copying or colourably imitating any portion of the above work will be proceeded against without further notice.

KAYE and GUEDALLA, Solicitors to Messrs. Longmans and Co., 21, Essex-street, Strand, London.[11]

At this point Bandmann's manager, Mr. John Lavine, entered the fray when, on July 29, *Lloyd's Weekly Newspaper* reported:

Last night we received the following letter:

TO THE EDITOR OF "LLOYDS."—DEAR SIR,—In the absence of Mr. Bandmann, who is expected hourly to arrive in England, allow me to state I am advised that the version of Dr. Jekyll and Mr. Hyde Mr. Bandmann intends to produce is no infringement whatever of Messrs. Longmann and Co.'s copyright, and that we have a perfect right to perform this version at the Opera Comique, on Monday, August 6, as advertised.—Respectfully, JOHN LAIME, Manager.[12]

In an attempt to contest the "sole authorised version" status now regularly accompanying Mansfield's advertisements, Bandmann's adverts began to include:

DR. JEKYLL AND MR. HYDE.—Bandmann's successful version. Endorsed by Mr. Robert Louis Stevenson as "a triumph of art and stage realism."—EVERY EVENING, at 8.15, commencing Aug. 6.[13]

The Mansfield camp countered with the following:

Mr. Mansfield and Mr. R. L. Stevenson.
Mr. E. D. Price, Mr. Mansfield's manager, requests us to publish the following correspondence:

"Skerryvore, Bournemouth, 18 June, 1886.
"My Dear Sir,—I have to thank you for your very polite communication. I am sure from its terms that Jekyll will be in good hands, and I have no doubt (as you say) that the venture can do me only good. I wish you all success in what appears to me a difficult undertaking, and, once more thanking you, remain yours very truly,
"ROBERT LOUIS STEVENSON.
"T. R. Sullivan, Esq."

"Saranac Lake, N.Y., 22 February, 1888.
"My dear Mr. Mansfield,—Many thanks for your agreeable letter, and for the cheques. I am still in bed and far from well, and I am sure you will excuse the baldness and brevity of this acknowledgement. Some day I shall hope to meet you, perhaps also Dr. Jekyll and Mr. Hyde; and meanwhile, I remain with thanks, yours very sincerely,
"ROBERT LOUIS STEVENSON."

"Saranac Lake, 12 March, 1888.
"To the Editor of the New York Sun.—
Sir,—It is my pleasing duty to inform you—and I am sure it will be yours to make the information public—that Mr. Mansfield has proved an exception to the general rule. From Mr. Sullivan (the author of Mr. Mansfield's version) I have met with every civility, and from Mr. Mansfield himself I am now in receipt of monthly cheques. That version is fully authorised by me.—I am, &c.,
"ROBERT LOUIS STEVENSON."

"Saranac, N.Y., 13 March, 1888.
"Dear Mr. Mansfield,—I hope you will not mind my having written to the papers. These misunderstandings make it necessary I should be very plain, and not only repeat that your version is duly authorised, but make public your handsome treatment of myself.—I am yours truly,
"ROBERT LOUIS STEVENSON."[14]

Mansfield's manager again went to press the following day with:

"DR. JEKYLL AND MR. HYDE."—Mr. E. D. Price, manager for Mr. Mansfield, writes from the Lyceum Theatre, July 30:—"To prevent any misstatement of facts, permit me to say Mr. Henry Irving was kind enough to secure the Opera Comique for a limited period on behalf of his tenant and friend Mr. Mansfield,

---

11. *Daily Telegraph*, July 27, 1888.
12. *Lloyd's Weekly Newspaper*, July 29, 1888. The same letter, this time with the correct spelling of Lavine's name, appeared in some of Monday's dailies, including the *Times* July 30, 1888.
13. *Daily Telegraph*, July 30, 1888.
14. *The Star*, July 30, 1888.

that the latter's Lyceum production of Dr. Jekyll and Mr. Hyde next Saturday evening should not be forestalled. If Mr. Bandmann had requested permission from Mr. Mansfield to use the Opera Comique stage for rehearsals, it would have been instantly granted. No such permission has been asked.[15]

This assertion was refuted by Lavine the next day:

> "DR. JEKYLL AND MR. HYDE."—Mr. John Lavine, manager for Mr. Bandmann, writes from the Opera Comique Theatre, July 31:—"Allow me to state facts in connexion with Mr. Bandmann and his London company and rehearsals on the stage of the Opera Comique. In a reported interview in an evening journal of July 27 I glean the following:—'Here Mr. Mansfield's eye twinkles merrily. "Well, Sir, until my first night at the Lyceum the Opera Comique has been taken by me, and before Mr. Bandmann can enter that house, even for a rehearsal, he will have to ask my leave." "Which of course he will get?" Again a merry twinkle.' To the above I would add that the stage-door keeper has informed our company that he has positive orders from Mr. Irving's representative not to allow any member of the company to enter the theatre, and that even our announcements on the theatre boards have been covered over with blank paper by his orders."[16]

Despite being thwarted in his efforts to gain early access to the Opera Comique, Bandmann played his final card in an attempt to upstage his rival. Believing he had secured a one-night tenancy, the actor invited members of the press and other notables to a full dress rehearsal of his *Jekyll and Hyde*, scheduled for Friday, August 3, at the Olympic Theatre. Perhaps mindful of impending court action, however, the management of the Olympic refused to allow public access to the theatre and, on the morning of the scheduled rehearsal the following notice appeared in the press:

> DRESS REHEARSAL OF DR. JEKYLL AND MR. HYDE.—OLYMPIC THEATRE.—A Card—In consequence of the positive refusal of the lessee of the above theatre to admit the Press and those invited, it is out of Mr. Bandmann's power on the short notice given to fulfil his promise. It is left to the public to draw their own conclusion. The play will positively be performed on MONDAY NEXT at the OPERA COMIQUE.[17]

August 3 also saw representatives of both sides meet in court, with the fullest details of the hearing appearing in the morning papers the next day:

> LAW INTELLIGENCE
> CHANCERY DIVISION, Aug. 3
> (Before Mr. Justice STIRLING.)
> LONGMANS V. BANDMANN.
>
> This is an action at the instance of Messrs. Longmans, Green, and Co., publishers, owners of the copyright in Robert Louis Stevenson's novel, "Strange Case of Dr. Jekyll and Mr. Hyde," and there was this morning a motion to restrain the defendant, Daniel E. Bandmann, the well-known actor, his managers, agents, or servants, "from printing or otherwise multiplying copies of a certain tale or novel, written by Robert Louis Stevenson, and published by the plaintiffs, entitled "Strange Case of Dr. Jekyll and Mr. Hyde," or any portion thereof, and from making any use of copies thereof heretofore illegally or unlawfully printed or otherwise multiplied, and from doing any act or thing in invasion, or infringement, of the plaintiffs' copyright in the said tale or novel until the trial of the action, or further order."
>
> Mr. Graham Hastings, Q.C., for the plaintiffs, said that he had to inform his lordship that the parties had come to an arrangement in regard to this matter. The allegation was that the copyright had been infringed by making a play which was announced to be performed on Monday, but Mr. Bandmann now said he was willing to give an undertaking in the terms of the notice of motion.
>
> Mr. Buckley, Q.C., (Mr. Ingpen with him), for the defendant, said he only wished to state this: Mr. Bandmann wrote this play about the month of March this year, but before writing it he communicated with Mr. Stevenson, the author of the book, and obtained his permission to dramatise the novel and perform the play. He wrote the play and produced it in America with great success, with Mr. Stevenson's knowledge and approval, and Mr. Stevenson witnessed the play and expressed his ap-

---

15. *The Times*, July 31, 1888.
16. *The Times*, August 1, 1888. Mansfield's comments referred to by Lavine in this letter can be found in the interview with *The Star*, July 27, 1888, reproduced in Appendix B of this volume.
17. *Daily Telegraph*, August 3, 1888. See also Appendix A (Winter Vol. I, p. 95–96).

proval of it. It took so well in America that Mr. Bandmann resolved to bring it over here, and he sent a copy over and had it lodged with the Lord Chamberlain. He himself was at sea, on his way over to this country, when it was first learned that Mr. Stevenson was not the sole owner of the copyright. That was learned after the writ in this action was issued, and as soon as he learned that Mr. Bandmann's agent withdrew the copy of the play which had been lodged with the Lord Chamberlain. Mr. Bandmann had, since then, rewritten the greater part of the play, and had removed all the passages that he had taken from the novel while he was under the belief that Mr. Stevenson was the owner of the copyright. He had now lodged the new book, which was not the same as the old, with the Lord Chamberlain, and it was this play that was to be produced. He wished to say also that it was to have been performed in full dress rehearsal to-night (Friday) at the Olympic; but the lessee of the theatre had in the circumstances raised objections, so that the rehearsal had necessarily been postponed.

His lordship: The order will not interfere with that now.

Mr. Buckley: Then I am quite willing to give that undertaking.

Mr. Graham-Hastings: Perpetual injunction, and with liberty to us to apply?

His lordship indicated ascent.

Mr. Buckley then added that the parties treated this as the trial of the action, and that the question of costs had been arranged.[18]

August 4 saw the following advice offered by the *Pall Mall Gazette*:

As the Fauntleroy case protects only the dialogue of a novel, not its plot and idea, Messrs. Longmans had to content themselves with Herr Bandmann's undertaking to re-write such portions of his "Dr. Jekyll and Mr. Hyde" as were "lifted" from Mr. Stevenson's text. The result, so far as Mr. Stevenson is concerned, is that in all probability a worse play will be fathered upon him than would otherwise have been the case. But how about the title? As soon as the Lyceum version is produced, Mr. Mansfield could surely (if he thinks it worth while) prevent Herr Bandmann from using the now famous name of "Dr. Jekyll and Mr. Hyde." It is true that Mr. Mansfield has no legal standing in this country until his play is produced to-night, and that between Saturday evening and Monday evening he can take no steps; but as soon as a judge is available he could probably vindicate his claim to the title. The better policy, no doubt, would be to let Herr Bandmann alone. The two plays will advertise each other.[19]

Such advice notwithstanding, the presentation of Bandmann's adaptation of *Jekyll and Hyde* at the Opera Comique on August 6 brought the parties back to court.

LAW INTELLIGENCE.
CHANCERY DIVISION, AUG. 9,
(Before Mr. Justice STIRLING.)
LONGMANS v. BANDMANN.

Mr. Graham Hastings, Q.C., for the plaintiffs (Longmans, Green, and Co.), in the action to restrain the defendant, the well-known actor and manager, from infringing their copyright in Mr. R. L. Stevenson's novel, "Strange Case of Dr. Jekyll and Mr. Hyde," mentioned the case before his lordship this morning. He said his lordship gave him leave to serve notice of motion to commit the defendant for breach of his undertaking not to infringe their copyright. Mr. Bandmann brought out the play at the Opera Comique on Monday, and, according to plaintiff's evidence, it was an infringement; but Mr. Ingpen, for the defendant, was willing to give an undertaking not to perform the play in London and the United Kingdom until over the second motion day in the next sittings.

Mr. Ingpen said that, owing to legal proceedings having been commenced in this court against himself and Messrs. Baring Brothers, and the course taken by Baring Brothers in consequence, defendant found it necessary to close the theatre last (Wednesday) night. It would be difficult to re-open it until he communicated with America; so that, without admitting that he infringed the previous undertaking, he would consent to the motion standing over, as his learned friend had said.

His lordship, without prejudice to any questions, thereupon allowed the matter to stand over.[20]

This action, and its continuance on November 30, 1888, effectively ensured that, after just two performances, Daniel E. Bandmann's adaptation of *Jekyll and Hyde* would not be repeated in London.

18. *Daily Telegraph*, August 4, 1888.
19. *Pall Mall Gazette*, August 4, 1888.
20. *Daily Telegraph*, August 10, 1888.

Dr. Jekyll and Mr. Hyde

A PLAY IN FOUR ACTS.[21]

This play is the sole property of DANIEL E. BANDMANN Garick Club, Garick Street, London.

Produced at the Opera Comique August 6th, 1888.

CHARACTERS

Henry Jekyll M. D.
Edward Hyde
J. G. Utterson, A lawyer of Chancery Lane
Rev. Wm. Howell, Vicar
Dr. Lanyon, Of Harley Street
Inspector Newcomen, Of Scotland Yard
Poole, Dr. Jekyll's Butler
Guest, Mr. Utterson's Clerk
O'Brien, A Policeman
Fielding, A Policeman
Bradshaw, Dr. Jekyll's Groom
Lilian Ross, Mr. Utterson's Niece
Mrs. Viley, A Hag
Maria, Dr. Jekyll's Housemaid
Sarah, Dr. Jekyll's Cook
Sybil Howell, The Vicar's Daughter
Choristers, Servants, Policemen &c.

ACT I

The Vicarage R. Jekyll's House L.
Church at the back with a low wall from J's House running to church, practical door. The garden must be full of flowers &c.

(At rise of Curtain Children heard singing grace in the Vicar's House at the end of song bell rings at little door in the wall from J's House.)

(Enter Poole — Butler to Dr. Jekyll)

---

21. This version of *Dr. Jekyll and Mr. Hyde* was granted Performance Licence No. 193 by the Lord Chamberlain's Office on July 23, 1888, for presentation at the Opera Comique Theatre, London. The manuscript is now part of the British Library's *Lord Chamberlain's Play Collection, ref: Add 53408K*. While obvious typing errors have been corrected, in order to convey a sense of Bandmann's style and the hurried rewriting of his script, the often peculiar punctuation , grammar and wording are reproduced in the following script.

POOLE. There's a ring at the back entrance they might leave us in peace on Sunday's; the doctor's life is not a bed of roses. (*Opens gate — Enter Servant in livery*) What do you want?

SERVANT. I want to see Dr. Jekyll.

POOLE. Well you can't see Dr. Jekyll. This is Sunday. Don't you know any better than coming in the back way. He is taking his tea at the vicarage and I am not going to disturb him, but I'll deliver your message as soon as he comes out. What is it?

SERVANT. Lady Dunsville sends her kind regards to Dr. Jekyll and wishes to see him at once if possible. (*Handing in card*)

POOLE. Alright, I'll deliver your message.

(*Exit Servant through door in wall L.*)

POOLE. By the way I think I'll go into the vicarage too, and have a cosy Sabbath cup of tea with Mira.

(*Exit Poole behind vicarage R.*)

(*Enter Vicar and Utterson from house R. Both coming down stage smoking*)

UTTERSON. Come, let us smoke our cigarettes in the open air and talk of the good old days when you and I used to take long rambles through the streets of London. Ah those were happy days.

(*Vicar Xing to L. and sitting*)

VICAR. Why should they not be as happy now? Are we not content in our quiet peaceful homes without excitements and their natural temptations, we have all we want.

UTTERSON. As for that William I'm not intolerant you know, I let my neighbour go to the deuce as he pleases.

VICAR. Hush, Utterson, what profanity.

UTTERSON. Its true I don't help mind a poor sinking devil occasionally. But on the whole I mind my own business and I my drude[22] work, have my long walks and shall no doubbtout out[23] a frizled up dried out matter of fact lawyer.

VICAR. Life is at the best but a dream, and there are some which appear to us more real than life itself, What would you say if I in my prosaic existence were to relate to an incident that pen can hardly describe.

UTTERSON. I would call it a very singular case but what is the incident?

VICAR. First let me ask you, have you ever seen a man without a soul.

UTTERSON. Certainly who has not.

VICAR. Every body in the sense you mean; but not in mine; for the first time in my life I have seen a being who has neither a soul or any thing human about him, and the memory of that vision produces a revulsion in my nature from which I shall never be relieved until my dying day—

UTTERSON. You excite my curiosity, let me hear your story.

VICAR. It was on a calm winter's morn, when I came home from a visit to one of my sick parishioners, It must have been five o'clock, and a very dismal morning too. The streets were quite deserted, and the dullness of the night was most oppressive. I began to feel nervous when suddenly a shrill cry sounded through the air which was evidently that of a child, I wending my steps to the place whence it came and turning to my right I saw to my amazement in a narrow court a figure standing over a little boy, and pounded away at him for a dear life. I took a hold of the ruffian and I looked into his face, such a face as I shall never forget as long as I live; It makes me sick to think of it, a miserable shrunken figure, half dwarf, half man, but with an expression of brutality so horrible that every sinew in my body seems to weaken at the very memory of it.

UTTERSON. Go on, this is exciting.

VICAR. I plucked up all my courage, and wrenched the stick from his hand in spite of his superhuman strength —"What do you want snarled he into my face with a voice I cannot describe. Half comic, half human, half animal, "I want you said I, I'll teach you how to pound away on this

---

22. "*drude*" is the text that appears in Bandmann's script
23. "*doubbtout out*" is the text that appears in Bandmann's script.

poor little half starved boy — and I'll hand you over to the police" — having quite recovered my usual equilibrium and seeing a crowd gather round us who were ready to back me, I became defiant. That word Police seemed to have struck him with terror so did the threatening glances of the crowd. "Police snarled he what's the good of that. Here are a few sovereigns for the brat's wounded feeling which are more sensible than your — police."

UTTERSON. (*Laughing*) A very logical remark.

VICAR. So it struck me looking at the poor little starving creature — Monetary compensation to him and his people would be far more practical than legal punishment to that wretch. But I was not going to accept a few sovereigns so I demand fifty pounds.

UTTERSON. (*Laughing*) Bravo William. You ought to have been a lawyer.

VICAR. He winced, bit his lips, and as there was but Hobson's choice for him hailed a cab invited me and the boy and his father who by that time had arrived to enter, and drove us to a busy street near Seven Dials where after alighting he suddenly disappeared before a dilapidated old house.

UTTERSON. And that was the last you saw of him;

VICAR. So I thought, but to my amazement after waiting for a few minutes in the cab, an old woman approached us handed us a cheque with the words "Here are your fifty pounds" and before I could question her she had withdrawn too.

UTTERSON. The cheque was a forgery of course.

VICAR. That's what I feared, but I wasn't to be done in such a clumsy manner; so I got out of the cab knocked at the door through which I had seen the old hag disappear and was about to make my demands heard when to my amazement the horrible creature approached me with the words; "I see you have some doubts as to the validity of the cheque — I will stay out here with one of you while the other can go to the bank and have it cashed.

UTTERSON. The deuce.

VICAR. I drove down to the bank with a full expectation of meeting with a forgery — when to my surprise the cheque was cashed and not a question asked.

UTTERSON. And what was his name?

VICAR. I shall never forget it — it has impressed itself with a horror upon my memory I seem him standing before me now, a being without a heart, soul or mind — an illustration of everything that is evil, in fact an incarnate Satan.

UTTERSON. But what was his name.

VICAR. Edward Hyde.

UTTERSON. Edward Hyde!!

VICAR. Yes, do you know him?

UTTERSON. Never saw him in my life —

VICAR. You may congratulate yourself upon that and I hope you never may.

UTTERSON. I say Amen with all my heart, but promise that you will never mention that name to me again.

VICAR. With pleasure! (*Children heard laughing from Vicarage*) But I must prepare for evening service, my lambs are calling.

(*Exit Vicar into house*)

UTTERSON. (*alone*) What is the meaning of this? Hyde! Hyde! I thought that name was erased from my memory I looked upon it as a myth — but know that I heard it again and described in such glaring colours brought before me once more in all its objectionable attributes. Jekyll has made a will in favour of this Hyde. Why and wherefore? What connections has he with this brutal man? What intimacy? The will says distinctly that all his fortune is to go to him if Jekyll should *suddenly* disappear, why disappear? And why in that case, should *Hyde* become his heir. A brutal, low bred fellow without soul, heart or mind as the vicar puts it. This is beyond my powers to understand. (*Enter Poole*) I say Poole is the doctor going out to day?

POOLE. I believe he is sir. I am ordering his carriage now.

UTTERSON. Tell him before he goes I would like to see him. (*Wrapt in thoughts*)

POOLE. Certainly sir.

Appendix D: Daniel E. Bandmann's Dr. Jekyll and Mr. Hyde

(*Enter Lanyon from Centre gate addressing Poole*)

DR. LANYON. Is the Vicar in?

POOLE. Yes Dr. Lanyon.

UTTERSON. (*Looks up at the word of Lanyon*) Lanyon, the very man I want to see.

DR. LANYON. Hulloa, Utterson, glad to see you.

UTTERSON. What brings you here?

DR. LANYON. I drop in occasionally on Sundays it's a easy day for us you know; besides Sybil is a favourite of mine; she is my little pet.

UTTERSON. No wonder she looks pale having two doctors to take an interest in her.

DR. LANYON. Ah! So Dr. Jekyll is here.

UTTERSON. Of course, of course.

DR. LANYON. That's one of my reasons for my visit here today.

UTTERSON. Ha! Ha! I see. Jekyll is getting dangerous eh?

DR. LANYON. Exactly.

UTTERSON. I say Lanyon I have perceived lately that you and Henry are no longer on the same good terms. Anything wrong?

DR. LANYON. Nothing whatsoever. My dear friend Dr. Jekyll and I are on the same footing as before, we merely differ in our scientific views, he has opinions of his own.

UTTERSON. You are well acquainted with all his friends, aren't you?

DR. LANYON. Certainly, so are you.

UTTERSON. Do you know one among them by the name of Hyde?

DR. LANYON. (*careless*) I can't say that I do.

JEKYLL. (*Jekyll outside*) Good bye Vicar I shall see you presently. Utterson! Utterson! (*As he Enters*) You want to speak to me. Hallo Lanyon how are you? Haven't seen you for an age. I never expected to see you here. You're growing a little grey my boy.

DR. LANYON. We're all subject to such changes, Henry, so you had better take a good warning in time. It's some time since we met.

JEKYLL. Your fault, not mine.

DR. LANYON. Perhaps, is the vicar at home?

JEKYLL. Yes, you'll find him inside with Sybil and the choir boys as usual on Sundays.

DR. LANYON. I'll go in for a moment shall I see you when I return?

JEKYLL. No, I'm called away professionally.

DR. LANYON. Then I'll say good bye to you now. Good bye gentlemen.

(*Exit in Vicar's house.*)

(*During this Poole has helped his master on with hat, etc and return into Jekyll's house.*)

JEKYLL. (*at table lighting a cigarette*) Well, Utterson, are you going to stay here?

UTTERSON. No, I have to take Lilian home.

JEKYLL. Then I may not see you again, then I will say good bye to you, too.

UTTERSON. One moment Henry, a word with you.

JEKYLL. Oh yes. You want to see me, anything particular?

UTTERSON. No, no. I merely want to ask you about that codial

JEKYLL. My dear boy don't bother yourself about that will, you would really oblige me to drop that matter and for ever.

UTTERSON. You know my opinion upon the subject.

JEKYLL. Of course I do and that is the very reason why I request you to drop it.

UTTERSON. I'm astonished that you associate with such a fellow

JEKYLL. Who says so?

UTTERSON. Nobody, but since you made a will in his favour, I take it that he is very dear to you.

JEKYLL. Have you ever seen him?

UTTERSON. Never! And never hope to.

JEKYLL. Why do you trouble yourself about him?

UTTERSON. Because I am your friend and adviser, and it is my duty to warn you,

Henry you know I would go through fire and water for you. Is there anything wrong?

JEKYLL. Oh no, no my friend. You are mistaken, you are really mistaken, there is nothing wrong, that man's life and mine have nothing akin to each other, he is merely a cipher in my existence, a cipher that I can wipe out at any moment I do so desire. Now, be content and don't ask any more questions, please.

UTTERSON. Well, I suppose I must, if you put it in that way.

JEKYLL. But there is one thing I do ask which you must sacredly promise.

UTTERSON. And that is?

JEKYLL. The execution of my will, whatever may happen. For you know that you are my executor.

UTTERSON. I will on my condition if you don't change your mind in the interval.

JEKYLL. Thanks, friend, thanks.

LILIAN. (*Lilian outside*) Good bye Sybil, I'll see you tomorrow. (*Runs on from house R.*) Well, Uncle I am ready if you are.

(*Poole Enters from house*)

POOLE. The carriage is at the door doctor.

UTTERSON. Poole, order me a four-wheeler.

JEKYLL. No need of that I'll take you home.

UTTERSON. If it is not to much out of your way.

JEKYLL. Not at all, and it will be a pleasure to enjoy Miss Lilian's company a little longer.

LILIAN. Oh Doctor, you make me blush I shall be as proud as a peacock to ride in the carriage of the famous Dr. Jekyll. (*Making curtsey*)

JEKYLL. Now, now, take care I shall punish you for that, and if you are not good I shall make you read this evening to us some of your uncle's dry divinity.

LILIAN. Don't say another word, doctor. I shall be as good as honey. (*Laughing running off L. 3rd U. E.*)

(*Jekyll and Utterson laughingly go off through door in little wall. Poole comes down steps.*)

POOLE. How everybody likes the doctor. No wonder. He is such a king, good genial man. By the bye I think I will go in and finish that cup of tea with Maria.

(*Exit Servant's Entrance at the Vicar's.*)

(*Boys heard laughing inside. Sybil Enters runs L to flower bed. Bus. Followed by Lanyon.*)

DR. LANYON. Sybil how is it that you have all these choir boys here?

SYBIL. Papa loves boys and occasionally I give them a Sunday tea between the afternoon and evening service. This is so kind of you Dr. Lanyon to gives us a visit. We see very little of you lately. Now, you will stay till after service and spend the evening with us won't you?

DR. LANYON. Impossible! I have but little spare time, you know we doctors are not our own masters.

SYBIL. I know that only too well I am sorry to say. Look what little time poor dear Dr. Jekyll has to himself. Two thirds of his life are devoted to his fellow men.

DR. LANYON. It is on that subject that I wish to speak to you. Will you forego for once the evening service and devote a few minutes to me?

SYBIL. With pleasure, if papa does not object. (*Bus. of Children to all run on laughing, followed by Vicar who comes Centre.*)

DR. LANYON. Vicar, I have asked Sybil to miss the service this evening, she does not feel well enough, and the beautiful air will benefit her.

VICAR. You are her medical adviser and she is but to obey, shall I see you after service?

DR. LANYON. I fear not.

VICAR. Then I will say good bye now. Don't be so long a stranger in the future my boy. Good bye.

(*Children together Good bye Miss Sybil.*)

SYBIL. Good bye boys.

(*Organ music — Bus. Hymn sung by the Children They file two by two into the church. Bus. of the Vicar &c. &c. Vicar Exits into church.*)

DR. LANYON. (*Dr. L and Sybil; come down*) So you don't see Dr. Jekyll often, Sybil?

SYBIL. No, he is always out, working for poor humanity.

DR. LANYON. Dr. Jekyll has a warm heart, but —

SYBIL. A warm heart indeed; I never knew a man so generous and unselfish. Why do you know doctor, he actually spends hours of his most valuable time playing and caressing little charity children and his office is always inundated with the poor and needful.

DR. LANYON. Indeed. I fear my advise comes too late. You seem to take a warm interest in Dr. Jekyll?

SYBIL. I do. And if it is on that subject you wish to speak to me and I strongly suspect it is, for I am no longer a child you need go no further, for I have fully made up my mind and I know what I do.

DR. LANYON. It is on that subject, but I fear I am too late

SYBIL. You are; we understand each other.

DR. LANYON. Perfectly?

SYBIL. No, but just as well.

DR. LANYON. But you are so young, think of the discrepancy in your ages, you twenty and he —

SYBIL. Oh I answer with Desdemona "I saw his visage in his mind"

DR. LANYON. Well, if it has gone so far, I say no more; I am too old to convince a woman in love against her will and to sensible to hold my tongue. God bless you my child, and although I do not like Dr. Jekyll for reasons I do not comprehend he certainly has a noble nature and may make an excellent husband; I sincerely hope he will.

(*Bus. and Exit.*)

SYBIL. He does not like Dr. Jekyll and yet he admits that he has a noble nature, how can he explain such a contradiction? Oh it is only a whim of the dear old doctor's which we must try to dispel; that will not be very difficult for Henry's influence over his fellow men his overpowering; he is so gentle and kind. How I love him, often I cannot understand my own self, since my childhood I have been wilful, daring, and high-spirited, but since I have met Henry my whole nature has under gone a change. (*Singing in church; Enter Jekyll*) How sweet are those sacred tunes, children's voices there dwells peace and love. Henry!

JEKYLL. My sweet girl alone not in church?

SYBIL. Dr. Lanyon asked me to stay and spend the evening with him.

JEKYLL. Oh that pedant! Were you not bored? He is so dull.

SYBIL. How is that two such brilliant men can have such bitter feelings towards each other?

JEKYLL. Things that you would not understand and that we had better leave untouched keep us apart.

SYBIL. Not understand, Henry; you say that, you who introduced me into the mysteries of our glorious arts taught me your science how to extract poison out of flowers, to read men's thoughts, how to love and be loved.

JEKYLL. Better had I not done so, Sybil. There are two natures in every man one of good and one of evil which divide and compound man's duel character, and he it is who can always keep the evil counterbalanced by the good who is the happiest and most deserving of men.

SYBIL. That is your nature, Henry, and for that I love you.

JEKYLL. You judge with loving eyes and therefore prejudice. Were I such a nature and could infuse it into others life would indeed be deprived of much that is unbearable. What good might not be done by one who could keep mankind from its inheirit[24] wickedness, needeth to a upright stedfast life and countercheck man's ingrafted evil.[25]

---

24. "*inheirit*" is the text that appears in Bandmann's script.
25. "*needeth to a unpright stedfast life and countercheck man's ingrafted evil*" is the text that appears in Bandmann's script.

SYBIL. But love Henry levels all these things the good as well as the bad.

JEKYLL. Not the bad Sybil. There must be some spark of good, some affection to lean upon or the most undying love finds no response. Look at an instance upon the story of Faust and Margerite Faust bargains his soul to the devil and is forgiven because of his undying love for Margerite. Margerite ascends to heaven, she had but sinned in loving Faust, the devil alone stands cheated of his bargain because of his satanic nature there is not one spot of love. Love reigns supreme throughout the universe, in heaven or on earth, in the airy regions or the masy substantials,[26] every animal cries, every bird sings, every animal that has the germ of life in it reads but in that one rapturous delight, that one little word love.

SYBIL. (*Running across stage*) And such shall be our ours.

JEKYLL. What are you doing?

SYBIL. Imitating Margerite.

JEKYLL. Great God what's this? A change is approaching I must rush into my room and get my powders or I am lost

SYBIL. You are not going yet.

JEKYLL. Only into my room; too late, too late. (*Change to Hyde — Stage darkens.*)

SYBIL. How dark it suddenly is growing I must run into the house. (*Turns and sees Hyde.*) Who are you?

HYDE. No matter.

SYBIL. What do you want here?

HYDE. You.

SYBIL. Get out of the way fellow; let me pass or I shall call for help.

HYDE. No you won't.

SYBIL. Dr. Jekyll!!

HYDE. Don't call him; I hate him; I'll kill him if he comes.

SYBIL. Why what has he done to you?

HYDE. No matter, I hate him.

SYBIL. Stand back fellow, and let me go.

HYDE. No I won't. I want you; your beauty excites me. I love you, I like you.

SYBIL. Father! Father!

(*Enter the Vicar from church in robes, comes down centre of stage rescues Sybil and recognizing Hyde.*)

VICAR. Ah, the fiend!

(*Hyde attacks him, stuns him with stick and after throttling him leaves him apparently dead on the ground, and Exits into house L.*)

(*Enter Poole Sarah, and Servant.*)

POOLE. I thought I heard Miss Sybil. Great Heavens is she dead!

SARAH. No, she has but fainted.

POOLE. She, she recovers.

SERVANT. But here lies someone dead.

SYBIL. (*recovering*) Dead! Oh horror, father murdered!

ALL. The Vicar!

(*Enter Jekyll from house L.*)

JEKYLL. Why, what's the matter?

SYBIL. Father murdered!

JEKYLL. Oh, by whom?

VICAR. (*gasping*) Hyde!

ALL. Hyde!!

Curtain.

---

26. "*masy substantials*" is the text that appears in Bandmann's script.

ACT II

Room at Utterson's.

(Discovered talking Detective and Utterson, the former standing Centre of stage, the latter seated R. of table L.)

DETECTIVE. This unnatural murder has shocked London, and you might aid us very considerably, no more saw this Hyde except Miss Sybil. She and this broken stick is the only evidences we have against him.

UTTERSON. Great Heavens! The same I gave to Jekyll.

DETECTIVE. Any evidence there?[27]

UTTERSON. No, no, no, What is this Mr. Hyde like?

DETECTIVE. From all accounts like nothing that has been seen before, at least so his landlady says; he lives in very comfortable lodgings by himself, near Soho, in a very disreputable quarter of London. Upon a thorough rout out of his room we found that he had evidently destroyed all evidence against him.

UTTERSON. And what did you find?

DETECTIVE. The remnant of a burnt pass book showing the deposits of two thousands pounds.

UTTERSON. And is this all you have so far discovered?

DETECTIVE. Yes at present. But I think we shall soon find out a great deal more, the old hag, his landlady has a good deal to say, we are pumping her and she will no doubt tell all.

UTTERSON. Don't be too sure of it. Know one has seen this Hyde all disagree as to his appearance[28] except as to one fact, he seems to be a dwarf.

DETECTIVE. And that's the clue I'll catch him on. No matter how many disguises he may assume, unless he is the devil himself I'll have him on the hip on the hunch I might say.[29] But when can I have an interview with the young lady?

UTTERSON. Today if you desire it, Mr. Newcomen. As the oldest friend of her father and his late legal adviser I took her into my house on that dreadful day, but she wishes to see you so you had better remain here Mr. Newcomen.

(Enter Servant)

SERVANT. Dr. Jekyll desires to see you, sir.

UTTERSON. Certainly, show the doctor up.

(Exit Servant)

Mr. Newcomen would you kindly step downstairs for a moment I'll send for you shortly.

DETECTIVE. Certainly, Mr. Utterson, certainly.

(Exit)

UTTERSON. What a labyrinth of mysteries.

(Enter Jekyll)

I'm glad to see you well again, Henry.

JEKYLL. Oh yes, I'm better in body.

UTTERSON. But in mind?

JEKYLL. There I am ill, quite ill.

UTTERSON. Henry, the vicar was our mutual friend, a villain has murdered him, an incarnate fiend. Where is he?

JEKYLL. Great Heavens, how do I know?

UTTERSON. He stands under your protection.

JEKYLL. No, no, I swear to you no. I know nothing of him. Want to know nothing of him. Have not seen him and never hope to meet him again. The very thought of him fills me with terror.

---

27. This line is a *handwritten* replacement for the typed but deleted text "*Will this led to anything?*" in Bandmann's script.

28. "*Know one has seen this Hyde all disagree as to his appearance*" is the text that appears in Bandmann's script.

29. "*I'll have him on the hip on the hunch I might say*" is the text that appears in Bandmann's script.

UTTERSON. How can I be sure of what you say?

JEKYLL. (*handing him a letter*) Read this.

UTTERSON. A letter from whom?

JEKYLL. Hyde!

UTTERSON. How do you come to have it?

JEKYLL. It was left in my study, by whom I cannot tell.

UTTERSON. And what do you want me to do with it?

JEKYLL. I want you to read it, to prove my innocence.

UTTERSON. (*reads*) "To Dr. Henry Jekyll.

When you read this I shall be far beyond the reach of human power, but I cannot depart without expressing my gratitude to one who has been kind and generous to me, perhaps, the only one who ever has or ever will be. Edward Hyde."

JEKYLL. Are you satisfied?

UTTERSON. I am. Why not hand this over to Scotland Yard.

JEKYLL. In that case how would that touch me?

UTTERSON. It might incriminate you, it is better in my safe. Ah Henry in what a fearful position you have placed yourself.

JEKYLL. I know it. I am like the wreck that drives rudderless before the wind — let it sink what matters it.

UTTERSON. But this devil would have killed you too.

JEKYLL. Perhaps, but that would not have been the worst, I have had an escape. Oh Heaven what an escape! Enough, Utterson, enough.

UTTERSON. Enough, the fellow now writes that he is beyond human reach this I take for a blind, I shall continue to look for him, and if I find him deliver him up to justice deliver him up — hand him over to the hangman's grasp[30]

JEKYLL. Do so, Utterson, do so, but search[31] no further into my life,[32] I have brought on myself a punishment over which God not man must judge. Suffer me to lead my own dark way, keep my silence Utterson if you love me keep my silence.

(*Exit Jekyll*)

UTTERSON. (*sitting down*) This is incomprehensible.

(*Enter Guest*)

GUEST. These papers require your immediate attention sir.

UTTERSON. (*Taking out letter*) Is it possible that he could have seen this man after all.

GUEST. (*Still holding papers*) Shall I return with them, sir?

UTTERSON. Never mind these papers now, Guest, they can wait. Sit down I want to speak to you. Of course you have heard of the death of the vicar?

GUEST. I am sorry to say I have sir. Killed by a lunatic poor old man. Has the perpetrator been found yet?

UTTERSON. No, but we are on his track, and I hold here in my hand a most notably evidence[33] against him, his signature.

GUEST. (*Taking it hastily*) That is indeed insignificant.[34]

(*Enter Poole*)

UTTERSON. Holloa Poole what brings you here?

POOLE. I beg your pardon Mr. Utterson, but I am the bearer of a letter which should have been delivered yesterday, but in the confusion of my master's illness was forgotten.

UTTERSON. (*reading it and laying it open on table*) All right Poole, it's only an invitation to dinner. I say Poole was there anyone in your house with a letter for your master yesterday?

POOLE. Not that I know of Mr. Utterson.

---

30. "*deliver him up — hand him over to the hangmans grasp*" is a *handwritten* insertion in Bandmann's script.
31. "*search*" is a *handwritten* replacement for the typed but deleted text "*spy*" in Bandmann's script.
32. "*life*" is a *handwritten* replacement for the typed but deleted text "*past*" in Bandmann's script.
33. "*a most notably evidence*" is the text that appears in Bandmann's script.
34. "*insignificant*" is the text that appears in Bandmann's script.

UTTERSON. That will do Poole.

(Exit Poole)

GUEST. (*Who has been looking at letters*) You say sir that this letter was written by Edward Hyde and this one is from Dr. Jekyll.

UTTERSON. Certainly, what of it?

GUEST. Oh nothing, it's only very extraordinary that both the signatures are alike.

UTTERSON. (*amazed*) What do you say?

GUEST. (*handing him letters*) Judge for yourself!

UTTERSON. Guest, remember that good old proverb.

GUEST. Yes sir. A silent tongue makes a wise head, a very good old proverb, very good indeed.

(Exit Guest)

UTTERSON. Great God! Henry Jekyll incriminates himself for a fiend like this, and I his friend I will see clearer into this then there is a mystery between these two men and I am determined to unravel it.

(Enter Sybil and Lilian.)

My dear child why have you left your room? You should take better care of her Lilian.

LILIAN. I could not help it uncle, she would come to your study.

SYBIL. Don't blame her, I could not remain there the suspense is killing me. What news have you?

UTTERSON. As yet not a single clue. He has disappeared out of the sight of the police as if he had never existed.

SYBIL. But has no one known him? No one seen him?

UTTERSON. No one.

SYBIL. And not a sign of his present whereabouts?

UTTERSON. Not one.

SYBIL. As[35] Dr. Jekyll been able to find out anything?

UTTERSON. I have not seen him yet.

LILIAN. Oh he has been here, and asked after you several times, hasn't he uncle?

UTTERSON. Yes, he was here but a moment ago and gave me some information which may led to his discovery.

LILIAN. Oh what clever people these lawyers are, they can tell a fib better even than a woman.

SYBIL. But why did he not stop?

UTTERSON. He was in a great hurry, and will no doubt return during the day.

SYBIL. I shall be so happy to see him after his illness, but now tell me the clue where and who is this horrible fiend.

LILIAN. Oh yes, tell us all I'm dying to know it.

UTTERSON. I must first confer with the detective and see what he has to say.

SYBIL. Do so Mr. Utterson he was your best, your truest friend, avenge my kind and good old father.

(Exits Sybil and Lilian)

UTTERSON. (*alone as he Exits L.*) It is easier said than done my child, this is one of the worst machiavellian cases known in criminal history.

(Enter Jekyll)

JEKYLL. My papers in Soho are all destroyed and I am safe in spite of Utterson's suspicions. But I am haunted by my thoughts, they draw me near her, where she dwells, innocent sufferer of my crime, but it was not my deed it was Hyde's, Hyde's who gloats upon his crime devises others for the future. Am I responsible for him, I stand aghast before his acts and shudder at his guilt. What then should I fear, there is no danger, the dead will not return, they sleep in peace, I may lay my busy brain against the bosom of my love and rest assured at night the tender clasp around my neck is not the hangman's grip; back then to thyself though selfish, peevish heart, be stilleth and watchful let not the secret stir from out its gloomy depths, I'm safe. But

---

35. "*As*" is the text that appears in Bandmann's script.

why cannot I sleep at night? Why lay awake and start and now[36] that I am guilty. Oh God hold me not answerable for his deeds, hear my prayers You who can look into the hearts of all, look into mine; it is as pure now as when a child I walked beside my mother in Thy house of worship, you have seen me went[37] face to face with death for others I have challenged danger, you have seen me drain my own heart's blood for my fellow men. Am I then answerable for the horrors of that damned night. What's this? The prayers are unheard my lying words still re-echo in my ears, my eyes are wild, my blood is cold, and my burning brain wanders[38] what ghastly mockery is this? See the crowd of hideous images they gather, they scream aloud, they clamour for my blood, see they point towards the snowy locks of that pale faced old man whom I have foully murdered, he lifts his mournful eyes up to the throne of heaven and pleads for justice against my damned crime. His prayers are heard I am condemned dragged to the gallows, shame and despair must follow, oh horrible, horrible, courage, Henry, courage, it is not too late, Hyde shall no more return it shall henceforth be impossible to me, I am resolved I have done problems back dark hellish past,[39] come future with Sybil by my side a better life is still in store for me.

(Enter Sybil L.)

SYBIL. I was told you were here, and I came to thank you Henry.

JEKYLL. For what love?

SYBIL. For the service you have rendered me in handing over to the police that guilty wretch.

JEKYLL. What in the name of Heaven are you talking of? I do not understand you.

SYBIL. You do not want to understand you wish to leave the honour of having found this fiend to others, it is your usual kindness that hinders you from speaking.

JEKYLL. Sybil, cannot you let this matter rest others will fight for you and do you justice, come let us talk of love and our future marriage.

SYBIL. So we will after this affair is settled. Bring the murderer of my innocent father to justice and you shall have my hand, but why do you look on me with that searching eye, that frowning brow.

JEKYLL. Oh no, no, no I have no frown for you but peace and love, but Sybil to revenge is unchristian like and out of the province of a woman.

SYBIL. In this case it is the most filial obligation of a child to her most outraged parent.

JEKYLL. To forgive is godly.

SYBIL. You say that Henry because you are beyond the average human race, a gentle noble self sacrificing nature, but I am human with all the spirit of a injured woman and I will not be content until I have seen the law in its minutest point executed an eye for an eye, a tooth for a tooth.

JEKYLL. Mercy for God, mercy,

SYBIL. Henry arise, this goes too far.

JEKYLL. You're right, I've gone too far; pardon me I'm not well he is not worthy of such compassion.

SYBIL. You are not well, I will go in and get you some refreshments, meantime compose yourself I'll soon return.

(Exit Sybil)

JEKYLL. Oh God! upon what an abyss do I stand another step and I am lost, she haunts the murderer and he stands before her, she seeks revenge and with the same breath thanks the slayer of her father. The curse is on my double life from which I never found release for Hyde is on my heels wherever I meet him, the spirit of hell was in me when I did that crime, but am I not safe? I'm not Hyde! I'm Jekyll! For how long? What's to become of me when I have

---

36. "*now*" is the text that appears in Bandmann's script.
37. "*went*" is the text that appears in Bandmann's script.
38. "*wanders*" is the text that appears in Bandmann's script.
39. "*I have done problems back dark hellish past*" is the text that appears in Bandmann's script.

lost the means to remain as Jekyll, and once more turn into the fiendish Hyde, a hunted, houseless murderer, whose certain fate must be ignominious death otherways or the hangman's hands, O horrible, I cannot die thus, I cannot end so meanly, so miserably my life, but what's to be done — who is to guide me out of this fearful danger? I must have a friend who will when I'm Hyde bring me the drugs to restore me back to Jekyll, but who, who? Lanyon. I'll go at once to notify him of my purpose ere it be too late, for I fear this terrible excitement will turn me into my other self before I am aware and I must hasten home where I have always my compound at my command. Farewell, Sybil, a long and sad farewell, perhaps for ever, since the slayer of your father must be punished your Henry's for every lost to you.

(Exit Centre)

(Sybil Enters)

SYBIL. Here Henry is a most refreshing drink. Gone! Poor Henry I feel he was too ill to stay. What could so have upset him?

(Lilian rushing in)

LILIAN. Sybil dear, sad again! What has a certain party promised me?

SYBIL. I know child but our hearts will not always keep pace with our tongues.

LILIAN. Mine will. If I make up my mind to be happy — I'm happy and nothing shall interfere with my intentions.

SYBIL. Not even your heart?

LILIAN. Not even that!

SYBIL. You have never loved!

LILIAN. No, and I hope I never will, if it makes me as unhappy as it does you.

SYBIL. Lilian you are wrong, my love makes me not unhappy it is in fact the only anchor to which I cling, it is the uncertainty which distresses me.

LILIAN. That is all the same, in love one can never tell of what one is certain, now this Dr. Jekyll who you all like so much I can[40] abide him.

SYBIL. Why?

LILIAN. I cannot tell, I don't feel comfortable in his presence.

SYBIL. Silence! Lilian you are insulting a noble man

LILIAN. Forgive me Sybil I didn't mean to hurt your feelings you know that I am a silly blab —

SYBIL. That's all right darling, I know you are but a chatterbox, and often speak of things you do not understand.

LILIAN. Oh I've got a surprise for you, the choir boys are down stairs and ask me to plead for them to have a peep at you.

SYBIL. Why certainly, let them come in, they'll cheer me up, I shall be delighted to see them, the dear boys, the last time I saw them was under very different circumstances.

LILIAN. *(outside)* Come in boys. *(Coming in with Children who rush to Sybil, shaking hands)* Good evening Miss Sybil.

SYBIL. Good evening boys, so you thought you would come to cheer me up. Well, that's kind of you, sit down make your selves at home, and Willie too, how are your parents is mamma better.

LITTLE WILLIE. Yes Miss Sybil, mamma is better, but my little sister has got the measles.

SYBIL. The measles, dear me. Well, that is not very dangerous, she'll get over that all right.

LITTLE CHARLIE. I had them once but I'm all right now.

FRANK. So had I!

HARRY. So had I, but I had them worse than you.

FRANK. No you didn't! I was in bed for a week.

(Boys all laugh)

SYBIL. Well, never mind boys, we won't discuss that subject any longer as you came to cheer me up I propose to have some music.

---

40. "can" is the text that appears in Bandmann's script.

OMNES BOYS. Oh yes, we'll have some music and you'll sing to us.

SYBIL. Oh boys I can't, I haven't the heart.

OMNES BOYS. Oh yes Miss Sybil do sing us something.

WILLIE. Please do Miss Sybil.

SYBIL. Very well, I will. But what shall I sing?

LILIAN. Sing that song that we like so much.

SYBIL. Oh yes, the one that father was so often of hearing you sing. I will, on one condition that you keep time.

(*Boys laughing We'll try. Bus.) (Of Boys placing themselves — Sybil goes to piano sings — Boys join in the chorus &c. At the end Boys altogether clapping hands how that was splendid. Enter Utterson from R. I. E*)

UTTERSON. Hulloa, here's a regular tea party have you come to study Law

SYBIL. They've come to cheer me up.

UTTERSON. That's very kind of them and I hope they have succeeded, but I have some important business with Miss Sybil in private for a few minutes. Lilian take the children to the billiard room and take care they don't cut the cloth.

LILIAN. Come along, boys, I'll show you how to make the balls roll.

BOYS. Oh that's jolly! Good bye Miss Sybil, good bye Mr. Utterson, good bye Miss Sybil! (*All laugh and run off — Little Willie coming back "Miss Sybil please may I come to morrow?"*)

SYBIL. Yes, certainly, dear, and let me know how your little sister is getting on. Now run along with the others.

(*W. Exits.*)

UTTERSON. (*who has beckoned on Detective*) Sybil, I have brought here to introduce to you Mr. Newcomen, chief detective in this case.

DETECTIVE. At your service, madam!

SYBIL. And so you think you are on the trail of this thing.

DETECTIVE. No doubt! I gave my views to Mr. Utterson and he entirely agrees with me.

SYBIL. May I hear them?

UTTERSON. He proposes to watch the vicarage tonight where we hope to catch him.

SYBIL. Why there?

DETECTIVE. He has been seen lurking there, lately. You see Miss, when a man commits a crime he often returns to the scene of his folly; it's the old, old story of the moth and the candle you know.

SYBIL. He intends to murder Dr. Jekyll he told me that he hated him.

UTTERSON. Don't be alarmed my dear, we'll watch and guard his house tonight.

DETECTIVE. I'll have already placed a detective inside and outside the premises.

SYBIL. And you expect him there to-night?

DETECTIVE. Yes ma'am!

SYBIL. Are you going to the vicarage as well?

UTTERSON. Yes!

SYBIL. And take me with you!

UTTERSON. Impossible!

SYBIL. Why so?

UTTERSON. To think of the danger child you waylaying a criminal.

SYBIL. The vicarage is my home, the spirit of my father hovers there. I shall be strong there whilst here in your absence the anxiety about Henry's safety would worry me to death, oh let me go why not?

DETECTIVE. Mr. Utterson you had better let the young lady have her way if it pleases her she can come to no harm, except catching a slight cold and she may be of some service to us as she is the only one who has seen this Hyde, we mustn't make a mistake you know.

UTTERSON. Well, you may go with us on one condition, you must promise not to leave my side.

SYBIL. I promise I'll be with you immediately.

(*Exit L.*)

UTTERSON. Come let's go, now we shall see clearly into this dreadful mystery.

Change to Act II. Scene II.

ACT II

SCENE II — Changes into Vicarage same as ACT I.
(Enter Officer O'Brien with a lantern from R. U. E.)

O'BRIEN. Well here I am! My instructions are to get into Dr. Jekyll's house and to watch from the inside and collar the devil Hyde without giving any intentions of mi[41] scheme. I'm to watch the inside of the house while the others watch the outside? Shure[42] and I don't mind if Sarah would only be here in time with one of her fine pies that she knows so well how to make. She knows the time, of my beat, what's that, I see the door opening there she is, that's her! Hist! Hist!

(Sarah from Jekyll's house at the door)

SARAH. Hist! Hist! Is that you Patrich O'Brien?

O'BRIEN. Shure isn't me it must be after being my ghost.

SARAH. (*coming to him*) Oh don't speak of ghosts in this dreadful place there're haunting me all night.

O'BRIEN. Never mind me darling, I'm here to protect to your[43] handsome O'Brien with my club in one hand and ye clasp to the true heart of Patrich O'Brien in the other.

(Bus.)

SARAH. Oh you're a dangerous man Pat, you talk just like those story books but I like ye. Now Pat let us set[44] on the step and have a quiet cosy talk.

O'BRIEN. Shure darling wouldn't it better safer[45] in the kitchen especially if you have any of those nice pies.

SARAH. Of course I have fine pies, but I couldn't think of going inside if the doctor or Poole were to hear of it I would lose my place.

O'BRIEN. Shure the doctor will never be after hearing of it, besides there is always room enough in the pantry for a policeman to hide.

SARAH. Well I'll risk it Pat, but mind if you're asked any questions say you've come for a glass of water

(Exit Sarah into house)

O'BRIEN. That's right my darling. I'm sure I've always been fond of a glass of — water.

(Follows her)

(Enter 2nd Policeman L. U. E. with bulls-eye on O'Brien.)

2ND POLICEMAN. There goes O'Brien with his cook, he'll be well taken care of the lucky devil, Pat's always there been[46] there's anything good to eat in the pantry. Pat'll do justice to it.

(Whistle of Detective outside)

That's the Inspector, here comes the party.

(As Detective, Utterson and Sybil come on)
(Bus)

DETECTIVE. You idiot what do you turn the bullseye on, turn your light the other way, where's O'Brien?

2ND POLICEMAN. Inside with a cook.

DETECTIVE. Then all is well! Mr. Utterson would it not be better for me to put the bracelets on him at once?

UTTERSON. No, I have my reasons for not doing so, I wish to satisfy myself if there is anything between these two.

DETECTIVE. I'm at your orders sir.

UTTERSON. Is all ready?

---

41. "*mi*" is the text that appears in Bandmann's script.
42. "*Shure*" indicating O'Brien's Irish accent is the text that appears in Bandmann's script.
43. "*to your*" is the text that appears in Bandmann's script.
44. "*set*" is the text that appears in Bandmann's script.
45. "*it better safer*" is the text that appears in Bandmann's script.
46. "*been*" is the text that appears in Bandmann's script.

DETECTIVE. Yes!

UTTERSON. Then all is right.

(Hyde heard outside.)

UTTERSON. *(Listening and turning round suddenly)* Stop! What's that thing hopping along there?

SYBIL. That's the horrible creature.

(General Bus.)

UTTERSON. Hush! Mr. Newcomen retire and be in readiness with your men. Go into the house child!

(Bus All retire. Enter Hyde)

HYDE. *(chuckling)* I love to torture women and children they are so helpless, this is the place where I killed the old chap serve him right. He'll never get another fifty pounds out of me because I was gently thrashing little brats, for spoiling my fun, how I do hate that goody goody fellow Jekyll, I'll kill him one of these days sure, he's another one of these church fellows, he prays and sings songs, I know what'll I do I'll go in and spoil all his holy books. *(Bus.)*

UTTERSON. Is your name Hyde?

HYDE. What's that to you!

UTTERSON. My name is Utterson. Dr. Jekyll's friend I see you are taking a stroll and I thought we might walk into the house together.

HYDE. Might we! Well you are very much mistaken, I don't care for company, and Dr. Jekyll is not at home.

UTTERSON. Sorry to hear that — would like to have had a chat with the doctor. But why do you hide your face from me?

HYDE. You lie! I do not hide my face from you.

UTTERSON. Come, come, you must be more civil!

HYDE. Go to — hell —

(Hyde Exits General Bus. All come forward)

DETECTIVE. That's exactly where I am going to send you to my friend! Come boys.

(Exit into house followed by Officer — Sybil who has been exploring Utterson excitedly cries)

SYBIL. Oh quick, quick, Mr. Utterson, before he does any injury to Dr. Jekyll!

UTTERSON. Don't be alarmed my child, have no fear. He'll do no more injury to any one, we have him safe!

(Sybil going down stage)

SYBIL. Oh but I fear, I fear for Jekyll! *(Turns sees Jekyll comes unconcernedly down.)* Ah, he is here! Thank God he is saved!

(General Bus. A Quick Curtain)

Tableau.

Curtain.

ACT III

SCENE I

(Utterson's Study same as Act. I. Detective Utterson, Poole, Two Officers discovered.)

DETECTIVE. *(discovered)* We're foiled once more! Mr. Utterson, but what can you expect when you are dealing with a pack of fools, this idiot *(At O'Brien)* insists that Hyde did not get out of the front door.

O'BRIEN. Nor did he!

DETECTIVE. Where did he get out of then?

O'BRIEN. Out of his skin, for all I know! But he didn't get out of the house!

DETECTIVE. Not out of the house you idiot, perhaps he is still there! What can you do with such a man. Had you followed my advise Mr. Utterson and allowed us to put the bracelets on him, he would of been in durance vile now.[47]

UTTERSON. I had grave grievances which I cannot disclose.

DETECTIVE. Well, you see the result, now Mr. Poole.

POOLE. Sir, sir!

DETECTIVE. When we rang the bell where were you?

POOLE. On the ground floor, looking out for the servants.

DETECTIVE. Oh yes, and where were *you* (*To O'Brien.*)

O'BRIEN. In the kitchen watching.

DETECTIVE. In the kitchen watching, more likely in the kitchen hiding. Well, did you see Hyde coming in?

O'BRIEN. Shure I did, and I followed him, and who should I see coming towards me.

DETECTIVE. Well, who?

O'BRIEN. Dr. Jekyll.

UTTERSON. Dr. Jekyll impossible.

DETECTIVE. Dr. Jekyll; Poole, didn't you say Dr. Jekyll wasn't at home?

POOLE. Now[48] was he, he came into the house by the back door after the bell was rung, the officer here is mistaken.

O'BRIEN. By the powers I'm not.

DETECTIVE. Oh you're not aren't you?

O'BRIEN. No sir, no sir, no sir.

DETECTIVE. Well how the deuce could he come towards you when he wasn't in the house.

O'BRIEN. I don't care whether he was in the house or out of it, I saw him coming out of his room.

DETECTIVE. Sure, you monkey. Mr. Utterson that man has been on the force for twenty years and were I not absolutely sure that he never touches a drop of liquor I should say he was either drunk or crazy.

O'BRIEN. Look here Mr. Inspector I'm a poor man but by the powers I won't stand that, I was neither drunk or crazy and if you discharge me on the spot I repeat I saw Dr. Jekyll going out at the front door when I saw Hyde sneaking in at the back.

DETECTIVE. Poor devil, he is has[49] crazy as a lune.

UTTERSON. Poole, after we rang the bell did you see anyone coming in by the back way?

POOLE. I did sir!

UTTERSON. Well, who did you think it was?

POOLE. Either Hyde or my master.

DETECTIVE. (*sharply*) What made you think it was Hyde?

POOLE. Hyde often comes and goes by the back way and we are told not to take any notice of him.

DETECTIVE. Hyde goes to Dr. Jekyll's, what relation is Dr. Jekyll to a murderer?

(*Enter Sybil & Lilian. Lilian is about to speak when Sybil stops her.*)

UTTERSON. I think I can explain this, Dr. Jekyll has for a long time been operating upon this poor specimen of humanity and has no doubt given him free access to his laboratory, although after the crime it was a daring thing for him to do.

DETECTIVE. (*rising and Xing Centre*) Mr. Utterson, this requires closer investigation and I shall place a stronger guard around the doctor's house.

(*Sybil comes down stage*)

SYBIL. Mr. Utterson may I speak to you one minute privately?

UTTERSON. Certainly my dear, Mr. Newcomen will you kindly take your men down stairs for a while, I will send for you.

DETECTIVE. Certainly, Mr. Utterson, certainly.

(*Exit followed by Poole & Officers*)

---

47. "*he would of been in durance vile now*" is the text that appears in Bandmann's script.
48. "*Now*" is the text that appears in Bandmann's script.
49. "*has*" is the text that appears in Bandmann's script.

UTTERSON. Well girls you look seriously,[50] anything wrong?

SYBIL. We were accidental hearers and have perhaps heard more than we should. Is it true that Hyde has access to Dr. Jekyll's house?

UTTERSON. It is.

SYBIL. Great Heaven! A murderer protected by Henry Jekyll and that murderer a slayer of his bride's father, impossible!

UTTERSON. So it seems.

SYBIL. You say so, the friend of my dead father who are pledged by faith and honour you do nothing in this matter but calmly say so it seems.

UTTERSON. Sybil you are unreasonable; I am powerless in this matter, some bond unites these men, some link unites their fate, some mystery prevails which I am utterly unable to unravel.

SYBIL. Now I see it all, and that is no doubt the reason why he fell upon his knees and prayed for pardon, this is indeed terrible and to think that I did love this man, it is the father for whom I mourn and does he counternane[51] his murderer, the very thought will drive me frantic.

LILIAN. Sybil, dear!

SYBIL. I know what I will do, I will go to him, I will tell him to choose between a murderer's companionship and mine.

UTTERSON. You will not find him dear, he has not been seen for days.

SYBIL. Not seen for days, where is he?

UTTERSON. That is the mystery which no one can unravel. He has not left London.

SYBIL. Then he must be still here and should be found.

(Enter Office Boy)

BOY. From Mr. Newcomen, Mr. Utterson.

UTTERSON. This may through[52] further light upon the matter. (*reads*) "Good news, Mr. Utterson, Hyde has been seen lurking in some of some[53] old dismal haunts, we're on his track again and this time he will not escape us." We mustn't be too sure of that, who says we are prosaic nation and that all the stories of the Arabianites[54] are but fiction, this one is most certainly clothed with the most terrible reality.

(Exit)

SYBIL. Lilian!

LILIAN. What dear?

SYBIL. I have made up my mind.

LILIAN. For what love.

SYBIL. I will look for Hyde myself.

LILIAN. Are you mad? What the entire force of Scotland Yard is unable to accomplish you hope to succeed in.

SYBIL. A woman's wit goes further than the police force of the entire world, this Hyde must be somewhere concealed and my instinct tells me his hiding place.

LILIAN. And that is?

SYBIL. At his old lodgings. His landlady is an avaricious hag who will do anything for money, if Hyde had communications with Jekyll is it not natural that she might have seen him there as well and if that is the case Jekyll must be guilty.

LILIAN. But how are you to find that out, she has so far been silent to all.

SYBIL. But she will not be to me. Money and persuasion and perhaps a little mercy for my position, for after all she is but a woman will go father[55] than the art of detectives.

LILIAN. Then you propose to send for her?

SYBIL. No, that would arouse suspicion I propose to go to her.

---

50. "*seriously*" is the text that appears in Bandmann's script.
51. "*counternane*" is the text that appears in Bandmann's script.
52. "*through*" is the text that appears in Bandmann's script.
53. "*in some of some*" is the text that appears in Bandmann's script.
54. "*Arabianites*" is the text that appears in Bandmann's script.
55. "*she is but a woman will go father*" is the text that appears in Bandmann's script.

LILIAN. Oh, you are mad? Do you know where she lives?

SYBIL. How many hundreds of good women visit the slums of London every day without fear or danger and why should not I do the same, besides it is my duty and Heaven will protect me.

LILIAN. Let uncle go with you.

SYBIL. No, I'll go alone.

LILIAN. Not alone Sybil; if you are determined I will go with you.

SYBIL. God bless you darling, no harm will come to us we'll be off at once.

LILIAN. Oh dear, oh dear, if I am murdered what shall I say to my uncle.

(Exit with Sybil.)

Change to ACT III. SCENE II

ACT III

SCENE II — Street in Soho.

Dilapidated house R. Enter O'Brien

O'BRIEN. Then there is not the slightest doubt on my mind that I'm dead. Well, it is better to be dead and alive than to be alive and dead. I drunk, I never drunk more than one glass of whiskey in my life, but that devil Hyde if I catch him I'll make him pay for it I'll hide the Hyde of him.

(Exit)

(Enter Lilian & Sybil)

SYBIL. For shame Lilian don't be so cowardly.

LILIAN. Oh I can't help it Sybil, I see that horrible Hyde everywhere. Why wouldn't you let the cab drive up here?

SYBIL. That would have been very foolish, indeed, this is not a street in which cabs are in the habit of stopping.

LILIAN. But now that you are here in this dreadful street what are you going to do?

SYBIL. Find out the lodgings keepers address.

LILIAN. But how?

SYBIL. You shall see *(Pause)* Mr. Officer!

(Enter O'Brien)

O'BRIEN. What can I do for you ma'am? A fine dress lady; by the powers that's Miss Sybil, and the other Mr. Utterson's niece.

SYBIL. We want to find the address of a certain lodging house keeper who lives in this neighbourhood a Mrs Viley.

O'BRIEN. *(aside)* That's Hyde woman; they don't know me but I know them — the police is awake.

SYBIL. Can you give us any information!

O'BRIEN. By jabis and I can; she lives right here.

SYBIL. Would it be safe to go in there?

LILIAN. *(frightened)* Oh yes Mr. Policeman would it be safe?

O'BRIEN. Well it would be safer to be out here, I'll call her out if you like, and have a watch while you talk.

SYBIL. Thanks!

(O'Brien knocks at the Hag's door, rattling of the chain heard and the bolt withdrawn after repeating knocking.)

HAG. *(inside)* I'm a coming, what do you want? *(Opens door sees Policeman and cringes)* Oh dear is it you Mr. Officer, any more news of that villain Hyde, won't you come in?

O'BRIEN. No, I want you to come out there are two ladies who wish to see you.

HAG. Two ladies, oh lor, I'm not in proper trim to see them.

O'BRIEN. Come out you old hag, and don't make such a fuss.

HAG. *(advancing)* Good evening, ladies, what can I do for you?

SYBIL. Are you the landlady with whom a certain Mr. Hyde stopped.

HAG. Yes madam! (*Looks around to see if Policeman is watching*) I is sorry I is, he was a wicked, a very wicked man, and I thank my Lord that he is gone.

SYBIL. Can you give us any clue of him?

HAG. How should I, I is a poor old woman who is aminding her own business and do what's right, I don't keep track of murderers.

SYBIL. Know[56] my good woman if I gave you a sovereign would you answer a few questions?

HAG. Of course I would bless your heart, of course I would.

SYBIL. (*giving her money*) Did Mr. Hyde go in and out of our house always alone?

HAG. Almost always ma'am, almost always.

SYBIL. What sort of company did he keep?

HAG. All sorts ma'am, all sorts.

SYBIL. Was there among those who came to see him a gentleman by the name of Jekyll?

LILIAN. Let's go Sybil.

HAG. Jekyll! Jekyll! Oh that's the gentleman he hated so. No ma'am, I often heard him speak of him and tell me that he would kill him, but never seen him ma'am, never seen him.

LILIAN & SYBIL. (*Lilian & Sybil looking at each other*)

He told you he would kill Dr. Jekyll?

HAG. Yes ma'am! And he would make faces at him and spit at him.

SYBIL. (*to Lilian*) This is incomprehensible and I am as wise now as I was before, but one thing I have learned Henry is innocent and all my suspicions have vanished, come let us go. Here my good woman here are ten pounds for you. I leave Hyde to the justice of a superior power now that I know that Henry is innocent.

(*Exit with Lilian*)

HAG. Well, I never! A ten pound note and from a Miss Sybil that was the name the other lady called her, and all because I told her that Hyde hates a certain gentleman by the name of Jekyll. Hyde was to be here to night to give me the other fifty pounds he promised me for being mum. If he doesn't pay me I'll betray him I was to give him notice of any danger, the officer is out of the way he is alright I hear a hansom that's Hyde.

(*Enter Hyde*)

HYDE. Well you old hag all safe?

HAG. Of course Mr. Hyde, or I would have given you warning.

HYDE. Get me some brandy, quick.

(*Exit Hag into house and returns with brandy*)

HAG. Won't you come in?

HYDE. No, I'm safer here, my cab is close by.

HAG. Well, there were two ladies enquiring after you, one of whom was called Sybil.

HYDE. Sybil! Sybil! what did she want?

HAG. She wanted to know something about Dr. Jekyll.

HYDE. And what did you say?

HAG. That you hated him.

HYDE. Good! (*laughs*) How did the vicar's daughter like that, eh, how did the vicar's daughter like that, eh?

HAG. The vicar's daughter! Then she was the poor child whose father you murdered!

HYDE. Shut up, you old hag!

HAG. I won't. That's the reason the poor thing gave me these ten pounds to squeal on you I suppose?

HYDE. (*snatching them from her and tearing them*) D — her ten pounds, I hate her.

HAG. He has torn my ten pounds. Police! Police!

HYDE. (*Taking her hold of her neck and forcing her down on her knees*) Hag, I killed the vicar, and if you give one sign, or one breath I'll kill you too.

---

56. "*Know*" is the text that appears in Bandmann's script.

(Exit leaving her almost lifeless.)

HAG. *(gasping)* Police! Police!

(Enter O'Brien.)

O'BRIEN. Well, you old hag what are you cleaning up the side walk for?

HAG. Hyde was here and nearly murdered me.

O'BRIEN. Hyde, where has he gone to?

HAG. *(pointing)* That cab.

O'BRIEN. Come along you old devil.

HAG. No I won't, my ten pounds he has torn.

O'BRIEN. Ten pounds—for you? Come along and show me the cab or I will break every bone in your body. *(Drags her off struggling and screaming)*

Change to ACT III SCENE III

ACT III

SCENE III — *Dr. Lanyon Reception Room.*

(Enter Lanyon and Poole, the latter with a small drawer.)

DR. LANYON. Come in Poole set it down there. *(To Servant)* James you can retire, I shall require you no more. Now Poole let me see your letter of instruction and compare it with mine. *(reads it)* Yes, exactly the same, what can he mean?

POOLE. I am sure I don't know, but we have fulfilled them to the letters.

DR. LANYON. Yes, we got the medicine he described, and the drawer and brought it here.

POOLE. Perhaps my master desires to make some experiment.

DR. LANYON. What, here?

POOLE. Yes doctor.

DR. LANYON. He does not say that in his letter, but he distinctly says someone will call for these drugs at twelve o'clock who will designate himself as a midnight messenger. Who is that someone?

POOLE. That's what puzzling me, he doesn't mention it in my letter, he only says I shall assist you in forcing open the cabinet and destroying the lock, I have obeyed his instructions and if you have no further use for me I think I had better go home as my master may turn up at any moment.

DR. LANYON. How long as[57] he been away Poole?

POOLE. Three days, but we don't mind that now it is not an uncommon occurrence for my master to leave his home.

DR. LANYON. Well, good night, Poole, you can use my cab outside.

POOLE. Thank you sir. *(Exit)*

DR. LANYON. Well, if I had not dined with Jekyll only a few days ago I should certainly consider him mad today. He is the most extraordinary individual of all my colleagues I wonder whether he is playing a joke with me, and yet he writes me so imploringly and gave Poole the same instructions as he gave me, made everything so clear that I cannot doubt the veracity of these letters, but who is this midnight messenger that I am to expect so secretly and why at such an unearthly hour? *(Looks at watch)* Midnight. Now for my man, I had better have my loaded revolver ready when this expected midnight caller arrives.

(Clock strikes twelve. Knock outside. Transparency shown Hyde seen outside the portico. Lanyon at door)

Who are you?

HYDE. Your midnight messenger.

---

57. "*as*" is the text that appears in Bandmann's script.

DR. LANYON. Come in quick!

(*Hyde Enters, slams the door in O'Brien's face as latter comes up — transparency darkens. Enter Lanyon into room followed by Hyde.*)

HYDE. Quick, quick! the drug, the drug!

DR. LANYON. Curb your impatience sir, I must first know who you are?

HYDE. A messenger from Dr. Henry Jekyll, your friend. He informed me I was to find here the — the —

DR. LANYON. On that chair! Control yourself sir.

HYDE. A glass of water. (*Lanyon gives it him*). A now Dr. Lanyon watch my mixture. When the tincture is complete say if you desire to see any more, here is the elixir of life. (*throws in powder*) See how it brightens. It will grow deeper (*throws in another*) Watch me, here is the last ingredient, moral power, how I hate it. (*throws in another*) My drink is brewed, and now before I proceed before I show you what science and progress has accomplished, over arrogance, ignorance, and darkness, swear to me by your profession and honour whatever you may see shall remain your heart's secret until your dying day, swear!

DR. LANYON. I swear!

HYDE. What fools you are who believe your cosmusdimedici[58] is the gospel of pathology I will prove to you by these few powders that there are powers in the brain of man beyond your logical A.B.C. you wise acres who dabble in the dark, and murder when you profess to cure.

DR. LANYON. I hear in your discourse but foul abuse, not proofs.

HYDE. Miserable bauble, you will bow before me as your master ere I leave this room, I have waited for this moment all my life, tis here, Lanyon the proud, imperious Dr. Lanyon will stand before me shortly as a school-boy before his tutor.

DR. LANYON. Enough of this, leave this room at once, or I shall hand you over to the police. (*places his hand on the bell*)

HYDE. One moment! Wait till you have seen the finale now Dr. Lanyon you who have grovelled in the ditch of darkness and unbelief, scorned and ridiculed dissenters behold your master!

DR. LANYON. Great Heavens! What do I see, it cannot be, yes, Henry Jekyll!

Curtain

ACT IV

SCENE I — *Room at Utterson's.*

(*Discovered Sybil, Lilian, and Utterson. Sybil reading.*)

SYBIL. "Dear Sybil,
   Pardon my sin and neglect but my health will not permit my visiting nor receiving you as often as of yore, consider it no lack of affection or want of feeling it is simply a matter of faith.

UTTERSON. That's exactly what he wrote me after my calling for the last four months in vain to see him.

SYBIL. What does he mean by it? Do you think he is ill?

LILIAN. I never knew him to be anything else.

UTTERSON. Perhaps your coldness may have driven him to this.

SYBIL. Could I do otherwise after his extraordinary behaviour. Why doesn't he give some explanation about this Hyde? Great Heaven! My future husband suspected

---

58. "*cosmusdimedici*" is the text that appears in Bandmann's script.

Appendix D: Daniel E. Bandmann's Dr. Jekyll and Mr. Hyde

even of knowing the hiding place of this man and instead of assisting us towards handing him to justice he proudly disdains all explanation and shuts himself up as the wronged and injured saint.

UTTERSON. True, true.

SYBIL. Well Dr. Henry Jekyll if you can be proud so can I and until you can clear your name of every vestige of suspicion so that not one speck remains upon it we must henceforth be strangers.

LILIAN. Bravo Sybil, that's the spirit I like to see you in.

UTTERSON. You take things too seriously; no doubt every thing will yet be explained to your perfect satisfaction; I wish I could give you better comfort but the sudden death of my old friend Lanyon as[59] quite unhinged me.

SYBIL. Have you yet discovered what caused his explicable[60] demise?

UTTERSON. It is said that a sudden shock paralyses[61] his powers the effect of which he never recovered from, here are his papers I have not opened them, I will do so now.

(Enter Poole)

POOLE. Good evening, ladies, good evening Mr. Utterson!

SYBIL. Why what's the matter Poole, you look as if you had seen ghosts.

LILIAN. It gives me the blues to look at him.

UTTERSON. Sit down Poole, and tell us what is the matter.

POOLE. Oh Mr. Utterson, oh Miss Sybil I should like to speak but I dare not, you see ma'am I dare not, I dare not, you see ma'am I'm afraid.

SYBIL. Now my good man be plain. What do you fear?

POOLE. The doctor has secluded himself in his study for five full days and allows no one to approach him and I, who for over twenty years have been his faithful servant and kept at a distance as if I were a stranger, sir, and that is breaking my heart.

SYBIL. Secluded himself, and does not even allow his servants, his faithful Poole to approach, that's strange.

POOLE. Strange! Yes ma'am, strange indeed!

UTTERSON. Come Poole, there must be something wrong, take courage and explain.

SYBIL. Yes Poole, try and tell us.

POOLE. Well I fear my master is gone!

SYBIL & LILIAN. Gone!

SYBIL. What does the man mean?

POOLE. Yes, murdered!

SYBIL & LILIAN. Murdered!

UTTERSON. Preposterous!

POOLE. You may say so, but I know what I know. Why does he pray to God for help and weep like a child and speak as if he was somebody else?

UTTERSON. How absurd! Do you think for one moment if Poole's preposterous story was true the murderer would remain at the scene of his crime.

POOLE. I have been for a score of years in my master's service and should be familiar with his voice and manner, and I hope you will not think me forward when I say I am familiar with every detail of my master's ways, and I know that that thing that is housed in his study is not my master.

UTTERSON. Why Poole who else should it be?

POOLE. How do I know, we cannot even get a glimpse of him, all we see of him whenever he wants anything are little notes that he throws out on the staircase for us to pick up and attend to. There was a certain prescription that he wanted badly, and I had to go for it as often as three and four times in one day and then it wasn't the proper thing.

UTTERSON. What has become of these notes?

---

59. "*as*" is the text that appears in Bandmann's script.
60. "*explicable*" is the text that appears in Bandmann's script.
61. "*paralysises*" is the text that appears in Bandmann's script.

POOLE. I have kept some of them because I thought they might give a clue.

UTTERSON. (*reading one*) "Dr. Jekyll most respectfully begs to state that the last medicine they sent was impure, and here is another. to Messrs Seal Nard & Co., Gentlemen, what is the reason I cannot get the real thing I am in a most distressing state, I beg of you to send by bearer the same I had some months ago."

SYBIL. These are strange notes.

UTTERSON. But how can you doubt your master still lives? When you see before your very eyes his own signature.

POOLE. I don't care, facts are facts. Didn't I see the horrible creature standing before me in all its ugliness

UTTERSON & LILIAN. What creature?

POOLE. Why the thing — the it — the dwarf, the monkey or whatever you may call it, I only saw it for an second[62] but that was enough it turn my blood to ice.[63]

UTTERSON. It's clear to me that Jekyll's suffering from a disease of the mind, a depression, a melancholia and as soon as that is passed his health will be restored.

SYBIL. God grant it may be so.

POOLE. Amen to that, but I know the difference who suffers from melancholia and one that is emaciated to a pulp, why Mr. Utterson do you think I am a child, I who have been for years in my master's service and not know his noble, fine and manly bearing compared to a miserable, humpbacked deformity? I tell you that I believe in my soul that he has been killed.

SYBIL & LILIAN. Horrible!

UTTERSON. If that is your belief there is but one thing left for me especially as this note proves him to be still alive, I'll demand to see him and if he denies me I'll demolish the door.

SYBIL. And we'll go with you.

UTTERSON. But will you promise me to be calm and collected.

SYBIL. My experience of the last few months has been so sad that it has turned me into a fearless and alas undaunted woman.

UTTERSON. You can stay with the housekeeper while Poole and I investigate the matter.

SYBIL. Come Lilian!

LILIAN. I suppose I must but I am sure I will never come out of that house alive.

UTTERSON. Let us be off. Now we shall find out whether Jekyll or Hyde.

CHANGE TO ACT IV SCENE. II

ACT IV

SCENE II

(*Hall of Dr. Jekyll's house — Maria the housemaid, Julia, the cook, Sarah, the parlour maid, Bradshaw, the footman, John, the coachman, George, the knife-boy, All huddled up together, pushing themselves into the door — when they are half on the stage they run off again — this business is repeated several times from L. I. E.*)

BRADSHAW. (*Very frightened*) What is you afraid of? Can't you have courage like me?

HOUSEMAID. (*Frightened*) If we were men undoubtedly we would.

COOK. I have seen it.

(*All turning in fright, coming near her*)

COOK. It has got horns.

---

62. "*an second*" is the text that appears in Bandmann's script.
63. "*that was enough it turn my blood to ice*" is the text that appears in Bandmann's script.

(All shudder)

And it's face is as white as snow. *(All shudder)*

And it certainly eats man's flesh. *(All shudder)*

And drinks man's blood. *(All shudder)*

And it haunts you in your dreams. *(All shudder)*

(Knocking heard outside — General Business — in fear the knife boy lets the knives and forks fall — Business of fear repeated; more knocking — Business repeated.)

BRADSHAW. *(To Sarah)* Go and open the door Sarah.

SARAH. Not for the world, you open it.

BRADSHAW. Give me a weapon, George. *(Takes knife from out of his hand)* Now I am armed. Is that you Poole?

POOLE. *(outside)* Yes that's me you fool! Open the door!

(Enter Utterson & Poole)

UTTERSON. Well, well, here's a goodly assembly, don't you know you are doing very wrong to leave your work and make fools of yourselves in this fashion.

POOLE. They're all afraid. Sarah go into the parlour and attend to the ladies, the rest of you attend to your duties, Bradshaw get me an axe and the kitchen poker, and now take my advice Mr. Utterson whatever you do don't enter the study, even if he should ask you to do so.

UTTERSON. Now Poole upon your oath whom do you think was the dwarf or the thing as you call it which you saw in your master's laboratory?

POOLE. *(Looking around frightened)* As I stand here before you, and as I am alive I swear to you Mr. Utterson it was Hyde and my solemn belief is, that Hyde is the sole occupant of Dr. Jekyll's cabinet at present.

UTTERSON. Then it is time to act. If Harry has been murdered he shall be avenged.

(Enter Bradshaw and Other)

Come boys pluck up your courage, given me the poker, take the candle Poole, now on to justice. *(Exit)*

POOLE. Come along now, you needn't be afraid ain't I with you. *(Exit)*

BRADSHAW. He said he was with us and he's gone and left us. *(drops axe)*

SERVANT. What did you do that for?

BRADSHAW. I couldn't help it.

SERVANT. Yes you did, you did it on purpose.

BRADSHAW. No I didn't, it was an accident.

(BUS and Dialogue. Exit)

CHANGE TO ACT. IV. SCENE. III.

ACT IV

SCENE III

(Dr. Jekyll's Cabinet)

JEKYLL. *(sitting before his study table papers in hand)* I have ransacked London in vain, I cannot get the original powders which proves beyond a doubt that the first supply was impure and the cause of all this misery, this then is the last time short of a miracle that Henry Jekyll can think his own thoughts or see his own face in the glass. Terrible, terrible! I am losing my original self and becoming more and more incorporated with my second worse, and thus I stand for ever despised and friendless, it is not the gallows that I fear but the horror of sinking back to the animal Hyde, the personification of evil, I go to bed as Jekyll and I awake as Hyde at any moment I may turn again into the brute that is within me. There was a time when I could foretell the indescribable sensations that heralded the change, but even that has left me now, and I may turn at any instance without warning into my other self, here is my full story to Utterson which I hope he will receive before Hyde destroys it out of malicious joy and hatred against me, in one half hour more after I have emptied this last mixture I shall again and then for ever enter into that horrid state. Will Hyde die upon the scaffold or will he find courage enough to release himself by taking this deadly poison, God knows. To vanish like a whisper without a friend, without one comfort it is too hard, I feel it coming now it is Hyde that stands near me, no, no, not yet. Oh if I had but a friend before I die an animal, a dog, to comfort me or lick my hand, but to die like a breath, a whiff oh 'tis sad. (*Knocks outside*) What's that? It cannot be my pursuers, has my hour already struck. (*Knocks again*) Who's there?

SYBIL. (*outside*) It is I your Sybil who on great peril comes to see you oh let me in.

JEKYLL. Oh joy 'tis she and I dare not see her but I hear her voice.

SYBIL. (*outside*) Open the door Henry, and let me in.

JEKYLL. I dare not love, it is impossible, and yet have I not yet one love yet with which I can secure a brief lease of my better self, if I could but steal her forgiveness and die in peace.

SYBIL. (*outside*) Open, Henry, open!

JEKYLL. I will if you promise to leave me when I bid you.

SYBIL. (*outside*) I swear it!

JEKYLL. (*takes drug*) Come friend I never clutched thee with so much joy before, now I am safe. (*Opens door. Enter Sybil*) (*At sight of him she stands amazed*)

SYBIL. This is not Jekyll!

JEKYLL. (*frightened and rushing to the mirror*) How so? (*sees his mistake*) True I am no longer Jekyll my sickness has made me very low.

SYBIL. Oh Henry why don't you let me nurse you?

JEKYLL. That is impossible; besides it is not the body's ailment, it is the mind's—I'll soon recover.

SYBIL. And then we shall unite and never more be parted, I am no longer head strong as soon as you are strong we will marry and be happy.

JEKYLL. As soon as I am well we will marry. Yes love. I dreamt last night that we were married and both in Heaven, there were green woods and lulling waters there as well as here and we saw the stars quite near; and we were so happy—no frowns—no starts—no chills—no horrid images—but everything was calm and bright and beautiful, your face was like an angel's, and your voice as pure and sacred as the children's in the choir.

SYBIL. Oh, how beautiful! Go on.

JEKYLL. And then we heard a voice so calm and clear which went right deep into your most inmost hearts; it said "How can you be so happy here when you know that there are other restless souls craving for pardon for their guilty lives?" It struck me as a warning, and when I awoke I forgave all who in this world had injured me.

SYBIL. And so will I. May all who injured me find pardon there as I forgive them there.

JEKYLL. (*solemnly*) Amen. God bless you for that prayer my child, may all who injured me find pardon there as I forgive them there. I feel so happy now and like a child could cry with joy. Good bye my love we'll meet again.

SYBIL. When, tomorrow?

JEKYLL. Perhaps!

SYBIL. To-morrow then.

(*As she is at the door he rises and goes to her*)

JEKYLL. Sybil, adieu, my love!

SYBIL. Husband! To-morrow.

(*Exit*)

JEKYLL. (*bolting door after her*) Tomorrow, a morrow on which no sun will ever rise for me, and now my soul is clear and I can die in peace. Twas time she went I felt unhinged. (*Chimes outside*) Oh those chimes, they do remind me of that dreadful night, oh God forgive me for my crime, it was wrong to tempt me thus and I am justly punished. William, you are avenged, oh I must pray to drive the fiend away, the fiend is coming, yes Hyde is here. Stop that organ and those chimes, stop them I say, I hate them, and that alas you have always been my enemy vanish into the hateful mists from which you never more shall rise. (*Breaks glass*)

UTTERSON. (*outside*) Jekyll let me in.

HYDE. You cannot come in, remain without or it will be the worst for you.

UTTERSON. (*outside*) That sounds like Hyde's voice. Force open the door, Poole.

HYDE. They are coming to take me to the gallows I will not die on the gallows whilst there is good poison here, I have killed two souls already here goes for the third, Jekyll I told you I would kill you. (*Drinks poison and falls centre.*)

(*The door falls open Enter Utterson & Poole*)

Curtain

Apotheosis

Curtain

Reviews of Bandmann's Dr. Jekyll and Mr. Hyde

Daily Telegraph, London, August 7, 1888

OPERA COMIQUE THEATRE

It has been urged, and certainly not without reason, that there is a demon of pantomime lurking somewhere in the folds of either Dr. Jekyll or Mr. Hyde. As the play proceeds, with its dark scenes and gauzes, we are conscious of the presence of the King of the Hobgoblins, and we long for the promised relief of "Hot Codlins" and "Tippity witchet" in the welcome by-and-by. The same idea seems to have struck Mr. Daniel E. Bandmann, who has entered heart and soul into the pure pantomime theory. Discarding the much-vaunted psychology and throwing the mental gymnastics of Mr. Louis R. Stevenson to the winds, he has, in the version which he produced last night, boldly introduced our old friends the marauding policeman, the affectionate cook, and the time-honoured rabbit pie! At one time the audience was tempted to believe that the rabbit pie would be discussed on a handy door-step, but the disappointing author backed out of it at the last moment, and the comic policeman discreetly went downstairs to discuss his purloined supper with the amorous domestic. But, as if this fine old crusted incident was not sufficient, we were presented in course of time with a pantomime rally that would have delighted the heart of Mr. Harry Payne. It is a most serious moment. Dr. Jekyll is supposed to have been murdered by the man-ape; Mr. Utterson and the confidential butler are prepared to break in the door; all is agitation and expectancy; when suddenly a crowd of pantomime servants files across the stage, some with brooms, some with carving-knives, all agitated with true pantomime terror, in order apparently to prove to Mr. Stevenson how truly "dramatic" was his book. Not content with the perambulating policeman, the effusive cook, the promised pie, and the "rally" that only requires a few cabbages and a clown to make it complete, the author of the latest version of Mr. Louis Stevenson's "Dr. Jekyll and Mr. Hyde" provides us with a transformation scene or apotheosis that is supposed to convey the notion of the good fairy, Dr. Jekyll, going up to heaven, and the bad demon, Mr. Hyde, descending to the lower regions. It is wonderful with what acuteness the psychological romance has been adapted by Mr. Bandmann to the requirements of good old-fashioned Christmas pantomime. Mr. George Grossmith and Mr. Burnand can hold their hands. Their comic work has already been done for them, for no funnier version of the much-discussed story has ever been given than that which provoked such genial merriment last evening.

The power of the law is, we believe, to be called into requisition in order to show how far the copyright in the brochure has been infringed by the play that was performed last night. How far has Mr. Bandmann imitated or reproduced the original ideas which have been imported into the story for dramatic purposes since Mr. Louis Stevenson left it alone? That is the question. Well, he has certainly done one thing that probably never occurred to Mr. Stevenson or Mr. Stevenson's first adaptor. He has for some occult reason made the genial Dr. Jekyll infinitely more repulsive than the revolting Hyde. Hyde may hop about the stage like "Spring-heeled Jack" of nursery memory, and decorate his face with monster teeth that remind one of the isolated almonds in a tipsy cake. Hyde may be a man-monkey or a babbling baboon, too ludicrously inappropriate in disguise even to frighten a well-ordered baby in its cot; but what are we to say to the mouthing, mannered, and equally toothless Jekyll, whose very presence is a shudder, and whose kiss on a young woman's brow and hair is an unpardonable insult? Psychology, or metaphysics, or some abstruse form of philosophy, may have urged Mr. Bandmann to this reckless course of piling horror upon horror; but, whilst the audience laughs outright at the merry demon with the tombstone-teeth, it positively shudders when the revolting and oleaginous Jekyll opens his mouth to rant and rave, and preach paltry platitudes in the most execrable English that has been heard on the stage for many a long year. Jekyll, as reconsidered by Mr. Bandmann as the mask of tragedy, may be the repulsive villain that he is represented to be, but even Jekyll, demoralised and debased as he is, should know the difference between "lay" and "lie."

In serious truth the new and "successful version" of "Dr. Jekyll and Mr. Hyde" is outside all criticism. If it be intended as a joke, it is not a very good one; if it is considered a serious flight into the domain of art, it is an unfortunate mistake. It can only be considered welcome as driving a strong nail into the coffin of psychological treatises adapted in an indifferent manner for the stage. The acting calls for little notice. Miss Louise Beaudet, who was introduced as the heroine of the drama, imitated the worst faults of the deplorable style of the combined Jekyll and Hyde, and seemed to consider that over-emphasis and stilted utterance are tolerable and effective. In order to give this curious dramatic exercise a namby-pamby contrast to the silliness that it called into action, Mr. Stedman's choir boys were introduced to sing a nursery ditty called "Rock-a-bye Baby," and to dandle an imaginary infant in their trencher caps. The song and the boys were ludicrously inappropriate. When at last the wearisome psychology was at an end, and the goblin Hyde, as well as the ghastly, grinning Jekyll, were fairly dead, Mr. Bandmann came forward, in response to an isolated and persistent shout, to make a speech full of sound that signified nothing. In the course of his remarks Mr. Bandmann said he had been all round the world, and that it rejoiced his heart to return to the blue skies, the enchanting sunshine, and the balmy atmosphere of the wonderful England that ruled such a majestic empire. At this inappropriate jest, the people who were approaching their dull August holiday laughed a hollow laugh. He went on to say that he was proud of the personal friendship and priceless regard of Mr. Louis Stevenson, whom he considered the genius of the age. Here the audience smiled. No doubt Mr. Stevenson, when he sees the "successful version of 'Dr. Jekyll and Mr. Hyde,'" will appreciate the compliment so gracefully given.

The Star, London, August 7, 1888

NOT AT THE OPERA COMIQUE.

Mr. Bandmann produced his version of "Dr. Jekyll and Mr. Hyde" at the Opera Comique last night, but we didn't go to see it, because we don't approve of the shifts by which he has fought against Mr. Mansfield. Now we have gathered some idea of the ludicrous character of his performance, we are doubly glad we were not there.

Pall Mall Gazette, London, August 7, 1888

THE PANTOMIME AT THE OPERA COMIQUE.

Mr. Stevenson, who appears to have been coquetting in his careless fashion with both the rival Dr. Jekylls, would have been sorry for his sport had he heard Herr Bandmann's speech at the Opéra Comique last night. He might have survived the actor's declaration of "devoted friendship and ardent admiration," but it would have been a shock to him to hear it asserted that he "warmly reciprocates" these sentiments. There is not a single redeeming feature either in Herr Bandmann's play or in his acting. The adaptor has adapted, not Mr. Stevenson's book, but Mr. Mansfield's play, annexing piecemeal the ideas of the other playwright, omitting all attempt to evolve the action logically from its initial postulate, inventing nothing (except an apotheosis of Jekyll!) and vulgarizing everything. As for Herr Bandmann's performance, it lacked even the ordinary adroitness of the "quick-change artiste." The stage was always darkened, without rhyme or reason, for his changes, and yet we could see the whole process; while the most hideous mechanical appliances could scarcely make his Hyde more unpleasant than his Jekyll. The production is as tedious as it is puerile.

Sunday Times, August 12, 1888

PLAYS AND PLAYERS.

To cry over spilt milk has always been considered a useless proceeding, and as we may regard Mr. Bandmann's harlequinade version of "Dr. Jekyll and Mr. Hyde" in the light of spilt milk, since it is not likely to be seen here again, no good purpose can be served by bewailing its production. Indeed, it seems to me that litigation in such a case was mere waste of money, for so bad a play and so indifferent a performance might have been allowed to perform the Happy Despatch. It wanted no legal injunction, no claim for infringement of copyright, to sound the death knell of such a ludicrous exhibition as that which was vouchsafed at the Opera Comique last Monday. The unwholesome gloom of the Lyceum version of Mr. Stevenson's supernatural story is excused, if not redeemed, by the extraordinarily powerful, although repulsive acting of Mr. Richard Mansfield in the character of the loathsome creature Hyde, the murder scene and the transformation scene being uniquely startling and marvellous as histrionic *tours de force*. But the Opera Comique version presented no redeeming features. From a dramatic point of view, neither version has any *raison d'être*, but at the Lyceum there is nothing absolutely ridiculous. Where it is not impressive, it is simply dull to a wearisome degree. At the Opera Comique, however, Mr. Bandmann contrived to make the whole thing outrageously ridiculous. His Jekyll was as nauseous as Mr. Mansfield's is maudlin, but there any possible comparison ends. Mr. Mansfield's Hyde is, however repulsive, an extraordinary piece of art; whereas Mr. Bandmann is excelled in his pantomime demon by Mr. George Conquest, jun., not to mention other pantomimists of lesser degree. Of Miss Louise Beaudet and the rest of the performers in this sorry affair, it were perhaps kinder to say nothing. The Opera Comique is now closed, and Mr. Bandmann promises not to do it again — till next time. Certain documents are expected from America, and until their arrival the lawyer's briefs are to be put on the shelf. *Requiescat in pace.*

Appendix E:
Jack the Ripper

The publicity attending Mansfield's Lyceum presentation of *Jekyll and Hyde* helped encourage the use of the dual character to illustrate a number of news items in the latter half of 1888.

The Prime Minister, Lord Salisbury, was portrayed as a Jekyll and Hyde character, when this supposed champion of improved housing for the poor was shown to be one of the worst slum landlords in the capital; reaping the rewards of renting 'disgraceful, insanitary, and dangerous' accommodation to poor Polish Jews (*The Star*, Aug. 15, 1888).

Salisbury's opposite number, the Liberal leader, was referred to as both "Gladstone-Jekyll" and "Gladstone-Hyde," when it came to light that during his tenure as Prime Minister in the early 1880s, while publicly denouncing "the unspeakable Turk," Gladstone was privately trying to encourage Turkish involvement in Egypt (*Pall Mall Gazette*, Sept. 21, 1888).

The "Hyde-Jekyll" characterisation of Sir Richard "Facing-both-ways" Webster was conjured by the press when the supposedly impartial Attorney General, acted as defence counsel for *The Times* newspaper in the O'Donnell v. Walter libel action, and the resulting Special Parliamentary 'Parnell Commission' (*The Star*, July, 4. *Pall Mall Gazette*, Sept. 18, 20, 1888).

A Jekyll and Hyde theme was also adopted by *Punch* on August 18, 1888, to portray the possible relationship between respectable and criminal elements in the quest for Irish Home Rule. Sir John Tenniel's illustration for *Punch* of M'Jekyll and O'Hyde is of particular interest here as it portrays a knife-wielding Hyde some three weeks before the Whitechapel murder sensation began to capture the public imagination. But, as will be seen from the following selection of newspaper reports relating that sensation, it was in reference to Jack the Ripper that Jekyll and Hyde seemed to become particularly relevant.

The Star, London, Saturday, September 1, 1888

HAVE we a murderous maniac loose in East London? It looks as if we had. Nothing so appalling, so devilish, so inhuman — or, rather non-human — as the three Whitechapel crimes has ever happened outside the pages of Poe or De Quincey. The unravelled mystery of "The Whitechapel Murders" would make a page of detective romance as ghastly as "The Murders in the Rue Morgue." The hellish violence and malignity of the crime which we described yesterday resemble in almost every particular the two other deeds of darkness which preceded it. Rational motive there appears to be none. The murderer must be a Man Monster, and when Sir Charles has done quarrelling with his detective service he will perhaps help the citizens of East London to catch him.

The Star, London, Thursday, September 6, 1888

DURING the Reign of Terror, death became so familiar to the Parisians that the inmates of the prisons amused themselves with farcical rehearsals of the scenes on the scaffold. They played at guillotining much as Mr. Mould's infants played at "berryin's." We shall soon be in much the same condition in this country. The Whitechapel murders, though quite as horrible as the celebrated Ratcliff Highway murders which drove St. George's-in-the-East almost wild with excitement and terror, have positively fallen flat. We are becoming *blasé*, like Macbeth: "Direness, familiar to our slaughterous thoughts, cannot once fright us." Men can no longer attract notice by mere murder and suicide. They despatch their wives with rifles, and make the slumbers of their children eternal with a saw, only to be arrested by one bored policeman and put off with four lines in the newspapers headed simply "Another Murder." A lady has cut a child's feet off, and a gentleman has gouged out his eyes; but we do not seem to mind. It is not midsummer madness; for there has been no summer. It is not the ugliness of London; for London was just as ugly last year. It is not "Dr. Jekyll and Mr. Hyde"; for America has not caught the infection, though it has read the novel. Whatever it is, it is not one of the successes of nineteenth century civilisation. Perhaps the British Association will devote a sitting to a discussion of the causes of the growth of despair in England.

Pall Mall Gazette, London, Saturday, September 8, 1888

ANOTHER MURDER—AND MORE TO FOLLOW?

SOMETHING like a panic will be occasioned in London to-day by the announcement that another horrible murder has taken place in densely populated Whitechapel. This makes the fourth murder of the same kind, the perpetrator of which has succeeded in escaping the vigilance of the police. The triumphant success with which the metropolitan police have suppressed all political meetings in Trafalgar-square contrasts strangely with their absolute failure to prevent the most brutal kind of murder in Whitechapel. The Criminal Investigation Department under Mr. MONRO was so preoccupied in tracking out the men suspected of meditating political crimes that the ordinary vulgar assassin has a free field in which to indulge his propensities. Whether or not this is the true explanation of the immunity which the Whitechapel murderer enjoys, the fact of that immunity is undoubted. Four poor women, miserable and wretched, have been murdered in the heart of a densely-populated quarter, and not only murdered but mutilated in a peculiarly brutal fashion, and so far the police do not seem to have discovered a single clue to the perpetrator of the crimes.

There is some reason to hope that the latest in this grim and gory series of outrages will supply some evidence as to the identity of the murderer. The knife with which he disembowelled his unfortunate victim and a leathern apron were, it is said, found by the corpse. If so, these are the only traces left by this mysterious criminal. Dr. ANDERSON, the new chief of the Detective Department, will now have an admirable opportunity of showing that wits sharpened by reflections upon the deeper problems of "Human Destiny" and the millennium are quite capable of grappling with the mundane problems of the detection of crime. The

"Dr. M'Jekyll and Mr. O'Hyde"— Stevenson's characters enter the realm of politics (*Punch*, August 18, 1888).

fact that the police have been freely talking for a week past about a man nicknamed Leather Apron may have led the criminal to leave a leather apron near his victim in order to mislead. He certainly seems to have been capable of such an act of deliberate preparation. The murder perpetrated this morning shows no indication of hurry or of alarm. He seems to have first killed the woman by cutting her throat so deeply as almost to sever her head from her shoulders, then to have disembowelled her, and then to have disposed of the viscera in a fashion recalling stories of Red Indian savagery. A man who was cool enough to do this, and who had time enough to do it, was not likely to leave his leather apron behind him and his knife apparently for no purpose but to serve as a clue. But be this as it may, if the police know of a ruffian who wears a leather apron in Whitechapel whom they have suspected of previous crimes, no time should be lost in ascertaining whether this leather apron, if it really exists, can be identified as his.

This renewed reminder of the potentialities of revolting barbarity which lie latent in man will administer a salutary shock to the complacent optimism which assumes that the progress of civilisation has rendered unnecessary the bolts and bars, social, moral, and legal, which keep the Mr. Hyde of humanity from assuming visible shape among us. There certainly seems to be a tolerably realistic impersonification of Mr. Hyde at large in Whitechapel. The Savage of Civilisation whom we are raising by the hundred thousand in our slums is quite as capable of bathing his hands in blood as any Sioux who ever scalped a foe. But we should not be surprised if the murderer in the present case should not turn out to be slum bred. The nature of the outrages and the calling of the victims suggests that we have to look out for a man who is animated by that mania of bloodthirsty cruelty which sometimes springs from the unbridled indulgence of the worst passions. We may have a plebeian Marquis DE SADE at large in Whitechapel. If so, and if he is not promptly apprehended, we shall not have long to wait for another addition to the ghastly catalogue of murder.

There is some reason to hope that the sentiment of horror which the peculiar atrocity of the present crime excites even in the most callous will spur the police into a display of vigorous and intelligent activity. At present the disaffection in the force is so widespread that, unless we are strangely misinformed, the police are thinking more of the possibility of striking against a system which has become intolerable than of overexerting themselves in the detection of crime. As for the community at large, the panic will probably be confined to the area within which this midnight murderer confines his operations. If, however, a similar crime were now to be committed in the West-end, there would be a panic, the like of which we have not seen in our time. From that, however, we shall probably be spared; but the public will be more or less uneasy as long as the Whitechapel murderer is left at large.

The Star, London, Monday, September 10, 1888

THE POLICE AND THE PRESS

The police, justly or unjustly, come in for a large share of the blame of these undiscovered crimes. It is true that Whitechapel is densely populated and difficult to cover, but it is also true that under anything like intelligent police management such a quartette of openly committed murders could hardly have occurred. One thing is absolutely certain, and that is that murderers will always escape with the ease that now characterises their escape in London until the police authorities adopt a different attitude towards the Press. They treat the reporters of the newspapers, who are simply news-gatherers for the great mass of the people, with a snobbery that would be beneath contempt were it not senseless to an almost criminal degree. On Saturday they shut the reporters out of the mortuary; they shut them out of the house where the murder was done; the constable at the mortuary door lied to them; some of the inspectors at the offices seemed to wilfully mislead them; they denied information which would have done no harm to make public, and the withholding of which only tended to increase the public uneasiness over the affair.

Now if the people of London wish murderers detected they must have all this changed. In New York, where the escape of a murderer is as rare as it is common here, the

REPORTERS ARE FAR MORE ACTIVE

agents in ferreting out crime than the detectives. They are no more numerous or more intelligent than the reporters of London, but they are given every facility and opportunity to get all the facts, and no part of any case is hidden from them unless the detectives' plan makes it necessary to keep it a secret. The consequence is that a large number of sharp and experienced eyes are focussed upon every point of a case, a number of different theories develop which the reporters themselves follow up, and instances in which the detection of a criminal is due to a newspaper reporter are simply too common to create any particular comment. Reporters are not prying individuals simply endeavoring to gratify their own curiosity. They are direct agents of the people who have a right to the news and a right to know what their paid servants the police and detectives are doing to earn the bread and butter for which the people are taxed. No properly accredited reporter ever wishes to know or print anything that will thwart the ends of justice, but he does desire and is fully entitled to the fullest scope in examining all the details of the case. The sooner the police authorities appreciate and act on this the sooner the Whitechapel fiend will be captured and human life in London rendered a little more safe.

A NEW SUGGESTION.

"T. C. M." writes: — May not the horrible murders of Whitechapel be the act of some insane butcher or dissecting-room porter? Mrs. Richardson's account of the ghastly sight of the last poor victim seems to bear out my theory of the crime being the deed of some miscreant who has been accustomed to some such work on the dead subject. As a medical man I am struck by the fact of the viscera being taken out and placed alongside of the unfortunate victim, as if for inspection by the demonstrator at a post-mortem examination. Anyhow, I think all dissecting room or post-mortem porters of the hospitals or mortuaries and even veterinary assistants should be scrutinised as to their state of mind also, and especially should some account be ascertained of all such persons who have lately left such situations, either of their own free will or by dismissal.

Pall Mall Gazette, London, Monday, September 10, 1888

It is to be hoped that the police and their amateur assistants are not confining their attention to those who look like "horrid ruffians." Many of the occupants of the Chambers of Horrors look like local preachers, Members of Parliament, or monthly nurses. We incline on the whole to the belief which we expressed on Saturday that the murderer is a victim of erotic mania which often takes the awful shape of an uncontrollable taste for blood. Sadism, as it is termed from the maniac marquis whose books sound the lowest depth obscenity has ever touched, is happily so strange to the majority of our people that they find it difficult to credit the possibility of mere debauchery bearing such awful fruitage. The Marquis de Sade, who died in a lunatic asylum at the age of seventy-four, after a life spent in qualifying for admission to gaol and escaping from prison, was an amiable-looking gentleman, and so, possibly enough, may be the Whitechapel murderer.

The Star, London, Tuesday, September 11, 1888

"MEANWHILE," writes an eccentric correspondent, "you, and every one of the papers, have missed the obvious solution of the Whitechapel mystery. The murderer is a Mr. Hyde, who seeks in the repose and comparative respectability of Dr. Jekyll security from the crimes he commits in his baser shape. Of course, the lively imaginations of your readers will at once supply certain means of identification for the Dr. Jekyll whose Mr. Hyde seems daily growing in ferocious intensity. If he should turn out to be a statesman engaged in the harmless pursuit of golf at North Berwick—well, you, sir, at least, will be able gratefully to remember that you have prepared your readers for the shock of the inevitable discovery."

The Star, London, Thursday, September 13, 1888

KILLED BY EMOTION.

Mrs. Mary Burridge, a dealer in floorcloth, at 132, Blackfriars-road, was standing at her door on Saturday, reading the *Star* account of the Whitechapel murder, and was so much affected that she retired to the kitchen, where she fell down in a fit. She regained consciousness for a short time on Monday, but afterwards relapsed and died yesterday.

The Star, London, Friday, September 14, 1888

THERE will be a perceptible tightening of public interest in the Whitechapel tragedies to-day. Nearly a week has passed since the final crime in the series, and still the police are at fault. Meanwhile, the epidemic of lawlessness continues. Three violent robberies have taken place within a hundred yards of each other, and midway between the scenes of the last two crimes. There has been one more mysterious crime in the West of London, to which again the police have no clue. The evidence at the inquest is bad—bad as can be. Mysterious personages flit through it like the shadowy and awful figures in POE'S and STEVENSON'S novels, or the stealthy and cunning assassins of GABORIAU and DU BOISGOBEY. The body of the woman is washed at the mortuary—nobody knows by whom. A ghostly pensioner starts into view and disappears again. Every new turn of this bewildering labyrinth reveals some fresh depth of social blackness, some strange and repulsive curiosity of human nature. What are we to do? Where are we to turn? The foreman of the jury indignantly echoes our demand for a large reward by the Government. The reply is that the Government have ceased to issue rewards. The local ignorance of the detectives, the glib carelessness of their methods, illustrate the absolute necessity for forming Vigilant Committees, which we recommended from the first, and which might have saved the neighborhood from the fresh spurt of criminal energy we record to-day. Neighborhoods go mad like individuals, and, while the West sits discussing the Whitechapel horrors over its wine, the East is seething with impatience, distrust, horror. What a situation!

Pall Mall Gazette, London, Friday, September 14, 1888

The medical evidence at the Whitechapel inquest yesterday was important as tending to negative the "maniac" theory. The doctor fortunately spared the jury and the public from hearing more about the murderer's mutilation of his victim than was absolutely necessary; but enough was said to show that the man went about his work in a way which if viewed in one light it was demoniacal enough, may yet in another be described as scientific. "There were indications," said Dr. Phillips, "of anatomical knowledge, which were only less indicated in consequence of haste." Here, then, we have two sets of fact. One is that the murderer has used the utmost ingenuity in concealing all traces of his whereabouts; the other, that he did his bloody work, with the lust it is true of the savage, but with the skill of a *savant*. Do not these facts point rather to Mr. Hyde than to a wandering lunatic?

The Star, London, Tuesday, September 18, 1888

ANOTHER THEORY.

With reference to the missing parts of Annie Chapman's body, Thomas Bolas writes:— "That biologists have been so infatuated by their pursuits as to cause murder to be committed in aid of their researches is a matter of history, and to my mind there is quite enough evidence of the last murder being the work of some half-mad physiologist in search of living tissues or organs from a healthy subject, for experiments on graftation, to justify certain investigations by the police."

The Star, London, Wednesday, September 19, 1888

A DETECTIVE'S DIARY A LA MODE.

MONDAY.— Papers full of the latest tragedy. One of them suggested that the assassin was a man who wore a blue coat. Arrested three blue-coat wearers on suspicion.

TUESDAY.— The blue-coats proved innocent. Released. Evening journal threw out a hint that deed might have been perpetrated by a soldier. Found a small drummer-boy drunk and incapable. Conveyed him to the station-house.

WEDNESDAY.— Drummer-boy released. Letter of anonymous correspondent to daily journal declaring that the outrage could only have been committed by a sailor. Decoyed petty officer of penny steamboat on shore, and suddenly arrested him.

THURSDAY.— Petty officer allowed to go. Hint thrown out in the correspondence columns that the crime might be traceable to a lunatic. Noticed an old gentleman purchasing a copy of "Maiwa's Revenge." Seized him.

FRIDAY.— Lunatic dispatched to an asylum. Anonymous letter received, denouncing local clergyman as the criminal. Took the reverend gentleman into custody.

SATURDAY.— Eminent ecclesiastic set at liberty with an apology. Ascertain in a periodical that it is thought just possible that the police may have committed the crime themselves. At the call of duty, finished the week by arresting myself!—*Punch*.

The Times, London, Saturday, September 22, 1888

STORIES OF CRIME.
TO THE EDITOR OF THE TIMES.

Sir,— It has long been the custom for provincial newspapers to publish serial stories in their weekly issues, generally of a more or less sensational character. These stories of late have in many instances taken the form of the lives and actions, most highly exaggerated, of notorious criminals—*e.g.*, "A Race to Ruin; or, the History of William Palmer the Poisoner," "Charles Peace, the King of Criminals," "Dick Turpin, the Prince of Highwaymen," "Prichard, the Poisoner of Glasgow."

It is only those whose duties cause them to

be mixed up with the lower and criminal classes who can really appreciate how great is the evil influence of this pernicious literature and how eagerly it is sought after.

Not long since some lads, children of honest parents, committed two burglaries; it was clearly shown by their own confession that they had been instigated to do so by reading "Dick Turpin, the Prince of Highwaymen." A youth of about 18, of miserable physical power, when arrested for larceny bit the constable's thumb and said, "I am as game as Charley Peace, and I will do as much as him before I die." The history of the "King of Criminals" was being published at the time by one of the local papers. Many similar instances could be furnished.

It is, to my mind, quite possible that the Whitechapel murders may be the fruit of such pernicious seed falling upon a morbid and degraded mind.

Although the law is powerless to repress such publications, they might be brought into disrepute and contempt if the attention of the better class of newspapers and the respectable portion of the community was drawn to this evil and its results by your powerful aid.

Your obedient servant,
K. T. A.

Illustrated Police News, London, Saturday, September 22, 1888

A contemporary asks (says the *St. James's Gazette*) if it is not "within the bounds of probability that to the highly-coloured pictorial advertisements to be seen on almost all the hoardings in London, vividly representing sensational scenes of murder, exhibited as the 'great attractions' of certain dramas, the public may be to a certain extent indebted for the horrible crimes in Whitechapel?" Everyone who walks much about the streets of London, or of any other large town, must have observed that during the last two or three years the illustrated posters on the walls have shown an increasing tendency to be grossly horrible and revolting. Theatrical advertisements sin most frequently in this direction. No detail is spared. We have the fiendish expression of the villain's countenance as he plunges a dagger into the bosom of the hero. The crimson stains upon the white shirt front are very effectively managed, and when the murderer withdraws his knife, as in some of the posters, there is sure to be a significant splash of red upon the point of it. In all great communities there are certain to be a number of small-brained creatures, only half human, whose minds, muddled by bad air and bad gin, readily take fire when they are confronted with the ghastly particulars of murder. Such pictures as these produce upon them the same effect that the taste of blood produces upon the tiger.

The Star, London, Monday, September 24, 1888

BLOOD MONEY TO WHITECHAPEL.
TO THE EDITOR OF "THE STAR."

SIR, — Will you allow me to make a comment on the success of the Whitechapel murderer in calling attention for a moment to the social question? Less than a year ago the West-end press, headed by the *St. James's Gazette*, the *Times*, and the *Saturday Review*, were literally clamoring for the blood of the people — hounding on Sir Charles Warren to thrash and muzzle the scum who dared to complain that they were starving — heaping insult and reckless calumny on those who interceded for the victims — applauding to the skies the open class bias of those magistrates and judges who zealously did their very worst in the criminal proceedings which followed — behaving, in short as the proprietary class always does behave when the workers throw it into a frenzy of terror by venturing to show their teeth. Quite lost on these journals and their patrons were indignant remonstrances, arguments, speeches, and sacrifices, appeals to history, philosophy, biology, economics, and statistics; references to the reports of inspectors, registrar generals, city missionaries, Parliamentary commissions, and newspapers; collections of evidence by the five senses at every turn; and house-to-house investigations into the condition of the unemployed, all unanswered and unanswerable, and all pointing the same way. The *Saturday Review* was still frankly for hanging the appellants; and the *Times* denounced them as "pests of society." This was still the tone of the class Press as lately as the strike of the Bryant and May girls. Now all is changed. Private enterprise has succeeded where Socialism failed. Whilst we conventional Social Democrats were wasting our time on education, agitation, and organisation, some independent genius has taken the matter in hand, and by simply murdering and disembowelling four women, converted the proprietary press to an inept sort of communism. The moral is a pretty one, and the Insurrectionists, the Dynamitards, the Invincibles, and the extreme left of the Anarchist party will not be slow to draw it. "Humanity, political science, economics, and religion," they will say, "are all rot; the one argument that touches your lady and gentleman is the knife." That is so pleasant for the party of Hope and Perseverance in their toughening struggle with the party of Desperation and Death!

However, these things have to be faced. If the line to be taken is that suggested by the converted West-end papers—if the people are still to yield up their wealth to the Clanricarde class, and get what they can back as charity through Lady Bountiful, then the policy for the people is plainly a policy of terror. Every gaol blown up, every window broken, every shop looted, every corpse found disembowelled, means another ten pound note for "ransom." The riots of 1886 brought in £78,000 and a People's Palace; it remains to be seen how much these murders may prove worth to the East-end in *panem et circenses*. Indeed, if the habits of duchesses only admitted of their being decoyed into Whitechapel back-yards, a single experiment in slaughterhouse anatomy on an aristocratic victim might fetch in a round half million and save the necessity of sacrificing four women of the people. Such is the stark-naked reality of these abominable bastard Utopias of genteel charity in which the poor are first to be robbed and then pauperised by way of compensation, in order that the rich man may combine the idle luxury of the protected thief with the unctuous self-satisfaction of the pious philanthropist.

The proper way to recover the rents of London for the people of London is not by charity, which is one of the worst curses of poverty, but by the municipal rate collector, who will no doubt make it sufficiently clear to the monopolists of ground value that he is not merely taking round the hat, and that the State is ready to enforce his demand, if need be. And the money thus obtained must be used by the municipality as the capital of productive industries for the better employment of the poor. I submit that this is at least a less disgusting and immoral method of relieving the East-end than the gush of bazaars and blood money which has suggested itself from the West-end point of view.— Yours, &c.,

G. BERNARD SHAW.

St. Stephen's Review, London, Saturday, September 29, 1888

Between the Whitechapel murders and the weird performance of *Dr. Jekyll and Mr. Hyde*, the mental condition of people with highly-strung nerves is becoming very serious. I was attracted by a crowd in the Strand the other night, and on investigating the matter, found that they surrounded a well-dressed young man who had bolted out of a 'bus while it was going at a rapid rate, and then fallen down in a fit. It appeared he had been to see Mr. Mansfield as Dr. Jekyll, and on getting into the 'bus found himself beside a most repulsive-looking man, whom he immediately concluded must either be the Doctor himself or the Whitechapel murderer. In a fit of fearful nervousness, he jumped from his seat, and came to grief as mentioned.

Daily Telegraph, London, Monday, October 1, 1888

On Thursday last the following letter, bearing the "E.C." post-mark, and directed in red ink, was delivered to the Central News Agency:

Sept. 25, 1888.

Dear Boss—I keep on hearing the police have caught me, but they won't fix me just yet. I have laughed when they look so clever and talk about being on the right track. Great joke about Leather Apron. Gave me real fits. I am down on whores, and I shan't quit ripping them till I do get buckled. Grand work the last job was. I gave the lady no time to squeal. How can they catch me now? I love my work and want to start again. You will soon hear of me, with my funny little games. I saved some of the proper red stuff in a ginger beer bottle over the last job to write with, but it went thick, like glue, and I can't use it. Red ink is fit enough, I hope. Ha, ha! The next job I do I shall clip the lady's ears off and send to the police officers, just for jolly, wouldn't you?

Keep this letter back till I do a bit more work, then give it out straight. My knife's so nice and sharp. I want to get to work right away if I get a chance. Good luck—Yours truly,

JACK THE RIPPER.

Don't mind me giving the trade name.

Wasn't good enough to post this before I got all the red ink off my hands; curse it. No luck yet. They say I'm a doctor now. Ha, ha!

The agency says: The whole of this extraordinary epistle is written in red ink in a free, bold, clerkly hand. It was of course treated as the work of a practical joker, but it is singular to note that the latest murders have been committed within a few days of the receipt of the letter; that, apparently, in the case of his last victim the murderer made an attempt to cut off the ears; and that he actually did mutilate the face in a manner which he has never before attempted. The letter is now in the hands of the Scotland-yard authorities.

The Star, London, Monday, October 1, 1888.

WHAT WE THINK.

THE terror of Whitechapel has walked again, and this time has marked down two victims, one hacked and disfigured beyond discovery, the other with her throat cut and torn. Again he has got away clear; and again the police, with wonderful frankness, confess that they have not a clue. They are waiting for a seventh and an eighth murder, just as they waited for a fifth, to help them to it. Meanwhile, Whitechapel is half mad with fear. The people are afraid even to talk with a stranger. Notwithstanding the repeated proofs that the murderer has but one aim, and seeks but one class in the community, the spirit of terror has got fairly abroad, and no one knows what steps a practically defenceless community may take to protect itself or avenge itself on any luckless wight who may be taken for the enemy. It is the duty of journalists to keep their heads cool, and not inflame men's passions when what is wanted is cool temper and clear thinking; and we shall try and write calmly about this new atrocity.

And, first, let us examine the facts, and the light they throw on any previous theories. To begin with it is clear that the BURKE and HARE theory is all but destroyed. There is no suggestion of surgical neatness, or of the removal of any organ, about the Mitre-square murder. It is a ghastly butchery—done with insane ruthlessness and violence. The gang theory is also weakened, and the story of a man who is said to have seen the Berner-street tragedy, and declares that one man butchered and another man watched, is, we think, *a priori* incredible. The theory of madness is on the other hand enormously strengthened. Crafty blood-thirst is written on every line of Sunday morning's doings, The rapid walk from Berner-street to Aldgate, to find a fresh victim, the reckless daring of the deed — in itself the most dangerous and cunning of all the murderer's resources — these all point to some epileptic outbreak of homicidal mania. The immediate motive need not trouble us now, except so far as it suggests the invariable choice of the poor street-wanderers of the East-end. It may be, as Dr. SAVAGE supposes, a plan of fiendish revenge for fancied wrongs, or the deed of some modern Thug or Sicarius, with a confused idea of putting down vice by picking off unfortunates in detail. A slaughterer or a butcher who has been in a lunatic asylum, a mad medical student with a bad history behind him or a tendency to religious mania — these are obviously classes on which the detective sense which all of us possess in some measure should be kept. Finally, there is the off-chance — too horrible almost to contemplate — that we have a social experimentalist abroad determined to make the classes see and feel how the masses live.

More important is the discussion as to the possible methods of the murderer. Granting that he has some rough knowledge of anatomy, it is probable that his hands only would be smeared by his bloody work, and that after doing the deed he would put on gloves. He must have done so in order to ensnare the second woman — if, indeed, the two deeds were the work of one hand. As a further precaution there might be the donning of an overcoat after the deed. As he nowhere stays to wash his hands, he probably does not inhabit lodging-houses or hotels, but a private house where he has special facilities — perhaps chemicals and a wash-hand stand communicating directly with a pipe — for getting rid of bloody hands and clothes. He must be inoffensive, probably respectable in manner and appearance, or else after the murderous warnings of last week, woman after woman could not have been decoyed by him. Two theories are suggested to us — that he may wear woman's clothes, or may be a policeman.

"JACK THE RIPPER'S" JOKE.

A practical joker, who signed himself "Jack the Ripper," wrote to the Central News last week, intimating with labored flippancy that he was going to commence operations again in Whitechapel shortly. He said he would cut the woman's ears off to send to the police. This morning the same agency received a postcard smeared apparently with dirty blood. It was written with red chalk. It says: —

"I was not codding dear old Boss when I gave you the tip. You'll hear about saucy Jacky's work to-morrow. Double event this time. Number one squealed a bit. Couldn't finish straight off. Had not time to get ears for police. Thanks for keeping back last letter till I got to work again. — JACK THE RIPPER."

The Daily Telegraph, London, Tuesday, October 2, 1888.

It is time that her Majesty's Government awoke to a proper sense of the responsibilities which weigh upon them as a consequence of the unprecedented series of atrocities that have produced almost a frenzy of panic at the East-end, and have spread alarm and apprehension throughout the length and breadth of this vast Metropolis. It is not assuredly the first time that a great city of the Empire has been angered and affrighted by the repeated occurrence of dreadful deeds of blood; still there is scarcely any analogy between the six appalling deeds of assassination and savagery which will be known in the black chronicle of crime as the

Whitechapel Murders and former cases of aggravated homicide, cruel and revolting enough in themselves, but which had still, from the beginning, an ascertained and palpable motive. Nearly sixty years ago Edinburgh first and London afterwards were convulsed with dread and horror by the fiendish deeds respectively of BURKE and HARE and of BISHOP and WILLIAMS. Then, however, from the first it was suspected, and the suspicion was very soon justified by certainty, that the miscreants who committed these horrible acts, and who decoyed cripples, drunken men, imbeciles, and poor Italian boys to their lairs, first to stupefy and then to suffocate them with pitch-plasters, were, in the cant language of the period, a monstrous development of the body-snatchers or "resurrection men," who found it easier and safer to murder their victims than to rifle graves in order to sell the corpses to the surgeons, whose anatomical studies were impeded by obstructive legislation. Still the hanging of the ruffians implicated in these atrocities was not the only cause of the immediate and definitive cessation of the crime of burking. Parliament passed an Anatomy Act, which enabled medical men to obtain "subjects" without resorting to any illegitimate means; and the scum of humanity, who had hitherto been the purveyors of the dissecting-room, found their profitable but ghastly occupation gone. While they flourished the burkers were a terror; but their whereabouts was guessed at, their intentions were patent, their movements were watched, and they were at last hunted down and consigned to the gallows; and the burkers, thank Heaven, are an extinct race of demons in human form. In the Whitechapel murders we have not, beyond the equivocal medical hypothesis broached by the coroner in the case of ANNIE CHAPMAN, one single clue, or even fragment of a clue — beyond the finding of a portion of the apron of one of the victims — which is likely to guide us either to the direction of the assassin or assassins or the possible motive which may have prompted the commission of these unspeakable crimes. The anatomical theory is, we repeat, almost entirely untenable; and we are thus left to weave the merest figments of fancy, and to form unpleasant visions of roving lunatics distraught with homicidal mania or bloodthirsty lust; of abandoned desperadoes wreaking their thirst for slaughter on forlorn and hopeless women, the wretchedest and most pitiable of their sex, to satisfy some inscrutably foul and crapulous vendetta; or, finally, we may dream of monsters, or ogres, and chimeras in the shape of wretched beings who catch from each awful story the contagion of senseless crime, and, out of a horrid imitativeness, repeat the abominable acts which they have seen described.

The Daily Telegraph, London, Wednesday, October 3, 1888.

"G. C." has a fancy "that the perpetrator is a being whose diseased brain has been inflamed by witnessing the performance of the drama of 'Dr. Jekyll and Mr. Hyde'— which I understand is now wisely withdrawn from the stage. If there is anything in this, let the detectives consider how Mr. Hyde would have acted—for there may be a system in the demonic actions of a madman in following the pattern set before him."

The Pall Mall Gazette, London, Wednesday 3 October 1888.

HOW TO CATCH THE MURDERER.
MORE SUGGESTIONS BY THE PUBLIC.

The suggestions from the public as to the Whitechapel murders, their perpetrator, and their prevention are becoming positively idiotic. Here are a few examples from the morning papers: -

A hint from Mr. Archibald Forbes.— That the murderer is the victim of a specific contagion, and is avenging himself. Possibly a medical student, from the knowledge of anatomy displayed in the murders.

Try the clairvoyant.— Several correspondents suggest that the spiritualists should be called in. Where are Messrs. Stuart Cumberland and Irving Bishop?

Handwriting expert.— Jack the Ripper's letters may be genuine. Why not have them photographed and widely circulated?

Baby-faced pugilists.— Policemen have beards, bass voices, and big feet. Give the pugilists a chance; there are numbers of well-trained pugilists in Shoreditch and Whitechapel, who are, many of them young, and, as is the custom in their profession, clean-shaved. Twenty game men of this class in women's clothes loitering about Whitechapel would have more chance than any number of heavy-footed policemen.

Jekyll and Hyde.— Possibly the culprit is an army doctor suffering from sunstroke. He has seen the horrible play, lives in Bayswater or North London, in perhaps a decent square or terrace, dresses well. Goes out about 10 P.M. straight to Whitechapel. Commits deed. Home again to breakfast. Wash, brush-up, sleep. Himself again — Dr. Hyde. Meantime, everybody scouring the scene of the tragedy for the usual type of a murderer.

The enterprising newspaper (½ d.).— Seek the person who profits by the crime. "I venture," says a correspondent, "to affirm that no one will be bold enough to deny that the occurrence of these murders has caused a very large some of money to be diverted into the pockets of the proprietors of some evening papers. The inference is obvious. The silly season is sillier than was ever known. A syndicate could easily be formed to provide the £20 which Mr. Wynne Baxter's experience as a coroner teaches him is a sufficient inducement to an unscrupulous person, and the amount of 'copy' produced by the expenditure of this moderate sum is practically unlimited."

The lunatic of Leavesden.— Twelve months ago an inmate of the lunatic asylum at Leavesden escaped. The local paper warned females against being out at night in the neighbourhood, as this man was dangerous only to women. Where is he?

The cryptogrammatic dagger.— In examining the chart representing the locality of the Whitechapel murders, says one, it is curious to observe that lines drawn through the spots where the murders were committed assume the exact form of a dagger, the hilt and blade of which pass through the scenes of the sixth, second, first, and third murders, the extremities of the guard making the fourth and fifth. Can this possibly afford a clue to the position of the next atrocity?

Letter to City of London Police, naming Mansfield as murderer, October 5, 1888.

Dear Sir

Now That these Horrable Murders are being Comited I think it the duty of Every one to let the Police know if they Suspect anyone. What I am going to Say Seems Allmost imposable but Still Strange things have Happend at times. I have A great Likeing for Acters So that I Should be the Last to think because A man take A dretfull Part he is therefore Bad but when I went to See Mr Mansfield Take the Part of Dr Jekel & Mr Hyde I felt at once that he was <u>the Man Wanted</u> & I have not been able to get this Feeling out of my Head. I have no Rest of <u>A night or day</u> I thought the dritfull manor he Works himself up in his Part that It might be Posable to work himself up So that he would <u>do it in Reality I do not think there is A man Living</u> So well able to disgise Himself in A moment as he does in front of the Public. <u>Who So well able to Baffel the Police</u>, or Public he Could be A <u>dark man. Fair man. Short man.</u> or <u>Tall</u> in A five Seconds if he carried A fine Faulse Wiskers &c in A Bag.

I thought it Strange this Play Should have Commenced before the Murders for it is Realy Something <u>after the Same Stile</u>. The Murders Take Place on <u>Saturday nights</u> Mr M never has A Preformance on <u>Saturday</u>. The Murders Once Took Place on Friday & once Mr M Was to ill to Preform at the <u>Saturday morning Preformance</u>. But weather it was at this time I dont know. I thought it Funney when <u>the Safe was Robed of £200</u> & no one knew by wolme it looks as if there was A <u>Bad Person about</u>.

I Read in the Globe the outher night that the Same <u>dretfull murders</u> took Place in <u>America</u> & were never discovered Mr M is I think <u>A American</u> But weather he Came from there I dont know.

As it has woried me So I thought it best to let you know for you could let A man watch him without Causing any Bother. ~~For I think~~ For I think you ought to know <u>where he Lodges</u> & what Sort of <u>A man he is</u>. I dont know Whats Put this into my Head I Can assure you it is not because I See him Take Such A dretfull Part for I have had Friends on the Stage Take Bad Parts but did not think they were bad in Conquence Yours one who Prays for the murdrer to be Caught. M. P. (Corporation of London Record Office, Police Box 3:16, No. 155)

Following four pages (181–184): A letter implicating Mansfield in the Jack the Ripper slayings sent to the City of London Police, October 5, 1888. (Corporation of London Records Office Police Box 3:16 No. 155)

Appendix E: Jack the Ripper

[155] Oct 5 1888   Not Acknowledged

Dear Sir
  Now that these
Horrable Murders are be-
ing Comited I think it the
Duty of Every one to let
the Police know if they
Suspect anyone. What I
am going to say seems
Allmost imposable but still
strange things have happend
at times. I have a great
Likening for Actors So that
I should be the Last to think
because a Man take a ruthe
Part
He is therefore Bad but
when I went to see Mr
Mansfield Take the Part
of Dr Jekel & Mr Hyde

CLRO Police Box 3.16 No. 155

I felt at once that he was the Man Wanted & I have not been able to get this Feeling out of my Head. I have no Rest of a Night or Day. I thought the dreadfull Manor he works himself up in his Part that It might be possable to work himself up so that he would do it in Reality. I do not think there is a Man Living so well able to Disguise Himself in a Moment as he does in front of the Public. Who so well able to Baffel the Police, or Public he could be a Dark Man, Fair Man, Short Man, or Tall in a few Seconds

of the Curse at pres Stanli
Wilkins & Co in X May.
I thought it strange this
play Shoulde have commence
before the Murders for it is
scaly something after the same
Style. The Murders take place
on Saturday Nights but
M Mener has X Preformance
on Saturday. The Murders once
took place on Friday. &
Once Mr M. was to ill to
preforme at the Saturday
Morning preformance. But
weather it was at this time
I don't know. I thought
it Funny when the Safe
was Robed of £200 & no one knew
by whom it looks as if there
was X Bad person about.
I read in the Globe the

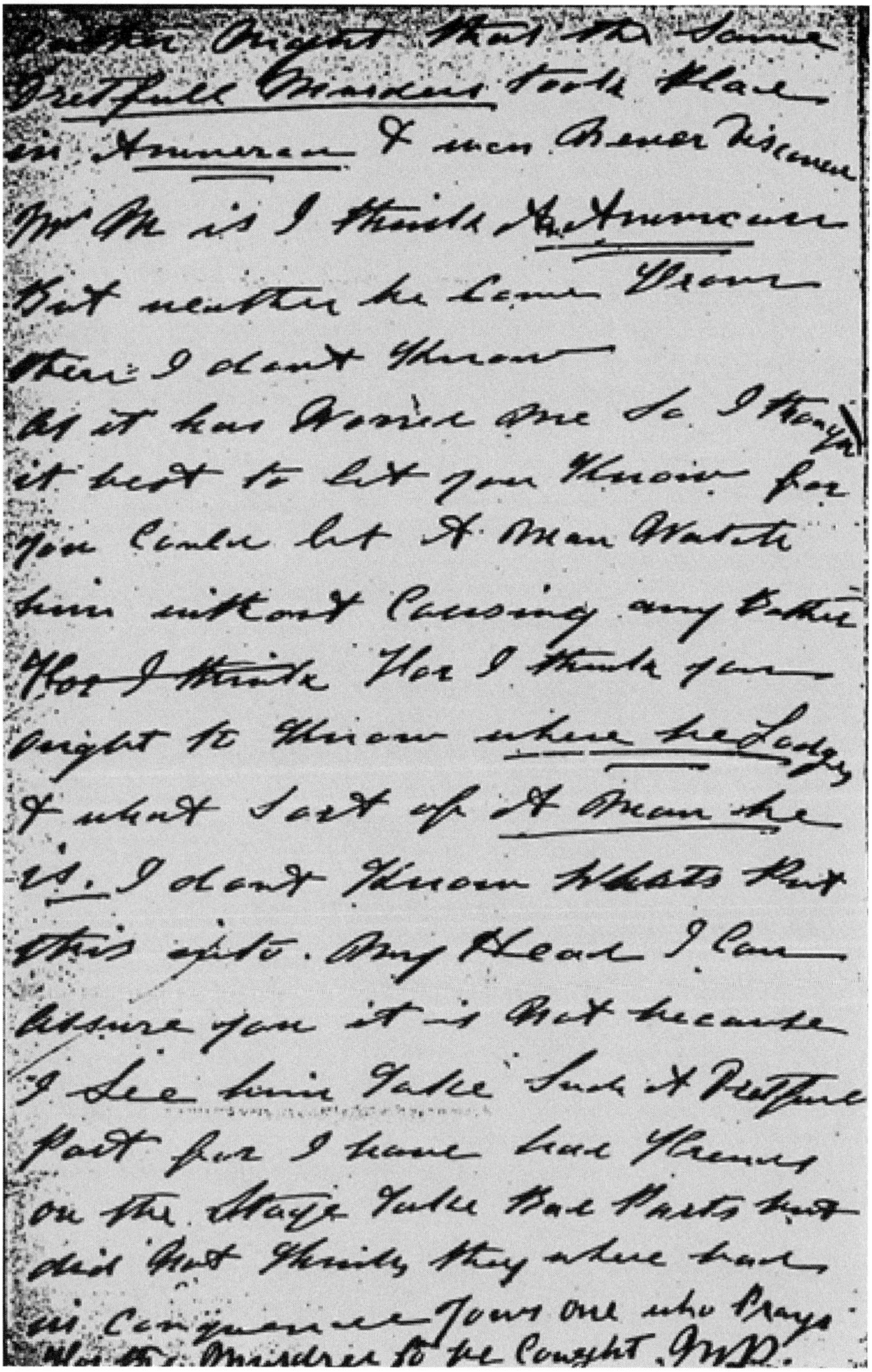

...ter Ought that the Same
Dreadfull Murders took place
in America & was never discovered
Mr Ma is I think An American
but neither he came from
there I dont know
As it has worried me so I thought
it best to let you know for
you could let A Man Watch
him without causing any bother
~~For I think~~ For I think you
ought to know where he Lodges
& what sort of A Man he
is. I dont know whats put
this into my Head I can
assure you it is not because
I see him take such A Dreadful
part for I have had friends
on the Stage take bad Parts but
did not think they where bad
in consequence Yours one who Prays
for the Murderer to be Caught. J.W.D.

The Star, London, October 6, 1888.

A Doctor's Clue.

He Gives Information of a Mad Medical Assistant.

A medical gentleman called at *The Star* office yesterday to give us some important information regarding a suspicion which he entertains as to the murderer. But his first words were of protest against the manner he was received at Scotland-yard. He went there in company with another medical gentleman and announced that he had some important information to communicate. He was shown into an underground room where two or three police clerks were standing about. He was not attended to, and after waiting some minutes he said to his friend, "Well, if this is the way we are to be treated I am going." Thereupon one of the subalterns said, "Beg pardon, sir, but we are very busy." This came from one of the men who was busy talking to his colleagues. At last the doctor received some, but not too polite, attention. He was conducted upstairs to see

"SOMEONE IN AUTHORITY,"

but that "someone" refused to see him. His statement was then taken down in a perfunctory manner. "The man," he says, "didn't put down half that I told him, and I was disgusted at the manner we were received and at the careless way Scotland-yard does its duty." The only explanation they gave to his protests was that "There's so many people call here, you know." Having extricated himself from Scotland-yard red tape and Warrenism, the gentleman came with his story to the *Star* office, not because he sympathises with the paper politically, for he is a "rank Conservative," but because of the importance he attaches to the news.

It has been more than once suggested that the murderer is a

MONOMANIAC WITH MEDICAL KNOWLEDGE

The doctor had an assistant who has gone mad recently, and who is exactly the sort of man Mr. Archibald Forbes had in his mind in his diagnosis of the murders. "Clearly," said Mr. Forbes, "the murderer is a man familiar with the geography of the Whitechapel purlieus. Clearly he is a man not unaccustomed in the manner of accosting these poor women as they are wont to be accosted. Clearly he is a man to whom the methods of the policeman are not unknown—the measured pace, the regular methodic round, the tendency to woodenness and unalertness of perception which are the characteristics of that well-meaning individual.

"Probably, a dissolute man, he fell a victim to a specific contagion, and so seriously that in the sequel he lost his career. What shape the deterioration may have taken, yet left him with a strong, steady hand, a brain of devilish coolness, and an active step, is not to be defined."

"The man's physical health ruined," continues Mr. Forbes, "and his career broken, he has possibly suffered specific brain damage as well. At this moment—I cannot use exact professional terms—there may be mischief to one of the lobes of the brain. Or he may have become insane simply from anguish of body and distress of mind. Anyhow, he is mad, and his mania, rising from the particular to the general, takes

THE FELL FORM OF REVENGE

against the class, a member of which has wrought him his blighting hurt, against, too, the persons of that class plying in Whitechapel, since it was from a Whitechapel loose woman that he took his scathe."

Now this exactly describes the man whom the doctor suspects. He is a man of about 35. He was not a fully qualified surgeon, but had a certain amount of anatomical knowledge, and had assisted at operations, including ovariotomy. He was the assistant to a doctor in Whitechapel, and

KNOWS EVERY ALLEY AND COURT

in the neighborhood of the places where the murders were committed. He has been the victim of "a specific contagion," and since then has been animated by feelings of hate, not to say revenge, against the lower class of women who haunt the streets. When seen about eight months ago he was mad. "What man," said the doctor, in concluding his story, "is more likely to have committed the crime than this maniac?" The matter is certainly one which should be sifted by the police, but Scotland-yard is perhaps too busy to attend to it, because forsooth "There's so many call here, you know."

The Philadelphia Inquirer, Wednesday, October 10, 1888.

THE WHITECHAPEL MURDERS.

THEORY STARTED THAT IT IS A JEKYLL AND HYDE CASE.

LONDON, Oct. 9.— The police have started the theory that the Whitechapel murders are the result of a case in real life of "Dr. Jekyll and Mr. Hyde."

Parallels are ingeniously drawn between the acts of the Whitechapel monster, who not only kills, but mutilates his victims, and the frenzied brutality with which the Mr. Hyde of the fiction stamps upon the girl, whom he knocks down and injures in the deserted and echoing streets at midnight, as told in the first part of the book.

Not only have the police been brought to this astounding position, through what they claim is direct evidence corroborative of such a theory, but they are industriously working with a particular individual in view, and they believe that they are truly upon the right track. A well known, prosperous resident of Grosvenor Square is the man thus under police surveillance. He moves in the best of society and is completely removed from derogatory suspicion among those who are his daily associates.

This man, however, has been tracked and traced until it is absolutely established that he does lead a double life. This "Dr. Jekyll" lives for the eminently respectable world in which he moves. The other self, like "Mr. Hyde," lives mysteriously, revoltingly. This latter self has been tracked to the Whitechapel district, and has been seen, in its form of man, skulking stealthily about dark corners and alleys, or stalking moodily through deserted side streets.

The Daily Telegraph, London, Friday, October 12, 1888.

DRAMATIC AND MUSICAL

Mr. Richard Mansfield has determined to abandon the "Creepy Drama," evidently beloved in America, in favour of wholesome comedy. The murderous Hyde will peer round the drawing-room windows and leap at his victim's throat for the last time during the forthcoming week; and in a few days we shall see no more at the Lyceum of the old satyr Baron Chevrial, who lives to love, and dies making hideous grimaces in an apoplectic fit. Experience has taught this clever young actor that there is no taste in London just now for horrors on the stage. There is quite sufficient to make us shudder out of doors.

The Star, London, Friday, October 12, 1888.

Look in the Ranks of the Respectable.

A solicitor writes us: I think that the detection of the Whitechapel murderer will be made impossible if the police and the public persevere in what appears to me a false scent. The general idea seems to be that the murderer lives in a low lodging house, or in some poverty-stricken den where the houseless and homeless gather together. This is absurd. The inmate of such a place would betray himself at once. The hour at which he returned would be recorded or remembered; and he would be observed washing the stains from his hands or clothes. No; the murderer is some man living with his wife and family; or, in rooms of his own or a house of his own, which he can enter with a latchkey without attracting the attention of anybody, and without anybody's permission or notice. In the quietness of his own bedroom he can calmly wash himself and his clothes, and go to bed without observation and without care. I think he must, however, live in the East and not in the West-end, as this theory might suggest. If he were living in the West-end, he would be almost certainly caught either walking away or driving away. A quiet house or private lodgings in the East-end — that's where the fellow skulks.

The Sensationalism of Our Day.

Sir. — We seem to be breathing nothing but the odor of the slaughterhouse. Is it necessary? The murders are horrible enough, and we must hunt, but we are getting too familiar with "ghastly details." What good end is to be served by that? Talking of this a few days ago, I took up a Leicester paper, with no special selection, and just as a test. Here is the result. The following headings appear in this one copy alone: — "Shocking affair at Chorley," "A priest's dead body burned to cinders in church," "Cut to pieces on the railway" (this was so relished that it was repeated in another part of the paper), "Cut to pieces at a railway station," "Sudden death of a child," "The Blackfriars mystery," "A cruel case," "A child worried by a pig," "Another suicide with carbolic acid," "The wife murder at Huddersfield," "The Whitechapel murder," "Attack on a Mormon agent in Wales," "A clergyman fined for drunkenness," "Another Thames mystery," "A human arm found in a timber yard," "Another railway accident in America — serious loss of life."

Why rake so much in one direction? It is becoming a serious question whether a decent and well-ordered household should go on admitting such buckets of slush. — Yours, &c.,

J. P. H.

Leicester, 6 Oct.

[We insert "J.P.H's" letter, but we confess we do not quite see his point. How can newspapers avoid telling their readers about these things. We admit that they should record them in a non-vulgar and truthful way, but it is useless to shut one's eyes to what daily happens. For instance, if clergymen get drunk why should they not be fined, and why should not their fine be recorded as an example to other clergymen. If terrible murders occur in the East, why should not the West be told of it, and why should not the public be instructed in the worst as well as the best facts? Truthful realism is good; it is only lying realism which should be avoided. — Ed. *Star*.]

Punch, London, Saturday, October 13, 1888.

Horrible London; Or,
The Pandemonium of Posters.

The Demon set forth in a novel disguise
(All methods of mischief the master-fiend
    tries)
Quoth he, "There's much ill to be wrought
    through the eyes.
I think, without being a boaster,
I can give their most 'cute Advertisers a start,
And beat them all round at the Bill-sticker's
    art.
I will set up in business in Babylon's mart,
As the new Pandemonium Poster!"
So he roved the huge city with wallet at
    waist,
With a brush, and a stick, and a pot full of
    paste,
And there wasn't a wall or a hoarding,
A space in a slum, or a blank on a fence,
A spare square of brick in a neighbourhood
    dense,
Or a bit of unoccupied boarding,
But there the new poster, who didn't much
    care
For the menacing legend, "Bill-stickers
    beware!"
Right soon was tremendously busy
With placards portentous in purple and blue,
Of horrible subject and hideous hue,
Enough to bemuddle an aëronaut's view,
And turn the best steeple-Jack dizzy.
Oh, the flamboyant flare of those fiendish
    designs,
With their sanguine paint-splashes and sinis-
    ter lines!
Gehenna seemed visibly glaring
In paint from those villanous daubs. There
    were men
At murderous work in malodorous den,
And ghoul-woman gruesomely staring.
The whole sordid drama of murder and guilt,
The steel that strikes home, and the blood
    that is spilt,
Was pictured in realist colours,
With emphasis strong on the black and the
    red,
The fear of the stricken, the glare of the dead;
All dreads and disasters and dolours

That haunt poor Humanity's dismallest state,
The horrors of crimes and the terrors of fate,
As conceived by the crudest of fancies,
Were limned on these posters in terrible
    tints,
In the style of the vilest sensational prints
Or the vulgarest penny romances.

That Bill-sticker paused in his work with a
    look
Which betrayed the black demon, and glee-
    somely shook
His sides in a spasm of laughter.
Quoth he, with a sinister wag of his head,
"By my horns, the good artist has lavished
    the red!
This home of coarse horror — this house of
    the dead
Looks crimson from basement to rafter.
How strange that a civilised City — ho! ho!
Tis their fatuous dream to consider it so! –
Which is nothing too lovely at best, should
    bestow
Such a liberal licence on spoilers!
These mural monstrosities, reeking of crime,
Flaring horridly forth amidst squalor and
    grime,
Must have an effect which will tell in good
    time
Upon legions of dull-witted toilers.
Taken in through the eyes such suggestions
    of sin
A sympathy morbid and monstrous must win
From the grovelling victims of gloom and bad
    gin,
Who gapingly gaze on them daily;
A fine picture-gallery this for the People!
Oh, while this endures, spite of School Board
    and Steeple,
My work must be going on gaily!"

Horrible London; Or, The Pandemonium of Posters. (*Punch*, October 13, 1888)

The East London Advertiser, Saturday, October 13, 1888.

Dr. Gordon Browne's evidence at the inquest on the woman discovered in Mitre-square establishes beyond a doubt the theory that the murderer is possessed of considerable anatomical skill. This belief had at one time grown weak, but it is now revived in full force. It is curious that he should have chosen quite a different organ to remove in the last instance. He clearly reads his papers and wishes to throw a new element into every case. However, we now know for certain that he is a skilled anatomist. There are not many such in Whitechapel, so that the investigations of the police are now very much narrowed. Dr. Browne's evidence disposes of a story which has just been telegraphed from America to the effect that a Malay some time ago declared that he had been robbed by a woman in Whitechapel, and that he intended to murder and mutilate every woman of the same class in that locality. Malay sailors are not as a rule skilled anatomists. The theories and stories which are still started every hour have, however, become too far-fetched to be worth notice.

Among the theories as to the Whitechapel murders, which start up one day and vanish the next, the one which is most in favour is the Jekyll and Hyde theory, namely, that the murderer is a man living a dual life, one respectable and even religious, and the other lawless and brutal; that he has two sets of chambers, and is probably a married man, and in every way a person whom you would not for a moment suspect. This theory derives considerable support from the opinion of Mr. George Lewis, the famous criminal lawyer, who holds it strongly, and is, I believe, prepared to defend it against all comers. Mr. Lewis's experience of criminal London is, of course, unique, and exceeds that of any living man with exception, perhaps, of Mr. Montagu Williams and Mr. Poland. He is, besides, a man of the world, of an extremely penetrating character, and sound though by no means narrow views.

The Star, London, Saturday, October 13, 1888.

ACTORS AND ACTING.
"SPECTATOR'S" NOTES ON THE DRAMATIC WEEK.

Mr. Richard Mansfield has shown a wise discretion in selecting a piece of pure comedy for his benefit performance next Friday in aid of the Bishop of Bedford's Home and Refuge Fund for the East-end Poor. The real horrors of Whitechapel have just now put the sham horrors of the stage to shame, and Mr. Mansfield is quick to recognise the situation.

Appendix F: H. B. Irving's *Dr. Jekyll and Mr. Hyde*

The Queen's Theatre, London, 1910

At the end of June 1889, Richard Mansfield left England owing £2,675 to Henry Irving in unpaid rent and loans, and harbouring the belief that his English season had been somehow sabotaged by Irving. This led to considerable ill-feeling between the two actors which culminated in Irving taking legal action to recover the debt, and securing from Longmans, Green & Co. the sole rights to perform *Dr. Jekyll and Mr. Hyde* in the UK. Despite depriving Mansfield of his hoped-for return to London in his most famous role, Henry Irving never performed the play, and it was left to his son, Henry Brodribb Irving, to return *Dr. Jekyll and Mr. Hyde* to the London stage, when he presented Joseph William Comyns Carr's adaptation of Stevenson's tale at the Queen's Theatre, London, in February 1910.

H. B. Irving's Queen's Theatre version, which was granted Performance Licence No 237 by the Lord Chamberlain's office on January 31, 1910, is presented in the following transcript with footnotes enabling comparison between this script and a partial *Dr. Jekyll and Mr. Hyde* script held by the New York Public Library.

This partial script consists of two holdings within New York Public Library's Billy Rose Theatre Collection: NCOF+ ZZ22022 "(Mansfield R. *Dr. Jekyll and Mr. Hyde* Typescript Acc No 312670B)" comprising Act I and Act IV complete; and NCOF+ ZZ22017 "(Mansfield R. *Dr. Jekyll and Mr. Hyde* Typescript)" containing nineteen pages of a complete Act III Scene 1, the first page of Act III Scene 2, and five loose, non-consecutive pages from Act II. (Act II Scene 1, pages 1 & 2; Act II Scene 2, pages 11 & 12; and Act II Scene 3, page 12.)

The library classification, and a handwritten note at the foot of the title page of Act I, attributing this script to "R. Mansfield & T. R. Sullivan," in contrast to the fact that the five loose pages from Act II constitute the only portion of the entire compilation which bears any resemblance to anything ever performed by Mansfield, has fostered the belief that this partial script is an "early draft" of Mansfield's *Jekyll and Hyde*."[1] As will be seen, however, a number of factors leave such a belief open to serious question.

---

1. Pinkston, C. Alex Jr. "The Stage Premiere of *Dr. Jekyll and Mr. Hyde*" *Nineteenth Century Theatre Research* 14:1/2 (1986) p.23.

The title page of Act I bears the stamp: "Office of Alice Kauser, 1402 Broadway, New York." Alice Kauser was recognized as a leading theatrical agent by the turn of the century. In 1887, however, probably the latest any "early draft" would have been circulated to agents, she was no more than sixteen years of age, and unlikely to be in business. The presence of an Act II Scene 3 among the only five pages actually taken from a known Mansfield script confirms this could not be an "early draft," as the addition of a third scene to Act II formed part of the revision of Mansfield's version, which took place after the Boston premiere in May 1887. In addition, the spelling of words such as "labours" (Act I p.5) and "neighbouring" (Act I p. 28), seem to indicate a British rather than an American author.

In view of this, despite some differences in layout and text, as noted in the following transcript, the overwhelming similarity of these two scripts seems to confirm that the New York Public Library's "early draft" is more closely related to H. B. Irving's 1910 Queen's Theatre presentation of J. W. Comyns Carr's *Dr. Jekyll and Mr. Hyde* than anything ever written by T. R. Sullivan or performed by Richard Mansfield.

DR. JEKYLL AND MR. HYDE[2]

(Dramatized by Joseph William Comyns Carr)

CHARACTERS

Dr. Jekyll

Mr. Hyde

Sir Danvers Carew

Mr. Utterson, a lawyer friend of Jekyll

Mr. Enfield, another friend.

Dr. Lanyon

James Wellaby, an Indian Army surgeon.

Mr. Greet, Utterson's clerk

Poole, Dr. Jekyll's butler.

Richard Hardman, formerly butler to Sir Danvers Carew.

Inspector Newcomen

Mr. Ransmead

Algie Bertram

Reginald Prout

Dick Faversham

Laura Jekyll

Lady Carew

Lady Hilda Holden[3]

---

2. H. B. Irving's Queen's Theatre script is held by the British Library's *Lord Chamberlains Plays Collection: 1910/4, Add. 65880C*. Throughout the following transcript, the Queen's Theatre script is referred to as QTS, while the New York Public Library's "early draft" is referred to as NMS. Footnotes record significant differences between these two scripts, with minor variations overlooked.

3. A further four characters, "*Evans*," "*Walters*," "*Ambassador*," and "*Butler*" are listed here in NMS. These characters appear in both scripts but are not listed at this point in QTS.

ACT I

SCENE: Room adjoining the drawing room in Doctor Jekyll's house. Folding doors at the back open[4] to the dining room. At L. hand corner at the angle of the front room, 3 steps descend to a corridor that communicates with the laboratory.[5] At R. hand corner[6] a door leading to a corridor — Door down stage R. Fireplace down stage L.)[7]

(As the curtain rises the folding doors are thrown open and Jekyll and his friends are seen round the table, from which they have just risen. Gradually in groups of 2 and 3 they come forward to the front room, evidently continuing a conversation)

LANYON. No, no, my dear Ransmead, the thing won't bear scrutiny. Where these so-called phenomena are not due to conscious imposture, they must rank as the hallucinations of a boundless credulity.

RANSMEAD. And would you dismiss with the same curt condemnation all the attested wonders wrought by the wizard doctors of the past?[8]

LANYON. Paracelsus and Doctor Faustus, are they your gods? Why should I concede to such mediaeval mountebanks what I deny to the spiritualists of our own day? They can claim no more than the added veil of mystery which time confers even on imposture. No, no, I say the whole thing is unscientific balderdash.[9]

UTTERSON. Well, that is definite, at any rate! But Lanyon is always definite.

RANSMEAD. Upon my soul, Utterson, I sometimes think the intolerance of science surpasses even the bigotry of the churches. Why even you lawyers are sometimes accessible to reason!

LANYON. But you poets are not! That is what I complain of. You suffer charlatans only too gladly.

UTTERSON. It is the old antagonism. The unscanned world that lies beyond the limit of things seen remains now as ever the promised land of the men of imagination. To that fee-simple, as we lawyers would phrase it, the man of science renounces all claim and title.

LANYON. Simple, as you rightly observe, my dear Utterson. The vast treasures of knowledge attested and proved by reason are heritage enough for those who seek only for truth.

(Jekyll now enters from the dining room with another of the guests.)

RANSMEAD. What does Jekyll say to that?

JEKYLL. Oh, my word would count for nothing with Lanyon! In these matters he regards me as a heretic. Science with Lanyon is concerned only with what the world knows to-day. The larger vision of to-morrow has no attraction for him.[10]

LANYON. If you include in that larger vision the peurile miracles of the professional medium and the table rapper, I plead guilty to the charge.[11]

(Jekyll goes down stage.)[12]

---

4 Typed direction *"the back open"* deleted and replaced by handwritten *"R. U. E."* in NMS.
5 Typed direction *"3 steps ... the laboratory"* deleted and replaced by handwritten *"window"* in NMS.
6 Typed direction *"hand corner"* deleted and replaced by handwritten *"I. E."* in NMS.
7 Further direction *"(Poole Enters through folding doors puts tray on table R. then Exit down R."* included here in NMS.
8 Stage direction *"(Enter Utterson)"* included here in NMS.
9 Handwritten stage direction *"goes to fire L."* inserted here in NMS.
10 Handwritten stage direction *"(Sits on couch L.)"* inserted here in NMS.
11 This entire portion of Lanyon dialogue replaced by *"You are right. I confess myself frankly a materialist. In my opinion the spirit of man owns but one world — the world his reason can apprehend. Take my own case for instance. I happen to suffer from an affection of the heart which I know one day will end my life as a spark is suddenly extinguished. But that fact has not prevented me from enjoying our host's excellent wine to-night nor does it lead me to traffic with the so-called miracles of the transcendentalist."* in NMS.
12 This direction replaced by *"(Enter Enfield and Wellaby R. U. E. stop by door. Wellaby takes book from table.)"* in NMS.

JEKYLL. The miracles of one age rank in the next among the accepted commonplaces of scientific belief.

LANYON. Until then they are fit food only for your poets and men of imagination like our friend Ransmead.

JEKYLL. There can be no true science without imagination, and never in the history of mankind was there greater need than now to keep our ears open to those half-whispered messages that are borne to us from that larger world beyond the world of sense.

LANYON. And why now more than in any other age since man first crawled over the broken crust of the earth?

JEKYLL. Because we are on the verge of great discoveries, which are destined to change our whole conception of existence, opening to those who shall come after us new realms of sense and spirit.

LANYON. A dream, my dear Jekyll, a dream! An age that has parted with faith is an easy prey to superstition and hungers again for the miracles it has shattered and destroyed.[13]

JEKYLL. I am no dreamer. I am speaking of what I know.[14]

LANYON. To the man of science nothing is known till it is proved. Where are your proofs, my dear Jekyll?

JEKYLL. They are already almost within our grasp, hidden only by a thin veil that the science of the future will tear away.

LANYON. Ah yes! It is always the future that is summoned to justify the credulous visions of to-day.

JEKYLL. It may be that the revolution I foresee will come within the lifetime of some of us here to-night. The secret which enshrines it is already half-revealed. It has come to me as the fruit of long and patient research and in a little while I shall gather my comrades about me to impart to them the result of my labours.

LANYON. I say again a dream, a vain dream.[15]

JEKYLL. What are we now but bundles of jarring elements bound together by the frail garment of the flesh? But science will find a way — it is already finding a way, — to set free the warring forces of good and evil that now make up our poor human nature, and loosening the shackles that bind them, to dissolve at last that hideous partnership which has made man till now at once an angel and a brute.

ENFIELD. If there is any question of a dissolution of partnership, we must invoke the aid of the law. Utterson, this is your chance!

UTTERSON. My experience of mankind does not make me very hopeful of the result. When that dissolution which Jekyll foresees is effected, I am afraid it will be found that the angel in man has occupied only a subordinate position in the firm!

RANSMEAD. You lawyers see only the seamy side of life.

ENFIELD. And yet remember that the business of the Courts is always in arrears. That gives some warrant for Utterson's cynicism.

LANYON. Can it be, my dear Jekyll, that your strange partnership with Mr. Hyde, who uses[16] your laboratory, has affected your mind with these pestilent heresies?[17]

JEKYLL. (*As though aroused from a reverie*) Who spoke of Hyde?

LANYON. I thought perhaps as a fellow comrade in research —

JEKYLL. With your permission, we will leave Mr. Hyde's name out of the discussion.

LANYON. With all my heart!

JEKYLL. Though it may be that he too has crossed the borderland that veils us from a knowledge of ourselves.

---

13. Further dialogue "*I say again a dream.*" included here in NMS.
14. *Handwritten* direction "*(Poole closes folding doors)*" inserted here in NMS.
15. "*a vain dream*" not included in NMS.
16. "*strange partnership with Mr. Hyde, who uses*" replaced by "*new fellow worker in*" in NMS.
17. Further dialogue "*This Mr. Hyde?*" included here in NMS.

RANSMEAD. (*Who has been talking apart with Wellaby*) Lanyon, I bring another witness into Court. Here is Wellaby, bronzed by Indian suns, who has come home his mind stored with all the occult science of the East.

WELLABY. We Army surgeons have little time for science, occult or otherwise, but I can give you a simple experience which you more learned gentlemen may digest and consider for yourselves.

RANSMEAD. (*To Lanyon*) I warn you it is a poser![18]

WELLABY. I can vouch for it anyway as a fact. It happened one night at Allahabad that a native was brought into the hospital who had been found dying in a swamp outside the town. The case came under my charge, and I am bound to confess that as he lay on the bed before me I thought him one of the most repulsive human beings it had ever been my lot to see. About half an hour after his admission, I was called downstairs to view[19] a commissioner of police, who told me he had reason to believe that the man I had been attending was a criminal who was wanted on a charge of a brutal murder. His description certainly tallied exactly with the appearance of my patient. We mounted to the ward, but as we entered, the nurse met us with an indescribable look of terror on her face. "Is he dead?" I enquired. "Yes, Doctor," she answered, "but it is not that. Look for yourself!" She drew aside the screen, and there on the bed lay a dead man, but it was not the man I had left half an hour before! It was not the man the police were seeking!

JEKYLL. (*Who has been listening with growing intensity of interest*) That you can swear?

WELLABY. That I can swear.

ENFIELD. They are a tricky lot, those Orientals!

JEKYLL. (*Impressively*) Dying men don't play tricks!

LANYON. And now for the solution of this bogus mystery!

WELLABY. There was none. The nurse admitted that she had left the bedside for about 10 minutes, but there the mystery remained.

RANSMEAD. I told you it was a poser!

JEKYLL. When did this happen?

WELLABY. It must be nearly two years ago. I left Allahabad that night, but as I passed through a month later the house surgeon told me that when the corpse was removed, there was found in the bed a small phial half-full of a greenish liquid. It seems he had sent it to a scientific friend in England who was curious in Oriental drugs, Bellingham[20] was the name.

UTTERSON. (*To Jekyll*) Your predecessor in this very house![21]

LANYON. You must have been working in this laboratory at the very time.

JEKYLL. (*With evident emotion*) Yes, I was working with him at the time.

(*He clutches at the chair for support.*)

UTTERSON. Jekyll, you are not ill!

JEKYLL. No, no, it is nothing, nothing.

(*A Voice is heard without calling "Henry"!*)

JEKYLL. Excuse me, gentlemen! My wife is calling.

(*He goes out door up stage R.*)

WELLABY. I am afraid something in my story distressed our host!

LANYON. You chanced upon a painful memory.[22] About that time[23] Jekyll was in the laboratory with Bellingham,[24] when an explosion occurred which cost Bellingham his

---

18. Stage direction "(*Joins Utterson*)" included here in NMS.
19. "*view*" replaced by "*interview*" in NMS.
20. Additional dialogue "*yes, Bellingham I think*" included here in NMS.
21. Additional line of dialogue with "*Jekyll (Rises)*" saying " *Yes, and my master, that is his portrait.*" included here in NMS.
22. Additional dialogue "*This man Bellingham was a singular character intent upon curious researches, the results of which he would impart to no one.*" included here in NMS.
23. "*that time*" replaced by "*the time you spoke of*" in NMS.
24. "*with Bellingham*" omitted from NMS.

life. At the moment of this terrible accident, Mrs. Jekyll had just entered the room, and the fragments of splintered glass destroyed the sight of both her eyes. Of course now you will understand.

WELLABY. Of course. I only wish I had known. I am sorry!

LANYON. Soon after poor Bellingham's death, Hyde became his associate in research, and ever since Jekyll has been a changed man. It was then that this craze for the supernatural first took possession of him. (*To Utterson*) You know this man Hyde?

UTTERSON. Enough only to distrust him. (*To Enfield*) That was the fellow you saw trample on a child in the street, and then hurry on heedless of her cries!

ENFIELD. Heedless! By the look on his face he seemed to gloat over the suffering he had caused!

LANYON. Well, I've never set eyes on the fellow and from what you tell me I've no great desire to meet him.

RANSMEAD. What on earth can Jekyll find in the companionship of such a man as that?

LANYON. The strange thing is, no one has ever seen them together and yet there must be some strong bond of union between them.

UTTERSON. There must indeed, as I have reason to know.

(*They all turn as Jekyll Re-enters*)

JEKYLL. (*To Wellaby*) I owe you an apology, but my wife was retiring for the night, and when I am at home she likes me to take her to her room. She suffers under a great affliction — she is blind.

WELLABY. It is I who ought to apologise, but I was ignorant, as you will understand.

RANSMEAD. It is now time we all followed Mrs. Jekyll's example. Wellaby, if you are going to the Rag I can drop you. I had no idea we had lingered so long over dinner.

LANYON. Because you had no idea science could be so interesting. You men of letters are so arrogant.

RANSMEAD. Another attack!

(*Jekyll meanwhile has crossed to Utterson*)[25]

JEKYLL. (*In an undertone*) You received my[26] instructions?

UTTERSON. This morning.

JEKYLL. Then let there be no delay. I want this will executed at once.

UTTERSON. You are quite determined to make this man Hyde your sole legatee?

JEKYLL. Absolutely. My wife, as you know, is already provided for. Good-night.[27]

RANSMEAD[28]. Good-night, Jekyll! A delightful evening, in spite of Lanyon!

ENFIELD. Utterson, we travel the same road, I think?[29]

JEKYLL. Good-night! Good-night! (*To Wellaby*) I hope to see you often here again![30]

(*They go out after exchanging farewell greetings with their host, Lanyon lingering behind*)[31]

LANYON. Can you spare me 10 minutes?

JEKYLL. Of course, but forgive me, — not to renew the discussion of this evening.

LANYON. No, no, nothing was further from my thoughts. The subject on which I want a word with you concerns myself.

JEKYLL. I hope that heart trouble you told me of has not increased. I warned you then, but of course you must have known it yourself that you will always have to be careful.

LANYON. No, no, I have been better, much better of late. Of course, we both know that

---

25. This direction is re-arranged to read "(*Utterson meanwhile has crossed to Jekyll*)" followed by an additional line of dialogue with "*Utterson*" saying "*Good-night.*" in NMS.
26. "*my*" replaced by "*Mr. Hyde's letter of*" in NMS.
27. Additional stage direction "(*Utter: shakes hands with Jekyll*)" included here in NMS.
28. Additional stage direction "(*Cross to Jekyll shakes hands*)" included here in NMS.
29. Additional stage direction "(*Both Exit*)" included here in NMS.
30. Additional dialogue with "*Wellaby*" saying "*Thank you Dr. Jekyll, good-night again.*" and "*Ransmead*" saying "*Come, Wellaby.*" included here in NMS.
31. Further direction "*goes to door R. and shuts it.*" included here in NMS.

JEKYLL. Good or bad, it is always at your service, old friend.

LANYON. A little while ago I had been attending a patient, a man well known in Society, whose symptoms caused me grave uneasiness. No treatment proved of any avail, and yet I could find no trace of organic disease. At last, I was forced to the conclusion that he was being poisoned,[33] and unhappily my suspicions fell upon his wife.

JEKYLL. I am afraid, Lanyon, that such cases are not so uncommon as the world supposes.

LANYON. At last I made up my mind to speak to her.

JEKYLL. A difficult task.

LANYON. Of course I made no direct accusation. What I said, indeed, was so veiled that it could only be understood by one to whom the truth was already known.

JEKYLL. And the result?

LANYON. Convinced me that my suspicions were well-founded. From that hour the unfavourable symptoms diminished and the patient recovered. But here comes the question upon which my mind is gravely exercised. Since that time, though we continue friends, this man has ceased to be my patient, and I am convinced this is due to the influence of his wife.

JEKYLL. My dear Lanyon, you will never regret the sacrifice.

LANYON. Oh, that does not trouble me. But I am haunted by the fear that relieved of my presence, this abominable attempt may be renewed, perhaps with fatal results. Now what in your opinion is my duty?

JEKYLL. Not an easy problem, a difficult problem — difficult to solve, impossible to evade!

LANYON. My own impulse is, without implicating anyone individually, to put this man upon his guard.

JEKYLL. A dangerous course!

LANYON. And yet I feel I cannot leave things as they are.

JEKYLL. No, your impulse is right, absolutely right. You must put this man upon his guard. In my opinion, it is your plain duty.

LANYON. (*Rising to go*)[34] I felt it, but I wanted your assurance to confirm me.

JEKYLL. In this matter I feel there can be no doubt.

LANYON. Well, good-night! And many thanks.[35] I am afraid in the heat of argument tonight, I was too insistent, too intolerant.

JEKYLL. No, no, don't think that, but in future we will avoid the subject. There, take a cigar to light you on your way.

LANYON. I will; but you have already lit me on my way by your wise counsel and advice. Good-night![36]

(*Lanyon Goes Out Jekyll goes to fireplace.*)

JEKYLL. (*Alone*) A wretched story. A wretched world. How[37] the brute in us crops up on every side.

(*Laura Enters quietly by door up stage R.*)

LAURA. I thought you were alone.

JEKYLL. (*Recovering himself*)[38] Yes, yes, quite alone.

LAURA. But surely you were talking as I came along the passage!

---

32. All dialogue from "*Jekyll I hope that heart ...*" to "*Lanyon ... none so good.*" omitted from NMS.
33. Additional line of dialogue with "*Jekyll*" saying "*Poisoned!*" included here in NMS.
34. This direction replaced by "*(Goes to corner of desk)*" in NMS.
35. Stage direction "*(Putting hand on shoulder of Jekyll)*" included here in NMS.
36. Stage direction "*(Shakes hands.)*" included here in NMS.
37. Dialogue "*How*" replaced by stage direction "*(Sits on sofa)*" in NMS.
38. Additional stage direction "*(Rises goes to her leads her towards sofa.)*" included here in NMS.

JEKYLL. That was to Lanyon. He outstayed the others, but has just gone. But why are you not asleep?

LAURA. I could not sleep without the touching of your hand again.[39] As you took me to my room it seemed to me that you were not yourself. Something has happened to disturb you!

JEKYLL. Nothing, nothing at all. It was your foolish fancy, no more.

LAURA. Henry, we blind people see so many visions in the dark. Sometimes I almost believe that I can see your face as I saw it when first we wed, and then a sudden fear falls upon me that it is not the same. I see dark lines about those eyes that used to look so lovingly into mine, and I can't see the old smile on those lips (*Passing her hand over his face.*) Tell me, is it the same, always the same?

JEKYLL. (*Bending over her and kissing her on the brow.*)[40] Always the same for you dear. While you are by there can be no change, no change.

(*There is a knock at the door*)

JEKYLL. Come in!

(*Enter Poole, who carries a card on a tray. Jekyll takes it, and looking at the name, starts with surprise.*)

JEKYLL. Is this person here?

POOLE. Yes, sir, in the morning-room.

JEKYLL. (*Returning the card*) Impossible, quite impossible to-night.

POOLE. I was to say, sir, that the case was very urgent, a matter of life and death.

(*Jekyll moves across the room, debating with himself.*)

JEKYLL. Well then, when I ring.

POOLE. Yes, sir.

(*Exit Poole*)

LAURA. It is cruel you should be disturbed at this hour!

JEKYLL. A doctor's fate and we must not complain. Is your maid there?

LAURA. She is waiting for me.[41] I know it is foolish, but since Mr. Hyde has been here so constantly, I am sometimes afraid to find my way about the house alone. I was never afraid before.

JEKYLL. This is a foolish fancy. Don't let me hear of it again.

LAURA. You are not angry?

JEKYLL. No, not angry; but I want you to understand that you can never have anything to fear from Mr. Hyde — never. And now, good-night!

LAURA. (*Raising her face to his*) I can never have anything to fear from anyone while you are with me.

JEKYLL. Nor I while you are by my side. You are my good angel.[42] Swear to me if ever I should seem to change to others, or even to myself you will hold fast to me still.

LAURA. You could never change to me, never.[43] Good-night.[44]

(*Jekyll opens the door, and calls*[45] *Walters. The maid*[46] *appears in the opening*[47] *and leads Mrs. Jekyll off. Jekyll closes the door, goes to the fireplace and rings bell*)

JEKYLL. (*Alone*) Isabel Carew, what brings her here to-night? Angel and devil — to-night I stand between the two.[48]

(*Enter Poole showing in Lady Carew Jekyll stands beside his desk motionless until the servant goes out and the door closes.*)

---

39. Stage direction "*(Putting his hand to her cheek)*" included here in NMS.
40. Stage direction "*kissing her on the brow*" replaced by "*cheek to cheek*" in NMS.
41. Stage direction "*(She goes to him)*" included here in NMS.
42. "You are my good angel." omitted from NMS.
43. Stage direction "*(Maid opens top door appears)*" included here in NMS.
44. Stage direction "*(At door turns)*" followed by further dialogue "*Good-night*" appears here in NMS.
45. Stage direction "*Jekyll opens the door, and calls*" omitted from NMS.
46. Stage direction "*The maid*" omitted from NMS.
47. Stage direction "*the opening*" replaced by "*door*" in NMS.
48. "*what brings her here … between the two.*" omitted from NMS.

JEKYLL. You have no right to be here.

LADY CAREW. Wait till you have heard what I have to say!

JEKYLL. Nothing you say can yield any excuse for your coming here to-night.

LADY CAREW. Nothing? Are you sure of that?

JEKYLL. Three years ago it was agreed between us that the past should never be renewed. Before the world we were still to pass as friends, but except in the presence of the world we were never to meet again. That was our compact.

LADY CAREW. Oh, don't think I have come here with any thought of winning you back.

JEKYLL. Win me back? No, thank Heaven those fetters are broken for ever!

LADY CAREW. Yet they held you once body and soul — they held you then![49]

JEKYLL. I had no soul. You never asked that of me. What you asked I gave. But you are right, I was your slave. We were fast chained together, as we sank lower and lower day by day. All that was base in me was in your keeping; the rest was dead. And you might have held me your slave to the end if you had been true. But you were false to me as you had been false to the man I betrayed.

LADY CAREW. You men set such store by constancy — in women!

JEKYLL. Oh, why should we renew the bitterness and the shame of those wretched days! We parted, that is enough.

LADY CAREW. Yes; and then you married. I was the fiend who had ruined you: she was to be the white angel to save you.

JEKYLL. We will not speak of her. Your message to me to-night was that you had come here on a matter of life and death. What have you to tell me?

LADY CAREW. That the past which we agreed should never be renewed has renewed itself. What we were to one another then is no longer our secret.

JEKYLL. You mean, Sir Danvers knows?

LADY CAREW. Knows nothing; but to-morrow, perhaps even to-night, he may know all.

JEKYLL. What does this mean?

LADY CAREW. Four months ago our butler, John Hardman left under suspicion of theft, and went abroad to South America. Two months ago he wrote saying that he was sailing for England and that he had a little account against me which he thought I should be glad to settle on his return.

JEKYLL. An idle threat.

LADY CAREW. Not idle. He said there were certain letters of mine he had taken by mistake which he was anxious to restore to me <u>or</u> to my husband.

JEKYLL. Is that true?

LADY CAREW. I went to the drawer in which I thought they were safely locked. They were gone.

JEKYLL. What did you do?

LADY CAREW. What I had often dreamed of doing. There was a month before his[50] ship could reach England. There was still time for my husband to die.

JEKYLL. To die!

LADY CAREW. And he would have died but because my plan was discovered; my purpose was foiled.[51] Do you understand?

JEKYLL. And you dare to tell me this?

LADY CAREW. I would dare more. A little while ago, by my advice, Sir Danvers decided to change his physician. If he chances to fall ill again, why should not you attend him?

JEKYLL. I will not hear you! I will not believe you! You shall not commit this terrible crime. I say, you shall not![52] The burden of the past is upon us and we must bear whatever punishment it brings! But this deeper infamy shall not be mine. By Heaven,[53] no, nor yours!

49. *Handwritten* stage direction "*Sits R. of desk*" inserted here in NMS.
50. "*his*" replaced by "*Hardman's*" in NMS.
51. "*my purpose was foiled*" omitted from NMS.
52. "*I say, you shall not!*" omitted from NMS.
53. "*By Heaven*" omitted from NMS.

LADY CAREW. That is how you men judge of life. You have two sides of your life, and you keep them apart.

JEKYLL. Pray God we do.

LADY CAREW. Yes, but we women have only one. The sins you allow yourself to commit are docketed and labelled. From what is bred of those sins you shrink back in horror. You halt there. We who have known what it is to love or hate know no such halting place.

JEKYLL. But you must, you shall!

LADY CAREW. What is this man to me? A profligate who has brought every humiliation upon my life from the first hour of our marriage. What is his life to me?

JEKYLL. If you take it, if you seek to take it, it will mean your life as well. I warn you, you shall not commit this insensate act of folly.

LADY CAREW. And what have you to propose?

JEKYLL. Is this man Hardman in England?

LADY CAREW.[54] He arrived a week ago. Yesterday I received this letter. You see he knows everything. (*She hands him letter*)[55] Your secret visits at night when Danvers was at Berlin — he watched you as you entered through the door at the back. You had the key then.

JEKYLL. I have the key still.

LADY CAREW. Who is to find this £5,000 he demands? Not I nor you. There is only one way.

JEKYLL. No, a thousand times no. I will see this man, and if my last shilling goes to save you I will pay it. If my life should be forfeit I will pay it. But you must go now at once. If Sir Danvers was to discover this visit!

LADY CAREW. Oh, there is no fear of that! To-night he has an official dinner at the Foreign Office, and then he will go to the Club and play at cards till 3 or 4 o'clock in the morning. That is his life.

JEKYLL. Go then. I will see this man Hardman to-morrow.

LADY CAREW. And I shall see you at our reception in the evening. You have avoided the house too long. This time you must come.

JEKYLL. This time I will come. (*Rings bell*)

LADY CAREW. One last word. He[56] will bleed you to death. In the end you will find that my way is the only way!

JEKYLL. (*Holding the door open*) Go, go!

(*Exit Lady Carew.*)

JEKYLL. (*Alone*) Her every word summons the devil that lurks within me. Till now that baser spirit, foul image of every deformed and hideous thought that lured me down to Hell has come and gone at my command — this supreme change which science at last revealed to me was mine to make or mine to resist. But to-night strange tremors shake me. I am no longer sure of myself. The blood that courses in my veins moves with another and a quicker pulse that is not mine. Have I wrung this secret from nature only to be its slave? No, I am master still! Master of my fate now and always.[57]

54. Stage direction "(*Taking letter from bag on desk*)" included here in NMS.
55. Further stage direction "(*Looks round the room*)" included here in NMS.
56. "*One last word. He*" replaced by "*This man Hardman*" in NMS.
57. This entire section of Jekyll dialogue replaced by "*My way is the only way — why do her words seem to rouse the devil that lurks within me — why to-night of all nights should Bellingham's name have surged up from the past. Yes it was you who first taught me to re-embody in forms separate and distinct those twin spirits of good and evil that lie hidden in the soul of man. You first taught me to mix that drug by whose aid I have summoned from the dark recesses of my soul the malignant spirit of Edward Hyde. Hyde — even now I feel his breath upon my face, and before my eyes hang the blackened records of his crimes. But they are his crimes, not mine. I am Jekyll, Henry Jekyll still. They are the crimes of Edward Hyde. Yes it was you who brought that curse upon me that has been my ruin. Your last confession given to me the day you died, I have it still. (Goes to desk sits L. of desk) It's every word is branded on my memory, but the warning it contains, (Rises Takes keys out opens drawer — Takes confession from drawer in desk) I need it now, yes more than ever now, for to-night I feel uncertain of myself. (Goes C.) Till now that baser spirit I had summoned, came and went at my command. That supreme change and transformation of myself which science had revealed to me was mine to make or mine to resist. (Gets to armchair) Ah! God! have I wrung this secret from nature only to be its slave?*"

(Knock at door)

Yes, what is it?

(Enter Poole bringing in bedroom candle-stick)[58]

POOLE. Is there anything more, sir?

JEKYLL. No, nothing. You can put out the lamp.

(Poole goes towards the lamp which stands on table R.)

POOLE. If you please, sir, Mr. Hyde was in the laboratory this afternoon.

JEKYLL. *(Speaking fiercely)* Well, what of it?

POOLE. Only sir, that[59] the light is still burning in the window. I thought perhaps that he might have fallen asleep. Shall I knock at the door?

JEKYLL. No, I am going there myself. If he is asleep, I will wake him.

(He goes towards candle and lights it with a spool, as[60] Poole extinguishes the lamp.)

POOLE. *(At door)* Good-night, sir!

JEKYLL. Good-night!

(Exit Poole)

JEKYLL. *(Alone)*[61] Would that he[62] were asleep, and would sleep for ever! But no, he wakes within me now. They come again those shuddering tremors that freeze my blood. I know them well, but never until now have they threatened me against my will.[63] But I will not yield.[64] I will not! Whatever power seeks to master me I defy it. But this time I will not.[65]

(He struggles towards door R. moving as if he were held back by chains.)[66]

Laura, Laura! Save me![67]

(With a cry the candlestick falls from his hand,[68] and the room is darkened except for the light of the fire.)

Ah! Too late, too late!

(He shrinks back towards the fire with a staggering gait, then turns, and the firelight discloses the features of Hyde. For a moment He stands facing the audience and then with a low chuckling laugh He slinks out of door L.[69] In the darkness the back of the scene disappears, and reveals laboratory.)

(To R. up stage a flight of steps descends into room. To L. down stage door leads to street. At back another door communicates with an inner chamber. A neighbouring church clock strikes the hour of 4. The click of the lock is heard in the door L. which opens and Hyde Enters stealthily)

HYDE. Wasted! Wasted![70] Four precious hours and nothing done.[71] If we had met to-

---

(Sits) Where is it? Ah, here it is! *(Reads:)* 'I found that once or twice the drug had seemed to weaken in its effect — and yet I gave no heed to the warning. This morning I woke in bed with an odd sensation. Something kept insisting that I was not where I seemed to be, but in another chamber where I am accustomed to sleep in the body of that other spirit I had created. As I wondered my eyes fell upon my hand and I saw, not my hand but that other hand I knew too well. I rushed to the mirror, there the horror of the thing stared me in the face. I had gone to bed Walter Bellingham and had wakened in the viler body of that fiend I had thought my slave. He had mastered me in my sleep.' *(Bus with hand)*" in NMS.

58. Further stage direction "*(Cross to Jekyll who takes candle alight from him)*" included here in NMS.
59. Additional dialogue "*as I came through the courtyard*" included here in NMS.
60. Stage direction "*He goes towards candle and lights it with a spool as*" omitted from NMS.
61. This direction is replaced by dialogue "*Hyde!*" in NMS.
62. "*he*" replaced by "*you*" in NMS.
63. "*They come again ... against my will.*" omitted from NMS.
64. Stage direction "*(Looking at portrait)*" included here in NMS.
65. "*I will not! Whatever ... this time I will not.*" replaced by "*You were conquered Bellingham, your spirit subdued against your will. But that shall not be my fate. I say it shall not. I defy your warning. (Tearing paper to pieces) I, Henry Jekyll remain the master and Edward Hyde my slave.*" in NMS.
66. This direction omitted from NMS.
67. "*Save me!*" replaced by "*I will not yield, I say I will not yield*" in NMS.
68. Stage direction "*With a cry the candlestick falls from his hand*" replaced by "*Drops candle and struggles towards door*" in NMS.
69. Stage direction "*L.*" replaced by "*C.*" followed by additional dialogue with "*Hyde*" saying "*Ah Sir Danvers Carew, she said you were playing cards at your club. Perhaps I shall find you there.*" in NMS.
70. "*Wasted! Wasted!*" replaced by stage direction "*(Mixing drug)*" in NMS.
71. Additional dialogue "*Sir Danvers Carew,*" included here in NMS.

night it would have been his last night!⁷² That is to come. Now for the drug and quickly!⁷³

(He lights a spirit lamp, which stands upon a table beside the door at the back. Then He starts.)

What's that? Nobody can be stirring now!

(The liquid simmers in the tube. He adds the salt and drains it off, as door at the head of the stairs softly opens and Mrs. Jekyll appears.)

HYDE. *(In whisper)* Has it lost its magic? No, no,⁷⁴ it works again, it works again.

LAURA. Henry, are you there?⁷⁵

(He turns and sees Her, and then steals out into the inner chamber at the back, as his wife feels her way down the steps.)

LAURA. Henry, Henry!

(He re-appears as Jekyll,⁷⁶ as She calls again)

LAURA. Henry! Then you are here?

JEKYLL. Yes, here, always at your call!⁷⁷

Curtain

ACT II.⁷⁸

The next night

SCENE:— *A large reception room at the house of Sir Danvers Carew. In back R. three French windows opening to the ground and leading to a small ornamental courtyard that is lit with electric lamps and decked with flowers. At back R. curtained archway leading to other reception rooms. At back L. another opening showing a small recess room with a writing table on which stands a lamp. Fireplace L.C. Down stage L. a door)*

(As the scene opens groups are passing to and fro from the corridor of stage R. from whence are heard strains of music from a band in the room beyond. As the stage clears Algie, Bertram and Prout are L.C.)

PROUT. Hallo Algie. Back from Berlin?

BERTRAM. Only for a few days. Had to come over for my cousin's wedding in Northumberland. Boring things, weddings.

(Enter Faversham)

FAVERSHAM. Did I catch the word "wedding"? I thought all that sort of thing was out of date.

BERTRAM. Our family is hopelessly old fashioned. They still marry and have children now and then.

FAVERSHAM. Wonderful! This old world moves very slowly.

PROUT. You can't bustle civilisation. *(Turning to Bertram)* But tell us about Berlin. Cheery?

BERTRAM. Well, after Stockholm I should call it hilarious.

FAVERSHAM. Berlin, my dear Prout, is fast taking rank as the most dissolute capital in Europe. It has been a tardy conversion, but, as the old maid said when she ran

72. "*it would have been his last night!*" replaced by additional "*if only we had met to-night*" in NMS.
73. "*Now for the drug and quickly!*" omitted from NMS.
74. "*Has it lost its magic? No, no,*" replaced by "*The drug, the drug,*" in NMS.
75. Additional dialogue "*Henry it's 4 o'clock, when you said good-night to me you didn't tell me you were working so late.*" included here in NMS.
76. Further direction "*shuts door*" included here in NMS.
77. Stage direction "*(Takes her hand)*" included here in NMS.
78. This Act, in its entirety, is missing from NMS. Five loose, non-consecutive pages from Act II of a revised version of Mansfield's Jekyll & Hyde are included, but bear no relation to the remainder of NMS.

away with her groom — it is never too late to go wrong!

BERTRAM. Oh Berlin's all right. Ask our host.

PROUT. Of course, of course, you were at the Embassy when Carew resigned. What is the story?

BERTRAM. The old story. An Austrian Countess, and a devilish handsome woman too.

(*Enter Lady Hilda Holden. Lady Hilda is a middle-aged woman, a little powdered and painted, but retaining youthful airs of fascination.*)

LADY HILDA. Now I am sure you were talking about me!

FAVERSHAM. My dear Lady Hilda, a very pardonable mistake, but this is another devilish handsome woman.

PROUT. (*Bowing to Lady Hilda*) Can there be another answering to that description?

FAVERSHAM. (*Gallantly*) Only in Lady Hilda's absence.

LADY HILDA. Very pretty, Dick Faversham! But when you wizened and withered philosophers wag your aged heads in concert, it is not for the sake of praising a woman's looks.

BERTRAM. We were talking about Carew and Berlin.

LADY HILDA. Oh, that is ancient history! I heard all about it from Tom Mildmay five days ago.

FAVERSHAM. And what does Madam say to it all?

LADY HILDA. Lady Carew? Nothing, and probably cares less. The only thing in Carew's career that could possibly interest his wife would be the end of it.

PROUT. And yet your were accusing us of talking scandal!

LADY HILDA. That is no scandal. There has never been a breath against our hostess — at least not that I have heard.

FAVERSHAM. I fancy Sir Danvers would be only too pleased if there were!

LADY HILDA. No, no; Sir Danvers has a due regard for the proprieties of English life — at least outwardly. He may desire freedom, but it must be by the intervention of the undertaker, not the President of the Divorce Court.

PROUT. And who is the candidate for the vacant post, that is, if it should fall vacant?

(*Sir Danvers Enters from R. and stands talking with a group. Bertram who has seen him, nudges Lady Hilda.*)

BERTRAM. Look out!

(*She turns and sees Carew*)

LADY HILDA. Oh my dear Sir Danvers! We were just talking about you!

SIR DANVERS. And wondering who was to fill the vacant post, eh?

LADY HILDA. At Berlin, Sir Danvers.

SIR DANVERS. Quite so, at Berlin. Well, I can satisfy your curiosity. I saw the Prime Minister this afternoon. Lord Marsden is to be your new chief, Bertram.

BERTRAM. Indeed, Sir.

SIR DANVERS. A good man, moderate intelligence, no initiative, always ready to exchange confidences without making any. In short, the ideal of what you must strive to become, my dear boy, if you want to rise in the service.

LADY HILDA. But what we want to know, Sir Danvers, if we were not too discreet to enquire, is why you should be thinking of deserting diplomacy?

SIR DANVERS. Weight of years, my dear lady.

LADY HILDA. Oh! Sir Danvers!

SIR DANVERS. Weight of years, and a cherished longing for the chastened pleasures of domestic life.

LADY HILDA. There are some people who are content to indulge their pleasures by abstaining from them!

SIR DANVERS. Lady Hilda, I shall not come to you for a character.

LADY HILDA. Do you suggest I have none to give away?

SIR DANVERS. None that would fit my simple nature, I am afraid.

LADY HILDA. You men have so many natures, in your case, I have no doubt, — all simple. We poor women, alas, have only one.

SIR DANVERS. Yes, but devilish complex!

LADY HILDA. I am routed, Sir Danvers, and shall seek consolation in music. I believe Fugolini is just beginning to play.

(She Goes up stage)

SIR DANVERS. You had better follow her, young gentlemen. Lady Hilda is a liberal education even for those engaged in diplomacy.

(As They move up stage, Lady Carew comes down with a Foreign Ambassador)

LADY CAREW. The Ambassador insists upon going away.

SIR DANVERS. So soon? The night is still young.

AMBASSADOR. Ah yes, but I remain old, so old. We cannot all boast your perpetual youth, my dear Carew.

SIR DANVERS. The poor reward of a blameless life!

(He moves with the Ambassador towards door L.)

But I want a word with you. I met Beckenheim at the Club this afternoon. He tells me that affairs in Tangiers are by no means settled.

(They Go Off talking through door L.)

(Lady Carew looks after them and then turns and encounters Jekyll, who Enters by one of the windows R.)

LADY CAREW. You have avoided me.

JEKYLL. No; I have waited for the moment to find you alone.

LADY CAREW. Have you seen this man?

JEKYLL. I went to his lodging. He was out. I am to meet him to-morrow.

LADY CAREW. And you think you can silence him?

JEKYLL. I think I can silence him.

LADY CAREW. To-night, just before dinner, Carew said something which made me think he suspected there was a cause for his illness of a month ago.

JEKYLL. You imagine these things.

LADY CAREW. There is no imagination. Something has roused the devil in him. His eyes, as he looked at me, were the eyes of a wild beast waiting to spring. I feel that my fate hangs upon to-night.

JEKYLL. Upon to-night? No, no he has no proof, no evidence.

LADY CAREW. An hour ago a letter was brought to him. I watched him as he opened it. I could see it disturbed him. What if it was from this man Hardman? What if they should meet to-night?

JEKYLL. Something within me tells me that they will never meet, either to-night, or to-morrow, or in the time to come.

LADY CAREW. You think that. But promise me you will see this man at once. To-morrow may be too late.

JEKYLL. Yes, to-morrow may be too late! Oh, why do you urge me on. That part you owned in me is yours again. I thought I had cast it away as a dead thing of the past, but to-night it leaps to life again.[79] There is no escape; would to God there were!

(Applause is being heard coming from the music room, for which Faversham now enters.)[80]

FAVERSHAM. Lady Carew, Fugolini absolutely refuses to play again. Won't you exert your influence?

LADY CAREW. I will try.

JEKYLL. Then I will say good-bye. I have some work that must be done to-night.

LADY CAREW. All my guests are deserting me.[81] *(Aside)* I shall hear from you to-morrow.

JEKYLL. To-morrow.

---

79. Dialogue "*It pursues me, it haunts me! This other self I thought I had crushed! I hear its whispered voice hissing in my ear. I am afraid to turn lest I should see those eyes staring back into mine.*" typed but deleted in QTS.
80. Additional *handwritten* direction "*with Prout & Bertram*" inserted here in QTS.
81. Dialogue "*Good night*" typed but deleted and replaced by *handwritten* direction "*(Shakes J. hand)*" in QTS.

(Lady Carew goes up with Faversham as Doctor Lanyon Enters through windows R.)

LANYON. Are you going?

JEKYLL. Yes. But I must have a word with you first. I have been thinking of what I said to you last night.

LANYON. I was deeply grateful for your advice.

JEKYLL. But I have reflected since that it would perhaps be wiser to wait, as you had no reason to believe that the symptoms you had noticed would be renewed.

LANYON. My dear Jekyll, I acted at once. This very morning I sought an interview with my former patient and warned him.

JEKYLL. Do you think he suspected the source of the danger?

LANYON. I am not sure.

JEKYLL. (*Vehemently*) Lanyon, we have done an infamous thing. What if your suspicions are unfounded? What if this woman you suspected is innocent?

LANYON. She is not innocent.

JEKYLL. So you say, so you think, but if she were — You can't tell, you don't know what you may have done! Pray God we may never have cause to regret it.

LANYON. My dear Jekyll, listen to me.

JEKYLL. No, no, not to-night. I have been overworked lately I am worn out. To-night I must sleep — if I can.

(Goes Out door L. as Utterson Enters)

UTTERSON. Is that Jekyll?

LANYON. Yes.

UTTERSON. He looks terribly ill. Everybody has been remarking it.

LANYON. Utterson, I am concerned about him, deeply concerned, of late he is a changed man, his nerves over-strung and overwrought. Just now he seemed almost to lose control of himself. I can't understand it.

UTTERSON. Nor I. But he *is* a changed man. I can speak in confidence to you. This morning he executed his Will, and he has left everything he possesses to whom do you suppose?

LANYON. To his wife?

UTTERSON. No, to that man Hyde.

LANYON. Hyde! I knew this man had gained some strong ascendancy over him. Ever since he took him into his laboratory, Jekyll has been a changed man. But this is infatuation! What can be the secret of it?

UTTERSON. I tried to dissuade him, but his instructions were imperative. He would listen to no advice or remonstrance. I was helpless. Whatever may be the source of this man's influence, I am convinced it is not for good.

(Sir Danvers Enters from door L.)

SIR DANVERS. Ah, my good friends, I have caught you red-handed! Yes, yes, I know what you have been saying.

UTTERSON. I am sure you don't, Sir Danvers.

SIR DANVERS. I challenge you both. (*Turning to Utterson*) You were saying as I came in that it had been a devilish dull evening, and Lanyon most cordially agreed with you.

LANYON. Emphatically no!

SIR DANVERS. And then you said, — "Well thank God, it is over at last"! And Utterson thanked God with equal fervour for the same cause.

UTTERSON. Wrong in every particular, Sir Danvers. As a matter of fact we were talking of our friend Jekyll.

SIR DANVERS. Looks devilish ill, don't he?

LANYON. That is exactly what we were saying.

SIR DANVERS. My dear Lanyon, you men of science all make the same mistake. You profess to seek knowledge, but you wait till the tree is withered before you pluck the fruit. In the hospital, the laboratory or the study you have but one life, and a damn dull one at that. Now we men of the world have at least two; one which we dedicate to a respectable British public, the other which we reserve for hours of recreation and enjoyment. In those two separate lives we are different men. That is what keeps us young.

LANYON. Well, Sir Danvers, you certainly do credit to your creed.

SIR DANVERS. But our poor friend Jekyll is only one man, and his life only one life. He has forgotten that to rank as a saint, one must first graduate as a sinner. He is now paying the penalty of a life of sustained self-denial, and having lived like an anchorite, he ends by looking like a ghost.

(*Sir Danvers goes to table and takes up a portrait.*)

This is what he was three years ago. Used to be a good deal about the house then. Look at him now!

(*Utterson takes the portrait and looks at it; then replaces it.*)

UTTERSON. Yes, the change in him has certainly been very rapid, almost alarming.

SIR DANVERS. He ought to have taken a leaf out of the book of an old reprobate like me. I have broken all the commandments that concern the sins of a gentleman, together with some others not specifically mentioned by Moses; and yet with 60 years to my credit, I can boast that I have had only one serious illness in my life. (*More seriously turning to Lanyon*) And that, perhaps, was not entirely my own fault, eh Lanyon?

UTTERSON. Well I am afraid my youth must have been as blameless and barren as poor Jekyll's, for I begin to find that I can't stand these late hours. I'll go and make my adieus to our hostess.[82]

SIR DANVERS. You will find her with Lady Hilda and her satellite followers. (*Turning to Lanyon*) Odd thing, Lanyon, that women like Lady Hilda, whose physical attractions, if I may say so, have fallen so sadly out of repair, should still have power to draw to her the youngest men in any company where she appears.

LANYON. (*Laughing*) Some of the young men of our day have achieved a sudden maturity that makes even Lady Hilda seem youthful by comparison.

SIR DANVERS. I believe you are right. Most of the youths of the present day must have been born old. They seem to live on lemonade and cigarettes. Their sins are all retrospective, and they pass into their dotage before they are out of their teens.

LANYON. (*Laughing*) We live in a degenerate age I am afraid, Sir Danvers.

SIR DANVERS. But we still live, we old 'uns, that is the point! But now, to be serious for a moment. Since you spoke to me this morning, I have received a strange letter, a very strange letter.

LANYON. From whom?

SIR DANVERS. Hear first what it says. (*Then reading*) "I can inform you of something which it is of vital importance that you should know. I shall enter to-night at the door at the back, of which I still retain the key, when your guests have gone, and you are alone, leave the window leading to the inner court on the latch. H."

LANYON. Do you know who could have sent it?

SIR DANVERS. I think I can guess. We had a butler named Hardman. That is his initial.

LANYON. Was he in your service at the time of your illness?

SIR DANVERS. No. He had been dismissed by my wife about two months before on a suspicion of theft.

LANYON. Strange, certainly. Do you intend to see him?

SIR DANVERS. Yes.

LANYON. Is it wise?

SIR DANVERS. You refused to tell me this morning on whom your suspicions rested.

LANYON. Sir Danvers, I went to the extreme limit of my duty in saying to you as much as I did. I may even have gone too far.

SIR DANVERS. You must judge for yourself. But there may be others this man perhaps, who know more, and who will be willing to tell what they know.

LANYON. A discharged servant, perhaps a thief as well, is hardly a trustworthy witness.

SIR DANVERS. Not unless he can prove what he says. During these last hours, Lanyon, my

---

82. *Handwritten* direction "(*Goes off L. Lanyon sits R.*)" inserted here in QTS.

mind has been like a sleuth-hound on the trail, and if I find out the truth, there is no appeal for mercy, no pity, no compassion that shall stay my hand. None, none.

(Lady Carew Enters from door up stage R. with Lady Hilda, Faversham and Bertram)

LADY HILDA. We are the last, positively the last, of your guests, but these boys are incorrigible.

FAVERSHAM. It is long past my bed-time.

BERTRAM. And mine. My hot bottle will be cold.

SIR DANVERS. Well, well, boys will be — old men, in these days.

LADY HILDA. As for Doctor Lanyon, I pity his patients to-morrow.

LANYON. (*Taking out his watch*) I am afraid Lady Hilda to-morrow is already with us. (*Bowing to Lady Carew*) Good-night Lady Carew.

LADY CAREW. (*Looking at him*) Good-night!

(They face one another, Sir Danvers watching them. Lanyon Goes Out as the Butler Enters)

BUTLER. Lady Hilda Holden's carriage.

LADY HILDA. (*To the two young men*) Well then, you shall both see me home, and you shall have one cigarette each as a reward, but mind, only one. Good-night, Sir Danvers!

(She Goes Out attended by Faver: and Bertram)

(Sir Danvers and Lady Carew are left alone He goes to fireplace and rings bell, Lady Carew watching his movements uneasily. Butler Enters)

SIR DANVERS. You can put out the lights in the other room and go to bed. I want nothing more.

BUTLER. Yes, Sir Danvers.[83]

(Butler goes up stage through curtained opening R. and as He goes through the electric lights are extinguished in the courtyard, where there is now a faint glimpse of moonlight)

LADY CAREW. Are you going to the Club?

SIR DANVERS. Very likely; but I have one or two letters to write first.

LADY CAREW. I noticed Monson brought you a letter this evening. It must have come by hand. I suppose it was important.

SIR DANVERS. It may be; but that letter needs no answer to-night.

LADY CAREW. I think I will go to my room; I am tired.

SIR DANVERS. And yet Thistleton said he never saw you looking so handsome or so young. I sometimes wonder, when I have sent my final resignation, who is the fortunate man who will be chosen to take my place!

LADY CAREW. I am afraid I am not in the humour for jesting to-night.

(She turns to go)

SIR DANVERS. Stay, let me look at you.

(He approaches her.)

Thistleton was wrong. You do look worn and tired! I dare say that all that nursing during my illness must have told upon you. If I should chance to fall ill again, I should send you away. The strain was too great.

LADY CAREW. There is no reason why you should fall ill again.

SIR DANVERS. True! I had not thought of that. There is no reason why I should fall ill again, — at least, none that I know of at present.

(He gazes at Her closely)

LADY CAREW. Nor I.

SIR DANVERS. Good-night!

LADY CAREW. Good-night!

(She goes up stage through the curtained opening R., and as she passes out of sight, He touches the switch and the light of the corridor is extinguished. He then loosens the band that holds up the heavy portiere which now falls over the entrance.)

---

83. Handwritten direction "*(Cross to French windows put out lights & go out of window & close same)*" inserted here in QTS.

SIR DANVERS. (*As He turns down stage*) But I may discover a reason and perhaps to-night!

(*He goes down stage and softly opens the window that leads to the courtyard. Then goes up to the recess chamber L.*)

And if I do, — well to-morrow will be time enough for that.

(*He unlocks the drawer of the writing-table and takes a letter from his pocket. He is about to put it in the drawer when a soft tap is heard on the glass of the window down stage. He replaces the letter in his pocket, and turns. As He does so, the face of Hyde peers into the room, but for the moment is unseen by Sir Danvers.*)

SIR DANVERS. Come in!

(*Hyde Enters as Sir Danvers goes down stage. He wears round his neck a black scarf loosely coiled.*)

SIR DANVERS. What is this? You are not Hardman!

HYDE. No, I am not Hardman.

SIR DANVERS. What brings you here? I do not know you. I have never seen you before.

HYDE. No; and it is likely you will never see me again, — after to-night!

(*Sir Danvers makes a movement towards the bell.*)

Do not ring Sir Danvers! If you do, you will repent it as long as you live. (*With a chuckle*) Yes, as long as you live.

(*He slides across the stage towards Carew.*)

I have something to tell you!

SIR DANVERS. (*Backing a little away from him*) Stand where you are, and tell it. Don't move another step or —

HYDE. Don't be frightened! You were expecting your old servant. Well, I have come in his place.

SIR DANVERS. Did he send you?

HYDE. No, no, not he! (*With a chuckle*) He would not like it if he knew I had come!

SIR DANVERS. It was he who wrote to me.

HYDE. No, it was I. That was my letter. He wants money out of yer. I don't!

SIR DANVERS. Then why are you here?

HYDE. Listen, Sir Danvers! I can tell you more than he could, — more that you want to know.

SIR DANVERS. Whatever you have to say, say it quickly.

HYDE. Why, you are pale, Sir Danvers! You are not afraid?

SIR DANVERS. Afraid! Of what?

HYDE. No, no, no! You are never afraid; but you have not quite recovered yet from your illness of a month ago. That is it! You are weak still. (*drawing a step nearer*) Poison leaves its mark even upon a constitution like yours!

SIR DANVERS. Poison!

HYDE. Come, come! That is no news to you! You have been warned of that already. But you don't know whose loving hand it was who set the poison beside your bed!

SIR DANVERS. If any man could tell me that —

HYDE. I can! It was your wife.

SIR DANVERS. Can you prove this? Whoever you are, — and you look more beast than man, — prove this and I'll —

HYDE. No, no! I told you I want no money. That is for Hardman. I shall claim another reward before we part, and that won't be long, Sir Danvers. (*Chuckling to himself.*)

SIR DANVERS. What reward?

HYDE. Wait and you shall know! You thought you were the only profligate in this respectable household. You did not know, you did not guess, that the woman by your side had caught the trick of infamy from you. Look back upon your past life, Sir Danvers, you have still time for that, — just time for that! From the day of your marriage you spurned her, insulted her, neglected her, flaunting your amours in the eyes of the world and in her eyes. But she had her revenge on you. She betrayed you!

SIR DANVERS. You lie!

HYDE. No, no, it is true, all true. You have been tricked and fooled, Sir Danvers, and by a friend, a friend you trusted. You thought you were the only Don Juan, but you were wrong. While you were abroad, he came to this house night after night secretly by the door through which I have come just now, opening it with this very key that I hold in my hand. (*He shows him the key*)

SIR DANVERS. Then you know him?

HYDE. Oh yes, I know him! He asked me to bring you back the key. He does not want it any more.

(*He flings it across the room.*)

SIR DANVERS. Who is it? Who is this man?

HYDE. Ask Hardman, your faithful servant. He can tell you. But he will want money, and I want none. I could tell you if I chose.

SIR DANVERS. (*Approaching him with a threatening gesture.*) Well, by Heaven, you shall!

HYDE. (*Half crouching as though about to spring*) Be careful!

SIR DANVERS. You shall not leave this house till I know his name!

HYDE. Look among the portraits upon that table!

(*He points to a table to the L. of Sir Danvers which among other ornaments holds a number of cabinet portraits in frames. Sir Danvers turns as He points, and makes a slight movement towards table.*)

You will find his amongst them.

(*Sir Danvers has approached the table.*)

No, not that one. Yes, where your hand is travelling now. Nearer, nearer!

SIR DANVERS. Not, — not, —(*touching the portrait of Jekyll which stands upon the table.*)

(*During this time Sir Danvers has his back turned to Hyde. Then with a wild leap Hyde coils the scarf about his neck and flings him to the ground.*)

HYDE. Yes, — Jekyll! Jekyll! Jekyll!

(*Sir Danvers gives one cry as he falls, and then with every repetition of the name of Jekyll, Hyde plunges a knife which he has drawn from his breast into the prostrate body of his victim. Then with a fierce, low chuckle He slides towards the window R.*)

(*Lady Carew appears at the curtained opening and stands transfixed with horror as Hyde Creeps Out. Then clutching at the curtain she falls senseless on the floor.*)

Curtain.

ACT III

SCENE I —(*Scene: The same as ACT I.*)

(*Time, the next afternoon. As Curtain draws up Dr. Jekyll Enters followed by Poole.*)

JEKYLL. Is my bag ready?

POOLE. Yes[84] sir.

JEKYLL. Then take a cab and leave it at Euston at once. I have a call to make on my way. I will pick it up there.

POOLE. Will you take nothing before you go, sir?

JEKYLL. Nothing.

POOLE. This is terrible news about Sir Danvers, sir!

JEKYLL. Terrible! Terrible! They were crying it as I came through the Square.

POOLE. I was reckoning it must have happened soon after you left sir.

JEKYLL. No, no. I left early, quite early; I was called away.[85] But when was it discovered?

---

84. "*Yes*" replaced by "*I am getting it ready now*," in NMS.
85. "*I was called away*" omitted from NMS.

POOLE. Not till this morning sir, when the housemaid went in to clean this room. It seems that after the guests had gone Sir Danvers remained downstairs writing letters.

JEKYLL. So that no one knows at what hour he died?

POOLE. So Mr. Utterson tells me.

JEKYLL. Mr. Utterson?

POOLE. He called about an hour ago, sir, while you were out, and said he would return at 4 o'clock.

JEKYLL. At 4 o'clock. What time is it now?

POOLE. Just turned half-past three, sir.

JEKYLL. Leave word with the maid to tell him I have been called to the country on an urgent case.

POOLE. Yes, sir.[86]

JEKYLL. And let a cab wait for me now at the door of the laboratory. I have some papers there I must take with me.

POOLE. Yes, sir.

(About to Exit)

JEKYLL. Stay![87] Give me a little brandy and cold water, quick! This news has shaken me.

(Poole fills a glass of brandy and hands it to him, as Jekyll draws a sealed letter from his pocket, then gulps down the brandy)

Listen to me! If while I am absent from home, either to-night or at any time, Dr. Lanyon should call with authority from me, open that envelope and you will find full written instructions what you have to do. See that you carry them out to the letter. To the letter, you understand?

POOLE. Yes, sir.

JEKYLL. Now go. There is no time to lose.

(Exit Poole)[88]

JEKYLL. *(Alone)* I am afraid to go, afraid to stay! That baser shape I once inhabited has grown horrible to me, and yet I dread lest those tremors should overtake me.[89] No, no, never again, never again! This one black night has shattered[90] the door upon the past. I will traffic no more with these hideous mysteries. What is left of life is all too short to expiate what is done. Laura, Laura! You alone can hold me to my vow. Come to me! Come to me!

(He throws himself in a paroxysm of sobs into the chair that stands by the table, burying his head in his hands. As the door down stage R. opens Lady Carew Enters. At the sound of her step he leaps to his feet.)

Laura!

(He sees Lady Carew and starts back. They stand facing one another in a momentary pause.)

JEKYLL. I know why you have come.

LADY CAREW. You do not, you cannot know.

JEKYLL. Yes, I know well why you have come and what you want of me.

LADY CAREW. I want nothing of you. Nothing.

JEKYLL. But you do. You said when we parted that your fate hung upon last night. Last night has saved you. While your letters were in that man's[91] hands you were afraid. They are in his hands no longer.

(He draws a packet of letters from his pocket)

Take them! Take them, I say!

(She takes them mechanically)

LADY CAREW. He gave them to you?[92]

JEKYLL. He gave them to one I can trust.[93] His lips are sealed. John Hardman will trou-

---

86. Stage direction "*(Goes to door.)*" included here in NMS.
87. "Stay!" replaced by "Poole!" in NMS.
88. Further stage direction "R. I. E. with bag." included here in NMS.
89. The dialogue "That baser shape … overtake me." replaced by "Hyde you have grown nearer to me since last night. I fear lest at any moment your shape should overtake me." in NMS.
90. "shattered" replaced by "shut" in NMS.
91. "man's" replaced by "man Hardman's" in NMS.
92. Additional dialogue "Hardman?" included here in NMS.
93. Additional dialogue with "Lady Carew" saying "To whom?" followed by "Jekyll" continuing "That I cannot tell you." included here in NMS.

ble you no more. Go back and face the world and leave me to the world I have to face. Henceforth there is a veil between us that sunders us for ever. It falls like fine rain in the air between us, and as it falls it takes the scent of blood.

LADY CAREW. Yes, yes, my husband's blood. You have heard…[94]

JEKYLL. I have heard.[95]

LADY CAREW. They are seeking for the murderer now.

JEKYLL. They will never find him; never, never!

LADY CAREW. Why not?

JEKYLL. Such a man has ways of escape that the law cannot trace and cannot follow. They will never take him, they will never take him.

LADY CAREW. They shall! They shall! Listen to me! I have only a moment to stay. Last night I would have given the world to have these letters safe back in my keeping. But I have changed since last night. I am withered and grown old; and if the man I wronged could come back to life again, I would kneel at his feet and give them into his hand.

JEKYLL. You!

LADY CAREW. Ah! I know what you would say — that I once thought to take his life. That is true, all true! But this blow that has fallen like a bolt from Heaven has shattered me. The horror of what I saw last night….

JEKYLL. (*Falling back with terror*) Of what you saw, of what you saw?

LADY CAREW. Of what I saw as he lay on the floor, lifeless and bleeding. What evil in his life had prompted this act of vengeance, who can say? I only know that from this day forth I will devote my life to find his murderer!

JEKYLL. You can do nothing, nothing.

LADY CAREW. I can. That is what I am going back to tell them now. The house was closed, I had gone to my room. He told me he had letters to write. I had put out my light when I heard a cry, so faint that I scarcely heard it, yet it seemed to draw me down to where I had left him. I crept along the corridor, and as I lifted the curtain — I saw….

JEKYLL. Yes, yes, I know. His dead body. Terrible, awful! Why speak of it?

LADY CAREW. Yes, his dead body; and crouching above it a hideous creature, striking wildly at his victim as he lay on the floor. Then, as he slunk away through the window, I saw his face. It was like the face of a beast, and as he went he uttered a fierce snarling cry like the cry of a beast. Then I fainted and fell.

JEKYLL. It was a dream. Forget it as a dream. You saw no one.

LADY CAREW. I saw him as plainly as I see you now.

JEKYLL. As you see me now!

LADY CAREW. How long I lay there I cannot tell. The clock on the mantelpiece struck the hour. That must have roused me. I crept back to my room, afraid to look again, and watched and listened till the dawn came and the house was astir. I heard a cry below, and then the hurrying footsteps as they came to my door. At first I think I was glad he was dead, and I determined to say nothing.

JEKYLL. And now you are determined to speak?

LADY CAREW. I must; something has changed me.[96] I must speak.

JEKYLL. It is useless, useless, I tell you! This man will never be found.

LADY CAREW. He will! In whatever corner of the earth he may lurk or hide I will seek him out.[97]

94. "*You have heard…*" omitted from NMS.
95. This entire line of Jekyll dialogue omitted from NMS.
96. "*Something has changed me*" replaced by "*This monster shall be tracked down and punished. If you had seen him as I saw him gloating in wild frenzy over the body of the man he had slain, you would understand, the sight of it blinds me still as though my eyes had been drenched with blood. No. The world shall be rid of such a fiend.*" in NMS.
97. "*In whatever … seek him out.*" replaced by "*He will!*" in NMS.

JEKYLL. Never, never, on this side of the grave! Listen to me! (*He struggles with himself as though half choking, then recovers*) No, no, I will say nothing. Do what you will. Go! Go!

(*The Voice of Mrs. Jekyll is heard outside calling "Henry!"*)

(*The door opens and Mrs. Jekyll Appears. There is absolute silence and stillness in the room, as Jekyll with a gesture motions Lady Carew to leave. Jekyll crosses softly to the door, and closes it with a slight click*)[98]

LAURA. Oh Henry! You have not gone?

JEKYLL. I have only just come in.[99]

LAURA. I hear you are called away to the country?

JEKYLL. Yes, I am called away.

LAURA. And you must go?

JEKYLL. I must go.

LAURA. I wish you could have stayed with me to-day. It is always a sad day to me.

JEKYLL. To you? No, no, not to you.

LAURA. Yes, to me. You have forgotten, but it was this day two years ago I saw your face for the last time. It was on this day I became blind.

JEKYLL. Forgotten? Would to God I could forget! If I could recall[100] that day, and all the days that have followed I should be happy now.

LAURA. The fault was not yours, dear.

JEKYLL. Yes, it was I who blinded you, but I have been punished—I have been punished.

(*He falls into chair by the table*)[101]

LAURA. Henry, I don't want you to think of it like that. Very often I do not think of it at all. There are hours and hours together when I forget that I am blind, and live again in the little sunlit garden where I met you first. But there are moments now and then when I would give the world to see your face once more. It is hard to think that time will never come.

JEKYLL. Perhaps it is better. You might not know it[102] again.

LAURA. Have you so changed? I do not believe it. I do not believe it would seem changed to me.

JEKYLL. No, no, not to you. While I am near you I feel I am back in those sunlit days, and whatever of good is left in me is yours always, yours to the end. (*He rises*) Now I must go.

LAURA. I want you to promise me something first. Last night I lay awake longing for your return. One after another the hours sounded, but I could not sleep. At last I heard a step in the passage that leads into the laboratory. I crept down and called you. There was no answer, but I felt something steal past me in the dark, and as it passed the air seemed suddenly to freeze my blood. It must have been Mr. Hyde.

JEKYLL. And if it were?

LAURA. I want you to promise that he shall never come to the house while you are away. That terrible murder of last night has frightened me. I could not sleep I could not rest, if I thought in your absence that man was free to come and go in the house. I dare say I am foolish, but I want your promise.

JEKYLL. You have it. Mr. Hyde shall never enter this house again. I have done with him.[103]

LAURA. Henry, have I asked too much of you?

JEKYLL. No, I will promise more. I swear to God that in this world I will never set eyes on him[104] again, never again! You shall hold me to my bond.

---

98. The direction "*Jekyll crosses ... slight click*" omitted from NMS.
99. This line of Jekyll dialogue replaced by "*No, no.*" in NMS.
100. "*If I could recall*" omitted from NMS.
101. This direction omitted from NMS.
102. "*it*" replaced by "*that face*" in NMS.
103. "*I have done with him.*" replaced by additional dialogue with "*Laura*" saying "*Then Poole may bolt and bar the door of the laboratory while you are away?*" followed by "*Jekyll*" saying "*Yes, yes.*" in NMS.
104. "*him*" replaced by "*Mr. Hyde*" in NMS.

(He folds her in his arms, straining her to his breast, and as they stand there a cry comes from the street below — "Murder of Sir Danvers Carew! Expected arrest of the murderer!")

JEKYLL. (*Suddenly breaking away from her*) I must go or I shall be too late!

LAURA. Good-bye then, till to-morrow!

JEKYLL. Till to-morrow!

(He passes through the door in the panel at back, as Mrs. Jekyll feels her way up stage R. and opens the door.)

LAURA. Walters!

(The Maid appears)

WALTERS. Have you heard, Ma'am?[105]

LAURA. Heard?

WALTERS. What the boys are crying in the street. It seems the Police suspect a former butler of Sir Danvers. He may be arrested within the hour.

LAURA. But what can have been the motive for such an awful crime?

WALTERS. There is nothing given in the papers except it certainly was not for gain, as nothing was taken from the body.[106]

LAURA. Lead me back to my room. I slept so badly last night, and I must rest. To-night I think I shall sleep in peace.

(They Go Out, and after a momentary pause Utterson Enters, followed by Poole)

UTTERSON. What time did your master leave the house?

POOLE. I left him here about 20 minutes ago sir, and his cab was waiting for him then at the laboratory door. He told me he had a call to make on the way.

UTTERSON. Unfortunate, most unfortunate! Did he say where he was going?

POOLE. No, sir; only that it was an urgent case in the country. He may have entered it in his diary. He most in general does — in case of telegrams.

UTTERSON. Look and see.

(Poole goes to desk and examines diary.)

POOLE. No sir, no word of any sort.

UTTERSON. Strange!

POOLE. If I may say so, sir, he did not seem in no way fit for travelling.

UTTERSON. Was he ill?

POOLE. Not to say ill, sir; but I think this terrible business had upset him.

UTTERSON. No wonder, no wonder!

POOLE. It seems that the Police suspect Hardman, the butler, who was discharged some three months ago.

UTTERSON. Yes, that is the suspicion — at present. A letter apparently signed by him was found on the body of Sir Danvers.[107]

POOLE. I used to see something of Mr. Hardman when he was in Sir Danver's service. I cannot say I ever greatly took to the man, but I should never have thought he would have committed a crime like that.[108]

UTTERSON. It is possible, quite possible, the Police are mistaken. That <u>has</u> happened before now.

POOLE. So I believe, sir.

(Going Out)

UTTERSON. By the way, I am expecting my clerk Mr. Guest in a few minutes. I appointed to meet him here, thinking to find Dr. Jekyll at home, and Inspector Newcomen of Scotland Yard. Perhaps you will be good enough to show them up.

POOLE. I hear the door now. I expect it is Mr. Guest.

(Exit Poole)

UTTERSON. (*Alone*) I wonder if he has found Hyde's letter?

(Enter Poole, showing in Newcomen.)

POOLE. Inspector Newcomen (*Exit Poole*)

---

105. This line of dialogue replaced by "*Yes, ma'am, I'm waiting.*" in NMS.
106. All dialogue from "*Laura Heard? ...*" to "*Walters ... from the body.*" omitted from NMS.
107. "*of Sir Danvers*" is a *handwritten* insertion in QTS.
108. This entire line of Poole dialogue omitted from NMS.

UTTERSON. Have you been able to trace this man Hardman?

NEWCOMEN. Two of my men are about it now. I left word at Grosvenor Square that when they returned they should follow me here. But I am afraid Mr. Utterson we are on the wrong track.

UTTERSON. How so?

NEWCOMEN. This morning Lady Carew was prostrated with grief, and could see no one. I have just seen her now.

UTTERSON. What can she know? She had retired to her room.

NEWCOMEN. She <u>saw</u> the murderer as he escaped through the window.

UTTERSON. Saw him!

NEWCOMEN. Yes sir; and if her description is correct, we are following a false clue. It was not Hardman that she saw.

UTTERSON. Not Hardman?

NEWCOMEN. That Lady Carew is prepared to swear.

UTTERSON. And yet the letter found upon the body....

NEWCOMEN. May have been a blind. It is possible this man Hardman was in the pay of someone who nursed a deadly enmity against the dead man, and that it was used by the murderer only as a means to gaining access to the house. They say Sir Danvers' way of life had not been beyond reproach.[109]

UTTERSON. True; and yet such a crime as this....[110]

(*Guest Enters hurriedly*)

Ah Guest! Here you are. Have you found it?

GUEST. I have it here, sir.

(*Hands letter which Utterson gazes at attentively.*)

UTTERSON. (*Still looking at the letter, but speaking to Newcomen*) Let me see again the letter that was discovered on the body.[111]

(*Newcomen gives him the letter, which he compares with the other.*) There it is Sir.[112]

What was Lady Carew's description of the man she saw?

NEWCOMEN. (*Referring to his notes.*) A crouching figure, short and slight in stature, with a face that in its ferocity of expression[113] seems to have filled her with terror.

UTTERSON. Then I was right! I felt sure of it. Yes, compare these two letters. The man who wrote that letter, the man who murdered Sir Danvers, was not Hardman, but Edward Hyde.

NEWCOMEN. Hyde? I have no such name on my notes.

UTTERSON. No. I thought it wiser to say nothing till I felt sure my suspicions were well founded. (*Turning to Guest*) Well?

GUEST. (*Handing back the letters*) Unmistakeably the same, though the handwriting in the second is disguised.[114]

NEWCOMEN. (*Looking at the letters*) I believe you're *right*, Mr. Utterson.

UTTERSON. This letter I received from Hyde three days ago, and that, when you showed it to me this morning, I felt sure I recognised as being by the same hand, but I wanted to be certain.

NEWCOMEN. We have lost time, and in these cases time is everything. Who is this man Hyde?

UTTERSON. A protege of Dr. Jekyll,[115] who for some time has assisted him in his laboratory.

109. The dialogue "*It is possible … beyond reproach.*" omitted from NMS.
110. This line of dialogue omitted from NMS.
111. Additional dialogue with "*Newcomen*" saying "*Here it is, sir.*" included at this point in NMS.
112. Newcomen's dialogue "*There it is Sir.*" omitted from NMS. and appears as a *handwritten* insertion in QTS.
113. "*in its ferocity of expression*" omitted from NMS.
114. Stage direction "*(Utterson gives letters to Newcomen)*" included here in NMS.
115. Stage direction "*(Enter Officer in plain clothes)*" included here in NMS.

(Enter Officer in plain clothes.)[116]

NEWCOMEN. Ah Evans! Were you able to trace him?

EVANS. No, sir. He[117] has given us the slip, sir; we were too late.

NEWCOMEN. Too late?

EVANS. We tracked him to his lodging in Chelsea. The door of his room was locked, but we forced it. There we found this man Hardman with his throat cut from ear to ear, and a razor lying on a chair by his side.

NEWCOMEN. Dead?

EVANS. Dead, Sir.

UTTERSON. What can this mean?

EVANS. Case of suicide, in my opinion, sir.

NEWCOMEN. You are not here to give opinions. *(Turning to Utterson)* Where does this man Hyde live?

UTTERSON. No one here knows. Jekyll could have told us.

NEWCOMEN. Is there no one else, no one? Think!

UTTERSON. Yes. Enfield. He's dining with me to-night.[118] He saw him once in Soho. *(Turning to Guest)* Was there any telegram at the office from Mr. Enfield?

GUEST. Yes, sir. *(He hands telegram)*

UTTERSON. *(Reading telegram)* "Sorry not to dine with you. Cannot reach Paddington till 11.23."

NEWCOMEN. *(Makes Note)* Paddington, 11.23. We must meet him there. Meanwhile I must go to Hardman's room. There may be papers there, that may help us. *(To Evans)* You left Derrick in charge?

EVANS. Yes, sir.

UTTERSON. This is a strange case!

NEWCOMEN. Strange as you say. But one thing I think is clear; if this man Hyde is the murderer of Sir Danvers Carew, Hardman did not commit suicide. He was murdered.[119]

UTTERSON. Then you think?—

NEWCOMEN. Nothing, sir, till I know. All I know at present is that we meet at Paddington at 11.23. Come Evans! I have work for you.

Curtain.

ACT III

SCENE II[120]—*(Scene: A dilapidated room on the first floor of a house in Soho. To R a window looking into the Street. To R. in backing a door. To L. of floor a table against the wall with a small gas burner upon it, and some bottles and test tubes. To L. up stage at angle of room a fireplace. On the side wall L. a low truckle bed. A washstand below the window against the wall R.)*

(As the Curtain Rises, Hyde is seated crouching over the fire. He rises and crosses to window, lifting the blind anxiously, and then returning to the fire with a low fierce snarling growl.)

HYDE. Two hours, two hours and more and the drug not here. It's no more than a mile to Lanyon's house: she ought to have been back an hour ago at the worst. If she has failed me I'll tear the flesh like ribbons from her bones.

(Looking cautiously through blind)

---

116. This direction does not appear at this point in NMS.
117. "*He*" replaced by "*Mr. Hardman*" in NMS.
118. "*He is dining with me to-night.*" is a *handwritten* insertion in QTS, and does not appear in NMS.
119. "*He was murdered.*" is typed in NMS but a *handwritten* insertion in QTS.
120. Apart from the first page, Act III Scene II is missing from NMS.

No, no, she wouldn't dare, she wouldn't dare. She has run many a filthy errand for me, has helped me to many a mad debauch here in this very house and has never failed me, never blabbed. She couldn't now. And what days and nights they were. Base and sordid joys you would call them, Jekyll, but they were too base, too bestial for me. And a trail of blood runs through them all, a trail that led me at last to Hardman's room. I can hear the gurgle in his throat as the razor leapt from ear to ear (*starting*) What's that? Is she here? (*looks through blind*) No, Hell's curse upon her! She doesn't know, she can't guess drunken sot that she is, that every moment counts against me — that this is the supreme hour of my fate and unless the drug reaches me in time there is nothing left but the gallows. No, Lanyon must come — he must — (*arranging the glass and spirit lamp on table*) Everything's ready — I only need the drug and I'm saved. And then I've money, yes money enough to escape to the other end of the world. (*Counting notes*) Fool that I was to bolt and bar the door against myself. Why couldn't I foresee that Bellingham's danger was my danger. I was scarcely half way to the station, when those dreaded tremors overtook me. I fled to the park and skulked behind trees till it was dark — then I crept back but the door was shut against me. There was no hiding place but this. I'm safe here but not for long.

(*Taking paper*)

"Short in stature with a low crouching gait and a face" — I know the rest. (*Throwing the paper away*) Lady Carew has spoken and they'll be upon my track. But they don't know this house — no one knows it as yet (*With a sudden start*) Hisht! I heard the door. She's coming. She's here at least. I'm saved! I'm saved!

(*breaks down, in chair with his head on table*)

(*Mrs. Leppery Enters*)

MRS. LEPPERY.[121] 'Allo (*seeing him with his head buried in his hands*) Gone to by-by? Hush, hush, don't wake the baby!

HYDE. Where have you been?

MRS. LEPPERY. Where have I been?

HYDE. Yes, where have you been?

MRS. LEPPERY. Lots of places—

"Up and down the City Road,
In and out the Eagle;
That's the way the money goes.
Pop goes the weasel!"

HYDE. If you do not answer me I will strangle you!

(*He seizes her by the throat*)

MRS. LEPPERY. (*Slipping from his grasp*) 'ere, 'ere! None of them familiarities! You ain't my 'usband, thank Gawd!

HYDE. Answer me! Did you go straight to Dr. Lanyon's house?

MRS. LEPPERY. Oh yes, I went there straight enough! But coming 'ome, well, I will not deceive yer Gov'nor! Coming 'ome was a bit of a zigzag.

HYDE. You left the letter?

MRS. LEPPERY. I left the letter sure enough.

HYDE. Then why didn't you come back?

MRS. LEPPERY. Why didn't I? Let me see. Oh! I know. As I was 'urrying back, it come over me all of a sudden as 'ow it was my birthday, and I always moistens my birthday. So there you have it at ono't!

HYDE. Well now you can go, you sot, and drink yourself blind! I want no more of you.

MRS. LEPPERY. No 'urry, no 'urry! I suppose you have heard of this murder?

HYDE. Go, I tell you! Or there will be another murder.

MRS. LEPPERY. There have been; there's two of them.

HYDE. Two? Who told you so?

MRS. LEPPERY. It's in the paper.

(*She hands Him a paper which She takes from her breast*)

---

121. Mrs. Leppery does not appear in the character lists of either NMS or QTS.

It's the talk of all the pubs, and there is quite a tidy lot of pubs between here and Cavendish Square.

HYDE. (*To himself*) She has spoken then, and it may be too late, too late!

MRS. LEPPERY. I always take to Literatoor when there is murder about. It's about the only bit of reading I find time for.

HYDE. Go, I tell you!

MRS. LEPPERY. You see they have got the description of the murderer right enough, and do you know what I says as I read it? I says "Gawd's truth, that might be the 'living pictur of my Guv'nor!'"

HYDE. You said that, did you? (*Tearing paper fiercely across*) Then listen to me. If you wish to see another birthday, keep your mouth shut and your tongue quiet.

MRS. LEPPERY. Lor' bless us! No harm done! For as I told 'em, it ain't my Guv'nor. 'E is as artful as Satan. You'd never be found out whatever you 'ad done, I'd go bail for that.

(*The bell sounds below*)

HYDE. There is the bell!

(*He peers through the blind again*)

Yes, it is Lanyon! Open the door quickly, and then go, — go home. I shan't want you again, never again!

MRS. LEPPERY. Well, so-long, wishing myself many 'appy returns of the day!

(*She Goes Out*)

HYDE. They will be on my track may be to-night. But he has come in time, just in time!

(*Lanyon Enters*)

Doctor Lanyon?

LANYON. Yes. Who are you? I came at the urgent summons of my friend Doctor Jekyll.

HYDE. I know it. He told me to expect you.

LANYON. Where is he?

HYDE. He will be here in a little while. Yes, in a little while he will be here again.

LANYON. Then I will wait till he comes.

HYDE. Have you brought what he asks for? There is no time to lose it.

LANYON. What I have brought I will deliver into his hands.

HYDE. No, into mine. If you refuse you imperil the life and honour of your friend. Both are at stake. If you refuse you will be false to the charge he gave you.

LANYON. What do you know of the charge he gave me?

HYDE. You shall judge for yourself. Two hours ago you received a letter signed by his hand. You cannot deny it.

LANYON. I have not denied it.

HYDE. In that letter he told you that he was at your mercy; that if you failed him to-night, he was lost for ever. Is that not so?

LANYON. You saw him write that letter?

HYDE. Listen, and you can answer that question for yourself. In that letter he prayed you, he commanded you, to go with all speed to his house, and break open the chest in his private cabinet that leads out of the laboratory, and to bring with you to this house the contents of the fourth drawer from the top.

LANYON. Even if what you say is true...

HYDE. It is true, and you know it. He told you the contents of the drawer were: some powders in separate packets, and a phial half-full of a blood-red liquor. Have you got them, have you got them I say? (*Sinking into a chair*) That is all I ask. Give them to me. Time presses. Give them to me.

LANYON. How can I know what use you will make of them? What assurance have I that in giving them into your hands I shall serve my friend?

HYDE. He told you in that letter that the blackness of despair was upon him, and he besought you to save him. Do you know what that means?

LANYON. I know no more than he said.

HYDE. Suppose your friend were hunted and trapped? Suppose that he had committed a crime for which the Law knows no penalty but death?

LANYON. It is not true! I will not believe it.

HYDE. Give me what you have there, and in a little while, — in the passing of a moment, he himself shall tell you if it is true. Refuse, and you will never see your friend on earth again!

LANYON. God help me if I do wrong! Take them! I dare refuse no longer.

HYDE. (*Seizing the drawer and opening it with trembling hands*) Yes, yes! The phial, the powders, all here. (*Then rising with an air of triumph*) Now, as to what remains, you shall decide for yourself. Will you be wise? Then leave this room and this house and forget that you have ever seen me. Remain to the end of your life the hide-bound pedant that you are to-day. You have your choice. Think well before you answer. If you stay here in this room upon the instant a new province of knowledge shall be opened to you. The mysteries of a world you have scorned shall be laid bare, and your sight shall be blinded by a prodigy mighty enough to stagger the unbelief of Satan. Think and choose.

LANYON. Such threats do not move me. Whatever happens I will wait here until my friend Henry Jekyll returns.

HYDE. Fool and idiot! I am Henry Jekyll!

LANYON. You — you lie.

HYDE. No, I speak the truth — a truth you have scoffed at too long. Here before you now stands the man you loved, of whose friendship you have boasted before the world. And here before you now stands the murderer of Sir Danvers Carew and the man who cut the throat of John Hardman, the same Henry Jekyll.

LANYON. A lie! An infamous lie.

HYDE. You don't recognize your friend in the man who speaks to you now. No, your purblind vision has never pierced beneath the shallow garb of flesh that hides the dual spirit of mankind. It was left to me — me whom you derided, to find the solvent drug which should set free the fiend that lurks in all of us. — Yes, convict or king, profligate or saint — they all own this same base twinship of good and evil, and it is I — I who have been the first since time began to cut the cord that has bound us together. Do you believe me now?

LANYON. No! I believe — I know that every word you say is false.

HYDE. Stay then and abide the proof.

(*He pours the contents of the phial into the test tube which He holds over the flame, then adds the salts.*)

LANYON. I will — this poor jugglery means nothing to me — I will stay to the end.

HYDE. Then you who have been content to dwell within the straightened limits of your mean material world, and have denied the secrets wrung from the heart of Nature by your superiors, wait and behold!

(*He drains the tube and there is a sudden flash. Then Hyde is seen reeling and staggering, then falls forward on his face.*)

LANYON. (*Rushing to him*) Dead?

(*He bends over the figure, which shudders and then slowly rises, and, pushing him aside, reveals the face of Henry Jekyll*)

LANYON. (*Starting back and leaning against the wall*) My God! My God! (*Then suddenly pressing his hand to his side*) Jekyll! My heart! My heart! Oh God!

(*He staggers back, and falls at full length on the bed.*)

JEKYLL. (*Rushing to the bed*) Lanyon! Not dead! Not dead! (*Puts his hand upon Lanyon's heart and falls kneeling beside him*) Lanyon! Speak to me! — Too late! Too late! — That loyal heart will never beat again — My friend, my boyhood's friend, the friend of my whole life, I have killed you. May Heaven forgive me!

(*He throws himself on the body with convulsive sobs, as knocking is heard below. It grows louder, then there is the sound of the breaking in of a door.*)

What's that?

(*He rises and draws the screen round the bed, so as to obscure the view of the body, standing motionless as*

Enter Utterson and Newcomen with Evans who waits in the entry of the doorway.)

UTTERSON. Jekyll! You here?

JEKYLL. Hush! He is dead.

UTTERSON. Jekyll, you are trying to shield this man, but it is useless.

NEWCOMEN. I hold the warrant of the law for the arrest of Edward Hyde.

JEKYLL. He is not here.

NEWCOMEN. Stand aside, sir! I must do my duty.

JEKYLL. Look for yourself. The man who lies there is Dr. Lanyon.

(*Newcomen draws aside the screen*)

UTTERSON. Lanyon! Lanyon dead!

JEKYLL. Yes, dead.

ENFIELD. But this is Hyde's house. I know it. I saw him enter here a month ago.

JEKYLL. It was Hyde's summons that brought me here. He had gone, but I found my friend. Too late! Too late! He is dead!

(*Falling on his knees beside the bed.*)

Lanyon! Forgive me! Forgive me!

Curtain.

ACT IV

SCENE — *The laboratory.*

(*Enter Mr. Utterson followed by Poole R.E.*)

POOLE. It was very good of you, sir, to come at once.

UTTERSON. I could see by your note you were disturbed.

POOLE. Of course, sir, I would have gone to your house, but I felt I daren't leave, even for a moment.

UTTERSON. Why man, you look alarmed! What is wrong?

POOLE. I do not know, sir. I can't tell. But I felt I could not bear it any longer alone.

UTTERSON. Alone? Is your mistress away?

POOLE. She has been staying with friends in the country. When he first took ill — that was more than a week ago — I suggested I should send for her, but he would not hear of it then; but last evening I found a telegram on the floor with instructions to send it at once.

UTTERSON. Was it to call her back?

POOLE. Yes, sir. I read it — "Come home at once or it may be too late."

UTTERSON. Then your master must be gravely ill.

POOLE. (*In low voice as He approaches Him*) Or may be, worse than that, Mr. Utterson!

UTTERSON. Worse! What do you mean?

POOLE. I mean that as I live, sir, I believe there is something wrong! I am sure of it.

UTTERSON. Nonsense, man! I will go to him at once.[122]

(*Making movement towards door*)

POOLE. He won't see you, sir. He will see no one.[123]

UTTERSON. He must, he shall![124] Is he in his room?

POOLE. (*Pointing to door up stage*) No, sir. He is there locked close in his cabinet, where he has been for three days, and he is there still — if he lives.

UTTERSON. If he lives! Surely you must know if he lives? Listen! I hear a footstep. There now!

---

122. "*I will go to him at once*" omitted from NMS.
123. This entire line omitted from NMS.
124. "*He must, he shall!*" omitted from NMS.

(He listens at the door)

Yes, I hear it plainly!

POOLE. I have heard it too, sir, any time these three days past. Sometimes I hear a voice moaning within, but is it my master's voice? Mr. Utterson, I do not believe it!

(There is a moan heard from the room beyond.)

UTTERSON. Quiet! Was that what you heard?

POOLE. Yes, sir; and once I heard it weeping, weeping — like a lost soul! That was two nights ago.

(The moaning is repeated, but louder.)

Now, sir, I ask you, was that my master's voice?

UTTERSON. Whose else should it be? You say he is ill and weak. In sickness a man's voice often changes. Suffering will sometimes make it seem like the voice of another man.

POOLE. No, no, sir. I have served the Doctor twenty years and cannot be deceived. That is not his voice. I swear it. Whoever it is that lives and moves in that room is not my master.[125]

UTTERSON. Poole, listen to me. This watching day and night has upset your nerve. But if you know anything more than you have told me, I insist, it is my duty to insist that you should tell me now.

POOLE. Of course you know, sir, that since Dr. Lanyon's death my master has never been the same. Even while he was up and about the house, he would see no one.[126]

UTTERSON. He has refused to see me again and again, and next to Lanyon, I suppose I am his oldest friend.[127]

POOLE. For days together he would scarcely see even his wife.[128] One night, about a week ago, when I took him his candle into the study, he said to me, "Poole, I am not long for this world." And to speak the truth, sir, he had the look of a dying man.

UTTERSON. I know he must have felt the loss of his friend terribly. They have been comrades from boyhood.

POOLE. When he locked himself into his cabinet three days ago, I thought little enough of it at first for that had always been his way, though never for so long a time.

UTTERSON. Has he been at work?

POOLE. He must have been, for he has sent me again and again, sometimes three or four times in the day, for a certain drug that I suppose he needed for his experiments.

UTTERSON. Did he speak to you then?

POOLE. No, sir. I would find the written instructions flung upon the floor beneath the window there. It had often been his habit when busy. Here is one of them.

(Takes up paper from the table.)

UTTERSON.[129] *(Reading)* "Doctor Jekyll begs to inform Messrs. Moore that the last sample is useless. They must search again for the exact quality as supplied to him on the 8th January two years ago. Nothing else will serve, him and his need is urgent — most urgent." A strange letter, but it is Jekyll's handwriting, undoubtedly his handwriting.[130]

POOLE. That is as may be, sir. But what matters handwriting? This morning I saw him.[131]

UTTERSON. Your master?

POOLE. No, sir. It was not my master.

UTTERSON. What does the man mean?

POOLE. This morning, about 6 o'clock, I came down, fearing he might be needing something. It was scarcely light, but as I stood

---

125. All dialogue from "*Utterson Whose else…*" to "*Poole … not my master.*" omitted from NMS.
126. "*Even while he … see no one.*" omitted from NMS.
127. This entire section of Utterson dialogue omitted from NMS.
128. "*For days together … even his wife.*" omitted from NMS.
129. Additional dialogue "*It's Jekyll's handwriting.*" included here in NMS.
130. "*A strange letter … his handwriting.*" replaced by "*The drug you have sent has lost "its physical effect." Physical effect, what does it mean? Have you seen your master?*" in NMS.
131. This entire section of Poole dialogue replaced by "*No, sir, I've only heard him, but this morning I saw —*" in NMS.

upon the stairs I saw a crouching figure making its way slowly to that cabinet by the wall, that one, sir, where the poisons are kept; but just as he was fitting the key into the door, I gave a cry, and the figure turned and fled back there, sir, like a rat into its hole, and then I heard the lock turn and the bolts go; and then the moaning began as before. And now, sir, just before you came, I heard someone inside rattling the lock, as though it would not open.

UTTERSON. Did you recognise the figure that you saw?

POOLE. Mr. Utterson, a week ago my master told me that Mr. Hyde was dead. Do you think it is sure that he is dead, or is he in there? (*Pointing to door*)

UTTERSON. Poole, this is folly! Madness! Put it out of your mind! Do you suppose that a murderer would come back here where he must know that he would fall into the hands of the Police?[132] You must have been deceived by the darkness. I will speak to the Doctor myself.

POOLE. You will get no reply, sir.

(*Utterson goes up to the door at the back*)

UTTERSON. Jekyll! Jekyll! Why don't you answer me? It is Utterson, your friend.

(*There is no reply*)

POOLE. I told you as much, sir!

(*At that moment the voice of Mrs. Jekyll is heard at the landing at the head of the stairs, speaking to her maid*)

LAURA. Thank you, Walters, I will find my own way down.

UTTERSON. Mrs. Jekyll! You must breathe no word of this folly to her.

(*Enter Mrs. Jekyll at the head of the stairs*)

LAURA. Is Poole there?

POOLE. Yes, ma'am.

LAURA. Please pay my cab. I had no change.

POOLE. Yes, ma'am.

LAURA. How is your master?

(*Poole is about to reply, but Utterson checks him*)

(*Poole goes quietly out*)

UTTERSON. Mrs. Jekyll!

LAURA. Is that Mr. Utterson?[133] I am glad you are here.

UTTERSON. I came at your servant's request.

LAURA. Take me to my husband. Lead me to him.

UTTERSON. (*Taking her hand which she extends*) Mrs. Jekyll, I am afraid my old friend is ill, gravely ill.

LAURA. You don't mean that he is dead? Don't say that he is dead.

UTTERSON. No, not dead.[134]

LAURA. Then take me to him. I am helpless in my blindness unless you help me. Take me to him, or it may be too late!

UTTERSON. Mrs. Jekyll, he is here.[135]

LAURA. Here?

UTTERSON. Yes, locked close in his room.

LAURA. Ah! Then I know my way.

(*She feels her way to door up stairs.*)[136]

UTTERSON. (*Detaining her*) Stay! I am afraid it is useless, at any rate for the present. He will see no one. Just now I implored him to open the door. He did not even answer me.

LAURA. (*Clinging to him*) Then he is dead! Do not deceive me if I am too late and he is dead. You must tell me!

UTTERSON. No, he is not dead, for as I listened at the door, I could hear him pacing up and down within.

LAURA. Thank God! Then I am in time.

---

132. "*Madness! Put it out ... of the Police?*" omitted from NMS.
133. Additional dialogue with "*Utterson*" saying "*Yes.*" included here in NMS.
134. All dialogue from "*Laura You don't mean…*" to "*Utterson … not dead.*" omitted from NMS.
135. Additional dialogue "*in his cabinet.*" included here in NMS.
136. This stage direction omitted from NMS.

UTTERSON. Pray Heaven it may be so.

LAURA. Mr. Utterson, leave me with him alone. He will see me. He has never refused to see me. He will see me now.

UTTERSON.[137] But if you should need help?[138]

LAURA. I will call you; but leave me now, I beseech you. If he is suffering, my place is by his side; if he is dying, he shall die in my arms.

UTTERSON. It may be she is right.

LAURA. Yes, yes, I know I am right. He will open the door when he knows I am alone.[139]

(Poole Enters down stage R. and holds out a card which he shows to Utterson)[140]

UTTERSON. *(Under his breath)* Inspector Newcomen![141]

POOLE.[142] He says he must see you at once.

UTTERSON. I will come.

(They Go Out quietly as Mrs. Jekyll advances towards the door)

LAURA. Henry! I have come back. Open the door to me! It is your wife. Oh, speak to me! Speak to me!

(As She crouches listening at the door, the window above slowly opens, and Hyde's face appears.)

HYDE. Is that Mrs. Jekyll?[143]

(She starts back with a half shuddering cry)[144]

LAURA. Henry! That is not his voice. No, that is not his voice![145]

HYDE. No, it is not his voice![146]

(She makes a movement towards the stairs.)[147]

LAURA. Mr. Utterson![148]

HYDE. Make no cry! Do not move a step, or your husband will be lost for ever.[149]

LAURA. Where is he? Where is my husband?[150]

HYDE. He is here. He is dying.[151]

LAURA. Then, whoever you are, let me come to him. Open the door, I beg you, I beseech you![152]

HYDE. The door won't open. The key is broken and jammed in the lock. If it were not, he would need no help but his own and mine.[153]

LAURA. Then I will call them to break the lock.[154]

HYDE. If you do, he will curse you. If you would help him in his sorest need, if you would save him from an end that is worse than death, do as he bids you — do as I bid you, and act quickly, or it may be too late.[155]

---

137. Additional dialogue "*It may be you're right.*" included here in NMS.
138. Additional dialogue "*I shall be within call.*" included here in NMS.
139. All dialogue from "*Laura I will call...*" to "*Laura ... I am alone.*" omitted from NMS.
140. Stage direction "*and holds out ... to Utterson*" replaced by "*UTTER: cross to Poole R.*" in NMS.
141. This entire line of Utterson dialogue omitted from NMS.
142. Additional dialogue "*Inspector Newcomen.*" included here in NMS.
143. This entire line of dialogue replaced by "*Hyde*" exclaiming "*Laura!*" followed by "*Laura*" exclaiming "*Henry!*" and then "*Hyde*" questioning "*You are alone?*" in NMS.
144. This stage direction omitted from NMS.
145. This line of Laura dialogue replaced by "*Yes, alone — but Henry, your voice sounds strange to me.*" in NMS.
146. This line of Hyde dialogue replaced by "*It is strange even to myself, but it is your husband who speaks to you.*" in NMS.
147. This direction omitted from NMS.
148. This line of Laura dialogue replaced by "*Oh, tell me what has happened.*" in NMS.
149. This line of Hyde dialogue replaced by "*I am changed — changed beyond recall, but it is I, Henry, who is trying to speak to you.*" in NMS.
150. This line of Laura dialogue replaced by "*Changed! Never to me. Let me come to you now!*" in NMS.
151. This line of Hyde dialogue replaced by "*No one can come to me. I must be alone now till the end.*" in NMS.
152. This line of Laura dialogue replaced by "*No, no, I implore you, open the door and let me come to you.*" in NMS.
153. This section of Hyde dialogue replaced by "*The door is fast — the key is broken in the lock.*" in NMS.
154. "*them to break the lock.*" replaced by "*for help*" followed by stage direction "*(She moves towards door R.)*" in NMS.
155. This section of Hyde dialogue replaced by "*If you do, you will bring upon me a fate that is worse than death. Do as I command — and quickly or it will be too late.*" in NMS.

LAURA. Then tell me what I can do. I would lay down my life to save him.[156]

HYDE. Takes these keys.

(He holds the keys out of the window. She reaches up her hand and takes them.)[157]

The largest on the ring will open the door of the cabinet that stands against the wall.[158] You can feel your way to it, but he said you would know it for[159] it is the same that stood there two years ago.[160] He said you would[161] remember.

LAURA. Yes, I remember.[162] The glass on the door is[163] labelled "Poison".[164] Why should he[165] want poison?

HYDE. There are poisons that cure as well as poisons that kill.[166] Quickly! Quickly! Or his curse will be upon you. It is he, not I, that asks this of you.[167]

LAURA. Now I must yield to whatever he asks.[168]

(She feels her way along the wall and reaches the cabinet and opens it with the key)[169]

HYDE. Run your hand along the lower shelf to the bottle that stands there. Yes! That one! That one! Now, quick! Give it to me! Quick, I say, or it may be too late![170]

(She goes back with bottle, which He seizes eagerly.)[171]

LAURA. *(With her head raised)* Oh! Beg him, pray him to let me go to him.[172]

HYDE. It may be he[173] will come to you before the end.

(Voices are heard without and the window closes.)

LAURA. What have I done? What have I done? Oh![174] Mr. Utterson! *(Calling)*

(Enter Mr. Utterson, Inspector Newcomen, Poole and an Officer.)[175]

UTTERSON. I am here, Mrs. Jekyll.

LAURA. Mr. Utterson, there is some one in that room besides my husband. He spoke to me just now, but it was not my husband's voice.[176]

POOLE. I knew it! I knew it![177]

---

156. This section of Laura dialogue replaced by "*Too late! No, no, not too late! Oh, tell me what is it I can do.*" in NMS.
157. This stage direction replaced by "*(She takes them)*" followed by "*Laura*" saying "*I have them.*" in NMS.
158. Additional dialogue with "*Laura*" saying "*Henry, you forget that I am blind.*" followed by "*Hyde*" saying "*No, I remember that you are blind.*" included here in NMS.
159. "*but he said you would know it for*" omitted from NMS.
160. Additional dialogue "*before my folly blinded you.*" included here in NMS.
161. "*He said you would*" replaced by "*Can't you*" in NMS.
162. Stage direction "*(Laura feels her way along the back then down L.)*" included here in NMS.
163. "*is*" replaced by "*was*" in NMS.
164. Additional dialogue "*Poison, Henry,*" included here in NMS.
165. "*he*" replaced by "*you*" in NMS.
166. "*as well as poisons that kill.*" replaced by "*when nothing else will cure. Trust me, I know my need. I am yours nor for a little, but in a moment I may be lost to you for ever.*" in NMS.
167. "*his curse will … asks this of you.*" replaced by "*it will be too late.*" in NMS.
168. This line of Laura dialogue replaced by "*I must obey you.*" followed by "*Hyde*" saying "*You must, you must.*" in NMS.
169. This stage direction replaced by dialogue with "*Laura (Feeling her way)*" saying "*I will! I am nearing it now.*" followed by "*Hyde*" saying "*Yes, yes, now — you have your hand upon the door.*" and stage direction "*(She opens it)*" in NMS.
170. "*Quick, I say, or it may be too late.*" replaced by "*As you love me bring it to me now.*" in NMS.
171. This direction omitted from NMS.
172. This line of Laura direction and dialogue replaced by "*Here it is. But Henry, let me come to you.*" in NMS.
173. "*he*" replaced by "*I*" in NMS.
174. "*Oh!*" replaced by stage direction "*(Enter Utterson followed by Enfield Poole Newcomen and Evans R.I.E.)*" in NMS.
175. This direction omitted from NMS.
176. This line of Laura dialogue replaced by "*He is there — he has spoken to me.*" in NMS.
177. This line of Poole dialogue replaced by "*My master has spoken to you?*" followed by "*Laura*" saying "*Yes, only a moment ago — but he is locked in — He won't let me go to him.*" and "*Utterson*" saying "*I am afraid, Mrs. Jekyll, there may be a reason for that — a reason it is better you should not know. Let me take you away.*" in NMS.

NEWCOMEN.[178] (*To Evans*) Have you posted your men beneath the window that looks on to the alley?

EVANS. Yes, sir.[179]

NEWCOMEN. Good; let no one leave this room.[180] (*Turning to Utterson*)[181] Mr. Utterson, I think Mrs. Jekyll should be informed of the course we propose to take. (*Turning to Poole*) Ask Lady Carew to come in.[182]

(*Enter Lady Carew*)

UTTERSON. (*To Mrs. Jekyll*) What you have just told me makes it more urgent that we should act not only in the interests of the law, but it may be in the interests of the man you love.

LAURA. What does it mean? Why are these men here? Oh! tell me what it means![183]

UTTERSON. Lady Carew, I must ask you to tell Mrs. Jekyll what you have told me[184] ten minutes ago.[185]

LADY CAREW. A month ago I swore to track down this man Edward Hyde, the murderer of my husband. A week ago, as I passed along the street I thought I saw his face at the window, but afterwards I felt I had been mistaken. Since then I have haunted this house, for what reason I could hardly tell myself, and this morning, not an hour ago, I saw plainly at the window[186] the face of the man whom I had seen bending over the murdered body of Sir Danvers Carew.[187]

LAURA. You mean that it is he, Hyde, who is hidden in that room?

LADY CAREW. Unless he has escaped since I saw him, I swear that it is Hyde.

NEWCOMEN. That evidence justifies me in the course that I propose to take. If this man will not yield himself up, I must break down the door.

UTTERSON. Wait! If Dr. Jekyll lives one rash step may imperil his life. Let me speak to him again.

(*He goes to the door*)

Jekyll! For your wife's sake, for your friends' sake I command you to speak to me!

HYDE. (*Speaking from within*) Utterson! For God's sake have mercy, have mercy!

UTTERSON. (*Springing back from the door*) You are right! It is not Jekyll's voice. It is Hyde's voice. Newcomen — do your duty![188]

NEWCOMEN. Derrick,[189] Evans, break down that door![190]

(*The two Men approach, one armed with a crow-bar. Two or three blows and the door flies backwards into the inner room, and the moment afterwards Hyde is seen in the*

---

178. Additional dialogue "*I am afraid, sir, I must ask you to remain and this lady too.*" included here in NMS.
179. Stage direction "*(Exit R.)*" followed by "*Laura*" saying "*Oh, what does this mean — who are these men?*" "*Utterson*" saying "*They are the officers of the law.*" "*Laura*" saying "*Officers of the law.*" and "*Utterson*" saying "*Mrs. Jekyll, there is reason to believe your husband is not alone in that room.*" included here in NMS.
180. "*Good; let no one leave this room*" omitted from NMS.
181. This direction is omitted from NMS.
182. Stage direction "*(Poole goes to door R.I.E.)*" followed by "*Enfield*" saying "*Utterson, I don't know why, but that strange story told us by Wellaby a month ago in this very house comes back to me now.*" and "*Utterson*" saying "*You mean of the Indian at Allahabad. I was thinking of it too. Strange indeed.*" included here in NMS.
183. All dialogue from "*Utterson (To Mrs.Jekyll) What…*" to "*Laura … what it means.*" omitted from NMS.
184. This line of dialogue attributed to "*Newcomen*" in NMS.
185. "*ten minutes ago*" replaced by additional dialogue with "*Lady Carew*" saying "*Mrs. Jekyll, you believe your husband is in that room?*" "*Laura*" saying "*I know it. I am sure of it.*" followed by "*Lady Carew*" saying "*Then as you love him, as I know you do, let that door be forced without an instant's delay. He is not there alone.*" and "*Laura*" saying "*Not alone! What do you mean?*" at this point in NMS.
186. "*A month ago … plainly at the window*" replaced by "*I mean that by his side, if he still lives is the murderer of my husband.*" followed by "*Laura*" saying "*Hyde!*" and "*Lady Carew*" saying "*Yes, Hyde. This morning in company with Mr. Enfield, I saw plainly at the window of that room which looks on to the street*" at this point in NMS.
187. Additional dialogue with "*Enfield*" saying "*And I can vouch for the truth of what Lady Carew has said.*" included here in NMS.
188. Further dialogue "*Break down the door.*" included here in NMS.
189. "*Derrick,*" omitted from NMS.
190. "*break down that door*" replaced by stage direction "*(Enter Evans)*" in NMS.

vacant entry.[191] *He holds in his hand the bottle that Mrs. Jekyll had given to him from the cabinet. His eyes, as He Enters are turned on Lady Carew.)*[192]

LADY CAREW. Yes, that is the man! That is my husband's murderer!

HYDE. Yes, and you have tracked me down as you swore you would track me down. You have ruined me at the last as you ruined me in the beginning![193]

(He drains down the poison, then, in the voice of Jekyll he cries:)

JEKYLL. Laura! Laura!

(He struggles towards his wife and falls at her feet.)

NEWCOMEN. We are too late! Too late![194]

LAURA. Henry! Look up! Look up! It is I — your wife.

UTTERSON. (*To Newcomen*) Hush! Say nothing. It is better so.[195] She is blind.

NEWCOMEN. (*To his men*) Lift him up.[196]

(The Officers lift up the fallen body,[197] *and as his face is turned to the audience, it is seen to be the face of Jekyll.)*

UTTERSON AND OTHERS. Jekyll!

LAURA. I knew it! I knew it! My love, my true love![198]

Curtain.

Review of H. B. Irving's Queen's Theatre Performance.

The Sphere, February 19, 1910

"Dr. Jekyll and Mr. Hyde" at the Queen's Theatre.
Mr. H. B. Irving's Interesting Impersonation of Robert Louis Stevenson's Famous Character

Everyone has read Mr. Robert Louis Stevenson's story, *Dr. Jekyll and Mr. Hyde*. It has been published at a shilling and even at sixpence. It has reached a far larger audience than most of Stevenson's books, and at least, if everyone has not read it, all will have read enough about it to know something of Stevenson's clever creation of a dual personality. Dr. Jekyll has been experimenting with drugs for years. At last he has succeeded in finding a drug which will drive all the evil dispositions in his nature into a separate being, so that when he wishes to be a model of virtue he can be so as "Dr. Jekyll," or when he wants to taste of the evil of life he can transfer himself into "Mr. Hyde." The subject lends itself, of course, to drama, and old playgoers talk of an earlier representation in which Mr. Mansfield excelled in the two parts. Mr. Comyns Carr has now written a four-act play for Mr. Irving in which he has introduced the feminine interest. We have a good woman, Laura Jekyll, the devoted wife of Dr. Jekyll; we have the bad woman, Lady Carew, and round these two the good and bad deeds of the hero villain centre.

The play opens in the library of Dr. Jekyll's

---

191. Additional dialogue with "*Enfield*" saying "*Hyde!*" included at this point in NMS.
192. Additional stage direction "*(Newcomen goes to arrest him Hyde shrinks back in doorway)*" included here in NMS.
193. All dialogue from "*Lady Carew Yes, that is...*" to "*Hyde ... in the beginning!*" omitted from NMS.
194. This entire line of Newcomen dialogue omitted from NMS.
195. "*It is better so.*" omitted from NMS.
196. This entire line of Newcomen direction and dialogue replaced by "*Laura*" saying "*Henry!*" in NMS.
197. Stage direction "*The Officers lift up the fallen body*" replaced by "*Jekyll turns over*" in NMS.
198. "*my true love*" replaced by "*my husband*" in NMS.

house. Some men have been dining with him and have been discussing this question of scientific possibilities. Dr. Jekyll tells his greatest friend, Dr. Lanyon, that there are more things in Heaven and earth than are dreamt of in his philosophy. In the next scene we are taken into the doctor's laboratory, and we know that he is the possessor of this wonderful drug that can transform his nature and also his appearance. Then there is a pretty scene with the wife, who has been blinded by one of her husband's experiments. Then we are introduced to the second woman in the case, Lady Carew, who had been in love with Jekyll and had been very anxious to get rid of her husband, Sir Danvers Carew, the diplomatist. Here in the second act we have Hyde's nature coming out in his strangling and stabbing of Carew.

Among the scenes in the third act we see Jekyll in his library again. We see Hyde in his lodgings in Soho—a wonderful transformation, reminiscent in some parts of Sir Henry Irving in *The Bells*. Then Dr. Lanyon, ably represented by Mr. Eille Norwood, is a witness to the transformation of his friend from Hyde to Jekyll, and the shock kills him, he having, as we have been notified in the first act, a very weak heart. The fourth act takes us back to the laboratory, where the unfortunate Hyde cannot find the drug which will restore him to his Jekyll state, and ultimately he dies.

We would have welcomed while we were in the region of melodrama a happier ending, but even as the play stands it makes capital material for Mr. Irving, who in so many particulars inherits his father's genius for acting. Mr. Charles Sugden is excellent as Sir Danvers Carew, and Mr. Frank Tyars as Poole, the butler, is quite superb. Miss Dorothea Baird is "sweet" as she always is. We are glad to learn that the play is a great success.

Select Bibliography

Primary Sources

Bandmann, Daniel E. *Dr. Jekyll and Mr. Hyde (A Play in Four Acts)*. 1888. Lord Chamberlain Plays Collection, Add. 53408K. British Library.

Carr, Joseph William Comyns. *Dr. Jekyll and Mr. Hyde (Play in 4 Acts)*. 1910. Lord Chamberlain Plays Collection, 1910/4, Add. 65880C. British Library.

Mansfield, R., and T. R. Sullivan. *Dr. Jekyll and Mr. Hyde* (Partial Script). Billy Rose Theatre Collection, refs: NCOF+ ZZ22022 & NCOF + ZZ22017. New York Public Library.

Police Box 3:16, No. 155. Corporation of London Record Office, Guildhall London.

Sullivan, Thomas R. *Dr. Jekyll and Mr. Hyde (A Play in Four Acts)*. American Play Co. Theatre Collection, RM 4894. New York Public Library Research Department.

Sullivan, Thomas R. *Dr. Jekyll and Mr. Hyde (A Play in Four Acts)*. 1888. Lord Chamberlain Plays Collection, Add. 53409B. British Library.

Sullivan, Thomas R. *Dr. Jekyll and Mr. Hyde (A Play in Four Acts)*. Mansfield Costume Collection. Smithsonian Institute, Washington D.C.

Main Newspaper Sources

Boston Evening Transcript. 1887.
Boston Globe. 1887.
Boston Post. 1887.
Daily Telegraph, London, 1888.
East London Advertiser, 1888.
The Era, London, 1888.
Illustrated Police News, London, 1888.
Illustrated Sporting and Dramatic News, London, 1888.
Lloyds Weekly Newspaper, London, 1888.
New York Tribune. 1887.
Pall Mall Gazette, London, 1888.
Philadelphia Inquirer. Philadelphia, 1888.
Punch, London, 1888.
St. Stephen's Review. London, 1888.
The Star, London, 1888.
Sunday Times, London, 1888.
The Times. London, 1888.

Secondary Sources

Begg, Paul, Martin Fido, and Keith Skinner. *The Jack the Ripper A–Z*. London: Headline, 1996.

Burr, David Holcomb. "Richard Mansfield: A Re-evaluation of His Career." Ph.D. dissertation, University of Michigan, 1972.

Chisholm, Alex, Christopher-Michael DiGrazia, and Dave Yost. *The News from Whitechapel: Jack the Ripper in the* Daily Telegraph, Jefferson, N.C.: McFarland, 2002.

Curtis, L. Perry, Jr. *Jack the Ripper and the London Press*. New Haven, Conn.: Yale University Press, 2001.

Danahay, Martin A., ed. *The Strange Case of Dr. Jekyll and Mr. Hyde by Robert Louis Stevenson*, Peterborough, Ontario: Broadview Press, 1999.

Evans, Stewart P., and Keith Skinner. *Jack the Ripper: Letters from Hell*. London: Sutton, 2001.

———. *The Ultimate Jack the Ripper Sourcebook*. London: Constable & Robinson, 2000.

Frayling, Christopher. *Nightmare: The Birth of Horror*. London: BBC Books, 1996.

———. "The House that Jack Built: Some Stereotypes of the Rapist in the History of Popular Culture." *Rape, an Historical and Cultural Enquiry*. Edited by R. Porter and S. Tomaselli. Blackwell, 1989.

Frick, John. "A Changing Theatre: New York and Beyond" in *The Cambridge History of American Theatre: Volume Two: 1870–1945*. Edited by Don B. Wilmeth and Christopher Bigsby. Cambridge: Cambridge University Press, 1999.

Harris, Melvin, *Jack the Ripper: The Bloody Truth*. London: Columbus Books, 1987.

Pierce, Jason Adam. "Penny-Wise and Virtue-Foolish: Robert Louis Stevenson and the Late Victorian Publishing Industry." Ph.D. dissertation, University of South Carolina, 1999.

Pinkston, C. Alex, Jr. "The Stage Première of Dr. Jekyll and Mr. Hyde." *Nineteenth Century Theatre Research* 14:1/2 (1986): 21–44.

Rumbelow, Donald. *The Complete Jack the Ripper*. London: W. H. Allen & Co., 1988.

Sugden, Philip. *The Complete History of Jack the Ripper*. London: Robinson, 1998.

Walkowitz, Judith R. *City of Dreadful Delight: Narratives of Sexual Danger in Late-Victorian London*. Chicago: Virago Press, 1994.

Wilmeth, Don B., and Christopher Bigsby. *The Cambridge History of American Theatre: Volume Two: 1870–1945*. Cambridge: Cambridge University Press, 1999.

Wilstach, Paul. *Richard Mansfield, the Man and the Actor*. London: Chapman & Hall, 1908.

Winter, William. *Life & Art of Richard Mansfield*. Moffat, New York: Yard & Co., 1910.

Internet Sites

Dury, Richard. *The Robert Louis Stevenson Web Site*. http://wwwesterni.unibg.it/siti_esterni/rls/rls.htm

Ryder, Stephen P. *The Casebook of Jack the Ripper*. www.casebook.org

Index

Always Intended 86

Bandmann, Daniel 2, 3, 15, 16, 36, 84, 85, 92, 93, 94, 99, 102, 103, 104, 105, 121, 133–138, 163–166
Beau Brummel 17, 87
Beaucaire 8, 19
Bernhardt, Sarah 11, 85, 92, 105
Booth, Edwin 7, 34, 93
Burr, David Holcomb 34–35

Carr, J. W. Comyns 2, 191, 192, 225
Combination company 29, 30
Cyrano de Bergerac 18

Derby School 9, 86, 87, 96
Devil's Disciple 18
The Doll House 17
Don Juan 17
D'Oyly Carte 10–12

Garrick Theatre, New York 18, 30
Gilbert and Sullivan 10, 11, 13
Globe Theatre, Boston 17
Globe Theatre, London 16, 86, 87, 96, 97
Gothic 22, 31, 33

Henry V 8, 19

Ibsen, Henrik 17, 19
Irving, Henry 7, 8, 11, 15, 31, 33, 84, 85, 86, 87, 91, 92, 93, 94, 95, 96, 97, 98, 104, 105, 118, 120, 122, 125, 129, 130, 133, 135, 136, 191, 226
Irving, Henry Brodribb 2, 7, 8, 11, 191, 192n, 225
Irving, Washington 11

"Jack the Ripper" 1, 2, 35–39, 121n, 128n, 167, 176, 177, 179
Jekyll and Hyde 1, 2, 3, 7, 11–17, 21, 22, 25, 31, 33–35, 37, 38, 43, 79, 81, 98, 100, 107, 108–132, 133–137, 165–167, 175, 178, 180, 186, 190, 191, 225
Jordan, Eben B. 9

Lesbia 131n
Lyceum, London (theatre) 1, 2, 15, 16, 37, 43, 84–86, 92–98, 102, 104–106, 120, 122, 123, 126–128, 130, 131, 133–137, 163, 167, 186

Madison Square, New York (theatre) 12–14, 82, 89, 92, 104, 115, 117
Mansfield, Beatrice (née Cameron) 18
Master and Man 17
Melodrama 1, 2, 17, 31–33, 89, 108–110, 124, 131, 226
Merchant of Venice 19
Monsieur 15, 17, 86, 89, 91, 116
Museum, Boston (theatre) 13, 82, 89, 108, 110, 112, 113, 117

Nero 17, 21, 22, 84, 89, 91, 96, 105, 107, 125
Niblo's Garden, New York (theatre) 92, 99

Offenbach, Jacques 11
Old Heidelberg 8
Opera Comique, London (theatre) 15, 84, 92, 94, 104, 133–138, 163, 165, 166

Parisian Romance 7, 12, 13, 16, 82, 86, 96, 105, 107, 125
Peer Gynt 19
Pinkston, Alex 43, 191n

Prince Karl 13, 15–17, 19, 31, 37, 86, 87, 89, 96, 116

Reed, German 10
Richard III 16, 17, 19, 84, 86, 87, 96, 97, 102
Rip Van Winkle 11
Rudersdorff, Erminia 8–10, 11, 33

Shaw, G. B. 18, 174–175
Sophia, Duchess of Baden 9
Stevenson, Robert Louis 1,3, 12, 13, 17n, 21, 23–25, 32, 33, 47, 81, 84, 90, 92–94, 98–100, 102–105, 108–117, 120–123, 126, 127, 130, 131, 134–137, 163–165, 172, 191, 225
Stock company 29
Story of Rodion, the Student 18, 89

Sullivan, T. R. 1–3, 13, 15, 17, 21–22, 25, 32, 47, 81, 89, 98, 99, 100, 102, 104, 108–115, 117, 122, 126, 131, 134, 135, 191, 192

Terry, Ellen 11
Theatrical Syndicate 30

Union Square Theater Company 12

Whitechapel murder 2, 35, 36, 37–39, 133, 167–190
Wilstach, Paul 2, 8, 13, 15–19, 31, 81–88
Winter, William 2, 7, 8, 33, 88–98, 105, 116n, 118n, 133n, 136n
World's Peace Jubilee 9